Pentecostal Manifestos

James K. A. Smith and Amos Yong, *Editors*

PENTECOSTAL MANIFESTOS will provide a forum for exhibiting the next generation of Pentecostal scholarship. Having exploded across the globe in the twentieth century, Pentecostalism now enters its second century. For the past fifty years, Pentecostal and charismatic theologians (and scholars in other disciplines) have been working "internally," as it were, to articulate a distinctly Pentecostal theology and vision. The next generation of Pentecostal scholarship is poised to move beyond a merely internal conversation to an outward-looking agenda, in a twofold sense: first, Pentecostal scholars are increasingly gaining the attention of those outside Pentecostal/charismatic circles *as* Pentecostal voices in mainstream discussions; second, Pentecostal scholars are moving beyond simply reflecting on their own tradition and instead are engaging in theological and cultural analysis of a variety of issues from a Pentecostal perspective. In short, Pentecostal scholars are poised with a new boldness:

- Whereas the first generation of Pentecostal scholars was careful to learn the methods of the academy and then "apply" those to the Pentecostal tradition, the next generation is beginning to interrogate the reigning methodologies and paradigms of inquiry from the perspective of a unique Pentecostal worldview.
- Whereas the first generation of Pentecostal scholars was faithful in applying the tools of their respective trades to the work of illuminating the phenomena of modern Pentecostalism, the charismatic movements, and (now) the global renewal movements, the second generation is expanding its focus to bring a Pentecostal perspective to bear on important questions and issues that are concerns not only for Pentecostals and charismatics but also for the whole church.
- Whereas the first generation of Pentecostal/charismatic scholars was engaged in transforming the anti-intellectualism of the tradition, the second generation is engaged in contributing to and even impacting the conversations of the wider theological academy.

PENTECOSTAL MANIFESTOS will bring together both high-profile scholars and newly emerging scholars to address issues at the intersection of Pentecostalism, the global church, the theological academy, and even broader cultural concerns. Authors in PENTECOSTAL MANIFESTOS will be writing to and addressing not only their own movements but also those outside of Pentecostal/charismatic circles, offering a manifesto for a uniquely Pentecostal perspective on various themes. These will be "manifestos" in the sense that they will be bold statements of a distinctly Pentecostal interjection into contemporary discussions and debates, undergirded by rigorous scholarship.

Under this general rubric of bold, programmatic "manifestos," the series will include both shorter, crisply argued volumes that articulate a bold vision within a field as well as longer scholarly monographs, more fully developed and meticulously documented, with the same goal of engaging wider conversations. Such PENTECOSTAL MANIFESTOS are offered as intrepid contributions with the hope of serving the global church and advancing wider conversations.

PUBLISHED

Frank D. Macchia, *Justified in the Spirit: Creation, Redemption, and the Triune God* (2010)

James K. A. Smith, *Thinking in Tongues: Pentecostal Contributions to Christian Philosophy* (2010)

Wolfgang Vondey, *Beyond Pentecostalism: The Crisis of Global Christianity and the Renewal of the Theological Agenda* (2010)

Beyond Pentecostalism

The Crisis of Global Christianity and
the Renewal of the Theological Agenda

Wolfgang Vondey

WILLIAM B. EERDMANS PUBLISHING COMPANY
GRAND RAPIDS, MICHIGAN / CAMBRIDGE, U.K.

Published 2010 by
Wm. B. Eerdmans Publishing Co.
2140 Oak Industrial Drive N.E., Grand Rapids, Michigan 49505 /
P.O. Box 163, Cambridge CB3 9PU U.K.

Printed in the United States of America

16 15 14 13 12 11 10   7 6 5 4 3 2 1

Library of Congress Cataloging-in-Publication Data

Vondey, Wolfgang.
    Beyond Pentecostalism: the crisis of global Christianity and the
    renewal of the theological agenda / Wolfgang Vondey.
        p.   cm. — (Pentecostal manifestos)
    Includes bibliographical references and indexes.
    ISBN 978-0-8028-6401-7 (pbk.: alk. paper)
        1. Pentecostalism. 2. Pentecostal churches — Doctrines. 3. Theology —
    History — 21st century.   I. Title.

BR1644.V66   2010
230'.994 — dc22

                                                    2010013942

www.eerdmans.com

To the
Society for Pentecostal Studies

Contents

Acknowledgments

The research and writing of *Beyond Pentecostalism* involved a large number of individuals, friends, colleagues, scholars, and institutions. Any omission in these acknowledgments is regrettable and entirely my responsibility, but perhaps unavoidable. Instrumental in giving me a solid foundation in Pentecostal faith and praxis as well as in theological research were the faculty and staff at the Church of God Theological Seminary, now called the Pentecostal Theological Seminary, in Cleveland, Tennessee. I am thankful for the spiritual formation and academic rigor of my teachers, who in one way or another have left their mark on this project. Also deserving special attention is the faculty at the theology department of Marquette University for directing my thoughts from my preoccupation with internal Pentecostal debates to broader theological concerns that address the theological academy at large. The Society for Pentecostal Studies has been a remarkable place to join together the variety of these ecumenical voices in and beyond the Pentecostal community that form the seedbed for this project. I am indebted to the many opportunities the members of the Society have given me to interact with and learn from the talented proposals and discussions at the annual meetings.

The completion of research and access to the resources of international and archival material were made possible through a generous contribution of the Lilly Theological Research Grants program, 2009-2010. This grant allowed me to process the rich array of documents on Pentecostalism made available by, among others, the Asian Pentecostal Society, Bund Freikirchlicher Pfingstgemeinden, David J. du Plessis Archive,

European Pentecostal Charismatic Research Association, European Research Network on Global Pentecostalism, Flower Pentecostal Heritage Center, Hal Bernard Dixon Pentecostal Research Center, Holy Spirit Research Center at Oral Roberts University, International Pentecostal Holiness Church Archives, Pentecostal Charismatic Theological Inquiry International, United Pentecostal Church Historical Center, and the Regent University Library.

The Ph.D. program in Renewal Studies at the School of Divinity of Regent University has been formative in crafting my ideas in the context of a global theological agenda. Students and faculty have repeatedly engaged the ideas of this project during the early phase of its completion. I am also thankful for the critical feedback on parts or all of the manuscript and its ideas from many colleagues and friends, particularly Dale Coulter, Ralph Del Colle, Andrew Grosso, Skip Jenkins, Frank Macchia, Kevin Spawn, Amos Yong, and my wife, Michelle Vondey. My graduate assistant, Bradford McCall, diligently read the manuscript and offered numerous editorial and constructive comments. I am particularly indebted to James K. A. Smith and Amos Yong for their encouragement in crafting the proposal and structure of this book, and for the opportunity to include a volume with the title *Beyond Pentecostalism* in a series entitled Pentecostal Manifestos. Finally, my appreciation goes to William B. Eerdmans Publishing Company for the opportunity to present the project to a larger audience.

Abbreviations

ACW	Ancient Christian Writers
AF	*The Apostolic Faith*
AHR	*American Historical Review*
AJPS	*Asian Journal of Pentecostal Studies*
AJS	*American Journal of Sociology*
AJT	*Asia Journal of Theology*
AL	*Archiv für Liturgiewissenschaft*
APB	*Acta patristica et byzantina*
AS	*Augustinian Studies*
AUSS	*Andrews University Seminary Studies*
BCSSCR	*Bulletin of the Center for the Study of Southern Culture and Religion*
BM	*The Bridegroom's Messenger*
BTZ	*Berliner Theologische Zeitschrift*
CC	*Cross Currents*
CD	*Church Dogmatics* by Karl Barth, 14 vols., ed. G. W. Bromiley and T. F. Torrance (London: T. & T. Clark, 2004)
CE	*Christian Evangel*
CH	*Church History*
ChrCent	*Christian Century*
COGE	*Church of God Evangel*
CPCR	*Cyberjournal for Pentecostal-Charismatic Research*
CTM	*Concordia Theological Monthly*
CurTM	*Currents in Theology and Mission*
Di	*Dialog*
EJEMR	*Exchange: Journal of Ecumenical and Missiological Research*
ELCGE	*Evening Light and the Church of God Evangel*
EQ	*Evangelical Quarterly*

ER	*Ecumenical Review*
ET	*Ecumenical Trends*
EuroJTh	*European Journal of Theology*
EvT	*Evangelische Theologie*
ExAud	*Ex auditu*
FT	*First Things*
GOTR	*Greek Orthodox Theological Review*
HTR	*Harvard Theological Review*
IBMR	*International Bulletin of Missionary Research*
ICHR	*Indian Church History Review*
IRM	*International Review of Mission*
JATL	*Journal für auserlesene theologische Literatur*
JBSM	*Journal of Black Sacred Music*
JEPTA	*Journal of the European Pentecostal Theology Association*
JES	*Journal of Ecumenical Studies*
JETS	*Journal of the Evangelical Theological Society*
JJRS	*Japanese Journal of Religious Studies*
JP	*Journal de psychologie*
JPT	*Journal of Pentecostal Theology*
JPTS	Journal of Pentecostal Theology Supplement Series
JRA	*Journal of Religion in Africa*
JRS	*Journal of Religious Studies*
JSOTSup	Journal for the Study of the Old Testament: Supplement Series
JSSR	*Journal for the Scientific Study of Religion*
JTS	*Journal of Theological Studies*
JTSA	*Journal of Theology for South Africa*
LJ	*Liturgisches Jahrbuch*
LM	*Liturgical Ministry*
MEJ	*Mid-Stream: An Ecumenical Journal*
MQRP	*Mind: A Quarterly Review of Philosophy*
MS	*Mission Studies*
MT	*Modern Theology*
MTSR	*Method and Theory in the Study of Religion*
NIDPCM	*The New International Dictionary of Pentecostal and Charismatic Movements*, ed. Stanley M. Burgess and Eduard M. van der Maas, rev. and exp. ed. (Grand Rapids: Zondervan, 2002)
NZSTR	*Neue Zeitschrift für Systematische Theologie und Religionsphilosophie*
OIC	*One in Christ*
ÖR	*Ökumenische Rundschau*
PE	*Pentecostal Evangel*
PHA	*Pentecostal Holiness Advocate*
Pneuma	*Pneuma: Journal of the Society for Pentecostal Studies*
PR	*Psychological Review*
PRS	*Perspectives in Religious Studies*

PS	*PentecoStudies*
PT	*Psychology Today*
QS	*Qualitative Sociology*
RAC	*Religion and American Culture*
RE	*Review and Expositor*
RUS	*Rice University Studies*
SA	*Sociological Analysis*
SC	*Social Compass*
SHE	*Studia Historiae Ecclesiasticae*
SHT	Studies in Historical Theology
SJT	*Scottish Journal of Theology*
SL	*Studia Liturgica*
SM	*Svensk missionstidskrift*
SPS	*Society for Pentecostal Studies*
STh	*The Summa theologica of St. Thomas Aquinas Literally Translated by the Fathers of the English Dominican Province*, 22 vols., trans. L. Shapcote (Westminster, Christian Classics, 1948; 1981)
SV	*Seminary Viewpoint*
TE	*Theological Education*
TG	*Theologie und Glaube*
Thom	*Thomist*
ThTo	*Theology Today*
TJ	*Trinity Journal*
TP	*The Pentecost*
TS	*Theological Studies*
TynBul	*Tyndale Bulletin*
UDC	*Unité des chrétiens*
USQR	*Union Seminary Quarterly Review*
WA	*D. Martin Luther's Werke: kritische Gesamtausgabe*, Weimar ed. (Weimar: H. Böhlau, 1883-)
WAW	*Word and Witness*
WCC	World Council of Churches
WCILR	*Worship: Concerned with the Issues of Liturgical Renewal*
WE	*Weekly Evangel*
WPKG	*Wissenschaft und Praxis in Kirche und Gesellschaft*
WTJ	*Wesleyan Theological Journal*
WW	*Word and Work*
YFS	*Yale French Studies*
ZJRS	*Zygon: Journal of Religion and Science*
ZK	*Zeitschrift für Kirchengeschichte*
ZKT	*Zeitschrift für katholische Theologie*

Pentecostalism and Global Christianity in the Late Modern World

Christianity at the beginning of the twenty-first century faces one of its greatest opportunities as well as one of its greatest challenges: the formulation of a global theology. Of course, the articulation and explanation of the gospel of Jesus Christ have always been globally oriented. In this sense, globalization is not a future goal but a perpetual context of theology. Broadly speaking, global theology is any theology that has an impact on the world beyond its own immediate context. It is not the opposite of "contextual theology" but rather its extension to the concerns and contexts of a global environment.[1] Christianity exists in this perpetual transition from the local to the global, from the particular to the universal, and the task of theology changes as the theological enterprise is faced with the continuing emergence of new global voices.[2] The chief question in the twenty-first century, therefore, is not *whether* Christian theology can be global but *what* that global theology will look like. At the same time, the unique task of contemporary theology is to come to terms with the forms and content of global Christian thought and praxis as it arises from one particularity and engages a myriad of other voices arising from other and different contexts. The success of this task is challenged by widespread skepticism ranging from the fear of oppressive homogeneity to accusations of indiscriminate pluralism and universalism.

In this book I propose that Pentecostalism plays a crucial role in the articulation of the global theological task in the late modern world.[3] Pentecostalism as a worldwide phenomenon unifies the theological enterprise and allows it to speak to the particularities of diverse contexts. How-

1

ever, rather than elevating Pentecostalism to a universal ideal, I suggest that Pentecostal thought and praxis function as indispensable catalysts for the development of global Christianity that Pentecostalism perpetuates at the cost of its own particularity. The articulation of Christian theology at the dawn of the twenty-first century is inevitably confronted with Pentecostal imagination and spirituality. Nonetheless, the path ahead leads not only toward but also beyond Pentecostalism.

Beyond Pentecostalism captures the essence of this thesis by attempting to integrate Pentecostal thought and praxis in the global Christian agenda. In so doing, it is possible to accentuate Pentecostalism as a manifestation of what has been called the late modern or postmodern theological crisis. In the following chapters I describe the elements of this crisis, identify how classical Pentecostalism has become a manifestation of the crisis, and suggest that the task of overcoming the crisis can be accomplished by integrating Pentecostal thought and praxis in the global theological agenda. This task, I propose, will inevitably push Christianity beyond the boundaries of the classical Pentecostal tradition. In so doing, global Pentecostalism enables the renewal of the global theological agenda. In the following chapters, I refer to this complex development as the crisis of theology in the late modern world.

1. The Crisis of Theology in the Late Modern World

Theology in the twenty-first century is in a crisis. Whereas the twentieth century was widely focused on the articulation of a unified theological task, quickly apparent in the prolific amount of literature dedicated to the endeavor in the wake of the two world wars, little has been said about the direction of the theological agenda in the twenty-first century. Globalization, postmodernism, intellectualism, secularization, and other buzzwords are quickly held responsible for this crisis. Christian theology, it appears, has simply become too large, too divided, too abstract, and too worldly to connect God and a pluralistic reality.

The theological crisis has been noted most vehemently in the European context, once the center of a so-called crisis theology that arose among Karl Barth, Emil Brunner, Friedrich Gogarten, and others in the wake of World War I. While the optimism immediately following World War II caused a gradual decline of interest in the concept of crisis, concerns about the secularization of the Christian faith and the desacralization of the church since the 1960s have revived the discussion.[4] The outward symptoms of this revived crisis resemble, in the words of Heribert Mühlen, "a climax or turning point in the development of salvation history that can no longer be repressed and . . . that does not return once it is missed."[5] For many, the symptoms are indications of a culture no longer influenced by Christian norms and values as well as of a theology unable to confront the origins of that crisis. Mühlen, in particular, understood the European predicament fundamentally as a crisis in the traditioning of the Christian faith that points to the secularization not only of the church and theology, in particular, but also of the idea of God, in general.[6] The result of this crisis, he predicted, is the collapse not of the church as such but of the historical idea and of the theologies supporting a church that exist in a vacuum.

The recent changes in Central and Eastern Europe over the last decades have further accentuated the conversation about the latent crisis. Ludek Broz remarks in his observations on the theological task in Europe that today's theology continues to lack "a political, social and economic objectivity."[7] Broz holds the illusory concept of a "Christian Europe" and the secularization of academic theology responsible for this crisis, "a situation in which either theology was shut in the ivory tower of its own superiority and unjustified sanctity, or those who practised theology were simply incapable of conducting a dialogue with the world, sharing its concerns and responding to its questions."[8] Theology has become a largely academic, philosophical, speculative, and secular exercise.

In the North American context, the extent of the theological crisis has been frequently noted with reference to evangelical and Catholic theology, black theology, liberal theology, biblical theology, ecclesiology, ecumenical dialogue, soteriology, and other areas.[9] In Latin America, theologians speak of the crisis of Latin American theology in general, and of liberation theology in particular.[10] The sharp words of Desmond Tutu, John de Gruchy, David Bosch, and others have pointed to the political, ecclesiological, and ministerial crisis in South African theology.[11] Asian theology, like many others, finds itself in a crisis of articulating a theology that is authentically Asian rather than inherently Western.[12] The crisis of theology, it can be said, has reached global proportions. While some of this crisis language is perhaps not always theologically motivated, I nonetheless want to take the notion of "crisis" seriously for an understanding of global Christianity in the twenty-first century.

Taking the idea of crisis seriously raises two questions: first, what is meant by crisis, and second, what is the significance of crisis in Christian theology? In addressing these questions, one can turn initially to the "crisis theology" of the early twentieth century. In his *Theology of Crisis*, Brunner outlines two meanings of the word "crisis": "first, it signifies the climax of an illness; second, it denotes a turning-point in the progress of an enterprise or movement."[13] While Brunner preferred the term in its second meaning, it nonetheless retains aspects of the first. The point he wished to make was both methodological and historical. The theological crisis does not denote some momentary illness but constitutes the last stage "of that tremendous intellectual movement which took hold of Christian European society at the close of the Middle Ages."[14] Theology finds itself "between the times,"[15] to use Gogarten's phrase, a designation that can be interpreted with reference to both a historical particularity and a broader eschatological dimension. In its basic meaning, "crisis" refers to both the end of something present and the beginning of something new. As a matter of fact, a crisis itself constitutes both the conclusion of the former and the possibility of the latter.

In the late 1930s, Edmund Husserl delivered a number of lectures in which the significance of crisis as a catalyst for progress becomes more readily apparent.[16] While Husserl certainly shared the concerns of his generation for the problems of the time, his purpose for identifying the crisis was not to present a cure for the imminent demise of a certain ideal. For Husserl, crisis is not fundamentally destructive. Rather, crisis contains in itself the means for progress. As James Dodd points out in his analysis of Husserl's work, such a definition is not "limited to a diagnosis of the crisis, but on the contrary [is] its intensification and, above all, its very manifestation."[17] Like his theological contemporaries, Husserl understood the crisis not only in its historical particularity but also as a universal element. "But this is to say that, ultimately, all modern sciences drifted into a peculiar, increasingly puzzling crisis with regard to the meaning of their original founding as branches of philosophy, a meaning which they continued to bear within themselves. This is a crisis which does not encroach upon the theoretical and practical successes of the special sciences; yet it shakes to the foundation the whole meaning of their truth."[18]

Martin Heidegger, a student of Husserl, made similar observations on the crisis of philosophy that suggest that crisis can indeed be understood in a positive and normative way, even if it indicates that something is coming to an end.

> We understand the end of something all too easily in the negative sense as a mere stopping, as the lack of continuation, perhaps even as decline

and impotence. In contrast, what we say about the end of philosophy means the completion of metaphysics. However, completion does not mean perfection as a consequence of which philosophy would have attained the highest perfection at its end. . . . The end of philosophy is the place, that place in which the whole of philosophy's history is gathered in its most extreme possibility.[19]

My own use of the term "crisis" in contemporary theology is motivated primarily by identifying these extreme possibilities for the theological task at the beginning of the twenty-first century. Similar to Thomas Kuhn's argument that crisis is a necessary precondition for the emergence of novel theories in the sciences,[20] I use the notion of crisis in Christian theology as a positive term defined as both turning point and prerequisite for the development of global Christianity.[21] This understanding of the term is consistent with the important role "crisis" plays in Pentecostal thought, where it is seen as a catalyst that "makes new and/or supplemental insights into the past, new expectations for the future, and, hence, a new present self-understanding."[22] In light of this characterization, I suggest that classical Pentecostalism is a particular manifestation of the contemporary crisis in theology and responsible for bringing about the turn of Christianity toward a global agenda. Pentecostalism, to be precise, is not itself the crisis. It is the manifestation of a crisis that shakes the foundations of Christianity and of the whole theological enterprise.

Since its visible conception at the beginning of the twentieth century, the manifestation of classical Pentecostalism has been frequently understood as a religious anomaly.[23] While this perception could easily be thought to support the idea that Pentecostalism (through its anomalous thought and praxis) contributed to the crisis of theology, the notion of anomaly makes Pentecostalism the object of theological study rather than a participant in the inquiry.[24] This view would understand Pentecostalism as a subject matter of the theological discipline, an anomaly to be resolved. Going "beyond" Pentecostalism would thus mean to extinguish its peculiarities, to integrate it in the orthodox theological landscape in which it would eventually disappear. Such a view misunderstands the role of crisis in Christian theology and, as a result, fails to acknowledge the significance of Pentecostalism.

Instead, the heart of this study suggests that global Pentecostalism offers indispensable resources to overcome the manifestations of the contemporary crisis. A programmatic integration of Pentecostalism in the development of global Christianity makes it possible to cast a vision for the future direction of the theological agenda in general that is decidedly global inasmuch as it is genuinely Pentecostal. I suggest that classical Pentecostalism itself emerged in *response* to social, cultural, economic, moral, and theological anomalies of the late modern world. It became associated with these anomalies because its response to the crisis came in the form of new paradigms that were not readily accepted by orthodox theology. As Kuhn reminds us, changing paradigms in the midst of a crisis requires "a reconstruction of the field from new fundamentals, a reconstruction that changes some of the field's most elementary theoretical generalizations as well as many of its paradigm methods and applications."[25] The ensuing crisis is therefore the result not only of the anomalies themselves and the Pentecostal response, but is also a consequence of the resistance of orthodox theology to the Pentecostal worldview. With Brunner one might say, "Orthodoxy errs in its insistence on the rigidity and finality of its form, which, because of its lack of critical insight, it assumes to be essential to its existence."[26] To say this is to direct the attention away from the anomaly as the sole perpetrator of the contemporary crisis and to locate a response in the joint action of both Pentecostalism and the broader ecumenical landscape. The critical issues cannot be understood as anomalies isolated from either the development of the theological disciplines or the broader sociocultural, historical, philosophical, and ecclesial context brought about by the emergence of Pentecostalism.

In the present volume, I expand on this thesis in six interrelated chapters that each consists of three main parts. Each chapter begins by examining one aspect of the crisis of Christianity from a broad historical-systematic perspective that aims at a critical reconstruction of the global state of affairs. The content of these sections is expansive in scope in order to address the shift of foundations that has taken place in global Christianity in the late modern world. This analysis is followed by a narrative that reveals classical Pentecostalism as a manifestation of that particular aspect of the crisis. In this second section I tell the story of Pentecostalism in North America from the broad perspective of theological affairs raised in the first section, and thus in ways in which the story has not always been told. In the final part of each chapter I begin to conceptualize a constructive and programmatic proposal for global Christianity that offers resources to overcome the crisis from within the Pentecostal tradition and thereby integrates Pentecostalism into the broader theological landscape. I suggest that the task of theology at the beginning of the twenty-first century requires an awareness of the critical issues of our time as they relate to both the established theological paradigms and the new directions suggested by Pentecostal thought and praxis.

The Pentecostal resources offered in this volume are seen as programmatic for the contemporary theological endeavor inasmuch as they hold the promise to take Christianity beyond its current crisis. This prospect holds inevitable consequences for both Pentecostalism and the global theological community. The title, *Beyond Pentecostalism,* suggests both that Pentecostal faith and praxis are significant *beyond* Pentecostal circles and that Pentecostalism, as it engages the global Christian agenda, is in the process of going *beyond* its own historical, theological, sociocultural, and institutional boundaries. Contrary to the idea that the origin of classical Pentecostalism in the early twentieth century represents the heart of the movement,[27] I argue that global Pentecostalism — in becoming conscious of its roots — is in the process of going beyond them. The following chapters serve to point out this distinction between the boundaries of classical Pentecostalism (as a manifestation of the theological crisis) and global Pentecostalism (as a gateway to end the theological crisis). The notion to go "beyond" Pentecostalism therefore implies a number of important consequences for the global Christian agenda:

- To go beyond the geographical, cultural, ethnic, and religious particularities of the North American Pentecostal tradition.
- To go beyond the notion that the historical roots of classical Pentecostalism form the heart of the movement.
- To go beyond the isolated ecclesial definition of Pentecostalism as one alternative to the established mainline Christian traditions.
- To go beyond the idea that Pentecostal theology is essentially synonymous with a theology of the Holy Spirit.
- To go beyond the perception that Pentecostalism is a limited religious phenomenon.

In this sense, the phrase "beyond Pentecostalism" emphasizes a shift of focus away from issues relating to the major emphases of classical Pentecostalism and toward a global theological agenda that is of broad ecumenical significance. Rather than debating topics that are of central importance in classical Pentecostal circles, often emphasized by the framework of salvation, healing, Spirit baptism, sanctification, and the coming kingdom of God, this book identifies themes that are of general theological significance. Nonetheless, this shift in focus does not mean a neglect of Pentecostal concerns. On the contrary, going *beyond* Pentecostalism suggests that the classical Pentecostal themes are defined by the larger theological contexts by which they were shaped. In short, Pentecostal theology can be described as a manifestation of dominant, global theological developments that continue to shape Pentecostal thought and praxis. What lies "beyond" is a new Christian era that is defined as much by a complex, multilayered, and globally diverse theological agenda as by a different Pentecostalism.[28] In this sense, *Beyond Pentecostalism* does not advocate the "end" of Pentecostalism but its transformation into a global movement. Beyond the boundaries of the classical Pentecostal tradition lies not only a renewed understanding of Pentecostalism but also — as part of that renewal — a renewed understanding of global Christianity. Theology "beyond Pentecostalism" is Pentecostal theology for the world.

2. Integrating Pentecostalism in the Christian Agenda

Pentecostalism has always been an elusive entity. Descriptions and definitions range from religious or social movement, spiritual revival, free church, charismatic denomination, restorationism, evangelical fundamentalism, and independent dogmatic tradition, to global culture or postmodern lifestyle.[29] A definition of the term "Pentecostalism" is notoriously difficult and further complicated by the global expansion of this once isolated phenomenon. My feeling is that "Pentecostalism" is a transitional term that designates variant forms of an emerging theology and life of faith on a global, transethnic, and multicultural level that center around the idea of renewal through God's Spirit and as such challenge established social, cultural, and religious forms of thought and praxis. This broad definition begs further clarification.

At the least, Pentecostalism can be defined as "a community of common origin, language or rhetoric, and theological interests which includes, or has as its circumference, considerable theological diversity."[30] Yet, the very nature of this statement arouses questions about the exact understanding of Pentecostal origins, the uniformity of Pentecostal languages, and the particularity of the Pentecostal community. Simply put, the same definition can be given to a number of confessional groups and churches.

The definition of Pentecostalism in contrast to other confessional communities continues to be widely debated. Some scholars see the term

"Pentecostal" as primarily a social scientific construct, an idea similar in scope to the vague definition above, which embraces "a variety of forms, to such a degree even that it seems difficult to determine exactly what they all have in common."[31] Others have distinguished between sociological aspects and theological aspects in their approach.[32] Yet, most arguments suggest a doctrinal definition of Pentecostalism and its experiential and practical implications.[33] In this vein, the anti-Pentecostal argument has generally focused on the Pentecostal commitment to Spirit baptism and glossolalia.[34] More sympathetic accounts of Pentecostalism have emphasized a "common fourfold pattern" of salvation, sanctification, healing, and eschatological vision as the basis of the theological and historical discussion.[35] Internal debates have focused on the particular distinctives of Pentecostalism, ranging from three to five, eight, and more elements particular to the movement.[36] Much of this debate has taken place in a white, male, middle-class North American context. The emergence of Pentecostalism worldwide, however, has shifted the debate away from what is *distinctive* to the movement in a particular context to what is *central* to the Pentecostal sensitivity in general. A chief result of this debate is the understanding that the North American context in the early twentieth century may be regarded as the origin but not the heart of global Pentecostalism.

In his classic study of worldwide Pentecostalism, Walter Hollenweger differentiates between classical Pentecostals, the charismatic movement, and Pentecostal or "Pentecostal-like" independent churches.[37] More recently, Allan Anderson highlighted that "we must sometimes distinguish between denominational or 'classical' Pentecostalism on the one hand, and those other movements like Charismatic movements within the older churches, autochthonous prophetic churches in the Majority World and the neo-charismatic independent churches on the other."[38] A similar perspective was also adopted by the *New International Dictionary of Pentecostal and Charismatic Movements,* which identifies as "Pentecostal" the so-called classical Pentecostals connected with the revival at the Azusa Street Mission in Los Angeles (1906-1909); the members of the so-called charismatic movements in the established Roman Catholic, Protestant, and Orthodox churches that surfaced in North America during the 1960s; and so-called neocharismatic groups, "a catch-all category that comprises 18,810 independent, indigenous, postdenominational denominations and groups that cannot be classified as either Pentecostal or charismatic but share a common emphasis on the Holy Spirit, spiritual gifts, Pentecostal-like experiences (*not* Pentecostal terminology), signs and wonders, and power encounters."[39]

This diversity in approaches to and definitions of Pentecostalism has led to a number of terminological suggestions. Four suggestions stand out in particular: first, the use of the term "Pentecostal" as a broad and inclusive category "for describing globally all churches and movements that emphasize the working of the gifts of the Spirit, both on phenomenological and on theological grounds — although not without qualification."[40] The broad use of the term by Anderson, for example, is intended to emphasize Pentecostalism's cultural diversity and *includes* classical Pentecostal, charismatic, and neo-Pentecostal groups. A distinction between groups is generally made only when a narrower definition is required. This attempt to broaden the definition of Pentecostalism has been met with disapproval particularly among those who identify "the classical Pentecostal movement with North American conservative evangelicalism."[41]

A second option is to use the term "Pentecostalisms," in the plural, instead of the singular. The choice of this terminology by Cecil M. Robeck, Jr., for example, comes in response to the North American tendency to interpret Pentecostalism mono-culturally from the perspective of American cultural history with little or no reference to the legitimate cultural divergence of Pentecostal faith and practice in other countries around the world.[42] Others prefer the plural designation "Pentecostalisms" to emphasize not only the sociocultural locations of these communities but also the differences in doctrine, liturgy, politics, or church government.[43]

A third option, suggested sometimes in response to the first two, speaks of "Pentecostal" in deliberate contrast to "charismatic." This rationale emerges from the understanding of Pentecostals as "those affiliated to specifically Pentecostal denominations committed to a Pentecostal theology usually including a post-conversion experience of a baptism in the Spirit."[44] Despite a similar theological emphasis, the term "charismatic" is then used as a descriptor of those who choose to remain affiliated with their respective doctrinal families. The term "Pentecostal" in this perspective has primarily ecclesiological undertones and expresses the initial emergence of Pentecostalism from the established ecclesial traditions, the development of hostility and an exclusive attitude toward Pentecostal faith and practice in those churches, and the resulting exclusion or deliberate separation of Pentecostals from the established denominations.[45] Consequently, the term "Pentecostal" in this definition refers primarily to the emergence of classical Pentecostalism in the twentieth century accompanied by the development of autonomous statements of faith as well as ecclesial forms of organization and praxis that eventually gave rise to new theological emphases.

Finally, a fourth option has been proposed recently by Amos Yong, who prefers the capitalized form "Pentecostal" to refer to the classical expression of Pentecostalism and the uncapitalized form "pentecostal" to refer to the movement in general or inclusively to its classical, charismatic, and neo-Pentecostal forms.[46] The rationale for this distinction becomes clear in Yong's exercise to speak sensibly of worldwide pentecostalism as it includes nonclassical (i.e., non–North American) expressions of pentecostalism that are culturally, ethnically, and theologically diverse.[47] The possibility of global theology from the perspective of world pentecostalism therefore requires a sensitivity to the cultural, racial, religious, and linguistic distinctions of global pentecostalism from its classical expression in North America.

These terminological suggestions essentially rely on the use of a single term to mark the diversity of Pentecostalism. The frequent result is, at best, a terminological confusion, and at worst the inability to dialogue with one another. Because Pentecostalism is not alone in its diversity, it seems helpful to remind ourselves that no one speaks of Catholicism or Lutheranism in the plural (i.e., Catholicisms or Lutheranisms); neither do we find terms such as "neo-Methodism," "Reformed-like," or "classical Orthodox." Likewise, the capitalization of terms (or the lack thereof) is not a common feature in the designation of confessional traditions and cannot be adopted in languages that require (or reject) the capitalization of nouns. Instead, it is precisely the designation of a tradition by a single term that marks its unity *and* diversity in a global context. Put differently, although there exist various forms of one tradition in the cultural and ethnic communities around the world, the importance is placed not only on the diversity of a tradition but particularly on its unity. It is this diversity in unity that is masked by any linguistic alteration of the term "Pentecostalism." In its place I want to preserve the consistent use of the term "Pentecostal" by pointing out its transitional character on a global level.

I suggest that there exist commonalities among Pentecostals worldwide that warrant the use of the term "Pentecostalism" in its singular, capitalized form. The plural or lowercase variations of the term emphasize the existence of other expressions of Pentecostal faith and praxis but do so at the expense of masking the diversity in those realms.[48] This diversity is an expression of what I want to call "transitional." It captures in many regards the early designations of Pentecostalism as a "movement." Yet, while the idea of movement from a sociological or ecclesiological perspective is often applied to Pentecostalism in its relation to other traditions (i.e.,

Pentecostalism moves through the churches), the reference to its "transitional" character emphasizes that Pentecostalism is itself moved and thereby continues to be transformed. In this way, by "transitional" I wish to celebrate the distinctions within Pentecostalism by pointing to its substantial unity (*one* Pentecostalism) and explicitly stating its inherent development (e.g., *North American* Pentecostalism, *classical* Pentecostalism, or *Asian* Pentecostalism). The heart of this argument is the proposal that Pentecostalism by its very nature cannot be static but remains subject to spiritual formation, imagination, and conversion. This is frequently expressed by Pentecostals in the idea that "Pentecostalism" is not a human organization but a work of the Holy Spirit "in the latter days." Any generalizations of form are foreign to the character of Pentecostalism and can at best grasp a rudimentary set of elements that are accurate within a set of particular historical, geographical, cultural, or ethnic coordinates. Pentecostalism as a "transitional" phenomenon, on the other hand, constantly points *beyond* itself, from a particular culture to the ends of the world, from one language to a variety of tongues, from the present time to the last days, from the church to the kingdom, from the world to the work of God in Christ and the Holy Spirit.

The various attempts at adjectival classifications confirm the transitional character of Pentecostalism. Among the earliest terms is the phrase "classical Pentecostalism," which I adopt here to designate the North American context of Pentecostalism and its origins as a spiritual rather than a theological community, an alternate worldview rather than a professing ideology, a movement rather than an organizational structure, a grassroots rather than a global phenomenon. Classical Pentecostalism is itself undergoing a transformational renewal on a global level that has taken the movement to the boundaries of its own (forced-upon and self-imposed) identity. In turn, the phrase "global Pentecostalism" is used to embrace the spiritual reality of so-called classical Pentecostalism but also indicates that the theological significance of Pentecostalism is not exhausted by its twentieth-century North American form. The notion of "global" Pentecostalism is not intended to designate either the sum total of the "worldwide" Pentecostal communities or a particular range of "international" communities in distinction to one particular national identity. Instead, the adjective "global" describes the dynamic of Pentecostalism as a theological, historical, and social movement. The fact that Pentecostalism is becoming more and more an ideological, organizational, ecclesiastical, and global entity witnesses to the transitional nature of Pentecostalism that can be more readily seen as an imaginative, teleological type than a descriptive, isolated event. As such, Pentecostalism, in fulfilling its theological vocation, tends to go beyond itself because it is fundamentally oriented toward God's presence in the world.

3. Revisioning the Theological Landscape

The integration of Pentecostalism in the global Christian agenda requires a broad theological vision. The following chapters begin to map out the terrain of this task through the lens of global Pentecostalism. However, the theological agenda envisioned here is not limited to the particularities of the Pentecostal community but addresses the global theological public. In other words, the goal is not a "pentecostalization" of Christianity but a revisioning of the global theological landscape in light of the significance of Pentecostal voices, thoughts, and practices worldwide. A broader metaphor is needed to reflect on the far-reaching implications of this task even beyond Pentecostalism, and to formulate a contrast between this vision and the orthodox forms of theology today. For this purpose, I employ the metaphor of "play."

On a general level, I suggest that the notion of play captures the essence of global Christianity, the dynamic of the theological disciplines, and the chorus of voices that characterizes the worldwide theological agenda. The notion of play is disinterested in any one particular theological perspective or community and thus is sensitive to the scope of the global theological task. At the same time, play reflects well the character, sensibilities, and practices of Pentecostalism; at the very least, both Pentecostalism and play are equally challenging dimensions in the dominant theological worldviews. In principle, "play" refers to any activity done for the joy of doing it and not for any performative, competitive, functionalistic, rationalistic, or utilitarian reasons. Theologically speaking, play is the joy of God in which we participate. These admittedly broad definitions will be further clarified in the context of each chapter with focus on addressing the various crisis moments of the contemporary theological agenda. My intention is not to develop a romantic idea of theology as play but to allow the image to shed light on the current theological ethos, both critically and therapeutically. This important realism shows that play itself has entered a substantial crisis in the late modern world. The nature of play is distinct from a game, as essentially a competitive exercise, and from dramatic play, as a performative act. In many ways, competition and performance delineate the extremes of play from which I wish to distinguish today's theological agenda.[49] On the other hand, play does not negate the reasonableness or earnestness of the theological task. By using the metaphor, I do not intend to make light of the sincerity and importance of Christian thought but rather to outline the emerging contours of global Christianity characterized by a distinct manner of being and self-understanding that stands in contrast to the dominant forms of the established theological "enterprise."

In the following chapters, the notion of play therefore serves as a guiding metaphor for reenvisioning, from the perspective of Pentecostalism, the shape of the global theological agenda, its focus, methods, concepts, and language. The goal of this volume is not simply to equate theology in general with the activity of play. Suggestions to that effect have been criticized in the past.[50] Instead, I propose that theology from a Pentecostal perspective can be characterized as play in contrast to both the realm of nonplay and the rational, performance-oriented, functionalistic, utilitarian, and institutionalized dimensions that describe much of the contemporary theological landscape. The perspective I advance thus challenges the circumstances that contradict or restrict the possibility and operation of theology as a participation in the joy of God. I examine these circumstances in the various dimensions of theology in general, and advocate that an understanding of the contributions of global Pentecostalism can serve the transformation of the theological ethos in the late modern world.

Based on this broad perspective, *Beyond Pentecostalism* intends a fundamental revision of the theological agenda by questioning its dominant sources and procedures in the context of the emerging face of global Christianity and by offering an alternative organization and orientation of theological loci. This revision emerges from a critical analysis of major theological headings *(loci theologici)*, their organization into systems of doctrine *(loci communes)*, and the foundational sources from which these doctrines are derived *(loci classici)*, an analysis that forms the starting point for each of the following chapters. While the loci of Christian theology in principle reflect the entire self-disclosure of God, theologians have repeatedly remarked on their actual restrictions and offered corrections and additions from the perspectives of their contemporary contexts.[51] In step with this extensive tradition, I suggest that global Pentecostalism offers a number of unique resources that address the challenges of theology in the twenty-first century: a revival of the theological imagination and its integration in the use of reason (chapter 1); a correction of the objectification of Scripture as text with a charismatic view of revelation (chapter 2); a reformulation of doctrine beyond the confines of creedal formulations (chapter 3); a transformation of the liturgy from a conceptually fixed, written, tradition-based framework into a liminal, antistructural notion of ritual (chapter 4); a revision of ecclesiality that understands the churches not as distinct, alternative institutions to each other but as dynamic, multicultural, and ecumenical movements (chapter 5); and an inherent emphasis on renewal that takes Pentecostalism beyond the boundaries of orthodoxy and, in so doing, offers a prototype for transforming the theological ethos in the late modern world (chapter 6).

What I envision, then, in going "beyond" the various aspects that define the current state of Christianity, is a fundamental attitude of flexibility and openness, a dynamic of playfulness, that repossesses and liberates traditional theological structures. I do not suggest that theology can escape the use of reason, Scripture, doctrine, ritual, and community, as might be suggested by the titles of the subsequent chapters. On the contrary, I propose that the resources provided by Pentecostalism are able to integrate orthodox theological structures and, by so doing, to transform them in an attitude that releases their full potential for a global Christianity. In this sense, the work presented here is intended, on the most fundamental level, as an invitation to play with Christian orthodoxy.

Pentecostals themselves have issued this invitation in a number of ways that I will introduce throughout this volume. The result can be no more than a programmatic proposal for a revisioning of the theological agenda. A full-scale "systematic theology" that is true to the Pentecostal ethos I describe in the following chapters has not yet been produced. For this to happen, there is need for a more foundational and critical self-evaluation among Pentecostals and of Pentecostalism in the global, ecumenical community. The following chapters initiate this kind of exercise and intend to stimulate the further integration of Pentecostal thought and praxis. The players I introduce along the way come from various traditions, sometimes unaccustomed to the idea of play and often with differing intentions and visions. This diversity enriches the kind of play we call "theology." It is a joyful, imaginative, risky, and richly rewarding exercise.

1 Beyond Reason

Theology, Story,
and the Crisis of the Imagination

Theology is the human pursuit of God. For centuries, those who have participated in this quest have acknowledged that its starting point is not the human being but God who chooses to reveal himself. Revelation is seen as the self-uncovering of the transcendent, mysterious God and the communication of the divine reality to the creature. This dominant emphasis on the divine self-manifestation has placed revelation effectively outside of the human being as that which comes to the created world from an uncreated and unknowable God. The human mind cannot arrive at the knowledge of the triune God without God's revelation. Left on its own, the mind always falls short of the full knowledge of God. Revelation, however, is said to offer the possibility of responding to and interpreting the divine existence. God's openness challenges the human being to open up in response to the God who would otherwise remain out of reach. The response to revelation is the rational interpretation of the experience of God's self-manifestation. Reason makes possible the human response to revelation, although the mind by itself could not arrive at the knowledge of God. The human being thus finds itself in a crisis: the mind is confronted with the unmanageable task of comprehending the divine, the unknown, and the uncreated, with the help of the human, the familiar, and the things that are made. Theology becomes a responsive and interpretive endeavor, always challenged to reach out to that which lies beyond the human but never able to participate fully in the divine. The mind waits for God to act. Apart from God's revelation, human beings are condemned to live with a limited idea of God that hungers for more but cannot satisfy its imagination. Reason becomes the abyss between the unveiling of God's self and the response of the human mind.

In contrast, some have resisted the understanding of revelation as an external event that subsequently has to be appropriated by human reason. Rather than an unveiling of God, revelation is understood by this perspective as an unveiling of the human soul. The self-manifestation of God calls, in the first place, for an exercise not of reason but of the imagination. Involved in this operation is not only the human mind but also the "spirit" — both the human and the divine — necessitating a relationship of the human being and God and making possible a participation of the human person in the divine self-manifestation. Revelation thus means not only communication but also transformation. The human being actively participates in the event by allowing the ascent of the soul to God. Revelation becomes a movement toward the beautiful, the good, and the holy by a soul that is itself made beautiful, good, and holy through its pursuit of the vision of God.

The historical emergence of these two movements manifests itself in the continuing juxtaposition of reason and the imagination cycling repeatedly from the elevation of one at the expense of the other. The movement that understands revelation as an unveiling of the transcendent God has its origins in the metaphysical argument of the autonomy of reason; the movement that understands revelation as an unveiling of the soul has its roots in the spiritual argument of the ascent of the soul. In this chapter I trace the development of these two movements by arguing that the crisis of global Christianity is at its foundation a crisis of the imagination that has come to its climax in the late modern world. The first part provides a historical overview of the role attributed to the imagination in the Western philosophical and theological traditions, tracing the development to its contemporary crisis. The second part analyzes the manifestation of the crisis in classical Pentecostalism. The final part explores the resources global Pentecostalism has to offer for a revival of the imagination.

1. The Crisis of the Imagination

The emergence of a crisis of the imagination from antiquity to the modern age is well documented.[1] The proclamation of a crisis is generally constructed by juxtaposing the use of reason with the use of the imagination. The elevation of one at the expense of the other can be outlined historically in the occurrence of five alternating cycles: (1) Plato's subordination of the imagination to the authority of reason, (2) the elevation of the imagination in patristic thought, (3) the discrimination against the imagination during the Middle Ages, (4) the triumph of the imagination in German idealism, and (5) the deconstruction of the imagination in the postmodern era. Rather than a disconnected alternation of views, subsequent cycles build on the opposing views of their predecessor(s). In this development, it is the rejection of the imagination that persists in Christian thought, making the imagination subservient to reason, a judgment attributed to the early formative influences of Neoplatonism and the skepticism exhibited in Western thought since the Enlightenment.[2] The Western philosophical tradition has repeatedly interpreted the imagination methodologically rather than theologically, thereby focusing on the practice of the imagination in light of the use of reason rather than the role of the imagination in the human relationship with God. Indebted to this interpretation, theology has eclipsed a number of fundamental attributes from its own agenda.

Plato's Subordination of the Imagination

The historical narrative of the imagination begins with Plato's systematic critical account, which has defined the imagination "in at least five fields of thought: in epistemology, in psychology, in ethics, in theology, and in aesthetics."[3] Epistemologically, Plato saw the imagination as confined to the world of sensory perception and unable to penetrate true reality. Psychologically, the imagination is found in the irrational soul, the place of human desires, appetites, and passions. Ethically, and as a result of the former, the imagination is a seduction to fabrication, untruth, and the irrational and is therefore inherently immoral. Aesthetically, the imagination is a mere reproductive faculty concerned with the material, the individual, and the transitional, distorting reality and unable to represent more than a reduced image of the truth.[4] Theologically, pure ideas exist only in the mind of God. Although the human being is recognized for its imaginative powers in dreams and visions, these remain subjective and unreal and as such not only unable to contemplate the divine truth but also inclined to replace the divine order with an idolatrous copy. Imagination is imitation, and humanity, insofar as it is unable to reach beyond the world of images, has become a race of imitators.[5]

Plato's negative view of the imagination stands in sharp contrast to his elevation of reason, a dualistic characterization illustrated most vividly in Plato's allegory of the cave.[6] For Plato, only reason is able to contemplate true reality, while the imagination is relegated to the mere reflections of the sensory world. The exercise of the imagination imprisons human beings in the illusory world of darkness and shadows. Reason alone is able "to lead the best part of the soul up to the contemplation of what is best among realities."[7]

This necessarily oversimplified summary of Platonic thought underscores the foundation for a dialectic that has also found, through Stoicism and Neoplatonism, entrance into Christian theology.[8] Moreover, with the separation of reason and imagination, theology took over its inherent contradiction. Despite Plato's seeming verdict to elevate reason at the expense of the imagination, he does not utterly condemn the use of the imaginative powers.[9] Instead, Plato suggests that "images may serve a positive heuristic purpose by providing the mind with quasi-intuitive representations of otherwise invisible truths."[10] Three aspects characterize this unexpected acknowledgment of the imagination. First, it appears in the context of Plato's urge toward the transcendent (thus giving the imagination a revelatory function); second, it places the epistemological discussion in the framework of the communication of truth (thus giving the imagination a discursive function); third, it portrays the quest for truth as a pursuit of the good and the beautiful (thus giving the imagination an ethical and aesthetic function). Here, the imagination sheds its purely reproductive function and takes on an active sense.[11] As such, the imagination can be a pathway to the transcendent and divine. The theologian is left with an apparent paradox. On the one hand, only reason is able to overcome the illusions of this world constructed by the imagination; on the other hand, only the imagination can behold the original beauty of divine revelation. The theological implications of this account were readily apparent to the writers of the patristic age who inherited Plato's views and, with it, the paradox of the imagination.

Patristic Elevation of the Imagination

The influence of Platonic thought is well documented in early Christian literature.[12] However, the patristic writers inherited alongside the philosophical tradition a biblical view of the imagination that focused the debate on its ethical dimension.[13] The imagination is an ambiguous notion in the biblical Scriptures. It does not exist as a technical term but must be inferred from a family of root words in the Old and New Testaments.[14] In the Hebrew Scriptures, as Walter Brueggemann shows, imagination when placed in the context of the human relationship with God contains the potential for both good and evil, so that "there is an awareness of the danger of the imagination which is autonomous, and at the same time a vigorous practice of *emancipated imagination which is obedient.*"[15] The New Testament writers contrast the imagination with reality but also emphasize that human reason falls short in understanding divine revelation. Paul, in particular, places the imagination in an ethical context and, in so doing, distinguishes the potential for good from its negative counterpart by virtue of the presence of the divine Spirit in the human being (see 1 Cor. 2:9-16; Gal. 5:16-25). The early Christian writers thus inherited both the dualism of the Platonic tradition between reason and imagination and the dualism of the biblical Scriptures between the spirit and the flesh.

The patristic writers considered the difficulty of comprehending God apart from the senses as one the greatest obstacles to theology. As one of the first, Tertullian questioned the Platonic rejection of the imagination and searched for some intermediary operation, "something that takes place between sensation and thought."[16] Irenaeus reflects on this possibility more explicitly through a Trinitarian perspective, "for God the Father is shown forth through all these [operations], the Spirit indeed working, and the Son ministering, while the Father was approving."[17] He insists that the triune God possesses a visible and audible dimension and that a righteous vision of God is therefore possible "by men who bear His Spirit."[18] Later authors continue this line of thinking with emphasis on the pneumatological dimension of the imagination.[19] The imagination can lead to a vision of God because it is an operation of the Holy Spirit. The patristic writers describe this aspect repeatedly as the pursuit of beauty by those who have themselves become beautiful, a Platonic concept cast in the Christian language of holiness and purity.[20]

Eventually, Augustine consolidated the patristic elevation of the imagination. Significantly, in his *Confessions* he laments that he had looked for an external vision of God while neglecting to seek the beauty of God on the inside of his person.[21] The concern about the possibly corruptive influence of the imagination remains, and Augustine emphasizes the importance of the purity of heart.[22] The ethical dimension, in particular, allowed Augustine to integrate rather than to distinguish the imagination from the use of reason. He insists that reason is a necessary component of the imagination in order to distinguish the true image from human fantasy and idolatry. In light of the potential of imaginative powers for both good and evil, any errors of the imagination are therefore based fundamentally on the operation of the will.[23] Augustine's distinction between the image and the imagination as ultimately an act of reason prepared "the way for a view of imagination as transcending the capacities of the simple reproductive faculty."[24] More precisely, the imagination is elevated to a spiritual activity that mediates between the senses of the body and the intellect.[25] The proper use of the imagination follows a hierarchy from the image itself to a spiritual vision and, eventually, to the interpretation of that vision by the intellect.[26] The imagination is necessary for prophecy, dreams, and visions, which all call on the operation of the mind for their interpretation.[27] Augustine therefore confirms the importance of both the ethical and the pneumatological dimensions, which form the backbone of the patristic elevation of the imagination.

The Medieval Discrimination against the Imagination

As we enter the medieval world, we find that Augustine's elevation of the imagination to a spiritual activity soon led to the counterassertion that the productive function of the imagination must not make the mind a mere passive recipient of sensory experience.[28] Medieval theology maintained Augustine's threefold order of image, imagination, and intellect. Yet, contrary to Augustine's intentions, by assigning the imagination a mediating position, medieval theology reinforced the Platonic dualism and undermined the pneumatological dimension of the imagination.[29] Three aspects are particularly significant to medieval thought: first, medieval interpretation of the biblical Scriptures revived the ethical suspicion of the imagination;[30] second, this suspicion was coupled with the rise of a secular and occult imagination and a resulting degradation of the imagination in general as diabolic, demonic, and heretical;[31] third, the imagination, although still a necessary corollary for connecting reason with the senses, is no longer seen as a spiritual activity but as purely instrumental to reason. The patristic emphasis on the imagination is exchanged for the medieval notion of meditative contemplation.[32]

The idea of contemplation is explained in detail by Richard of St. Victor, whose distinction of six kinds of imagination illustrates well its devaluation in the medieval period.[33] The imagination is shifted again to the lowest level of human faculties and is seen as merely a "handmaid" and "vestment" for the mind.[34] Similarly, Bonaventure describes the imagination as mere "shadows, echoes and pictures . . . vestiges, representations, spectacles . . . exteriorly given" through which "we are disposed to reenter the mirror of our mind in which divine realities shine forth."[35] For medieval mysticism, influenced as it was by the scholastic emphasis on reality and rationality, contemplation, not the imagination, represents the productive faculty. The beautiful, therefore, as Thomas Aquinas puts it, "has to do with knowledge."[36] Although the knowledge of beauty still proceeds from images, beauty is now understood as "a reference to the cognitive powers" and the imagination is judged by intellectual habits.[37] The patristic emphasis on a pneumatological dimension of the imagination as a pursuit of holiness disappears. Ethically and epistemologically, reason is reestablished as the highest human faculty. The medieval discrimination against the imagination persisted throughout the Renaissance period, when confidence in the cognitive function of the imagination finally disappeared entirely.[38]

German Idealism and the Triumph of the Imagination

Only the German idealists of the eighteenth and nineteenth centuries reconsidered the creative function of the imagination, albeit not by a revival of patristic thought but through a genuine interest in the role of the imagination in human existence, cognition, and aesthetics. Immanuel Kant is widely credited with the liberation of the imagination from its reproductive role, declaring it to be not only a productive faculty but also the presupposition of both sensation and understanding.[39] Although Kant continued to grant the imagination a halfway position between sense experience and the intellect, he distinguished between the empirical imagination, which is entirely reproductive, serving a posteriori to identify and associate ideas, and the transcendental imagination, which is productive and creative, serving a priori as the condition of all knowledge.[40] With this distinction, the way was opened for German idealism to discover the imaginative power as a driving force in, as F. W. J. Schelling puts it, "the original, still unconscious, poetry of the spirit."[41] Fichte, then, understood the creative imagination as the "capacity" that determines "whether one philosophizes with or without spirit."[42] This idea was solidified in detail in Hegel's philosophy of spirit.[43] The immediate result was the reestablishment of greater credibility regarding the imagination in epistemology, aesthetics, and moral judgment.

Nonetheless, with the reference of the transcendental imagination to an activity of "spirit," Kant and his followers referred to the realm of the human mind, a synthesis of sensible experience and intelligence, and not, like the patristic authors, to the Holy Spirit and the presence of the divine in the human being.[44] The imagination is transcendental by being a creative incentive of the human intellect that produces objectivity and thereby represents all objects of possible experience.[45] The transcendental imagination operates as an act of the understanding on an "inner sense"[46] that makes possible the experience of beauty and goodness, that is, aesthetic and moral judgment. The imagination is thus free to move within its own productive activity, bound by no rules other than its own (i.e., those of the senses and the intellect). Those who imagine are able to experience not only the beautiful but also the sublime in the very fact that in the use of the imagination the person is confronted with the intricate idea that there is *more* than can be imagined.[47]

In this sense, the imagination is seen as an ecstatic power that can arouse the mind to become aware even of God's sublimity insofar as one's attitude conforms to God's will.[48] Similar to the patristic rejection of Plato's dualism, for the idealists the imagination is subject to an ongoing task of moral improvement, and beauty is "the symbol of the morally good."[49] The highest good is a moral ideal to which the "mighty" imagination strives.[50] As Philip J. Rossi observes, it is "the moral imagination by which the social authority of reason empowers us to hope."[51] This hope of the imagination is able to transform our experiences and judgments and has no limits other than the inadequacy of human images for the sublime.

The Postmodern Deconstruction of the Imagination

Despite these concessions, the flight of the imagination in German idealism did not last beyond the rise of what Paul Ricoeur has called the "hermeneutics of suspicion."[52] Fueled by the growing disillusionment of modernization and industrialization, an attitude of suspicion turned against the extravagant freedom granted to the subjectivity of the human mind. As one of the first, Ludwig Feuerbach's unprecedented critique of religion in the nineteenth century accused the theological imagination of being noth-

ing but a projection of human self-consciousness.[53] Not only did his critique influence revolutionary thinkers such as Marx, Engels, Ruge, Bauer,
Stirner, and Strauss, but echoes of Feuerbach's thought are also found
throughout the works of Friedrich Heinrich Jacobi, Friedrich Nietzsche,
Martin Heidegger, Jean-Paul Sartre, and other late modern thinkers.[54] For
these writers, the use of the imagination had produced a sensuous theology that had to be tempered again by reason. However, the path beyond
idealism, as Jacobi explained, became an attempt to reconcile the imagination with scientific reasoning that ultimately dissolved both into nothing.[55] Nietzsche most forcefully declared that all truth was consequently an
illusion and, in formulating a case against the Christian imagination, accused Christianity of the explicit practice of nihilism. Christian theology
was declared guilty of masking its imagination as truth while failing to acknowledge the complexity of understanding human existence.[56]

Nietzsche and Kierkegaard, both essential figures of nineteenth-
century existentialism, rejected the optimism of idealism and its trust in
the imagination.[57] Eventually, Heidegger took on the project to transform
the idealist notion of the imagination to fit the confines of phenomenological existentialism in the twentieth century.[58] He argued that Kant's
own concept ultimately led him to reject the notion of the transcendental
imagination on the grounds that it questions the very possibility of transcendence.[59] The notion of "pure" reason, so to speak, "deprived itself of
its own theme if pure reason transformed into transcendental imagination."[60] For Heidegger, the imagination is fundamentally a mode of the existence of a finite human being, and as such a temporal act that cannot
project itself beyond the nothingness of human existence.[61] Jean-Paul
Sartre consolidated this interpretation and declared images to be essentially nothing, turning the imagination fundamentally into a negating activity that ceases to exist the moment its object becomes real.[62] The modern world turned the objective of the imagination from the pursuit of
beauty into the abyss of the nothing. The use of the imagination became a
pathological, neurotic activity that is condemned to remain aesthetically
empty and ethically absurd.[63] The pursuit of God through the imagination
had thus become an impossible task.

In the late modern world, the imagination found itself finally at the
heart of a full-blown crisis. As Richard Kearney remarks in his account of
postmodern culture, "across the spectrum of structuralist, post-
structuralist and deconstructionist thinking, one notes a common concern to dismantle the very notion of imagination."[64] While the patristic

imagination found its origin in the divine, and the transcendental imagination in the human being, the postmodern account dissolves the imagination into the unidentified processes of human language.[65] As one of the first, Ferdinand de Saussure, the father of twentieth-century linguistics, reduced images to arbitrary signs that receive their meaning only within the autonomous system of language.[66] The role of the imagination is insignificant because it does not affect the existence of the sign, which is made possible entirely by the fixed code of the community.[67] The social theorist Jean Baudrillard further restricts this code to govern only certain signs, rejecting the existence of a universal system.[68] Language itself, to follow Jacques Derrida, is merely the product of an autonomous, impersonal, and artificial process of mimesis.[69] Imagination is once again seen as nothing but imitation, an isolated process that inevitably leads to what Jean-François Lyotard has called the postmodern "incredulity toward metanarratives."[70]

Lyotard's observation relates primarily to the nature of the claims made by those who legitimate their narratives "by an appeal to a supposed universal, scientific reason."[71] The rejection of the imagination has contributed to the proposal of grand narratives based on a rationalist definition of knowledge and an appeal to a universal, scientific reason in which the story itself is dispersed into anonymous processes of language and universal, scientific codes. From a theological perspective, the postmodern incredulity toward these claims has become one of the most challenging tasks, since the imagination is central to both the biblical narratives and the traditioning process that resulted in the biblical Scriptures.[72] The biblical story, and with it the story of God's people, is not based on a scientific metanarrative but on the unfolding drama of God's story in the church and in the world.[73] A revival of the imagination comes at the cost of juxtaposing this story with the critical inquiry and universal claims that have come to govern the late modern world; its existence stands in contrast to the eclipse of the imagination from theological criteria and expectations and thereby from the life of the church. At present, as postcolonial theology would put it, the imagination has lost its historical, dialogical, and diasporic dimensions.[74] The imagination is defined neither anthropologically nor theologically: it has no memory, no meaning, no ethnicity, no culture, no language, and no text.[75] The use of the imagination has no revelatory, spiritual, aesthetic, or ethical function. As a result, theology has been deprived of a genuine language and formulation of the Christian story.

2. The Pentecostal Story and the Revival of the Imagination

Classical Pentecostalism emerged in conflict with the modern rejection of
the imagination. This opposition was not formulated explicitly but crafted
and developed in testimonies, songs, sermons, and pamphlets circulating
largely within the movement. Pentecostals at the turn of the twentieth century were neither trained philosophers nor professional theologians and
were mostly unacquainted with the challenges of conceptual, systematic
theological inquiry.[76] A definition of the Pentecostal self-understanding in
terms evading and even contradicting the established philosophical categories and theological traditions did not emerge until the rise of the charismatic movement in the 1960s and the growth of Pentecostal scholarship
since the 1970s. Instead, the origins of classical Pentecostalism are marked
by an austere skepticism of the human intellectual capacities and a dependence on the use of the imagination.

Classical Pentecostalism erupted in pockets throughout the late nineteenth century until the more broadly recognized Azusa Street revival in
Los Angeles, California, in 1906.[77] A trademark of these pioneers was the
lack of conceptual and communicative tools to process and evaluate their
own experiences. Most of them had neither the training nor the time to in-
vestigate and explain the occurrences, yet they were convinced that their
experiences were from God.[78] This conviction was based not on logical arguments or defined doctrinal persuasions but on an imagination that approached God and the world in seemingly precognitive, unmeditated,
counterintuitive, and unreasonable ways. Nevertheless, Pentecostals were
aware of the various elements of their own experiences that allowed them
to be recognized by one another and by those who rejected them.[79] What
was lacking for the community as a whole was a comprehensive narrative
that would offer a self-understanding of their own identity that could be
communicated to the orthodox theological establishment of the day.

The Pentecostal Story

The theme for a narrative of Pentecostalism was provided by the biblical
images of holiness, sanctification, and consecration. The immediate origins
of Pentecostalism in North America coincide with the rise of the Holiness
movement in the nineteenth century.[80] The established churches, and the
Reformed view of the Christian life that was dominant in colonial America,

were frequently opposed to this theological emphasis, since the political economy of the mainline churches did not provide the means with which it could be interpreted and integrated.[81] Theology in the early twentieth century assigned a negative value to the imagination of the Holiness movement and its emphasis on individual transformation (a second crisis) as a continuation of salvation (a second work of grace) and the claim of Christian perfection.[82] Pentecostals, on the other hand, found in the imagination of the Holiness movement the roots for their own story, usually expressed in sermons, testimonies, and songs.[83] Frequently, the image of a holy and righteous God who called the world to repentance carried over into spontaneous songs that could be heard long after the worship services. As C. E. Jones explains, "a new genre of Holiness-experience songs emerged" that "drew worshipers into sympathy one to another at the same time they were reinforcing teaching from the pulpit and creating a common doctrinal and behavioral standard."[84] These songs became the initial outlet for the communal imagination of early Pentecostals:

> The people sang in the Spirit, and such singing as we had never heard before. The very air was laden with the spirit of these songs; and as we returned home from the meeting that night, we could hear the different crowds going down their respective road singing.[85]

The shared expression of the holiness imagination formed the thematic backdrop for the formation of the Pentecostal self-understanding:

> When I first heard of holiness I thought it must be right;
> It seemed to fit the Bible, And be the Christian light.
> I heard the people singing and testifying too;
> They seemed to love their Savior, As Christians ought to do.
>
> I little thought of joining, I said I could not stand,
> To be among that people, That's called the "holy band."
> The world looked down upon them, And said they were so rash,
> They often spoke against them, And said they were but trash.
>
> But as I went to hear them, And saw the way they did,
> I saw they had a treasure, From worldly people hid.
> They seemed to be so happy, And filled with Christian love;
> When people talked about them, They only looked above.

My heart began to hunger, And thirst and burn within:
I wanted full salvation, A freedom from all sin.
I went to God for holiness, And called upon his name;
He cleansed my heart completely, And filled it with the same.[86]

The emphasis on holiness permeated early Pentecostal literature, frequently clothed in biblical language and imagery of repentance, sanctification, and perfection.[87] However, while holiness provided the overarching
theme for the emerging self-understanding of classical Pentecostalism, the
eschatological emphasis of the biblical Scriptures, coupled with a pessimistic
outlook on the progress of history and the expectation of the imminent return of Christ, provided the overarching worldview for the Pentecostal
imagination.[88] The primary illustration for this imagination was the battle
imagery provided by the apocalyptic texts of Scripture. Hymns such as "On-
ward, Christian Soldiers," "Battling for the Lord," and "On to Victory" became popular expressions of the eschatological sentiment among classical
Pentecostals. The root for this imagination remained the holiness theme,
which now became woven into a larger story of warfare between good and
evil, God and Satan, holiness and sin, a drama that involved God's people
under the command of Christ as the primary actors on the battlefield.

There is need of valiant soldiers in the army of the Lord,
To rally round the standard of the cross;
With a holy consecration and unwavering faith in God,
Oh, rally round the standard of the cross!

Strongly guarded and defended are the battlements of sin;
Oh, rally round the standard of the cross!
But with Christ our blest Commander, we the victory shall win;
Oh, rally round the standard of the cross![89]

The eschatological urgency and apocalyptic vision among classical
Pentecostals further hardened the fronts to the established churches. For
Pentecostals, the biblical texts and the apostolic community provided "a
photograph as it were"[90] of the Christian life lived in expectation of the
end of the world. The Pentecostal imagination envisioned the last days as
the unfolding of a cosmic drama of hope and judgment that constituted
an irreversible break with the world and became the heartbeat of the Pentecostal self-understanding.[91] The church was an "army with banners,"[92] a

missionary movement, standing at the dawn of the world's final crisis.[93] Combined with this missionary zeal were eschatological images that were soon adopted to describe the movement as a whole, among them "Apostolic Faith" (with its emphasis on the restoration of the church before the end of the age), "Latter Rain" (with its emphasis on the realization of the final dispensation of history), "Full Gospel" (with its emphasis on the impending consummation of the kingdom of God), and "Pentecostal" (with its emphasis on the fulfillment of God's promises in the last days).[94] Among these, the events of Pentecost reflected particularly well the experiences of the holiness-eschatological imagination and were soon adopted as the plot for what now became, more explicitly, a "Pentecostal" story.

Pentecostals found in the New Testament narrative of Luke-Acts a comprehensive plot for those who recognized their own experiences in the events of the day of Pentecost and who counted themselves among those addressed by the prophecy of Acts 2:17-21 and the promise to succeeding generations in Acts 2:39. However, the biblical narrative was typically transmitted orally among Pentecostals rather than in written form.[95] As a result, the story of Pentecost was integrated into the larger biblical story, alongside other narratives, and there formed a dynamic tradition that expressed not only the biblical story itself, but also a person's understanding of and participation in that story. New members added to this imagination, bringing with them the likes and dislikes of their former religious backgrounds and forming a multifaceted narrative that was as much a reflection of the biblical texts as of their own experiences.[96] In the biblical narrative, Pentecostals found a common emphasis on dreams, visions, ecstatic utterances, words of knowledge, words of wisdom, spiritual discernment, and a prophetic imagination that provided the fundamental framework for articulating their own story.

> On the day of Pentecost, when the Holy Ghost was seen, heard and felt, thousands were brought into the spiritual kingdom of God. Peter stood up in a blaze of Holy Ghost power and glory, and said when God poured out His Spirit on His sons and daughters they would see visions and dream dreams and prophesy. He told them that these signs would be sure to follow the outpourings of His Spirit.[97]

As this retelling of the story of Pentecost illustrates, the biblical narrative provided Pentecostals with the plot for the articulation of their own imagination. It placed the theme of holiness and the drama of the last days in the specific context of the continuing manifestation of God in history, which a person had now encountered. Although deeply committed to the revelation of God in Jesus Christ, the story of Pentecost shifted the theological emphasis to the continuing eschatological and sanctifying activity of the Holy Spirit.

At the heart of the Pentecostal story stood the outpouring of the Holy Spirit. Pentecost was seen as both a unique, historical event and a continuing renewal and realization of that event in the subsequent unfolding of history. The biblical narrative opened up the realization of the prophecy of Joel 2:28-32 to those present in Jerusalem on the day of Pentecost and to "all who are afar off" (Acts 2:39).[98] Classical Pentecostals, as Steven J. Land has emphasized, "saw themselves as recovering and re-entering that Pentecostal reality."[99] As those afar off, Pentecostalism was seen as a participation in the ongoing story of Pentecost and, as such, in the unfolding of the story of God in the world through Christ and the Spirit. Pentecost became "a liturgical paradigm, an existential reality, and a dispensation of the Spirit in the last days."[100] The biblical narrative was cast in the light of the Pentecostal imagination, which placed less emphasis on the literary sequence of events than on the overarching imagery. The hallmark of this imagery was the oral manifestation of what Pentecostals interpreted as "evidence" that the Spirit of Pentecost continued in their midst.

Speaking in tongues, in a fundamental sense, became the oral manifestation of the Pentecostal imagination.[101] Some Pentecostals have described the phenomenon in terms of the affections characteristic to Pentecostalism. Land, for example, explains these affections as objective, dispositional, and relational constituents of the Christian life.[102] God is the immediate source and object of the Christian affections. More precisely, the biblical imagination of a holy God in relation to a world confronted by the coming of God's kingdom informs, shapes, and directs the expression of the affections.[103] Those who engage this imagination are overwhelmed by gratitude, compassion, and courage expressed in worship, prayer, and witness.[104] The holiness theme and eschatological drama underlying the story of Pentecostalism transformed the classical Pentecostal imagination into a catalyst for worship and evangelism.[105] The realization of one's own involvement in the unfolding story of God in the world was at times so overpowering and uncontainable that the person erupted in stammering sounds that, Pentecostals were certain, did not originate in the mind.[106] It was the biblical narrative of Pentecost that provided the initial framework for an understanding of these sounds as "tongues." Speaking in tongues became the unexpected and spontaneous outflow of the Pentecostal imagination, a release of the affections and language of worship and mission that could not be defined by any existing formal, conceptual, or linguistic system. Tongues speech expressed affectionately and orally the imagination that had come to shape classical Pentecostalism.

The Revival of the Imagination

The revival of the imagination among Pentecostals and its oral, affectionate expression in tongues clearly exposed the crisis of the imagination in the late modern world. The inability to integrate the phenomenon in the existing conceptual (i.e., cessationist) categories of the orthodox establishment led to an irreversible rejection of the traditional code of meaning and to the formation of an understanding of the imagination that developed internally among classical Pentecostals and that was rejected or ignored by the larger theological academy.[107] Tongues speech was the central element of the Pentecostal articulation of meaning, a means to communicate the Pentecostal self-understanding more tangibly than the imagination that nourished it. Dreams, vision, prophecies, words of wisdom, spiritual discernment, and other spiritual gifts were seen in light of the dominant position occupied by glossolalia. To articulate the significance of tongues and the charismata, in general, Pentecostals could not find a systematic account able to contain the Pentecostal story or the concept of narrative but instead turned to an image that would reflect both their personal experience and their understanding of the divine self-disclosure.[108] The image the biblical narrative provided was a baptism in the Spirit.

Spirit baptism was from the outset conceived as an image rather than a theological concept. Classical Pentecostals relied in particular on the biblical imagery that illuminates the promise of a baptism with the Spirit in light of, as well as in contrast to, the established baptism with water (e.g., Mark 1:8; Acts 1:4-5) and the events in Acts that were interpreted as the fulfillment of that promise (Acts 2:1-4; 8:12-17; 10:44-46; 11:14-16; 15:7-9). The practice of baptism as the immersion into water allowed Pentecostals to see Spirit baptism similarly in terms of an immersion, a "clothing" (Luke 24:49), "filling" (Acts 2:4; 9:17), "outpouring" (Acts 2:17, 33), "falling" (Acts 8:16; 10:44), and "coming upon" (Acts 1:8; 19:6) of God's Spirit.[109] However, the parallels to water baptism were interpreted primarily in an analogical sense and not in the established sacramental sense. To be "baptized" with the Spirit meant to receive the Spirit of God "without limit" (see John

3:34), an overwhelming experience often compared to the floodwaters of
the sea or the consuming flames of a raging fire.

> My soul today is thirsting for living streams divine,
> To sweep from highest heaven to this poor heart of mine;
> I stand upon the promise, in Jesus' name I plead;
> O send the gracious current to satisfy my need.
>
> I see the clouds arising, the mercy clouds of love,
> That come to bring refreshing down from the throne above,
> The earnest of the shower, just now to us is given,
> And now we wait, expecting the floods of grace from heaven.
>
> The shower of grace is falling, the tide is rolling in,
> The floodtide of salvation, with pow'r to cleanse from sin.
> It's surging thro' my being and takes my sin away,
> It keeps me shouting glory! thro' all the happy day.
>
> It's coming, yes, it's coming down this hour,
> A torrent of salvation in saving, cleansing pow'r:
> I hear the billows surging, I see them mount and roll;
> O glory, hallelujah! they're sweeping thro' my soul.[110]

The essence of this imagery lay not in its understanding of baptism as a
rite of initiation but in its explication of forgiveness, repentance, salvation,
and sanctification, which through the Pentecostal imagination became associated less with the rituals of the church than with the individual and
communal experience of the Holy Spirit. For Pentecostals, there was little
need to "explain" this imagination; it was experienced in the inexplicable
terms of joy, power, and glory.[111] It appeared as a baptism for sanctification, empowerment, and missionary zeal. For the established churches that
were unprepared to engage the Pentecostal image of another "baptism," on
the other hand, this hesitation to engage the debate conceptually only contributed to the hermeneutics of suspicion.

The image of Spirit baptism cut once and for all the ties of classical
Pentecostalism with the mainline churches.[112] The established theological
traditions approached the idea from the outset conceptually and systematically rather than as a product of the imagination and could not integrate
this "baptism" in the existing theological categories. As a product of the

imagination, Spirit baptism, despite its sacramental undertones, did not fit in the conceptual framework of twentieth-century sacramental theology.[113] It was not to be confused with water baptism or confirmation, rituals traditionally associated with the gift of the Holy Spirit.[114] There was no "act" or "celebration" of Spirit baptism that could be incorporated into the traditional liturgical framework in which the minister acts in the person of the whole church.[115] Although manifested repeatedly, Spirit baptism could not be administered or reproduced by human hands. The traditional network of meaning and its rejection of the imagination, on the other hand, forced the established churches to interpret Spirit baptism as a conceptual construct rather than as an image. As a result, the Pentecostal understanding of glossolalia as "sign" was changed by the systematic, linguistic categories of traditional theology into a semiotic model rather than an expression of the imagination.[116] For classical Pentecostals, tongues speech transcended rational approaches to truth while for the established traditions the Pentecostal "tongues" were devoid of truthfulness.[117]

The reaction of the mainline churches further consolidated and isolated classical Pentecostalism, which often "was denounced as 'anti-Christian,' as 'sensual and devilish,' and as 'the last vomit of Satan.' Its adherents were taunted and derided from the pulpit as well as in religious and secular press. . . . Those ministers and missionaries who embraced the Holy Spirit baptism were removed from their pulpits or dismissed by their mission boards."[118] The anti-Pentecostal sentiment ranged from eccentric but harmless ideology to excessive emotionalism and "the work of the devil."[119] The main argument focused not on the Pentecostal imagination but almost exclusively on the validity and credibility of its most tangible oral expression, speaking in tongues. Glossolalia was rejected as a form of "enthusiasm" that resides beyond the control of reason. However, as a result of the rejection of tongues speech, Spirit baptism was also disregarded, and with it the entire Pentecostal story. With the rejection of the Pentecostal story, the door was shut to the integration of the Pentecostal imagination in the larger theological enterprise of the twentieth century.

The formalization and conceptualization of the various elements of the Pentecostal imagination dissociated the theme of holiness, the eschatological drama, the plot of Pentecost, and the image of "Spirit baptism" from their original imaginative and narrative framework.[120] A conceptual explanation of the Pentecostal story required, first of all, a shared epistemological presupposition with the modern era "that only what is historically and objectively true is meaningful."[121] The Pentecostal imagination, however, reflects a "hierarchy" of truths different from that of the theological traditions of the twentieth century.[122] Meaning in the Pentecostal story depends neither on the ability of the mind to conceptualize nor on the capacity of language to express it as truth. Instead, the Pentecostal imagination is an invitation to experience God's Spirit despite these human limitations. The foundations of the crisis of theology in the twenty-first century consist of the conceptualization of the imagination as a purely formal, cognitive, and performative act. Pentecostalism is a particular manifestation of this crisis by turning its constituents on their head, rejecting the dominance of reason (e.g., conceptualization, formalization, organization, etc.), and declaring the rule of the imagination by God's Spirit as a pursuit of holiness in a world confronted with the coming of God's kingdom. This combination of pneumatology, eschatology, and ethics is fundamental to the Pentecostal imagination. Nevertheless, classical Pentecostalism exacerbated the crisis by resisting the formulation of a systematic account of their story of the imagination, focusing instead on the significance of individual elements (Spirit baptism, glossolalia, etc.) as dictated by the demands of the orthodox theological enterprise.[123] Methodologically, this choice has forced Pentecostals to objectify the scriptural witness in order to create a biblical support for their faith and praxis (see chapter 2). Doctrinally, this preference has led to a subordination of pneumatology as a theology of the third article to the dominant theologies of the first and second articles of the creed (see chapter 3).[124] Practically, it has forced Pentecostals into an often artificial synthesis of existing doctrinal proposals rather than permitting them a creative contribution to Christianity based on the Pentecostal imagination (see chapter 4). Overall, the ecumenical community missed the opportunity to formulate the significance of classical Pentecostalism for the theological enterprise, and thereby to direct the attention away from the primary occupation with doctrine to a broader theological agenda.

3. Theology as Play of the Imagination

Resources from Pentecostalism to overcome the crisis of the imagination stem primarily from the movement's connection of the imagination with the Christian life understood as a story of the Holy Spirit. Despite a number of recent attempts to revive the role of the imagination, twentieth-century theology has placed little emphasis on the pneumatological dimension of the imagination.[125] A focus on the narrative aspect of theol-

ogy, on the other hand, has become one of the most significant developments at the end of the twentieth century, encompassing such fields as
biblical studies, hermeneutics, ethics, and doctrine, and pursued most emphatically by the proponents of narrative theology.[126]

The Drama of Doctrine

The main concern of narrative theology has been the reestablishment of
the biblical narrative as story and the relocation of the authority of that
story in the particular faith community. Narrative theology, for Hans Frei,
means that Christians are specified "not by a quality of 'narrativity' inherent in our picture of self, world, and transcendence at large"[127] but by relation to the biblical narrative and by the conceptual retelling of that narrative, which George Lindbeck characterizes as "an overarching story that
has the specific literary features of realistic narrative exemplified in diverse
ways."[128] Lindbeck's cultural-linguistic paradigm understands these diverse features as expressions of the living traditions of language and culture that form the subjectivities of individuals in the communities of the
"story-shaped church."[129] In the stories of these particular communities,
we relate our faith to the multiplicity of experiences and process the ultimate questions and problems of life.[130] Lindbeck's widely acknowledged
proposal invites Pentecostalism to participate in the global theological enterprise not only as one confessional community but in the variety of its
worldwide particularities. The most crucial challenge of the cultural-
linguistic turn to theology is the notion that a global community, such as
Pentecostalism, is always confronted with a variety of narratives rather
than a single, universal performance of the biblical story. On the other
hand, Lindbeck's proposal shows not only a "pneumatological deficit"[131]
but also a neglect of the role of the imagination and of the performance of
the variety of Christian stories in the life of the churches.

The most rigorous adaptation of Lindbeck's cultural-linguistic proposal to date is Kevin J. Vanhoozer's *The Drama of Doctrine*. The concept of
drama exposes the shortcomings of the notion of narrative. In place of a
cultural-linguistic turn to doctrine, Vanhoozer offers a canonical-linguistic
approach that seeks to reestablish biblical authority not in the ecclesial culture but in the biblical canon.[132] To address the shortcomings of narrative
theology, he reconceptualizes Christian theology as attending "both to the
drama *in* the text — what God is doing in the world through Christ — and

to the drama that continues in the church as God uses Scripture to address, edify, and confront its readers" (p. 17). The resulting dramatic theology combines the narrative understanding of theology as ecclesial practice with the idea of biblical interpretation as performance in order to conceptualize the task of theology as the continuing drama of the biblical story (p. 22). Significantly, the performance of this "theo-drama" requires not only the intellectual assent of the individual but also the direction of the Holy Spirit and the involvement of the imagination of the faith community.

Vanhoozer offers a postconservative theology that employs a "cognitive-poetic" imagination in contrast to Lindbeck's cognitive-propositional theology (p. 278). Faulting Lindbeck for his neglect of the imagination, Vanhoozer redefines theology as dramaturgy that is based on the authority of the biblical script and confronted with performing that script in new and different contexts (see pp. 243-362). Echoing Hans Urs von Balthasar's emphasis on "theo-drama" as the life of the church in the action of God, Vanhoozer underlines the superiority of dramatic theory over narrative theory, since drama integrates narrative with propositions and experiences into performative action (pp. 100-102). "The drama of doctrine consists in the Spirit's directing the church rightly to participate in the evangelical action by performing its authoritative script" (p. 102). Vanhoozer consequently locates the work of the Holy Spirit in the practices of the canon and makes the Spirit the director of the divine drama of Scripture played out in the life of the church. God's Spirit opens up the eschatological horizon of Scripture by summoning the reader into God's story of redemption and generating "a performance tradition that reenacts the same drama in *new* ways" (p. 235, italics in original). The Christian life thus exhibits the drama of doctrine by acting out canonical practices that serve as the norm for all theological praxis. Theology, in turn, faces the dual task of making sense of the script (exegetical *scientia*) for both the community of faith and its audience (practical *sapientia*) by serving in a dramaturgical role as the adviser to both the director (the Holy Spirit) and the performers (the church) (pp. 243-63).

Significantly, the imagination is central to both exegetical *scientia* and practical *sapientia*. Vanhoozer understands the imagination as "the power of synoptic vision: the ability to synthesize heterogeneous elements into a unified whole. *The imagination is that cognitive faculty that allows us to see as whole what those who lack imagination see only as unrelated parts*" (p. 281). The imagination and its products — metaphors and stories — serve as cognitive instruments indispensable to the exegetical task, since they make possible the configuration and emplotment of the Christian narrative (pp. 281-

82). In turn, the narrative provides the basis for performing the theo-drama in confrontation with new situations and problems (p. 335). These new tasks demand that theology is consistent with the biblical script and none-theless acts meaningfully in situations and cultures that differ from that script. Vanhoozer, among others, points to the dramatic tool of improvisa-tion to speak faithfully in different contexts.[133] Improvisation with the ca-nonical script requires the use of the imagination in order to be able to dis-cern both the larger picture and the need of the specific situation that cannot be directly addressed by the script.[134] Although scripted, improvisa-tion is a spontaneous response to the demands of the moment that reveals our spirituality, that is, our freedom to respond to the given situation in ways obvious and fitting by either rejecting or accepting and incorporating the offers of the new context into the larger story of the script.[135] The script itself is the product of divine improvisation that is based on a covenantal theme whose action is propelled forward by the word of God and exempli-fies the key assumptions of the Christian theo-drama.[136] "Indeed, every at-tempt to render Christianity playable today involves improvising the canonical-linguistic action in new cultural-linguistic contexts."[137] The task of theology is to discern the principle of what is at stake in both the canoni-cal texts and the contemporary situation. Theology is therefore "ultimately a matter of right *judgments,* not concepts."[138]

Vanhoozer's proposal resonates with the emphasis Pentecostals place on the authority of the biblical text for all matters of faith and praxis and on the role of the Holy Spirit in the drama of the Christian life. *The Drama of Doctrine* gives a voice to the Pentecostal sentiment that theology is not only storytelling but also participation in and performance of the Chris-tian story in new and different contexts. The idea that theology goes be-yond concepts toward right judgments is akin to the Pentecostal emphasis on the role of spiritual discernment in the Christian life in general. The space reserved for improvisation, in particular, reflects the Pentecostal as-piration to escape the strict boundaries of formal liturgies, creeds, and sys-tems in Christian faith and praxis. At the same time, Vanhoozer's reconfig-uration of theology as dramatic performance directed by God's Spirit challenges Pentecostals to go beyond a mere narrating of a single Pentecos-tal story to a theological reflection on the performance of the multiplicity of stories as dramas in various contexts of the late modern world.

In turn, Pentecostals are likely to be critical of the concept of drama since it does not resolve the pneumatological deficit of narrative theology. Pentecostals see a much closer connection between the imagination and the

Holy Spirit, an involvement of the Spirit in the drama and the life of the participants themselves. Pentecost (i.e., the story), Pentecostalism (i.e., the drama), and Pentecostals (i.e., the participants) are themselves seen as expressions of the Holy Spirit's imaginative action. Vanhoozer understands the imagination primarily as a cognitive skill rather than a pneumatic activity. Echoing the revival of the imagination in idealism, the imaginative faculty is located in "the multiplicity of the mental"[139] rather than the diversity of the spiritual realm — higher but not different in kind from other intellectual activity. As such, the imagination is seen as a faculty of cognitive performance rather than an integral part of the drama itself. However, the performance of a script leaves little room for the margins of the imagination that constitute "the fading fringe found at the outer limit of specific imagined content."[140] Pentecostals see themselves as living within these margins formed by the unexpected, unscripted, unutterable, transforming work of God's Spirit. Put differently, for Pentecostals there exists an inherent narrativity in the sanctified, eschatological imagination, which emerges from the spirit of the biblical texts, and yet is carried by that spirit beyond the text.[141] The experience of that narrativity, although grounded in the biblical revelation, is governed by a person's openness to the work of the Holy Spirit that culminates in a new experience of that revelation, captured in the image of the baptism of the Holy Spirit.[142] Beyond scripted performance, theology requires not only *scientia* and *sapientia* but also *energeia*. Vanhoozer's theo-drama remains in essence a cognitive-linguistic performance of the canonical script that lacks an explicit energetic, kinesthetic dimension. Spontaneity, in particular, rather than the act of readiness of the actor or the result of disciplined preparation, is found in a (sometimes unexpected) corporeal, kinesthetic response to the presence of the Holy Spirit that propels forward the imagination intellectually, practically, and communally. For Pentecostals, theology is not "Christo-dramatic fittingness,"[143] as Vanhoozer puts it, but Spirit-energetic freedom.

A major contribution to the correction of the pneumatological deficit in the account of the imagination comes from Pentecostal theologian Amos Yong.[144] He defines the "pneumatological imagination" as a synthesis of passive and active elements that emerge from an experiential and metaphoric dialectic of specific encounters with the Holy Spirit. The biblical imagination provides the basis for such encounters from three basic dimensions: first, the capturing of the primordial experience of the Spirit in the image of "power"; second, the integration of the relational quality of the Holy Spirit expressed in the images of the "spirit of God" and "spirit of Christ"; and third, attention to the diversity of spirits operative in the world. The pneumatological imagination, for Yong, is creative in its greater sensitivity to the various dimensions of reality; its holistic approach to the world on the affective, valuational, and spiritual levels; and its discernment and engagement of the various facets of life. The imagination, informed by God's Spirit, exemplifies the metaphysical categories Yong considers foundational to pneumatology itself: realism, relationalism, and social dynamism (p. 146).

Yong's pneumatological proposal revives the emphasis on the role of spirit in the imagination and expands that emphasis to include also the pragmatic, affective, and spiritual effects of the Holy Spirit on the transformation of God's people. Building on Peircean epistemology, Yong connects the imagination with what Scripture calls "living in the Spirit," a transformation of the believer into the character of Christ (see pp. 151-84). The pneumatological imagination leads the faithful in the process of sanctification toward the goal of being transformed into the image of Jesus. This process is not a mere performance of the script but is also an axiological, affective, and spiritual encounter with the living Christ. Although the category of narrative occupies a place of epistemic priority in the understanding of this encounter, the pneumatological imagination gives greater privilege to the operation of God's Spirit as the Spirit of truth (see 1 John 5:6) that is in all respects "open to the ongoing encounter with novelty and surprise — no a priori limitations can or should be imposed on what life in the Spirit might bring about" (p. 160). In Vanhoozer's terms, the Spirit enables us to participate in the script and thus in God's story and in the divine nature itself (p. 175). The Spirit of truth is the divine mind who reveals the truth of the Father and the Son narratively, epistemically, and ontologically, thus enabling us both to know and to participate in that relationship in order to be conformed to them affectionally, materially, and spiritually. As the Spirit of truth, the Holy Spirit has the ability to transform the imagination in order to confront the materialism, nominalism, and positivism of the world with the truth of God in Christ (p. 216). The personal and ethical (rather than abstract and totalistic) presence of the Spirit of truth *as* truth "is transformative and directive toward eschatological fulfillment" (p. 175). Put differently, the Spirit is not the director of a scripted drama but the moral and eschatological imagination of the story itself and of its performance in the world. Although Yong does not suggest that his proposal is peculiar to Pentecostalism, the notion of the pneumatological imagination is consistent with a Pentecostal narrative. The Pentecostal imagination is the pneumatological, eschatological, and ethical pursuit of God.

From Yong's perspective, global Pentecostalism understands the Christian life not as a "performance" of the biblical script, and thus not primarily as dramatic activity, but as a transformative encounter with the Holy Spirit as the biblical imagination that engages the human being and the world factually, corporeally, relationally, communally, morally, and spiritually.[145] The priority given to narrative in classical Pentecostalism has made for a broad debate about the nature of the concept of narrative itself, the sustainability of the privilege given to narrative Scripture, the influence of narrative on normative practices, the role of communities and rituals in the narrative, and the experience of that narrative as story beyond the text itself.[146] Yong and other Pentecostals have integrated narrative theology into a broader context that involves the interplay of the biblical canon, the community of readers, and the work of the Holy Spirit. Theological reflection, in this broader context, is mediated as drama only insofar as that activity is inspired by a particular pneumatological imagination as the enduring yet unfinished dynamic that is oriented toward an encounter with God through the Holy Spirit. Dutch Pentecostal Jean-Jacques Suurmond has suggested that this imagination is best described not as a story or performance of a drama but as play.[147]

The Play of the Imagination

The notion of play is akin to, yet also more fundamental than, drama.[148] Storytelling and drama are at their root playful activities before they become performative acts. More substantially, while the theo-drama is performed *within* culture, Suurmond points out that culture itself *is* play.[149] From this perspective, "the world is not merely a stage on which the drama of life is acted out. The material world itself is built up according to the structure of play."[150] In this cultural-cosmic play, the imagination takes on a central position as the creative spontaneity and randomness that make possible novelty and surprise. Here, theology is not the dramatic performance of a script in which we find ourselves inevitably involved but a voluntary, and not always determinative, activity that is meaningful within its own imaginative freedom. For Suurmond and others, the Word of God provides the necessity and structure of the play, while the Spirit supplies dynamism and chance.[151] Word and Spirit at play in the world create their own order of play in which the outcome is open and everything is possible so that God's own imagination is fulfilled.[152] Play is carried out in constant tension between one's own identity and the integration of that identity in a relationship with the context and environment in which one is confronted with new and different situations.[153] It is thus not only the biblical text itself but the use of that text in the tension of play that provides what Walter Brueggemann has called a "counterworld" to the "givens" that "prevail because they are accepted as beyond criticism."[154] In their place, theology as imaginative play is able not only to interpret but also to reconstruct the world differently, that is, to offer a biblical, critical, poetic, and ethical alternative to the orthodox establishment.[155] Conceived as play, theology offers what has been labeled a "conversion of the imagination" and "remapping" or "reconfiguring" of the world of nonplay and corrupted play, subordinated to the players' ends and degenerated into a violent game that inevitably leads to the world's destruction.[156] Theological play thus takes on a critical function, even iconoclastic role, which challenges the established conventions. With critical play theology engages the world not only theoretically and doctrinally but also physically, materially, spiritually, aesthetically, and morally. Simply put, play always requires a playground.

Jürgen Moltmann has described play itself as the playground of the imagination where we "move from a merely reproductive imagination, which in its leisure recapitulates the rhythm of the working world, to an imagination productive of a more liberated world."[157] In this sense, play demonstrates the freedom of the imagination to leave purely pragmatic, instrumental, and purpose-oriented attitudes that suffocate play for the sake of joy, curiosity, spontaneity, risk, and dreams, all of which are neither meaningless nor dangerous. Hans-Georg Gadamer can therefore speak of play as a model of the imagination, since the essence of play is located in the movement of play itself rather than in the consciousness of the participants or some other dimension underlying the play.[158] In other words, the playground of the imagination is "pure self-presentation."[159] Theology as play becomes a suspension of the roles and rules of the world for the sake of what Harvey Cox has called a celebration of the "feast of fools."[160] Cox offers a juxtapositional approach for theology that is "out of step" with the postulations of its age and emerges instead from the tensions between the present situation and theology's own symbols as the occasion for the play of the imagination.[161] Theology as play involves the risk to challenge both the dominant order of the world and theology's own symbols and rituals for the sake of liberating them for play with God. For Pentecostals, the freely accepted patterns of this play are established by a desire for holiness and an eschatological worldview that stand in tension with the reasoning and order of the world. The pneumatological imagination creates a holy play of hope that involves God, the church, and the world in the fellowship of the Holy Spirit. Its goal is a transformation of the present crisis in light of the eschatological future breaking open the present conditions for the renewing work of God's Spirit.

The tension at the foundation of play keeps theology vulnerable to the temptations of breaking the boundaries of play for the sake of the account-ability and reasonableness demanded by the norms of the age. The continu-ing presence of this tension emphasizes the importance of not interpreting everything as play but of preserving the relationship of play and nonplay.[162] If everything is play, then play itself ultimately devolves into the idea of what Lionel Abel has popularly termed *metaplay,* a dramatic form in which the dramatic situations are created by the self-consciousness of the drama-tists themselves, since all external reference to play has ceased to exist.[163] Consequently, theology as liberated play does not reject or forsake the world of nonplay, work, and suffering, but seeks to invite and integrate that world into play. Play in the context of suffering is irrevocably confronted with the inability of the world to enter into play and participation in the Christian story.[164] Pentecostal appropriations of the images and narratives of urban violence in Brazil, for example, show not only an attempt to inte-grate the reality of nonplay but also to transform the rationality of violence for the sake of play informed by a sanctified, eschatological imagination.[165] The pneumatological imagination emerges not immediately from Scripture or the presence of the Holy Spirit but from the tension between play and nonplay that exposes Word and Spirit as dimensions of both realities. This confrontation of the realities of play and nonplay sheds particular light on a Pentecostal engagement of the world.

In the remaining chapters of this volume I suggest that the tension be-tween the understanding of theology as performance and the Pentecostal notion of theology as play represents the most fruitful engagement of Pentecostalism in the revision of the theological task facing a global Chris-tianity. Pentecostalism presents, first and foremost, an imagination: a play of expectations and affections, improvisation and transformation, self-determination, and mission. The Pentecostal imagination is thoroughly theological in character and, as such, nourishes the spiritual, liturgical, doctrinal, and ecclesial commitments of Pentecostals to the playground of the world and to the freedom of creation.

The freedom of play is a significant aspect of Pentecostalism; it em-phasizes that theological pursuit cannot be pure performance. In play, there is no audience; it is not a dramatic act but an invitation to participate in a shared corporeal, spiritual, intellectual, and ethical celebration.[166] Nonplay does not observe play for the sake of study or entertainment. Conversely, play is not aimed at a performance to "nonplayers"; it is interested in playing *with* others, not *for* others. As Wolfhart Pannenberg puts it, the freedom of play is characterized by the "fascination" of the players with being outside of themselves.[167] In the enthusiasm of play, all players are equal. For theology conceived as dramatic performance, on the other hand, the distinctions between the performance and its performers, the performers and the audience, the director, cast, and script are necessary and inescapable. Although play conceived as an unbound invitation to participate is inevitably confronted with those who do not play or who wish to play by different rules, this confrontation provides the creative ground for the exercise of the imagination. The reluctance of Pentecostalism to engage theology systematically stems from a deep-rooted aversion to Christian thought as a purely performance-oriented, structured, and pragmatic exercise of an established group of imaginative players. The concept of theology as drama could have the potential to enhance that aversion. The imagination, however, like play, is at the disposal of all who wish to engage in the joint activity. The differences between the players (i.e., their relationships to the play itself and to the world of nonplay) are overcome fundamentally by the use of improvisation as a resource of the entire playing community.

The worldwide variety of Pentecostalism portrays improvisation less as a "scripted" performance or "scriptural" recital and more as a "jazz" concert.[168] Jazz understands itself not as a performance-oriented process that seeks an adaptation or reenactment of a script in different circumstances but as the playful cooperation of a community characterized by a wide variety of styles and stories.[169] Improvisation here is similar to Vanhoozer's notion, what ethicist Samuel Wells describes as "a community formed in right habits trusting itself to embody its tradition in new and often challenging circumstances."[170] To use a phrase of Stanley Hauerwas, improvisation requires a "community of character" in which the theologian plays in tune with the script yet is allowed to play a version that is not an exact performance.[171] However, for Pentecostals improvisation is possible because it is based on habits that arise from a pneumatological imagination nourished by a pursuit of holiness in a world confronted with the coming of God's kingdom. Although the story of Pentecost provides the "tone" for the imagination, this provision is not a script, and theology can play and improvise the tone and rhythm of that story in a variety of ways. Improvisation from the perspective of jazz, in Pentecostal terms, is a "singing in the Spirit" with psalms, hymns, and spiritual songs that can evolve with the history, culture, and language of each community. This aspect is particularly important in a community as diverse and migrant as global Pentecostalism.[172] Improvisation in the Spirit is therefore both community-forming and community-formed.[173] In the freedom of the imagination, human beings are liberated to meet each other not only as "I" and "thou" but also in the "we" of play.[174] Theology opens up to the encounter with God in the life experiences of the playing community.

The notion of play as improvisation corrects the classical Pentecostal emphasis on the heuristic centrality of a single Pentecostal story, understood from the perspective of a universal narrative. In its place, global Pentecostalism presents itself as a community joined together by a shared vision and imagination, a multiplicity of voices and languages that nonetheless plays together for the enjoyment of God. This joint improvisation develops from the moral and eschatological habits of the community informed by Scripture and the challenges of the present reality. The imagination is therefore as much a theological improvisation (with God) as it is a biblical improvisation (of Scripture) and an ecclesial improvisation (in the church). It is paradigmatic for Christian theology, in general, and determinative of the ecumenical vision of the church. Improvisation is a pathos that is not afraid of approaching the limits of the imagination. Steven Land has referred to this moral and eschatological praxis of Pentecostals as an "action-reflection" in the Spirit or, more technically, orthopathy.[175]

Improvisation, from Land's Pentecostal perspective, points to the importance of integrating orthodoxy and orthopraxy with orthopathy. Play informed by right pathos is neither purely conceptual nor purely practical but, as many Pentecostals have repeatedly emphasized, orthopathy forms a bridge between both worlds.[176] The Christian pathos is rooted in a pneumatological sharing in the "heart" of God, where intellect and experience are joined together and mutually inform one other, for the sake of participating in both joy and suffering in the story of God. Samuel Solivan has shown that, in Hispanic Pentecostalism, orthopathy establishes a bond between the suffering of God and humanity for the sake of liberation.[177] Catholic systematician Ralph Del Colle suggests that the emphasis on orthopathy is essential to the role transformation plays in the Pentecostal community in general.[178] Pathos is seen not as a medium of theological performance for the sake of doctrine but as the heart of theology for the sake of transformation. For Pentecostals, theology is an affection of the heart that invites God and the world into play without mediation or limitation. As Del Colle acknowledges, "When translated into Pentecostal practice, this may very well mean that the perceived immediacy of divine presence trumps mediated modalities with consequences all across the theological spectrum from spirituality to ecclesiology."[179] The eschatological goal of theology is the transformation of all suffering and the liberation of all nonplay into participation for play with God.

The immediate consequence of understanding theology as a play of the heart, informed by a holy and eschatological imagination for the sake of transformation and fellowship, is the insight that a solution to the crisis of the imagination goes beyond the realm of conceptualization, formalization, systematization, analysis, or synthesis (and therefore beyond the confines of this chapter). A purely "rational" definition is foreign to the idea of play. Rather, theology as the play of orthopathy is an openness to the transrational world of the pneumatological imagination, the realistic, relational, and dynamic realm of spirit and human creativity that frees theology from the dominance of universal reason, technological efficiency, and the abstractions of the mind.[180] In the play of the imagination, theology expands to the realm of the good, the holy, and the beautiful that enter the world through visions, dreams, and prophecies — habits of orthopathy that are the objective, relational, and dispositional operations of the Holy Spirit in the Christian life.[181]

The exercise of the imagination in the form of orthopathy frees the imagination from the Platonic confines of sensory perception, subjectivism, and imitation. The interplay of pathos, doctrine, and praxis seeks to overcome the dialectic of reason and the imagination inherited by theology and sheds light on the cognitive and practical sense of the imagination as a pathway to the transcendent and the divine. The revival of the patristic emphasis on the Holy Spirit avoids the pitfalls of elevating the imagination above or subordinating it to the intellect or the world of sense perception. Instrumental to the exercise of the imagination is a vision of both its character of holiness and its eschatological orientation toward God and the world. As an active link between the realms of human and divine existence, the pneumatological imagination overcomes its "transcendental" prison in the inner self and becomes the playground for sanctification, contemplation, and praxis. Theology as play of the imagination escapes Feuerbach's fundamental critique of religion by placing the imagination in a pneumatological dimension of a historical, dialogical, and diasporic community. As a pneumatological act, the imagination can project itself beyond human existence, doctrine, and praxis — as mere elements of the structured world of signs, languages, institutions, productivity, and performance — to the realm of play. The imagination is not another structural element that can now be brought into dialogue with existing concepts of the ordering of theological loci. Instead, theology that invites the play of the imagination challenges us to reimagine our understanding of theological authorities and structures. On the most basic level, the imagination always seeks to transcend the structures of orthodoxy imposed by reason alone. It does not reject them, but makes them available to change, expansion, and growth located in a theology of the heart. With orthopathy as the playing field of the imagination, theology develops exclusively from neither a doctrinal nor a practical perspective but from the realm of the heart. In its heuristic function, the imagination thus remains connected to both the realm of divine play and joy and the realm of nonplay and human suffering. The imagination is not only anticipation of play with God and the world through visions, dreams, and prophecies, but already participation in and transformation for the full realization of that fellowship in the kingdom of God.

In the remaining chapters I want to begin the conversation about a revisioning of the theological enterprise that acknowledges the play of the imagination. Any such endeavor must begin with the question of revelation, or the authoritative sources that initiate and sustain the theological agenda. In the present chapter I have taken for granted the significance of the biblical story for the self-understanding of classical Pentecostalism and the transformation of global Christianity. However, the contrast I have painted between playful and performative notions of theology begs the question how exactly the Bible is perceived by Pentecostals and what shape a reimagining of Scripture from the perspective of the imagination would take. These considerations are the focus of the next chapter.

2 Beyond Scripture

Sola Scriptura, *Word of God, and the Crisis of Revelation*

The preceding chapter examined the resources Pentecostalism provides to address the crisis of the imagination. I suggested that the tension between a systematic account of theology as performance and the Pentecostal approach to theology as play represents the most fruitful engagement of Pentecostalism in the revision of the global theological agenda. Most tangible from the preceding chapter has been the insight that a revival of the imagination as foundational for global Christianity inevitably leads to a revisioning of the authoritative sources and structures that inform the global theological enterprise. In this chapter I wish to initiate this conversation by reflecting on how the play of the imagination informs the understanding of the authority and role of revelation. My particular focus is on Scripture as an objectified dimension of the divine self-disclosure. The crisis of global Christianity, I advocate, is also a crisis of revelation.

The notion of revelation has encountered a crisis in the late modern world exemplified in the divisions over the doctrine of Scripture. A discussion of this crisis was in full steam during the latter half of the twentieth century on the European continent, but has since lost momentum. The full concerns of the birthplace of the Reformation only recently reached the North American context, where the complex discussion has surfaced in the revival of the Protestant Scripture principle.[1] At heart, the Scripture principle is a dogmatic axiom that represents not only a theological and hermeneutical perspective but also the faith and praxis of the community that embraces its application. In this light, the discussion of the Scripture principle offers several advantages to the current project. It represents one of the chief axioms of Protestantism that emphasizes the centrality of revelation for the Christian life. The affirmation of the central place of Scripture in the life of faith is also a hallmark of contemporary Evangelicalism and classical Pentecostalism. In addition, the principle has been critically reviewed by all major ecumenical traditions.[2] It thus offers a concise entrance to a larger, ecumenical discussion of the role of revelation in the development of global Christianity. From that perspective, and with focus on the manifestation of the crisis in classical Pentecostalism, I suggest that Christian theology demands a substantive revision of the notion of revelation and the role of Scripture.

The first part of this chapter addresses the complex field of meaning associated with revelation from the perspective of Scripture and recaptures the development of the Scripture principle from its origins in the Protestant Reformation. The task here is not to retrace the history of the doctrine of Scripture but to locate the position of Scripture in revelation and to formulate the implications of the crisis of the Scripture principle for the contemporary task of theology. This section highlights the development of a performative understanding of the Scripture principle manifested primarily in an artificial distinction between form and content. The second part illustrates the manifestation of the crisis in the North American context by highlighting the problems associated with the adaptation of the performative notion of Scripture by classical Pentecostalism. On the basis of these observations, I suggest in the final part that Christianity can address the crisis of revelation by going "beyond" Scripture to interpret revelation from the perspective of the interplay of Spirit and Word in the community and thus, in contrast to the notion of performance, as an actualization of God at play.

1. The Crisis of Revelation

The notion of revelation has received renewed attention throughout the twentieth century.[3] A prolific amount of literature bears witness that the significance and meaning of Scripture in the context of revelation have entered a critical phase.[4] Much of the literature focuses on two interrelated areas: the relationship of Scripture and revelation, and the relationship of Scripture and tradition.[5] Twentieth-century theology has posited between each of these constituents an either-or relationship, intensified not only by the rise of critical methods and the renewed focus on history as the premier context for biblical interpretation but also by the increasing absence of the Bible from everyday life. The first part of this chapter approaches this intricate situation from the perspective of Scripture, and with focus on the dimensions of revelation and tradition, and seeks to illuminate the crisis of revelation from that phenomenological perspective rather than from a conceptual approach to the idea of revelation as such. I begin by tracing the critical developments from the advance of *sola Scriptura* by Martin Luther to the alteration of the concept during nineteenth-century Protestantism and its application to the modern theological agenda, which will then allow me to analyze the implications of the alteration of the Scripture principle for the contemporary theological agenda.

Sola Scriptura *and Word of God*

The origins of the Scripture principle are usually attributed to the Protestant Reformation generally, and to Martin Luther in particular. Although Luther was not the first to acknowledge the authority of the biblical texts, he elevated the status of Scripture to a theological principle, later summarized in the motto *sola Scriptura,* or "Scripture alone," which represented a general consensus among the Protestant reformers.[6] The advocacy of this principle indicated a wide-ranging concern with the theological or dogmatic function of revelation in the church and in history that overshadowed questions about the proper interpretation of the biblical texts.[7] As important as Luther's desire that the Bible should be read, in the first place, and his advocacy for a proper understanding of the biblical texts, is Luther's identification of this task with the quest to discover the authentic sources of revelation.[8] Simply put, Luther was concerned both with what the Bible said and with what it represented. Yet, in praxis, these aspirations were not always readily reconcilable.

Luther's understanding of the Bible is complex, and for the purposes of this chapter I will focus only on the significance that his understanding of revelation and Scripture bears for the formulation of Christian doctrine.[9] From this perspective, the role of Scripture is most clearly described in Luther's idea of the Word of God. By "Word," Luther meant a complex relationship of Jesus Christ, the biblical texts, and the proclamation of the gospel, all of which can be designated as "Word" without contradiction and form but one Word of God in different dimensions.[10] In this context, *sola Scriptura* implied that the Bible is always revelation before it serves as principle. More precisely, Luther's understanding of revelation exhibits a logical distinction, which proposes that Scripture, *because* it is the Word of

God and therefore the "first principle of the Christian life,"[11] represents the "sole rule and norm of all doctrine."[12] Put differently, Luther distinguished between the biblical texts *(Scriptura)* and the authority attributed to Scripture by the church *(sola)*. Only with the addition of *"sola"* could Scripture serve as a principle of Christian doctrine.

The addition of *"sola"* painted a sharp contrast between the established Roman understanding and Luther's own concept of the sources of doctrine.[13] On the one hand, Luther rejected the dominant two-source theory that accepted both the biblical revelation and an extrabiblical, oral authority as reliable resources for the theological task.[14] On the other hand, although Luther held to the long-standing single-source theory, which located the unique authority of the Bible in the exegetical tradition of interpreted Scripture, *sola Scriptura* posited that the biblical texts received their authorization and interpretation from themselves before being applied to and interpreted by Christian doctrine.[15] In this sense, the Scripture principle was not intended to juxtapose Scripture and tradition as two antithetical institutions of revelation or to separate Scripture from the established exegetical tradition. Rather, *sola Scriptura* was designed to attribute authority to Scripture from an internal principle in order to integrate it from that perspective into the theological agenda.

The uncontested internal principle of Scripture for Luther was the revelation of Jesus Christ, who stands as the incarnate Word of God at the center of the biblical Word that is proclaimed in the churches. The principle of *sola Scriptura* is overwhelmed by its own witness to Christ.[16] In the plain and literal sense, a dominant form of interpretation since the Renaissance,[17] the written Word does not reveal itself but points to the self-disclosure of the hidden God in the person of Christ. For the Reformer, the Scripture principle was at heart a christocentric principle, which advocated the gospel of Christ as the sole content of the biblical revelation and thus as the center of Christian doctrine. Scripture occupies a major place in the divine self-disclosure since it plainly and clearly presents Christ to the believer.

Luther's idea of the plainness and perspicuity of the Bible was tied to the idea of Scripture as "Christ's spiritual body,"[18] which is made present by the Holy Spirit in the preaching of the Word of God and its reception by faith.[19] In Christ and the Spirit, God remains in unrestricted authority over Scripture.[20] The Bible as the Word of God consists of this unity-in-tension of Spirit and letter before it is made subject to interpretation by the church. The authority, certainty, and perspicuity of the biblical texts are attributed to God's Spirit who enters the dynamic of the Word of God, and in this manner allows Scripture to emerge as the fountainhead for the theological task.[21] Luther upheld the authority of the text but submitted it to the liturgy of the Word as a "living voice"[22] in the Christian life that is not only read but also seen, heard, and experienced. Luther's Scripture principle did not reject the judgment of the theological tradition, but it demanded that all doctrine conform to the witness of the Spirit in Scripture.[23] In the praxis of the Reformation, Scripture functioned as the chief principle for the promulgation of Christian doctrine, albeit not primarily as text but as the living reality of the Word of God.

Nevertheless, the authority granted to the Word of God as the highest principle of doctrine did not mean that the Reformers embraced a radical biblicism. Particularly in response to more radical reformers, Luther rejected the idea of a restoration of the entire Christian life to the doctrines and practices of Scripture. Revelation was a basis for proclamation, conversion, and worship, but not for the reinstatement of the biblical world.[24] Jaroslav Pelikan highlights the importance of this distinction for an understanding of the role of Scripture in Luther's thought. "[I]t is inaccurate to designate his work as that of restoring the Bible to the church. It would be more accurate perhaps to interpret it as the task of restoring the gospel to the Bible. For he did not seek to repristinate New Testament Christianity. When he thought that Zwingli was trying to do something like that in his mode of celebrating the Lord's Supper, Luther repudiated this mode as irrelevant."[25] Relevant to Luther was the postulation of the Word of God as the center of the authority of Scripture and thus as the living principle for the doctrines of the church. The idea of *sola Scriptura* represented for Luther, and for much of early Protestant dogmatics, the indisputable standard of theology but not the underlying principle of the Reformation.[26] The peasant wars and the iconoclasm of the Reformation, although often justified by an appeal to the Scripture principle, were not its proper focus and intention.[27] The goal of *sola Scriptura* was not to create a "religion of the book"[28] but to shape a theological tradition that was consistent with the biblical witness of the Spirit to the gospel of Christ.

The Alteration of the Scripture Principle

The Formula of Concord is one of the earliest indications of departure from Luther's original intentions. Significantly, it posited next to an affirmation of the authority of Scripture the adherence to the Augsburg Confession and Luther's Small and Large Catechisms. Whereas Luther saw Scripture as the principal ground of doctrine, because it revealed the hidden God in the person of Christ and elevated the Word of God to the fountainhead of the theological task, the Lutheran formula segregated the text of Scripture to function as a heuristic model of theological method that included other authoritative sources.[29] The general rationalization of theology during the Enlightenment began to derive the authority of Scripture no longer from the idea of the Word of God or from the testimony of the Holy Spirit but from various scientific reasons based on an increasingly rationalistic concept of revelation.[30] As a result, the texts of Scripture became part of demonstrable scientific knowledge and the performance of the hermeneutical and theological enterprise. The authority of the canonical texts was legitimized by rational means, and the Scripture principle in its original form began to be rearranged.[31] The revival of Aristotelian metaphysics, and its distinction between form and matter, provided the most significant tool in the theological pursuit of the essence of biblical revelation.

The quest to define the essence of revelation in the light of Scripture lent itself to an adoption of the distinction between form and matter for an understanding of the nature and authority of the biblical texts.[32] From this perspective, the divine authority of Scripture is located not in the "content" of revelation, the collection of the biblical texts, but in their inner "form," a term not always clearly and consistently defined.[33] The form was elevated to the internal basis of revelation and became the rational explanation of Luther's designation of Scripture as the Word of God. This tendency was most pronounced initially in the work of Johann Gerhard,[34] whose influential systematic account of orthodox Lutheran doctrine provided a major impetus for the resurgence of neo-Aristotelian categories in the elaboration and defense of the Scripture principle. Gerhard demanded strict harmony between form and matter and rejected the elevation of revelation above the historical, human, or written dimensions of Scripture.[35] Nonetheless, the distinction between form and matter as such led to the erroneous conclusion that the doctrine of revelation could be seen from the perspective of such a division and, consequently, that one could speak of a formal and material principle of Christian doctrine in the first place.

Most influential in perpetuating the fundamental distinction between a material and formal principle of theology was J. W. Baier's *Compendium of Positive Theology*. This essential textbook of systematic theology for generations of Lutheran pastors since the end of the seventeenth century advocated a strict division:

The object of revealed theology is two-fold: Material and formal. The material object is the content . . . of revelation, which is known in revealed theology. And this applies not so much to the subject of the operation and the cause and means of the following goal, but also to the goal itself, in so far as it is known by the aptitude of theology. The formal object, or principle and ground of knowing, from where also the knowledge of things comes, things which are put forward in revealed theology, is divine revelation.[36]

The impact of this distinction reached its climax in the debates of the nineteenth century about the role of Scripture in the Protestant religion. In 1875 Albrecht Ritschl provided an influential summary of the development during his century, which emphasized the tension between rationalism and positivism as a chief catalyst for the alteration of Luther's *sola Scriptura*.[37] Ritschl highlights the work of Johann Philipp Gabler, who argued that the only material foundation of the Christian religion could be a doctrine that would serve as the source of all other teachings.[38] He concluded that it was impossible to offer such a highest material principle as long as doctrine was to keep its positive character and not to become a religion built on mere rational principles. As a consequence, Luther's doctrine of justification could be seen as the chief teaching of the Christian faith but not as the overarching principle of theology.[39] Gabler insisted that the theological task was guided by a formal principle, and not by a matter of content.[40] This emphasis opened the way for an elevation of the twofold distinction to an integral principle of Protestant thought.[41] The motto *sola Scriptura* was now placed in a much broader historical context and confessional environment. And the distinction between formal and material allowed the biblical revelation to remain in a place of formal authority for the theological task, albeit at the cost of disassociating this authority from any particular scriptural content.

Subsequent theological discussion attempted to reconcile the identity of Scripture as a formal principle of doctrine with the material content of Scripture, yet with no substantial efforts to forsake the fundamental distinction itself. In light of this tendency, Scripture could function as a formal principle for Christian doctrine without dictating a particular matter of concern. In turn, theology could be allowed to critically assess the content of the biblical texts without thereby threatening the formal authority of revelation. However, as Ritschl concluded, in contrast to Luther's intentions, the Scripture principle served the historical evaluation of the Reformation and the resulting confessions; it delineated a formula for contemporary

Protestantism and not a principle of understanding for the theological agenda.[42] The idea of the Scripture principle is maintained only on formal grounds. More precisely, Scripture was no longer seen as the indisputable methodological basis for the formulation of doctrine in general, but as the formal principle of the Protestant worldview, which, in turn, must be supplemented by a material counterpart from within the system of Protestant doctrines. In this way, the doctrine of justification was elevated beyond Luther's intentions to the material principle of the theological enterprise, which, understood as a compendium of propositional, dogmatic truths, demanded adherence to the authority of Scripture only on formal grounds.

Ritschl's essay points to the fundamental impasse of reconciling a formal principle with a material principle of revelation in contemporary thought. Either both principles are given equal authority, which would elevate doctrine to the same status as Scripture, or one principle supersedes the other, which would undermine the authority of the theological enterprise that is responsible for the designation of the principles in the first place.[43] In each case, the original intentions of *sola Scriptura* are eliminated. The only logical alternative is a separation of the formal element from the material. Although Ritschl emphasized his rejection of this alternative, his essay provided the fundamental basis for the adoption and explication of Scripture as the formal principle of Protestantism.[44] The crisis of revelation is manifested most tangibly in this crisis of the Scripture principle.

A chief result of this development was that the biblical texts were disjointed from the idea of revelation and cast into the open field of modern science. On the one hand, theology became one science among others, concerned only with a particular aspect of revelation as the formal criterion for the formulation of doctrine. On the other hand, the collection of the biblical texts was opened up to the scrutiny of scientific methodology. The idea of the formal and material dimensions of revelation became de facto two irreconcilable principles of Protestantism. These developments catapulted the dissolution of the doctrine of Scripture and its consequences beyond the realm of the Protestant world into the global arena of a world post-Christendom.

The Contemporary Crisis of the Scripture Principle

In a number of publications during the 1960s, Wolfhart Pannenberg illustrated the implications of the crisis of the Scripture principle for a broader theological context.[45] Convinced "that the dissolution of the Scripture principle is very closely connected to the failure of theology in its universal task,"[46] Pannenberg warned that the horizons of revelation and the theological task had been permanently separated. Although he did not directly speak to the historical division of form and matter, Pannenberg's publications reflect the broad impact of that separation on the modern view of theology. On a foundational level, the distinction separated the content of the biblical writings from the essential concerns of the biblical revelation and the authority attributed to both. While for Luther the two were intimately connected in the revelation of Jesus Christ, contemporary theology emphasizes the distinction between the texts themselves and the person and history of Jesus that stand "behind" the text as the formal principle. "The nineteenth-century quest for the historical Jesus based itself on the history of Jesus, but in such a way that the connection between Jesus and the apostolic proclamation of Christ became obscured. The kerygmatic theology of our century countered this approach by declaring that the historical attempt to go behind the text was theologically irrelevant, and that the texts are theologically binding only in their witnessing character."[47] While the dissolution of the Scripture principle may be attributed to the rise of biblical criticism, the cultural shift to secular modernity, the emphasis on religious experience, the rejection of ecclesial dogmas, or the questioning of the supernatural character of the Bible,[48] the underlying factor responsible for the crisis of revelation remains the artificial separation of the function of Scripture into two autonomous realms.

The distinction of two self-governing principles of doctrine has dissolved any "material" agreement that hitherto had been assumed among the biblical writings. Moreover, it created a distance between the substance of the primitive Christian faith and the content of contemporary theology. *Sola Scriptura* became the slogan for a religion of the "Book" that took "the scriptures" as the objectified form of the faith removed from concerns about content — dimensions that can now be related only at the cost of ignoring the differences between the primitive Christian community and the present situation.[49] During much of the twentieth century, attempts to fuse the horizons emphasized the centrality of history for a rational ordering of revelation and its adaptation to the Christian community.[50] History thus became the primary hermeneutical lens of Protestantism. While the *sola Scriptura* of the Reformers attributed authority to Scripture from a self-evident, internal principle that was then attributed to the task of Christian doctrine, the alteration of the Scripture principle has led to a denial of the final and comprehensive reliability of the biblical witness for contemporary thought. Instead, theology itself becomes the stage for the performance of Scripture, and apart from doctrine, revelation has neither depth nor vitality.

The idea of the performance of Scripture mirrors the notion of the formal principle of biblical authority. As Kevin Vanhoozer points out, "some have rushed to the conclusion, therefore, that it is this certain way of using the Bible, and not the Bible itself, that is authoritative."[51] Ultimate significance is given to the performance of doctrine as the material principle of the Christian life and not to Scripture, which represents only the formal principle for the direction of the theological performance. Since the biblical texts are not self-performing, they demand an external principle for the proper ordering of this performance. The doctrines of the church are consequently reintroduced, as the material principle, into the biblical witness, where they function as "a canon within a canon"[52] that ultimately determines the purpose of the biblical writings. The result has been, among other things, a positing of the New Testament against the Old Testament, the kerygma against other biblical genres, the sayings of Jesus against other words of Scripture, a central biblical message against the totality of the canon, or a "normative supermotive" against the diverse range of the biblical writings.[53] The stories, letters, prophecies, visions, and songs of the Bible have been disconnected from each other and from the idea of the Word of God, which functions as the formal principle of the authority of the Scriptures that remain essentially void of content. A misplaced notion of the performance of Scripture has introduced a competitiveness into the biblical witness that is foreign to the playful character of the biblical imagination.

The Protestant consensus on the authority of Scripture has been replaced by a wide range of differing opinions. In their recent comprehensive treatment of the Scripture principle, Clark Pinnock and Barry Callen portray the current situation as "a great divide . . . not so much between Catholics and Protestants, but between classical Christians of every kind and liberals who seem bent on shifting the church from her scriptural foundations."[54] The contours of this divide are formed neither by a complete denial of biblical authority nor by the diversity of its definitions.[55] Consequently, recent attempts simply to redefine biblical authority, its object and scope, do not address the heart of the problem and have essentially failed.[56] Instead, at the bottom of the crisis of revelation lies the fundamental distinction between form and matter. This distinction has created an impasse that isolates revelation as a mere formal component from the object and content of the theological agenda. The perception of this formality takes various forms, ranging from the notion that revelation does not contribute anything to the body of rational knowledge to the idea that revelation constitutes merely an inner experience. The former removes the concept of revelation to an abstract idea; the latter makes it an isolated internal stimulus. In both cases, the truths of revelation are removed from the context of the biblical narratives and emptied of their cognitive content.[57] As a result, revelation manifests the authority of Scripture but does not communicate any information for the development of doctrine. The chief consequence is an essential separation of revelation from the theological task altogether. Any solution to this crisis must begin not by reconciling the idea of formal and material principles but by abandoning the distinction altogether.

2. Classical Pentecostalism and the Word of God

In this section I trace the contours of the crisis of revelation from the perspective of classical Pentecostalism. My chief concern is to define the presuppositions that inform the role of Scripture in Pentecostal thought and praxis rather than to trace the contours of a particular Pentecostal hermeneutic. The Pentecostal situation illustrates with particular clarity in the North American context the implications of the alteration of the Scripture principle described in the previous section. I begin with an overview of the understanding of Scripture in classical Pentecostal circles of the early twentieth century, describe the adaptation of the Scripture principle and its impact on Pentecostalism, and analyze the contours of the resulting impasse of Pentecostal hermeneutics. This analysis forms the background for an understanding of what it means to move "beyond Scripture" in the revision of the global theological agenda advanced in the title of this chapter.

Revelation and Scripture in Classical Pentecostalism

The consensus of the Reformers that the Bible constitutes the Word of God remained largely uncontested in the North American context until the middle of the nineteenth century. *Sola Scriptura* typically meant "no creed but the Bible" — a popular slogan that sought to establish the authority of

Scripture from sometimes quite different perspectives but always with emphasis on the clarity and self-interpreting capacity of the Bible, the centrality of Jesus Christ, and the activity of the Holy Spirit.[58] A "populist hermeneutic" affirmed the availability and perspicuity of the biblical writings that could (and should) be read and understood with common sense by everyone.[59] This commonsense approach appealed to a broad constituency, members of the Holiness movement as well as adherents of Protestant liberalism and North American fundamentalism.[60] Yet, the rise of rational biblicism, the right to private judgment, and the accompanying individualization of conscience eventually brought an end to the general consensus.[61] Evangelical historian Mark A. Noll describes the outcome concisely. "In 1870, most Americans, including most academics, agreed on *what* it meant for the Bible to be the Word of God. By 1900, Christians contended with each other as to *how* the Bible was the Word of God. And the academic world at large has asked *if* it was."[62]

Among classical Pentecostals, the conviction that the Bible is the living Word of God stood at the heart of the movement.[63] The restorationist tendencies among the earliest Pentecostals were often accompanied by the slogan "Back to the Bible!" or "Back to the Bible standard!"[64] Adherence to this motto typically meant a reading of the biblical texts that was widely criticized as literal, ahistorical, uncritical, or pietistic by the established exegetical traditions.[65] For Pentecostals, however, the Bible offered the primary affirmation of the experiences that ostracized them from the Christian orthodoxy, most importantly Spirit baptism and the speaking with tongues, a fact frequently emphasized in early Pentecostal publications by phrases such as "Bible evidence," "Bible testimony," and "Bible witness." This emphasis on the Bible as a whole rather than on individual passages or books reflected the common notion that "the only safe rule" in the use of one biblical idea was "to make it harmonize with all other scriptures."[66] As I have shown in the previous chapter, the Bible contained the basis for Pentecostal aspirations of a holy and sanctified life and presented the primary resources for their eschatological expectations (see chapter 1).[67] As Steven Land suggests, Pentecostals were recovering and reentering the entire biblical story of redemption in their own lives.[68] What Land emphasizes is the Pentecostal reception of the dynamic, critical, and prophetic quality of the biblical narratives themselves. From that perspective, the biblical stories were not seen as "Scripture" or "text" but as experienced reality. That is, Pentecostals accepted the biblical reality as the Word of God that was to be taken at face value so that it guided and interpreted their own lives in the present.[69] The Bible represented the original experiences of the revelation of God's presence in the world that continued to intrude upon the immediate context and experiences of present-day believers.[70] Pentecostals were not "readers," "observers," or "interpreters" of Scripture but "evidence" and "testimony" of the continuing realization of God's Word. In the language of the previous chapter, God's Word engaged Pentecostals in the realm of the imagination, orthopathy, and the affections.

More precisely, for the Pentecostal imagination the Bible was the charismatic and affective revelation of God's Word rather than a historical compilation of human records. The Bible was seen as "living and active" (Heb. 4:12), a reality that fused the horizons of human existence and experience with the presence of God's Spirit in the world. This encounter emerges from a human sharing in the pathos of God, where intellect and experience are joined together and mutually inform one other for the sake of participating in God's self-manifestation. Official statements on the authority of Scripture were rarely made by Pentecostals during the first half of the twentieth century.[71] Pentecostal pioneers did not participate in the debates over the validity and veracity of the biblical texts or questions of the inerrancy and infallibility of Scripture.[72] Little or no significance was given to the history of the texts or their distinction from the contemporary situation. This blending of the horizons of God's revelation in the recorded stories and the world of Pentecostals was epitomized by a this-is-that hermeneutic,[73] derived from Acts 2:16, which stripped the biblical revelation from any relegation to events in a distant past or the expectation of a far-off future by attributing to the biblical narratives primary significance for the lives and actions of the present-day community. This-is-that meant: the events within the Pentecostal community were seen as none other than a continuation of the events of the biblical community. This collapse between the historical distance of Scripture and the present day was nowhere more evident than in the understanding of the narratives surrounding the day of Pentecost and the outpouring of the Holy Spirit, events that were seen as enduring in the lives of Pentecostals. The Bible was seen as the persistent revelation of God rather than a closed canon, and it was a story that still unfolded and continued to be experienced in the church and in the world.

In many respects, the Bible was seen as "Word" rather than "Scripture." This distinction was a matter not simply of the hermeneutical perspective of the reader with regard to the biblical texts but of the position of the believer with regard to God's actual self-disclosure: Pentecostals did not *look at* the Bible in order to read and interpret it as Scripture; they sought to *hear from* the Bible as God's Word in order to understand their experiences and find direction and meaning in their encounter with God. Revelation was an event that included speaking and hearing rather than written verbalization; it represented the story of God's dealing with humankind as much as the personal experiences of Pentecostals.[74] The Bible was seen as "recorded" divine speech; yet Scripture did not merely "contain" the records of God's story, it *was* the actual Word of God itself. In this intimate relationship of biblical record and divine speech, God was seen as dynamically present.[75] Through the Word of God, Pentecostals felt addressed by God's Spirit in ways that transcend the written texts and that suggest that Scripture was not merely "an object which we interpret, but a living Word which interprets us and through which the Spirit flows in ways that we cannot dictate, calculate or program."[76] At least initially, this perspective may be described as a charismatic understanding of revelation.

At the heart of the charismatic understanding of revelation among Pentecostals stood the conviction that revelation is transmitted by the Holy Spirit to the church, and that any genuine experience of the Spirit cannot be contrary to the witness of Scripture.[77] The biblical narratives as well as the experiences of Spirit baptism, tongue speech, prophecy, and other charismatic manifestations testified to the idea that the Holy Spirit continues to form the church as a prophetic community through which the Word of God is proclaimed.[78] The Pentecostal imagination characterized these communities as charismatic signs of salvation, sanctification, judgment, and hope that announce the initiation, continuation, and completion of God's work in the world.[79] This charismatic dimension fused the encounter with God at the heart of the biblical story with the Pentecostal experiences of the Holy Spirit. The pleasure and pathos of the Bible were found in the affective, charismatic, and prophetic claims of the biblical witness on the present-day believer. In this sense, the early Pentecostal approach to the biblical texts was precritical since it was preceded and consumed by the passionate claims God's Word makes on the believing community through the Holy Spirit. No distinction is made between the form and matter of revelation, since both are fused in an encounter of the imagination with the divine Word. There is no distinction between written Word and charismatic speech, since both are fused in the affective work of God's Spirit. And no distinction exists between the revelation of God in the biblical texts and the words of the community, since in both charismatic manifestations God continues to speak.

The notion of the speaking of God points to a fundamental conviction among early Pentecostals on the nature of revelation. The mode of orality placed the emphasis on the memory of human experience, the story line, the characters, and the transformative power of the Word of God rather than on the history, structure, textuality, rhetoric, or form of the biblical texts.[80] Orality characterized revelation as self-manifestation through prophetic witness, testimony, preaching, songs, poems, prayers, and charismatic speech that together form a multifaceted story that discloses God in communion. Revelation was considered the interaction of the speaking and hearing of the Word of God in the charismatic community. The divine self-disclosure therefore was considered to be not merely *about* God or *from* God but to happen in the human encounter *with God*. Revelation has no independent, formal identity apart from what is said and heard. In this sense, revelation constituted for Pentecostals the *living* Word of God, and Scripture, insofar as it is written revelation, is living and active by the continuing process of the speaking and hearing of God in the church. In principle, therefore, prophecies, tongue speech and interpretation, preaching, and other forms of revelation held the same authority as Scripture.[81] Central to the significance attributed to revelation in any form were the promise and potential it contained for a face-to-face encounter with God. This notion emerged from and confirmed the charismatic worldview of early Pentecostal thought and praxis.[82] More precisely, the character of revelation as an oral and aural event arose from an imagination at the heart of the Pentecostal community that expects not only the speaking and hearing of God's Word but also, as a result, the transformation of the entire community of faith.

As a transformative event, the encounter with revelation is not immediately dependent upon linguistic structures, narrative progression, historical coherence, or literary requirements but on the imaginative acceptance and wholehearted engagement of revelation as the self-disclosure of God. At the root of the spoken word stands not the sound made but the image that sound intends to convey. In this sense, revelation does not address the eye or the ear but the heart. For early Pentecostals, the event of Spirit baptism and tongue speech rendered an irrevocable experience of a kind of revelatory act that conveyed no intelligible sound yet was perceived by the imagination and transformed by the affections.[83] The orality of this encounter did not so much serve to construct or perform reality as to imagine the Christian life from the perspective of the pathos of God.[84] Prophetic utterances, testimonies, poems, songs, and prayers served as expressions of dreams and visions that captured the heart of God as much as the affections of the faithful. Their primary intention was not the preservation but the proclamation of the encounter with God. The imagination at the root of this proclamation is interested less in facts than in relationship, action, and worship. It is not a record or performance of a completed act but an expression of the continuing possibility of revelation as an encounter with God that calls for a response in the present. The revelation of God is not objectified as Scripture — revelation *is* the presence and pathos of God.

The Objectification of Scripture as Text

The historical turn in the Pentecostal understanding of Scripture is best characterized as the adoption of a performative notion of revelation manifested in an objectification of Scripture. The epistemological roots of this development have been attributed to the Enlightenment ideal of objectivity transmitted to Pentecostals through the encounter with fundamentalism and modernism in the 1920s.[85] While classical Pentecostals and fundamentalists have different historical origins, it is particularly the non-Wesleyan branch of Pentecostalism that adopted early fundamentalist thinking in general, and dispensational thinking in particular.[86] The widely influential publication of the fundamentalist position in a series of books, *The Fundamentals,* sought to reaffirm the Scripture principle by defending it against modernist ideas of higher criticism.[87] However, the foundation of the fundamentalist approach to the Bible and its affirmation of *sola Scriptura* were rooted in the objectification of Scripture. C. Norman Kraus describes the development succinctly: "Fundamentalists viewed the Bible as the intellectual source book for theological data which it used to form a system of definitions and doctrines. Then in turn it equated its fundamental definitions, which were extrapolated from Scripture, with the Scripture message itself. . . . In order to guarantee the Bible as an infallibly trustworthy source for theology they insisted on the theory of verbal plenary inspiration and inerrancy of the text."[88] Fundamentalism responded to the challenges brought to the idea of biblical authority with a strict adherence to the literal interpretation of Scripture and introduced a new hermeneutical scheme that interpreted the biblical material as projecting a series of dispensations.[89] Classical Pentecostals were accustomed to a biblical literalism. However, the Pentecostal community understood as "literal" the prima facie application of the Word of God, regardless of its form, whereas fundamentalists used the term exclusively as a reference to the biblical narratives, bound inevitably to the written texts of Scripture.[90] For Pentecostals, revelation was the dominant category of meaning, whereas fundamentalists focused exclusively on the historicity of the biblical truth.[91] Pentecostal literalism aimed at understanding the meaning of their own circumstances in light of the continuing unfolding of the biblical revelation; fundamentalist literalism looked for a comprehensive methodology for "rightly dividing" the scriptural content. Both desires merged in the application of a dispensational reading of the biblical material.

The theological roots of classical Pentecostalism show an early influence of dispensational thought in the work of William H. Durham and the work of John Fletcher.[92] Pentecostals found in the idea of progressive dispensations a welcome emphasis on the present work of the Holy Spirit that yielded a much-needed theological basis for the doctrine of Spirit baptism. Another influential factor for the acceptance of dispensational teaching was the eschatological orientation that permeated the early Pentecostal revivals.[93] A dispensational understanding offered Pentecostals a systematic structure that could express their eschatological imagination by arranging biblical history in a manner that affirmed their predominant "this-is-that" hermeneutic. However, fundamentalist dispensationalism represented a performative method that submitted the biblical texts to historical and grammatical considerations apart from the concerns that emerged from the Pentecostal self-understanding. The adoption of this dispensational hermeneutic directed Pentecostals to an objectification of Scripture that dispensed the biblical narratives into the realm of history and equated the notion of revelation with the idea of historicity. Revelation now *contained* the Word of God, and Scripture was no longer seen as a charismatic event but fully embodied as text.

Fundamentalist dispensational thought succeeded in shaping a consistent objectivist epistemology among Pentecostals that repressed the charismatic dimensions in their original understanding of revelation. Forsaking the charismatic understanding of revelation for a literalistic approach to Scripture, Pentecostals replaced their oral-affective participation in the self-disclosure of God with a historical-grammatical interpretation of the biblical texts. The result was a "textualization" of revelation that reserved primary status to the written canon and suppressed the function of the imagination in the charismatic community and its affective-prophetic way of being.[94] The concept of revelation was reconceived from the literalistic perspective of Scripture without questioning whether this idea of the Scripture principle was able to contain the charismatic, prophetic, and affective dimensions that Pentecostals associated with the divine self-disclosure. This uncritical adoption of biblical and theological presuppositions has been frequently labeled as the Evangelicalization of Pentecostalism.[95] The adoption of the evangelical mind-set has been described as exerting a negative impact on classical Pentecostalism, particularly on the role of sanctification, Spirit baptism, and speaking in tongues, as well as on the larger perspective of christological and pneumatological themes.[96] Foundational to these concerns is the objectification of the nature of revelation in the form of Scripture and its impact on Pentecostal thought and praxis.

The influence of fundamentalism perpetuated among classical Pentecostals the implications of the performative concept of *sola Scriptura,* which separates the formal authority of Scripture from the content of its revelation and demands an external principle for the proper ordering of its performance. Dispensational theory presented itself as such a principle by allowing Pentecostals to arrange the content of the biblical narratives in a manner consistent with their eschatological imagination, the experience of the outpouring of the Holy Spirit, and the manifestation of spiritual gifts. At the heart of the dispensationalist activity stands the compartmentalization of the biblical material that, while emphasizing the unity of Scripture, invites questions on the principal purpose of the overall content of God's revelation.[97] Pentecostals responded to this challenge by developing "a hermeneutical and exegetical perspective informed explicitly by Luke-Acts"[98] and using it as a quasi canon within the canon, a model, and pattern for the ordering and understanding of the biblical material. As a result, classical Pentecostals have tended not only to lose sight of the whole canon by emphasizing particular books, genres, patterns, and passages but also to legitimize this selective reading of the biblical texts by arguing that the Lukan epic continues in their own lives.[99] In turn, Pentecostal scholarship is hard pressed to reintegrate Luke-Acts into the rest of the New Testament,[100] to reconcile the text with the historically reconstructed world behind the text as well as with the thought world of the contemporary reader,[101] to reintegrate the critical interpretation of the text with the shared charismatic experience of the interpreting community,[102] and, consequently, to defend these concerns as genuine elements of a uniquely Pentecostal hermeneutic.[103] The objectification of Scripture has directed that task toward the resources of philosophical hermeneutics and away from the charismatic notion of revelation and the exercise of the imagination.

The hermeneutical enterprise among classical Pentecostals thus finds itself at an impasse: the idea of the formal authority of revelation objectifies Scripture in the form of the canonical texts and engages only with difficulty the affective, prophetic, and charismatic dimensions of the divine self-disclosure. While early Pentecostals viewed the biblical witness from a holistic perspective of revelation as the continuing and self-fulfilling Word of God, the adherence to fundamentalist doctrine has separated the formal authority of the Scriptures from their content and forced Pentecostals to bring the literal arrangement of the biblical narratives into harmony with a textual and objectified notion of revelation. This notion views God's self-disclosure as mediated scripturally with a focus on "reading" and "organizing" the biblical texts that bypasses the imagination in favor of conscious and critical interpretation.[104] The object of interpretation is the Book, seen largely as a compilation of doctrines rather than the relational and interpenetrating reality of the divine self-manifestation. The task of hermeneutics is the objective "understanding" of Scripture as text and its performance in the church rather than the personal, affective, charismatic, and communal encounter with the living Word of God.

This objectification of Scripture suppresses the unfolding of the Pentecostal imagination and its pragmatic, affective, and spiritual dimensions. The longing for a genuine Pentecostal hermeneutic is faced with the difficulty of reconciling the multidimensional phenomena of a pneumatological imagination with the two-dimensional world of the written texts.[105] The biblical texts represent the confines of the activity of the Holy Spirit, subsumed under the notions of inspiration and illumination. These formal dimensions are expected to emerge immediately from the engagement with the biblical content. Such performative expectations of exegetical practices contradict the dynamic of the imagination, the enduring quality of revelation, the expectation of hearing the Spirit's voice, and the improvisational quality of applying God's Word to the situation of life of the community as they were characteristic of early Pentecostal thought.

The neglect of the charismatic community as the overarching framework of revelation has separated the authority of Scripture from the personal and communal experiences of Pentecostals and relegated it to the formal dimension of an autonomous, theological principle. With the collapse of the notion of revelation into writing as the single revelatory channel of the biblical witness, the charismatic community has been relegated to the realm of reception. The Scripture principle overrules the idea of participation in the revelatory act, since that act is already completed in the written product of Scripture. In other words, the idea of revelation cannot move beyond the concept of Scripture as text. The suppression of the oral character of revelation has moved the affective, charismatic, and prophetic engagement of revelation by the community into the background of organized exegetical performance. Prophetic utterances, testimonies, tongues, songs, and prayers of the community assume an identity apart from the biblical revelation that subsequently needs to be reintegrated. As revelation loses its relational character, so also the prophetic community disengages from the reading and hearing of Scripture as a relational act. The community as con*text* stands over against revelation as text and is no longer able to open up this horizon for a face-to-face encounter with God.

3. The Play of Spirit, Word, and Community

The crisis of revelation, described on the previous pages, has not gone unnoticed in theological circles. A general consensus seems to exist that a solution to the crisis consists of a redefinition of the boundaries of *sola Scriptura*.[106] In this section I give voice to this task by advocating that theology go beyond Scripture. This seemingly provocative statement does not suggest theology forsake the biblical witness altogether but that the notion of "Scripture" be redirected in two foundational ways: first, by a reenvisioning of revelation that forsakes the objectification of Scripture as text, and second, by a reconceiving of *sola Scriptura* that forsakes the distinction of formal and material principle as a designation of biblical authority. Contemporary Pentecostal scholarship, in particular, abandons the artificial distinction between the form and content of revelation by redirecting the definition of Scripture toward a pneumatological and communal understanding of the Word of God. I suggest that, from this perspective, the pneumatological imagination is operative in and beyond Scripture as a charismatic imagination that moves beyond the confines of the textuality of Scripture and the centrality attributed to the performance of the written text toward a dynamic, relational, and affective understanding of revelation that is better characterized as play. I begin by tracing proposals to resolve the crisis of revelation from the work of Karl Barth to contemporary suggestions of the performance of Scripture. I then bring these proposals into dialogue with suggestions from global Pentecostalism that regard the notion of revelation not as performative action but as the playful interaction of the Holy Spirit, the Word of God, and the community.

The Performance of Scripture

Karl Barth may serve as a starting point in this endeavor, since the notion of Scripture he formulated is embedded in the larger doctrine of the Word of God with the precise intention to establish the authority of God's self-disclosure over the authority of the written text.[107] The basis of Barth's concept of the Scripture principle is the idea that God in his revelation is identical with the act and effects of that revelation.[108] In Barth's discussion, Jesus Christ functions as the objective reality ("act") and the Holy Spirit as the subjective reality ("effects") of revelation. Scripture functions as the primary witness to God's self-manifestation in Christ and through the Holy Spirit. That means, however, that Scripture is not identical in all regards with the acts and effects of revelation.[109] This assertion is rooted in Barth's fundamental notion of the freedom of God over his own self-disclosure, a notion that echoes Luther's dictum of God's lordship over Scripture. For Barth, a false notion of the Scripture principle robs Scripture of the sovereignty of God's self-manifestation and encloses the authority of the Word of God in the confines of the written text and the closed body of the biblical canon.[110] Instead, Scripture exists not only as "the text of the biblical witness"[111] but also as "the event or the events of the presence of the Word of God in our own present."[112] Without separating from the biblical witness, God's self-disclosure extends beyond the canon into the present life of the church. Barth is emphatic in his description of the freedom of God's self-disclosure. Even so, he offers little concrete reflection on the expansion of revelation beyond the actual text of Scripture.

In response to Barth's influential account, twentieth-century theology has offered an array of proposals to address the essential problem of revelation, now represented in Barthian terms as the distinction between Scripture and the Word of God.[113] Among the most prolific proposals is the idea of revelation as symbolic disclosure offered by such respected thinkers as H. Richard Niebuhr, Paul Tillich, Karl Rahner, and Avery Dulles. While these thinkers exhibit various approaches to the concept of revelation, a common basis of their symbolic notion is the emphasis on the imagination. The idea of symbolic mediation finds common properties in revelation and the imagination that address the false dichotomy between a biblical and imaginative starting point of theology.[114] In Scripture, divine revelation and human imagination coincide without collapsing into each other. The former removes Scripture from the realm of human fantasy and self-centeredness; the latter reintegrates the divine self-disclosure in the life of the human being by appealing to what Niebuhr calls the "internal history," the "heart," and the "living memory" of the community of faith.[115] Revelation as symbolic disclosure, in the words of Tillich, is at once representation and manifestation of the power of God.[116] These events, as Rahner would say, are expressions of the self-communication of one person to another that are real not only in a historical but also in a salvific sense and resist "any attempt by man to shut himself up in a world of his own categories."[117] Revelation as symbolic event thus gives "participatory knowledge" that "has a transforming effect," as Dulles explains, and therefore "stirs the imagination" by bringing the human being into a new realm of reality with God.[118] In Barth's terms, the freedom of God's self-disclosure is manifested not in the biblical texts, literally, but in the symbolic mediation of the Word of God through the biblical witness, thus liberating the human imagination from its preoccupation with the textual reality of Scripture alone.

The emphasis on the imagination is essential, since it allows the symbol to function beyond a utilitarian view of the biblical texts. At the same time, however, the use of the imagination in the symbolic approach exhibits the same fundamental dichotomy as the one underlying the broader crisis of revelation. From the perspective of Scripture as symbolic mediation, the imagination is essentially synonymous with the idea of inspiration. Although the strict emphasis on the textuality of Scripture is redirected toward the revelatory events that ultimately resulted in the biblical texts, the imagination designates only the form for those events that represent the actual content of the revelation. Scripture is thus God's Word only in a metaphorical sense (as linked to the original revelatory events); the symbols are purely performative (as linking to the revelatory events); and the imagination (as the act of linking Scripture to the original events) is disconnected from the life of the present community.

David Kelsey has thoroughly criticized the symbolic reconstrual of the performative notion of Scripture.[119] He is particularly critical of the functionalist interpretation of symbolic mediation that remains indebted to some property of the texts themselves. Kelsey argues that if "biblical texts are taken as 'Scripture' in virtue of their *doing* something,"[120] then the acting subject is not the text but the church that adopts these texts in order to preserve and shape its own identity. Scripture then designates not a particular property or accommodation of the divine revelation but the use of the canonical texts "in the common life of the church in ways such that they can decisively rule the community's forms of life and forms of speech."[121] In short, the life of the church and its use of Scripture mutually define one another without reducing the biblical texts to pure functionalism. Scripture operates in the church based on the "imaginative judgment" of "what Christianity is basically all about . . . shaped by imaginative characterizations of the mode of God's presence among the faithful."[122] This kind of imagination is rooted in the community as it has shaped Scripture and as it continues to be shaped by the patterns of the biblical witness.

Kelsey's account provides a starting point for the thought of Kevin Vanhoozer, initially discussed in the previous chapter. In a number of larger works, Vanhoozer rethinks the notion of Scripture as communicative acts that "undo" and ultimately "redeem" the biblical canon from the exclusive focus on textual mediation.[123] He revisions the relationship of Scripture and tradition from the perspective of Scripture as "script" and tradition as "performance," arguing "that the canon is itself a performance — an act of discourse — before being script (a design for further performance)."[124] The Christian life "performs" Scripture by representing the past performances of the canonical practices and by submitting them as the norm for the performance of contemporary theology. The biblical script and its performance in the church are thus incomplete without one another.

Vanhoozer's work echoes the wider discussion on the role of performance in general, and the idea of "performing texts" in particular.[125] He is critical of any notion of the performance of Scripture that isolates the canon from the interpretative community by positing the performative act against the authority of the biblical texts and neglecting to render God as the essential communicative agent of revelation.[126] Instead, a revitalized Scripture principle would contain the response and enactment of the drama of redemption as it is both inherent in the biblical text and intended by the divine author. Scripture is an invitation to participate in the "communicative act" of the triune God. As the script for this enactment, the biblical "canon specifies just those patterns of divine communicative action . . . in which the church is to participate."[127] The church is thus not simply an extension of the text, the Christian life not only the pathos and praxis that celebrate the divine drama in Jesus Christ, but the Christian is engaged in a "vital" theater that demands the attention of the entire person.[128]

Vanhoozer's account of performance is significant in its integration of Scripture and community as mutually dependent means of God's revelation. The concept of Scripture as "script" designates the content of revelation, its form, and its function, thereby significantly expanding the idea of Scripture as "text." Moreover, the emphasis on revelation as speech act frees theology from a literal and textual approach and directs the attention to the performance of the communicative action of the biblical canon. Textuality, it can be said, "is no more the dominant criterion in theological understanding."[129] However, the revised notion of performance continues to be based on functional and utilitarian terms that operate on the cognitive-linguistic level of the canon and its interpretation rather than the play of the imagination. In the performance of the script, faith seeks understanding *for the sake of* participation; pathos, transformation, and imagination are relegated to the effects of God's self-communication rather than admitted to form the essence of God's actions. As I pointed out in the previous chapter, for Pentecostals, it is orthopathy that bridges the conceptual and the practical dimensions of participating in God's self-manifestation. The consideration of the divine and human pathos in revelation takes the idea of Scripture beyond the notion of communicative action. While the taxonomy of speech acts attributes assertive, commissive, expressive, directive, and declarative dimensions to God's self-communication,[130] similar to Barth's thought, it suggests that these illocutionary acts do not become *effective* apart from their performance by the church.

More precisely, script and symbol are similar designations that introduce a functional distance between the revelation that occasioned the biblical witness and the experiences in the life of the present-day community of faith. Script and symbol are both performative notions in the sense that they define Scripture as the *expression* of the occurrence of an original revelatory event and the *occasion* of a dependent revelatory experience.[131] Although this kind of distinction is assumed to be justified on conceptual grounds, it remains unclear how exactly these two dispensations are related to each other in the reality of Scripture and its use by the community. To overcome this impasse, both notions turn to the pneumatological dimension of revelation. Since Scripture itself is not self-performing, God's self-disclosure in the original revelatory event is effective beyond the illocutionary dimensions listed above only if these are ascribed to an intermediary agent who realizes and regulates the performance of the dependent revelatory event in the life of the present-day community.[132] The Spirit of God, as that communicative agent, thus becomes a substitute for the pathos of God contained in (and by) Scripture. The church, in response, is an "empty space"[133] in need of being filled with practices that perform Scripture in light of the Spirit's direction. However, these practices are occasioned by the original revelatory events and the performance of its scripted or symbolic reality. The performance of Scripture remains bound to the text rather than to the operation of the Spirit or the community. The possibility is excluded that Scripture is not merely the form of expression or the occasion of revelation but the play of the divine self-disclosure as such.

Beyond Scripture as Performance

Pentecostal scholarship has struggled to overcome the boundaries set by the uncritical acceptance of a textual and performative notion of Scripture and the resulting objectification of the biblical texts. Of course, Pentecostals do not ignore the fact that Scripture exists in written, canonical form. Nonetheless, from the perspective of the Pentecostal experience, the revelation of Scripture confronts the human person not only — and not primarily — as text. That is, the canonical writings are not understood as the sole and final form of revelation but exist as revelatory events in the dynamic play of God's self-disclosure to humanity. Barth's notion of the freedom and authority of God over his own revelation, the emphasis of the symbolic interpretation of revelation on the pathos of God, the imagination, and the transformation of the human person, as well as the pneumatological directions of performance theory, are all reflected in Pentecostal thought. The contribution of global Pentecostalism lies in the integration of these components into a dynamic concept of revelation as the interplay of Spirit, Word, and community.

As one of the first Pentecostal scholars, Rickie D. Moore suggested that there exists a "dialectical and complementary relationship between canonical word and . . . charismatic revelation."[134] Revelation is mediated not only through the canonical text, or script, but also through charismatic speech, thus creating a "revelatory synergism"[135] that redefines the engagement of Scripture in terms of charismatic participation in a "theophanic encounter."[136] This idea resists the conceptualization of Scripture as an object of hermeneutics "and points more to the actualization of a relationship . . . to the manifest presence of God."[137] Scripture is the continuing actuality of the self-disclosure of God that captures the community as a voice from the outside.[138] For Moore, it is this experience of the voice of God in, through, and beyond the biblical canon that "commands and centers the deepest commitments of the heart."[139] The person and community thus captured by God's pathos participate in the divine self-disclosure not by performing but by being themselves transformed into a voice that brings together the witness of Scripture and the Spirit of God.

Moore's view is echoed by a variety of Pentecostals who reenvision revelation apart from functional and performative notions in dynamic and relational terms. This tendency has directed the attention away from an objectification of Scripture as "text" and toward the pneumatological and communal dimensions of revelation. The Spirit, from the perspective of play, is the pathos of God's revelation, not a communicative agent but the actualization of the divine self-communication in the imagination of the community. The church, in this sense, is not the context of interpretation of the biblical texts but the deposit of God's self-disclosure apart from which the Word of God cannot be actualized in its revealedness. Put differently, the community is that realm that makes possible the play of revelation, and as one of its possible realities (though not the only one) the role of the charismatic community far exceeds that of a mere circumference for the hermeneutical exercise.

John McKay highlights the dynamic interaction of Spirit and Word in the church as a shared participation in a charismatic or prophetic experience that refers not only to the self-disclosure of God in Scripture but also to the community that participates in the same revelatory event.[140] For Pentecostals this participation means that "beyond the bounds of the text lies the God of the text,"[141] and, as Larry McQueen underlines, the prophetic dimensions of God's voice beyond Scripture require an equally prophetic hearing and speaking in the prophetic community.[142] Most emphatically, Roger Stronstad challenges the commonly accepted assignment of "a *dispensational* limit to the charismatic activity of the Spirit,"[143] and calls for a recovery of the charismatic theology of Luke-Acts that entails not only the prophetic dimensions of the biblical witness itself but also the prophethood of all believers.[144] John Christopher Thomas adds that "in this hermeneutical model the text does not function in a static fashion but in a dynamic manner, making necessary a more intensive engagement with the text in order to discover its truths in ways that transcend the merely cognitive."[145]

The sentiment of these diverse Pentecostal scholars is echoed throughout the global Pentecostal community and its tendency to speak of revelation less in terms of canonical performance than in terms of the charismatic activity of the Holy Spirit. Particular importance has been assumed by the notion of revelation as prophecy. Swiss Pentecostal Matthias Wenk remarks that the communal experiences of the Spirit are guided not only by the content of Scripture but also by "the nature and the process of biblical prophecy as role model."[146] Miroslav Volf highlights the role of the prophetic community in its historical, theological, pedagogical, doxological, charismatic, and eschatological dimensions.[147] Eldin Villafañe stresses in the context of Hispanic American Pentecostalism the prophetic community as a model of transformed relationships that realize and demonstrate the prophetic reality of the biblical witness in fellowship, worship, proclamation, and service.[148] In Brazil, André Corten suggests that this prophetic reality can make use of the biblical revelation without necessarily involving meaning, understanding, or interpretative scholarship but by appealing "to the imagination of the people."[149] For Corten, the prophetic community exists inflamed by the revelation and pathos of God only in their prophetic actualization of Scripture.[150]

In the African context of Pentecostalism, Sunday A. Aigbe argues that the prophetic mandate issued by Scripture calls the Christian community to bridge the distinctions between biblical, cultural, and evangelistic ministry.[151] The prophetic mandate exists for the sake of an "inclusive holism" that reaches "the spiritual, social, psychological, political, private, public, sacred, and secular dimensions of the individuals and the society."[152] In the prophetic community the charismatic nature of Scripture is realized, contextualized, and applied to the Christian life. Similarly, Madipoane Masenya indicates that for Pentecostalism in Africa biblical prophecy and contemporary prophetic practices are intimately linked to form a joint prophetic witness that speaks to the injustices and sinful structures in the world and in the church.[153]

In Asia, Pentecostals have called for a broader prophetic and vocational role of the charismatic community. Joseph L. Suico links this role with the possibility of social change in the Philippines.[154] In Hong Kong, Lap-yan Kung proposes that the community confront the challenges of globalization, competitiveness, and transitoriness with a spirit of solidarity.[155] In Singapore, Tan-Chow May Ling similarly emphasizes the importance of prophetic responsibility and criticism for the future of the church and its mission.[156] This prophetic dimension of today's church is intimately connected with the prophetic community of Scripture. May Ling thus remarks on the need to expand the biblical paradigm for the reconception of the prophetic community beyond the confines of Luke-Acts.[157] In other words, the prophetic dimensions open up Scripture beyond the boundaries of the fixed text,[158] regardless of form or content, and expand the notion of revelation to the realm of the imagination of the prophetic community. Scripture and prophecy are therefore not two distinct channels of revelation. On the contrary, Pentecostals would emphasize that both actualize oracles of judgment, words of knowledge, words of wisdom, calls to repentance, tongues, interpretation, spiritual discernment, and other charismatic gifts.[159] Even references to the written texts of Scripture within Scripture refer to those texts not to limit the realization of revelation to the form or content of those texts alone. Instead, Scripture points to revelation "as it is written" also as a referent to the continuing actualization of the received tradition beyond the confines of the literal text.[160] The actualizations of revelation in the present community go beyond the text, not forsaking the biblical authority or its canonical tradition, but making manifest the written self-disclosure of God by expanding the canonical witness into the life of the church.

The expansion of Scripture from the confines of the written and canonical text is an endeavor not immediately based on interpretation but on the play of the imagination. For a number of Pentecostal scholars, this form of play develops from the idea of revelation as an oral and aural event,[161] a perspective that initially resonates with the idea of Scripture as performative speech acts. However, as play, the imagination of Scripture is more than oral discourse in written form: as the speech of God the imagination cannot be contained by the written text but constantly breaks out of the textual mold and its performance. Lee Roy Martin speaks of the "radical affective transformation of the hearer"[162] who is interested not only in understanding but also in discernment, faithfulness, obedience, and worship. Whereas linguistic, literary, narrative, and canonical approaches to Scripture seek to hear God's voice *through* the text, the prophetic community encounters God also always *beyond* the text. In fact, revelation as charismatic and prophetic event does not emerge from the written text itself, its letters, grammar, or syntax, but from what occurred and continues to occur in the community as God's presence seen, heard, spoken, and experienced. In other words, Scripture can be neither performed nor played. Instead, it is revelation itself as the play of God's imagination that invites the community to encounter God in the Word and in the Spirit.

The biblical text and the community of faith are thus placed under the norm of the Spirit's work that continues to extend God's voice beyond the written canon. For James K. A. Smith, the incarnation is the predominant exclamation of "God's refusal to avoid speaking."[163] The actualization of this event does not negate the importance of Scripture as text but only of the canon as written norm. For Smith, "prophecy is not subject to the standard of written Scripture but rather the *kanon* of the Spirit as it operates in the discernment of the community."[164] Kenneth Archer speaks similarly of a triadic negotiation of meaning that involves Scripture and the Spirit in the life of the community.[165] "Scripture" is the product of the relational and dialogical validation of the meaning of revelation that unfolds over time and extends "past the canon" to "be embraced and lived out in the community."[166] "Beyond Scripture" are the continuing authentic experiences of the same divine self-disclosure in the community. The church not only hears God's voice through Scripture but also becomes itself a manifestation of the play of God's continuing revelation.

More forcefully, Amos Yong has argued that all theological interpretation proceeds within a triadic framework of Spirit, Word, and community that rejects any single hermeneutical principle, such as *sola Scriptura*. Instead, Yong argues for a replacement of the Scripture principle with a prophetic understanding of revelation that sees the Word of God "not only as inspired speech, but as a complex interactive process between God, the prophet, the inspired utterance, and the audience to which such utterance is directed."[167] This rejection of *sola Scriptura* is not a denunciation of biblical revelation as a whole but only the refutation of a one-sided focus on the textuality of Scripture: "The written word, it is arguable, was never meant only to be read. . . . Scripture as the written Word of God was always meant to be experienced — imagined, spoken, heard, recited, memorized, interpreted, and obeyed — and that as directed toward a variety of liturgical, social, devotional, formational, and spiritual ends."[168] For Yong, the authority of Scripture as God's self-disclosure lies in the multidimensional reality of God's Word as encountered by the church "behind," "within," and "in front of" the biblical text.[169] This revision of the meaning of revelation beyond the textuality of Scripture relies on the "interplay" of Spirit, Word, and community as "three moments [that] are inter-structurally given, interdependent, interconnected, interrelated, interpenetrating and inter-influential."[170] The subject and object, form and content, text and context of revelation *coexist* only in this dynamic relationship of Spirit, Word, and community that is best characterized as play.

The nature of play provides significant insight into the ontology of revelation. Play is a useful metaphor for a characterization of revelation that further overcomes the distinction between form and content. Understood as play, the divine self-disclosure extends beyond the performance of Scripture without thereby forsaking the biblical revelation. Gadamer's in-

sights into the nature of play, noted in the previous chapter, are again helpful to illuminate this point. He describes the essential nature of play as the
ability to absorb everything into its own reality.[171] From that perspective,
the essence of play is located in the actuality of play itself rather than in the
consciousness of the participants or some other dimension underlying
play. Play is thus realized only if all participants and constituencies give up
themselves for the sake of play.[172] In the context of revelation this means
that in the triadic interplay of Spirit, Word, and community, none of these
three occupies the position as the subject of the divine self-disclosure. Play
is found neither in the Spirit, nor in the community, nor even in the Word
of God itself (understood in its manifold sense) but only in the play of
God's revelation as such. In God's self-disclosure, Word, Spirit, and community find themselves lost in the play of God and, emptied of themselves,
are carried away and transformed into a new reality.

Pentecostal scholarship speaks of this transformation in its anthropological, charismatic, communal, intellectual, moral, sociological, and spiritual dimensions.[173] The notion of play reflects this radical change wrought
by God's self-disclosure, to use Gadamer's terms, because it seeks to transform everything that existed before and apart from play into something
that now exists due to its absorption into the reality of play.[174] The world
of play is a transformed world that exposes the essence of everything else
for its own sake. Revelation as play is not performance but "pure self-
presentation"[175] that has an absolute autonomy in relation to everything
else. The players are not performers; instead, play becomes present
through them regardless of whether and what they perform. In other
words, play is not a kind of activity that conditions the effects of revelation
but a mode of being in which that revelation is actualized.[176] Spirit, Word,
and community are not the performance of revelation, nor do they perform the divine self-disclosure, but they are so captured and transformed
by God's revealedness of being that revelation becomes reality through
them. This transformation into realization can also be described as a self-
emptying of Spirit, Word, and community into each other for the sake of
God's self-manifestation. It is this act of *kenosis* that lies beyond the capacity of Scripture as text.

The *kenosis* of the canon for the sake of the divine revelation challenges the traditional notion of Scripture, since both form and content of
revelation cannot be actualized apart from the interplay of Spirit, Word,
and community. Put differently, this triadic interplay is always both form
and content of the divine self-disclosure. God does not reveal something

else through the pneumatological, scriptural, and communal dimensions, but in the play of Spirit, Word, and community it is God's self that is revealed. The attention is thus directed away from the actualization of play to that which intends to be actualized by the play. Form and content of revelation are constantly re-presented by the dynamic nature of play. That means, as Johan Huizinga points out in his seminal work on play, "while it is in progress all is movement, change, alteration, succession, association, separation."[177] Revelation as play is not merely re-presentation of but identification with God's self-disclosure "which is then not so much *shown figuratively* as *actually reproduced* in the action."[178] The moment theology attempts to hold on to the essence of revelation in Scripture alone, the movement of its play ceases and the actualization of the divine self-manifestation is redirected in an endless cycle to the literal texts.

These admittedly very general observations can offer no more than a programmatic direction for contemporary theology. The integration of Pentecostal voices into this task indicates that the hermeneutical enterprise in the late modern world has to address more fully the place of revelation and the nature of Scripture before it is in a position to offer a viable and consistent hermeneutical method. The focus on Scripture as a special form of God's self-disclosure robs revelation of its rhythm and obscures the charismatic dimension in the Christian life. *Sola Scriptura* understood as a reference to the textuality of Scripture delimits the freedom of revelation to a supervised performance within the boundaries of the Bible as book. The passion of God must then be performed outside of the Bible in order to break out of the text instead of already existing beyond it. God's self is enclosed in the book and must be disclosed through the exegetical and hermeneutical task. In the performance of Scripture, the human being therefore effectively takes on the task of disclosing God. In contrast, revelation as play directs the hermeneutical endeavor not first to the canonical text but to the interplay of Spirit and Word in the community. The confrontation with this dynamic actualization of revelation dissolves the misleading distinction between form and content, since neither aspect is sufficient by itself to identify with the charismatic character of the divine self-manifestation. If Pentecostals refer to the revelatory event as a charismatic encounter, then this emphasis embraces the dynamic interplay of the Word and the Spirit of God in the community. It is in this interplay that the Scripture principle can endure as the heartbeat of Christian doctrine. How this task affects the formulation of doctrine is the subject of the next chapter.

3 Beyond Doctrine

Trinity, Oneness,
and the Crisis of the Creed

In chapter 1, I argued that global Christianity, when perceived at heart as a rational, conceptual, analytical, and systematic institution, is facing a crisis in the late modern world. The integration of Pentecostal voices suggests, instead, that the imagination is foundational to Christianity, both in theory and praxis. This proposal inevitably leads to a reimagining of the authoritative sources of Christian theology — a task initially approached in chapter 2 and its attention to the role of the Bible. In that chapter I showed how the impact of the crisis of the imagination is reflected in a crisis of revelation exemplified by the alteration of the Scripture principle. I suggested that global Christianity is constrained by a misleading separation of the form and content of revelation that binds Scripture to a static reality of the text alone. Resources from global Pentecostalism that engage the crisis emphasize the oral, affective, and prophetic nature of the divine self-disclosure and point to the need to go beyond Scripture as text to the play of revelation in Spirit, Word, and community.

In the present chapter, I continue to pursue the idea of the play of the imagination as foundational to global Christianity. The reimagining of the notion of revelation attempted in the previous chapter inevitably questions whether it is compatible with contemporary orthodox notions of the development of doctrine. Reflecting the previous observation on the confinement of revelation to the textuality of Scripture, I argue here that the formulation of doctrine is similarly confined to the formal structure of creedal proclamations. The crisis of global Christianity is also a crisis of its creedal tradition. I therefore engage in a critical evaluation of the formulation of doctrine in the context of the history of Christian creeds. The first part of this chapter outlines the main elements of a crisis of the creed manifested in the Trinitarian discussions surrounding the composition and interpretation of the Nicene-Constantinopolitan Creed and most sharply in the so-called *filioque* controversy. In the second part, I analyze how this crisis is manifested in classical Pentecostalism and its rejection of creedal articulations, represented most clearly in the history and doctrine of Oneness Pentecostalism. The final part of the chapter offers resources from global Pentecostalism that point the task of doctrine beyond its structural articulations to the character of play.

1. The Crisis of the Creed

It is not difficult to find support in arguing for a crisis of creedal theology in the late modern world. Twentieth-century theology, in particular, has lamented the widespread disconnect of the formulation of Christian doctrine from the life of the church, its liturgy, and the spirituality of the faithful. The single most dividing issue, and the most dominant and persistent problem of theological discourse, has been the addition of the *filioque* clause to the Nicene-Constantinopolitan Creed.[1] This section seeks to approach the crisis of creedal theology by clarifying the actual nature of the *filioque* controversy. That is, the question is asked, what exactly constitutes the heart of the "controversy," and how does this issue manifest a critical moment in Christian theology of the late modern world? I propose that more light can be shed on the crisis by examining the theological propositions of the creed from the perspective of its ecclesiological significance, thus exposing the motivation behind the church's formulation of creedal doctrine, and from the viewpoint of epistemology, thus questioning if the methodology and structure of the creed are appropriate for the formulation of its theological content.

The Ecclesiological Significance of the Creed

The *filioque* controversy is typically seen as first and foremost an issue of doctrinal concerns. The Nicene-Constantinopolitan Creed, the classic formulation of the common faith of the Christian community and expression of its teaching and worship, was expanded in the West by the addition of a

Latin clause to reflect the theological conviction that the Holy Spirit proceeds from both the Father "and the Son" *(filioque)*. Immediate concerns over this teaching did not arise from theological convictions.[2] Before it became a subject of division, the East did not protest the profession that both the Father and the Son are involved in the eternal procession of the Spirit. Instead, the controversy was unleashed only with the accusation of the West that the East had suppressed the addition of the clause. In turn, the East argued that any addition to the creed was an inadmissible alteration of the church's common teaching. Both arguments were motivated primarily by ecclesiological concerns, which are immediately visible when we consider the origins of the creed in the liturgical and catechetical setting of the early Christian community.[3] In his classic study of early Christian creeds, J. N. D. Kelly has provided a detailed analysis of the development of the creeds from their association with the preparation of the baptismal rite and the initiation into the Christian fellowship to their establishment as public declarations of faith. The most prominent metaphor for this function is the term "symbol."

From the outset, the term "symbol" has carried strong ecclesiological overtones.[4] The most widely accepted interpretation of the term is the exposition of the Apostles' Creed by Rufinus.[5] When discussing the apostolic composition of the creedal text, he offers a twofold meaning of the designation: "*Symbol* in Greek can mean both 'token' and 'collection,' that is, a joint whole to which several persons contribute."[6] While the exact reasons for the choice of the term remain unclear, Rufinus illuminates the scope of its meaning and offers an explanation accepted by a number of subsequent writers by suggesting that the recitation of the creed was understood as a "token" or "password."[7] Here, the "symbol" is understood as an instrument of identifying the person of faith rather than the doctrinal content proclaimed. From the perspective of the West, Augustine further suggests that the Latin language of "symbol" establishes an analogy to legal contracts and business agreements into which people enter with one another.[8] In their initial association with the baptismal rite, creeds were a token and sign of the Christian community, a declaration of adherence to the church. The doctrines expressed in the creeds served first and foremost as ecclesiological instruments that ascertained and confirmed the catholicity of the church's traditioning process in order to authenticate the orthodoxy of a person's faith. Put differently, the symbol functions as a rule of faith only insofar as it is the communal deposit of faith. The creed as a declaration of faith is first and foremost the symbol of the church.

The ecclesiological dimension of the creed as symbol forms the basis for a broader understanding of its theological function. First, the creed is a *product* of the Christian community. This aspect could be understood in terms of the oneness, holiness, catholicity, and apostolicity of the church.[9] The creed represents the unity, orthodoxy, comprehensiveness, and continuity of the community's teaching. Second, the creed is the *distinguishing sign* of the church, setting apart the Christian teaching from the non-Christian. The relatively slow movement toward fixed forms of the creed contradicts the common expectation that its primary use was in the church's battle against heresy.[10] Third, the creed is a *summary* of the church's teaching and therefore an expression of the common faith.[11] As such, whether used in interrogatory or declaratory form, it represents the essence of the church's traditioning process.[12] Finally, fourth, used by the faithful, the creed becomes a *declaration* of acceptance of the church's teaching, a public signal of initiation into and identification with the Christian community. In this sense the creed can also be seen as a *covenant pledge.*[13] It is the personal response ("I believe") to the revelation of God and the invitation of the church, and it establishes a formal bond with God and among the faithful. As the creeds became fixed and dissociated from their original liturgical and catechetical setting, the wording of the text further emphasized this communal aspect. Characteristic of the Nicene-Constantinopolitan Creed, the text begins with an ecclesial confession of faith in the first-person plural: "we believe," rather than a private expression of faith.

The immediate proclamation, "we believe," places the entire content of the creed in the epistemological realm. More precisely, as recent scholarship has pointed out, the creedal statements are originally performative and require both the relation to God and the integration in the community of faith.[14] As such, they are not automatically effective. From an ecclesiological perspective, the question is not whether religious performatives are true or false but whether they are used correctly or incorrectly.[15] Embedded in the communal proclamation of the church, the performance of creedal statements is intimately connected with the baptismal rite. The historical witness to the detachment of the creeds from the catechumenate therefore raises serious questions about the use of creedal statements as foundations for the theological enterprise, since theological statements presuppose other, nonperformative arguments.

Modern expositions of the creed have largely neglected its performative and communal dimensions.[16] An exception is Heribert Mühlen, who has noted the ecclesial "we" among the most significant aspects of the creedal proclamation.[17] For Mühlen, the "we believe" is not simply spoken by a number of individual selves who then unite to a community of common doctrine. Rather, the performative "we" includes and presupposes the ecclesial "we" as the joint confession of the entire church. Although this "we" is open to theological differentiations, it is not open to a separation of the individual from the church or of the churches from one another.[18] In this sense, Mühlen suggests the need for a more detailed reflection on the "we" and its function in the ecclesial and ecumenical community before addressing the theological doctrines of the creed. A resolution to the *filioque* controversy emerges from an affirmation of the oneness and catholicity of the Christian "we" in one place, time, and act that allows for an unfolding of the universal presence of the Holy Spirit among the churches.[19] Necessary for doctrinal agreement is ecclesial convergence, a process of union *among persons* that only subsequently affects unity in doctrine.[20]

From the perspective of the ecclesial "we," the addition of the *filioque* clause disrupted primarily the nature and fellowship of the Christian community before it confronted the univocal explication of its doctrines. This disruption goes beyond the community expressed by the authority of the ecumenical councils to what Jaroslav Pelikan calls the "ecclesiastical enactment"[21] of the whole community of faith. As a symbol of the church, the creed is not merely an objective good or the rational sum of revealed truths but is the dynamic expression of the living we of the entire church.[22] A change in the creed means therefore first of all a change in the ecclesiality of the church and only subsequently an offense against the authority of the council and alteration of its doctrine. However, dominant ecclesiologies do not offer a dynamic concept of ecclesiality and, as a result, imply a rather static image of the development of doctrine, often disconnected from ecclesiological concerns. Illustrative of this dilemma is the fact that the West has located the authority of the creed *in* the church, particularly the papal authority, that is, *outside* of the symbol, while the East has placed the authority of the creed *above* the church, and thus *outside* of the ecclesial community.[23] The contemporary discussion continues to seek a resolution to the doctrinal controversy in isolation from the ecclesiological roots of the debate and implies that any act on the doctrinal formulation of the *filioque* clause will also alleviate the divisions among the churches.[24] Creed and church are thus separated conceptually, leading to the development of doctrine apart from the concerns of ecclesiology.

The conceptual separation of church and creed has contributed to an isolation of the faith from the praxis of the Christian community. The creedal texts are depersonalized and largely emptied of their relationship to the community and to the tradition that contributed to their formation. This isolation of creedal theology from the life of the church has led to a detachment of doctrine from its kerygmatic and charismatic heritage. Separated from the life of the church, the creeds came to be seen as independent systems of doctrine.[25] The decision to commit the declarations to writing further removed them from the heart and memory of the living community and made them a *depositum fidei* rather than a *symbolum ecclesiae*. As a written deposit of faith, the creeds became a formalized script of doctrinal propositions, documents of declaratory statements formative of the church's identity rather than emanating from its faith, history, and doxology. The debates about the addition of the *filioque* clause have further removed the creedal formulations from their original argumentative contexts and turned them into propositional formulas prescriptive of the church's teaching and of the manner in which it was to be conducted.[26] In the late modern world, the creeds are no longer proclaimed by the "we" of the church but are preserved as an "it" of faith, often constitutive of the private faith of the individual and widely estranged from the history and life of the Christian community.

The Epistemology of Creedal Structure

The structural composition of creedal formulae has stimulated little debate, and the *filioque* controversy has raised more questions about doctrinal content than about the theological form and method employed in the composition of the creeds. Discussion has focused primarily on the doctrine of the Trinity and the divine processions, while concerns regarding the adequacy of the creedal structure for that purpose have been largely ignored. This neglect has sidestepped the question whether the structure of the Nicene-Constantinopolitan Creed was at all composed for the purpose of Trinitarian thought and whether it does justice to the creed to identify it essentially as a Trinitarian document.

Scholarly consensus has shown that the work of the pre-Nicene fathers was primarily apologetic in character and did not attempt to formulate an explicit doctrine of the Trinity.[27] At the heart of doctrinal debates about the inner structure of the faith stood the union of God and man in the person of Jesus Christ, which also served as a vantage point to thoughts about the Trinity.[28] The most urgent tasks of the patristic era concerning the formal development of Trinitarian theology did not emerge until the third and fourth centuries, when the conciliar teaching began to occupy a more central position in the methodological and structural development of doctrine.[29] During the pre-Nicene era, no technical debates about the concepts of "person," "substance," or "procession" took place, and no evidence exists of a comprehensive progress of Trinitarian thought. The writings of the pre-Nicene fathers reveal few attempts to formulate a Trinitarian doctrine built on the thought of previous writers and generally show a digression rather than progression of orthodox Trinitarian thought.[30] In turn, the Nicene Creed found neither a theological nor a structural foundation in the patristic thought of the first two centuries. The Council of Nicaea reflects little of the debate on nature, essence, energy, operations, or processions that marks the later discussion, and the composition of the Nicene Creed remains dominated by an intentional complexity of meaning and lack of Trinitarian focus.[31] The coeternal and consubstantial divinity of the Holy Spirit was not explicitly confirmed until the Council of Constantinople (A.D. 381).[32] In other words, the triadic structure of the Nicene-Constantinopolitan Creed does not have an explicit basis in a Trinitarian tradition. The *filioque* controversy, however, has overshadowed this aspect with Trinitarian concerns foreign to the original intentions of the creed. In this sense, the *filioque* is an addition, not an interpretation, a divergence, not a defense of the original intentions of the creedal tradition.

As a result of the lack of Trinitarian heritage, the Nicene-Constantinopolitan Creed is interpreted typically from the perspective of the doctrinal debates that *followed* it and with little account that the document was not designed to meet the demands of subsequent Trinitarian debates.[33] The addition of the *filioque* was therefore not within the intentions of the creed, since the clause is exclusively a Trinitarian concept and reflects neither liturgical nor ecclesiological concerns. As a result, many contemporary paradigms have shed a false light on the history of patristic theology and developed a number of concepts artificial and anachronistic to the history of creedal composition. The most far-reaching among these paradigms is the theory advanced by Theodore de Régnon, who distinguished between different methodological approaches among Greek and Latin authors, the former beginning with the oneness of the divine nature and working toward the distinction of three persons, the latter beginning with the persons and moving toward the unity of being.[34] Theological scholarship during the twentieth century widely employed this paradigm and proposed its value in outlining the epistemological options available for the formulation of Trinitarian thought. From that perspective, one has to choose either the unity of being or the diversity of persons as a starting point for the formulation of Trinitarian doctrine. However, recent scholarship has shown that no such universal dichotomy existed in the history of Greek and Latin approaches to the Trinity.[35] Even if the paradigm of de Régnon were historically substantiated, the triadic structure of the Nicene-Constantinopolitan Creed can be explained by neither an approach from the unity of nature nor one from the distinction of personhood, nor from a progressive correlation between the two.

In the context of its liturgical origins, the creed was sometimes described as the "symbol of the Trinity,"[36] yet this designation referred primarily to the threefold interrogation and response of the catechetical process and contained no explicit profession of Trinitarian doctrine. The triadic structure gradually emerged as a stationary element of creedal composition as new situations demanded clarification and modification of the original content. The method of modification typically consisted of insertions in the basic threefold structure, keeping the triadic arrangement intact yet expanding and interpolating its content and rhythm.[37] The triadic structure of the creed seamlessly fit the defense of orthodox Trinitarian thought and dictated where modifications and additions could be made without offering, at the same time, a theological justification for the preservation of the threefold creedal composition.

Only in medieval and scholastic literature do we find a deliberate discussion of the compositional structure of creedal doctrine, often discussed under the notion of "articles."[38] In his *Summa Theologiae*, Thomas Aquinas offers a justification for the concept and its usefulness for the articulation and organization of Christian doctrine in general.[39] Relating the term to its etymological heritage in denoting the "joints" *(articulus)* of the body, Aquinas defines "articles" as the parts that "fit together" distinct compositions of speech. While this definition can be seen as belonging properly to the work of Aquinas and to scholastic methodology, Aquinas does explicitly connect his explanations with the creedal tradition. From this perspective, the reason to use an articular structure in the formulation of Trinitarian doctrine is primarily epistemological.[40] Since the human intellect is able neither to grasp nor to express the revelation of God in its fullness, the divine truth must be divided into distinct articles that make it possible to formulate individual aspects and to associate with one another those aspects of doctrine that belong together.[41] Aquinas distinguishes between the ontological order of God and the epistemological realm of faith, with the former containing no separation of articles.[42] However, since we cannot access the ontological order except through the epistemological realm, the "formal aspect of matters of faith" makes a distinction of articles necessary.[43] The doctrine of the Trinity forms for Aquinas the heart of the primary matters of faith and thus the guideline for the basic distinctions of articles.[44] While he acknowledges that epistemologically we have only one knowledge of the three divine persons, he justifies the triadic distinctions by pointing to the economy of salvation, which ascribes different works to each of the three persons, and to the misunderstandings of the ontological order in the history of doctrine, which made a separate treatment of each person necessary.[45] Hence, Aquinas highlights the epistemological tension between the unity of being and the diversity of persons in the theological description of God. Yet, he gives no indication of the theological starting point for a doctrine of the Trinity in the creed and does not show how the distinction of articles provides an explicit Trinitarian structure or methodology.

Although it may seem implicit, the Nicene-Constantinopolitan Creed does not claim to postulate an ontological order of the Trinity. The three articles express no ontological distinction between immanent and economic Trinity, a paradigm that developed only as a result of the development of Trinitarian thought after the Council of Nicaea.[46] The epistemological distinctions advanced by de Régnon also do not apply, since the creed shows no movement from the unity of being to the diversity of persons or vice versa. Instead, as Aquinas points out, the reference to "one" God is placed within the first article of the creed, which also introduces the Father. Neither the word "three" nor the technical term "trinity" is used in the text. As a result, the question of the unity of being and the trinity of persons is conflated in the first article to a profession of faith in one God and the Father without relating the oneness to the Father, the Son, and the Holy Spirit collectively. Another reference to singularity in the second article is concerned entirely with the union of the two natures in the person of Christ and carries only implicit Trinitarian repercussions.[47] While the term "God" is used in this context for both the Father and the Son, an explicitly Trinitarian designation of the Holy Spirit by the use of the same term is absent. Aquinas mentions that this conflation can be justified on the epistemological grounds that there is only one knowledge of the three persons, yet this justification also collapses the triadic structure into essentially one article. The single reference to "one" God reflects the use of the biblical concept of God but is not qualified on the basis of Trinitarian justifications, since the debates that would make such a qualification possible had not yet taken place.[48] Moreover, the postulation of articles, while epistemologically justifiable, is an essential obstacle to the formulation of Trinitarian thought.

The distinction of persons seems to be reflected more readily in the triadic articulation of the creed. In fact, the articles take the place of a proper theological distinction of persons, which is only implicit in the structural division. The postulation of faith in the Father, the Son, and the Holy Spirit in three articles is not substantiated by a definition of personhood or elaboration of the relation of the three persons to the one divine nature. On the contrary, due to the distinction of articles, the councils are at pains to establish the relations between the divine persons more explicitly with the language of generation and procession. This language, however, had to be added to the content of specific articles, dealing with one person respectively, thus attributing the relation *between* persons to the property of one person. No indication is given for the principle or the order of the processions, and thus for the manner of being of all three persons in relation to one another. While the order may be implicit in the semantic sequence of the three articles, no explanation is found for the distinction of generation and procession or for the consequences these terms bear for an understanding of the Son and the Holy Spirit.

As a result, the articles remain static in their identification of the three persons and show no intention to move from the distinction of persons to the unity of being. By assigning the relations to each person respectively, the unity of being is defined between the Father and the Son in terms of the generation of the Son from the Father, and between the Father and the Holy Spirit in terms of the procession of the Spirit from the Father. The second and third articles of the creed thus correlate to the first article. No explicit relation is established between the second and third articles, that is, between the Son and the Holy Spirit. The addition of the *filioque* clause manifests the desire of the Latin Church to make that relation explicit and thereby to make unequivocal in the proclamation of the creed the unity of the divine being in all three divine persons.[49] However, while its addition was epistemologically justifiable, the clause was structurally embedded in the article on the Holy Spirit and thereby sharpened the contrast between the three articles while blurring their structural weakness. This association of the *filioque* with the Holy Spirit has decidedly impeded the development of pneumatology. Nonetheless, the question about the appropriateness of articular formulations with regard to pneumatology in particular, or to Trinitarian theology in general, has not been raised and has remained the foremost theological task of Christian doctrine to this day.

The lack of primary Trinitarian data in the creed has led to an epistemological distinction in the form of articles that further perpetuate not only the crisis of Trinitarian theology but also its immediate impact on the ecclesial "we." In light of the ecclesiological significance attributed above to the creed as a symbol of the church, this criticism further elevates the importance of creedal theology for the global theological agenda. In the following I suggest that the impact of the crisis of creedal theology is illustrated with particular clarity in classical Pentecostalism. Rather than perpetuating a theology of articles, Pentecostal thought can be seen as a critical catalyst in addressing the shortcoming of such an endeavor and thereby contributes to a solution of the crisis of the creed.

2. Oneness Pentecostalism and the Articles of Faith

This section addresses how classical Pentecostalism is a manifestation of the crisis of the creed. The goal is to illuminate the history and doctrine of early Pentecostal theology from the viewpoint of the creedal affirmations. From this perspective, I argue, the Oneness Pentecostal tradition offers a valuable illustration of the crisis of creedal theology. The history of divisions between Oneness and Trinitarian Pentecostals sheds further light on the ecclesiological and epistemological perspectives of creedal composition presented in the first part of this chapter.[50] The current section does not aim at justifying Oneness Pentecostal doctrine but at integrating it into an ecumenical analysis of the crisis of creedal theology. This intention is admittedly carried out from my own commitment to Trinitarian thought. I do not intend to assimilate the two positions but to analyze the Oneness Pentecostal critique of creedal theology. On this basis, the final section of the chapter offers resources from both Trinitarian and Oneness Pentecostals to address the challenge of critically evaluating the traditions in their task of formulating Christian doctrine.

The rejection of creeds is a well-known trademark of early Pentecostal history in North America. The doctrines, rituals, and creedal statements of the church presented for early Pentecostals an often insurmountable obstacle to spiritual freedom and the priesthood of all believers. Pentecostal pioneers boasted in having "no creeds, rituals, or articles of faith,"[51] and no creed but Christ or the Bible. Few Pentecostals, however, have voiced concrete doctrinal grounds for their rejection beyond concerns about the institutionalization of church structure and the formalization of doctrine at the cost of practical ministry.[52] Most classical Pentecostals do not reject the content of the creedal confessions and have little concern about using the creeds to support their own beliefs. The stereotype that the rejection of creeds forms the basis for a broader rejection of academic and systematic theology among classical Pentecostals can therefore not be sustained.

A fundamental concern among early Pentecostals was not the doctrine or wording of the creed but its ecclesiological significance. Creeds were seen as destructive to the life of the church and synonymous with "isms" and "schisms"[53] among God's people. Replacing God's law of unity with "men-made creeds,"[54] the Council of Nicaea was made primarily responsible for the initial disruption of the Christian fellowship. The challenge to adhere to the creedal proclamation of faith confronted first-generation classical Pentecostals with the ecumenical ecclesiology that was fundamental to their own movement. Pentecostals saw the creeds as ecumenical fences, a "test of fellowship"[55] in opposition to the "unity of the Spirit,"[56] separating the faithful from one another. In this sense, it did not matter whether the creedal statements were true or false, since they broke the law of love and unity. This separation was often experienced among Pentecostals in the harsh reality of persecution at the hands of the established churches.[57] Ecclesiological and ecumenical concerns governed much of the Pentecostal hostility toward the adherence to creedal formulations. The birth of Oneness Pentecostalism and the rise of the so-called new issue in 1914 illustrate with particular clarity the crisis of the creed in the twentieth century.

Oneness Pentecostalism and the Creed

The "new issue," or Oneness controversy, arose from the liturgical context of classical Pentecostalism early in the second decade of the twentieth century and led to a division of Pentecostals into Oneness and Trinitarian camps. The emphasis on the liturgical origins of the debate is important on at least two levels. First, the debate emerged amidst the widely attended camp meetings that shaped the early Pentecostal liturgy and the cultural and ecclesiastical diversity of classical Pentecostalism.[58] Second, it emerged in the explicit context of the administration of water baptism, the understanding of the baptismal mode, and the question of the correct baptismal formula.[59] The origins of Oneness Pentecostal doctrine mirror the liturgical seedbed of the creeds.

Unlike most Trinitarian Pentecostals, Oneness Pentecostals understand conversion as reflected in Acts 2:38 to comprise repentance, water baptism, and baptism in the Spirit, and the liturgical practices of Oneness congregations typically include opportunities for all three activities.[60] Water baptism "for the remission of sin" obtained an essential role in the order of salvation and in the theological reflection of early Oneness teaching.[61] Moreover, most early Pentecostals embraced William H. Durham's teaching of the "finished work of Calvary," which rejected the idea of sanctification as a second crisis separate from salvation and instead ascribed to the full efficacy of Christ's death that finds its application in one inseparable event of conversion (see chapter 2).[62] The "finished work" theology concentrated the *ordo salutis* essentially in one experience that was identified by Oneness Pentecostals with Christian initiation.[63] Hence, the recent Oneness-Trinitarian Pentecostal dialogue (2002-2007) acknowledged "that the struggle over the biblical formula for baptism and, ultimately, the meaning of baptism, initiated historically our divisions as Oneness and Trinitarian Pentecostal churches,"[64] and granted the topic of baptism primacy in the dialogue toward reconciliation.

At the heart of the historical debate about Christian initiation stood the reconciliation of the triadic baptismal formula in Matthew 28:19 with the apostolic practice of baptism in the name of Jesus, as recorded in Acts 2:38 and elsewhere.[65] The discussion inquired about the "correct" paradigm of water baptism in the church, a task typically seen among early classical Pentecostals as identifying the "biblical" paradigm in the New Testament. In its doctrinal concerns, the debate questioned which baptismal formula should be used in the movement that saw itself as restoring the apostolic life. The consequences of this debate did not immediately emerge as Trinitarian questions but unfolded on the basis of a distinction in liturgical praxis between the single name of Jesus and the three titles "Father," "Son," and "Holy Spirit." In this context, the triadic structure of the creed emerged as a dividing line between adherents of the Oneness and Trinitarian Pentecostal positions.

The Council of Nicaea clearly emerges as a watershed between the Oneness and Trinitarian views of God.[66] David Bernard, senior theologian of the United Pentecostal Church International (UPCI), the largest Oneness Pentecostal organization, sees the primary reason for the ascendancy of the triadic formula of the creed in the impact of the baptismal practice on combating heresy, while he emphasizes that a distinctively Trinitarian language and doctrine did not develop until the fourth century.[67] His analysis of the Nicene Creed begins by pointing to the lack of Trinitarian theology despite the apparent triadic structure. "While this confession was threefold, it was not explicitly trinitarian, for it did not state that Father, Son, and Holy Ghost were three distinct persons. Rather, its fundamental purpose was to affirm the deity of Jesus Christ against the Arians. . . . The phrase 'God of God . . . very God of very God' may imply two divine persons, but it can also be understood as simply referring to the Incarnation."[68] While Oneness doctrine would reject the Trinitarian interpretation of the creed as implying the eternal procession of the Son, Oneness Pentecostals are able to "use the same words to mean the one God came in flesh and therefore God who dwelt in Jesus is the same as God before the Incarnation."[69] In addition, the profession of faith in the Holy Spirit in the third article of the creed is not integrated in any explicit Trinitarian theology of divine personhood,[70] leaving open the interpretation of the exact relation between the oneness of God and the manifestation of God as Father, Son, and Holy Spirit even among the supporters of Trinitarian thought. In other words, the creedal formulation is in *content* acceptable to both Trinitarian and Oneness thinking.[71] The point of contention is the triadic sequence in the *structure* of the creedal confession and its implications for distinguishing three separate divine persons.

There are at least two fundamental reasons why Oneness Pentecostals can accept the content of the creed. First, Oneness Pentecostal doctrine does not completely reject a triadic aspect of the Godhead. Garfield T. Haywood, a pioneer of first-generation Oneness thought, admitted a triadic manifestation of God in the world as creator, redeemer, and sustainer.[72] His contemporary, Andrew D. Urshan, did not hesitate to speak of "the Three-One God," a "Tri-Unity," or "a divine three-ness of being."[73] The content of the creedal confessions continued to be reflected in publications and statements of faith for many years, since it did not explicitly contradict Oneness Pentecostal doctrine. Second, the history of the creeds was interpreted as leaving room for non-Trinitarian interpretations of the doctrine of God.[74] Oneness Pentecostals found in modalistic monarchianism of the fourth century a historical ancestor that affirmed the two central aspects of their own doctrine of God: "1) there is one indivisible God with no distinction of persons in God's eternal essence, and 2) Jesus Christ is the manifestation, human personification, or incarnation of the one God."[75] Oneness Pentecostals argue that the creed can be read from this perspective, since its affirmation of "oneness" relates explicitly only to the unity of the divine being and the unity of natures in Jesus Christ and not to a unity of divine persons, a distinction of persons that is not made in content, in the first place.

On the other hand, the rejection of the structure of the creed by Oneness Pentecostals as implicitly Trinitarian is based on at least two observations. First, a dismissal of the creedal structure emerges from the significance attributed to the apostolic community for matters of faith and praxis among classical Pentecostals in general, and from an observation of the apostolic practice of baptism in particular. Oneness Pentecostals emphasize the widespread use of baptism "in the name of Jesus Christ" as the original apostolic formula before the age of the Greek apologists. Even when the formula was expanded to a triadic form, it continued to include the name of Jesus — not in opposition to the threefold structure but as convocation of the grace of God that included the grace of the Father and the sanctification of the Holy Spirit.[76] Oneness Pentecostal doctrine juxtaposes the practice of baptism "in the name of the Father, and the Son, and the Holy Spirit" (Matt. 28:19) with the proclamation of "one baptism" (Eph. 4:5), highlighting the identity of singularity in name and baptism and the difficulty of the church to reconcile the oneness of God with a threefold immersion. This tension is ultimately consolidated in the triadic structure of the Nicene-Constantinopolitan Creed and its proclamation of "one baptism," which reflects the emphasis on "one God," "one Lord," and "one church" but does not reconcile this oneness with the distinction of the Father, Son, and Holy Spirit.

Second, the triadic structure of the creed is seen as resulting from an inadmissible combination of the radical monotheism of the Old Testament and the redemptive manifestation of Father, Son, and Holy Spirit in the New Testament on the basis of a philosophical distinction between economic and immanent Trinity.[77] This departure from the biblical revelation and subjection of Scripture to philosophical reasoning is a chief reason for the Oneness Pentecostal rejection of the creedal tradition.[78] While the biblical witness affirms the tri-unity of the Father, Son, and Holy Spirit in the economy of salvation, a distinction of "economic" and "immanent" is foreign to Oneness Pentecostal doctrine, and the conceptual distinction of three manifestations does not translate into an ontological argument of the Trinity.[79] The supposed rejection of the notion of "person" and denial of economic and ontological arguments for the doctrine of God form the main reasons for the manifestation of the crisis of the creed in contemporary Pentecostalism. The theological consequences of both views for the task of theology need to be further elaborated.

The preceding overview highlights only the central issues dividing Oneness Pentecostals from the Trinitarian creedal tradition. The fact that the divisions are based on structural or methodological concerns rather than on the content of the doctrinal confession has generally been overshadowed by what the Oneness-Trinitarian Pentecostal dialogue has called the "passions" of the early debate.[80] Yet, the report of the dialogue itself also does not contain a section on the respective methodological approaches to the doctrine of God and does not consider the epistemological consequences of de Régnon's distinction of starting points in the unity of being or the diversity of persons for an understanding of either side's theological approach. As a consequence, while the five-year study illuminates many of the commonalities of and differences between the traditions, it does not offer a proposal to overcome the impasse. This path would inevitably confront both sides with the reconciliation of content and structure of Trinitarian thought or, more precisely, with the questions of divine personhood and the eternal processions.

Central Issues of the Oneness-Trinitarian Impasse

Although the belief is widely held even among supporters, Oneness Pentecostals do not reject the concept of "person" as such but see God as "a personal being, not a generic, abstract substance."[81] However, Oneness Pentecostal doctrine makes no distinction of persons (plural) in the Godhead and attributes personhood (singular) only to Jesus Christ. This choice seeks to speak to the difficulty in Trinitarian doctrine to reconcile the distinction of three persons with the unity of the divine being, generally addressed in the concepts of the interpenetration *(perichoresis)* of the three divine persons and the eternal procession of the Son and the Holy Spirit. In the place of these Trinitarian ideas, Oneness Pentecostals speak of one God who is one being in the person of Jesus Christ and encompasses in this person all three manifestations of the Father, Son, and Holy Spirit. This understanding is supported by reading Matthew 28:19 not as a command to distinguish in baptism three separate persons but to identify the Father, Son, and Spirit as a single being identified by a single name.[82] This "name" does not merely represent the character, authority, rank, or power of God, but it is "the indispensable part of the *personality*" of the divine being, that is, in God "the name and the person are synonymous."[83] This ontological equivalence seeks to address the challenge of Trinitarian theology to reconcile the univocal use of the term "person" with the personhood of three divine persons and the distinction of each person from the other two. Oneness Pentecostal doctrine replaces the idea of three "persons" with the single "name" of God manifested in the person of Jesus Christ. In other words, from a Oneness Pentecostal perspective, the person of Jesus *is* the name of God.[84] It is therefore possible (and necessary) to confess faith in the Father, Son, and Holy Spirit among Oneness Pentecostals.[85] However, this confession is summed up in the act of water baptism "in Jesus' name" so that theologically and practically Jesus Christ is proclaimed as the only personification of God.

In light of the preceding considerations, Oneness Pentecostals have been frequently labeled incorrectly as a "Jesus only" movement — a label that applies more correctly to their baptismal formula than to their doctrine of God. Yet, while their approach to the doctrine of God is certainly christocentric, Oneness Pentecostal faith and praxis are after all a reflection of the profoundly christological orientation of the Pentecostal affections in general, and the emphasis on the name of Jesus is not synonymous with a rejection of the Father or the Holy Spirit. At the same time, the prominence of Christology emerges from a more profound acknowledgment of the Jewish heritage of the Christian doctrine of God[86] and should not be confused with a doctrine of the second article. While that approach would account for the personhood of Jesus, it also presupposes the distinction of more than one divine person through the essential application of the terms "Father," "Son," and "Spirit." Oneness Pentecostals, on the other hand, reject the identification of these terms with the personhood of three distinct divine persons and propose that "the titles of Father, Son, and Holy Spirit describe God's redemptive roles or revelations, but they do not reflect an essential threeness in His nature."[87] The three manifestations are therefore necessary, coexistent redemptive roles in the economy of salvation proclaimed in the doctrine of God as creator, savior, and sanctifier[88] and centered in the experience of Jesus Christ.

The Oneness-Trinitarian Pentecostal dialogue brings attention to Christology immediately following the discussion of water baptism. While subscribing to the joint affirmation of the incarnation and the full humanity and deity of Christ, the Oneness Pentecostal team rejects the definition of the Son as the "second" divine person on the basis that this definition "results in two Sons — an eternal, divine Son who could not die and a temporal, human Son who did die."[89] To escape this dilemma, the Oneness Pentecostal team affirms that "Jesus is not the incarnation of one person of a trinity but the incarnation of all the identity, character, and personality of God."[90] In other words, Jesus is not the eternal second person but the eternal God who became Son in a "begotten Sonship"[91] manifested in the economy of salvation. The incarnation marks the beginning of the work of the Son, whose redeeming role will end when the present world ceases to exist.[92] While Oneness Pentecostals insist that this perspective can in principle be reconciled with the content of the creedal confession of faith in Jesus Christ, Oneness Pentecostals see a "single-clause, Christological pattern"[93] as more consistent with the intentions of the creed and refute a representation of the christological emphasis as a "second article." In contrast, the Oneness Pentecostal view would account for only one article in the creed, which is identical with the confession in Christ and comprises at the same time the redemptive manifestations of God as Father, Son, and Holy Spirit. A label of Oneness Pentecostal thought as a doctrine of "one article" emphasizes that Oneness and Trinitarian thought are like-minded in content but, in principle, incompatible in structure.

The implications of the last sentence for creedal theology have to be worked out in more detail. In this context, the statement of faith of the UPCI offers at least a starting point for understanding one alternative that Oneness Pentecostalism offers to the triadic structure of the creed. "We believe in the one ever-living, eternal God: infinite in power, holy in nature, attributes and purpose; and possessing absolute, indivisible deity. This one true God has revealed Himself as Father; through His Son, in redemption; and as the Holy Spirit, by emanation. . . . Before the incarnation, this one true God manifested Himself in divers ways. In the incarnation, He manifests Himself in the Son, who walked among men. As He works in the lives of believers, He manifests Himself as the Holy Spirit. . . ."[94] In this statement, the three articles of the creed are combined into a single proclamation of faith in the three redemptive manifestations of God. This focus on the economy of salvation is symptomatic of classical Pentecostalism in general, and is a significant aspect for understanding the Oneness Pentecostal doctrine of God.[95] It carries primary implications for the rejection of a distinction of persons in God's eternal being.

Oneness Pentecostal doctrine resists the distinction between immanent and economic Godhead primarily because it is contingent on substance metaphysics, that is, more precisely, the distinction is based on the concept of the eternality of the undivided divine substance and a distinction of sub-stantial manifestations (i.e., persons) in the economy of salvation. Bernard shows that Oneness Pentecostals give priority to the biblical concept of "spirit" in the place of the philosophical notion of "substance" and uphold a threefold distinction of manifestations while rejecting the idea of three dis-tinct persons. "The Spirit of Jesus existed from all eternity because he is God Himself. However, the humanity of Jesus did not exist before the Incarna-tion, except as a plan in the mind of God. Therefore we can say that the Spirit of Jesus preexisted the Incarnation, but we cannot say the Son preexisted the Incarnation in any substantial sense."[96] This pneumatological perspective on the redemptive manifestations of God illuminates the desire of Oneness Pentecostal doctrine to speak of the Father, Son, and Holy Spirit as simulta-neous rather than successive manifestations. From the perspective of the re-demptive experience of the work of God, Christians "do not experience three personalities when they worship, nor do they receive three spirits, but they are in relationship with one personal spirit being."[97] Therefore, the Spirit of God can be called "simply God," "God himself," or "the one God."[98] "Father" is the designation of the Spirit as a "transcendent God" and synon-ymous with the Spirit in the "Son" or with the deity of Christ.[99] From the perspective of Oneness pneumatology, in the incarnation, the transcendent "Father" and the omnipresent "Spirit" are manifested in the flesh in the hu-man person of the "Son." As a consequence, the "Holy Spirit" is the Spirit of Jesus and "does not come as another person but comes in another form (in spirit instead of flesh) and another relationship ('in you' instead of 'with you'); the Holy Spirit is actually Jesus coming to dwell in human lives."[100] The single-clause, christological pattern of Oneness Pentecostal doctrine is therefore in a fundamental sense pneumatologically oriented. From the per-spective of the creedal structure, the single clause would have to parallel the affirmation of the oneness of God's being proclaimed in the first article, cen-ter in the confession of faith in Jesus Christ as divine-human person asserted in the second article, and proclaim the activity of the Holy Spirit as declared in the third article. From the Oneness Pentecostal perspective, these affirma-tions would have to be made in a single clause that avoids both a triadic structure of the doctrine of God and the necessary consequence of relating each aspect of the triad to the other.

At this point, the Oneness-Trinitarian controversy has reached a meth-odological impasse. From a Oneness Pentecostal perspective, the triadic structure of the creed unnecessarily perpetuates tritheism. The Trinitarian distinction between one substance and a threefold division of persons in

God makes necessary the notions of *perichoresis* and procession that are ultimately held responsible for the *filioque* controversy. However, the creed does not make use of either concept since full development of them belongs to the post-Nicene era. Oneness Pentecostals, on the other hand, basically ignore both concepts because they presuppose the distinction of persons and are based on a notion of interaction among the persons in the immanent Trinity of which we have no experience. An examination of the biblical witness to the interpenetration of redemptive manifestations of the Father, Son, and Holy Spirit or of the applicability of the concept to the economy of salvation in general, has not been attempted among either Trinitarian or Oneness camps.[101] The question whether the Oneness Pentecostal doctrine of God is essentially "perichoretic" in nature might offer a direction for further discussion if the concept can be loosed from the notion of personhood and applied to God's activity in the world, with particular emphasis on a pneumatological orientation.

Oneness Pentecostals would consider "procession" an economic term that denotes a "sending" or "appointment" in "the supernatural plan and action of God,"[102] but that does not refer to a distinction of the divine substance or a preexistence of persons apart from the economy of salvation. When applied to the Son, "the sending . . . emphasizes the humanity of the Son and the specific purpose for which the Son was born."[103] The Son does not proceed eternally from the Father but is begotten by the Spirit as the human manifestation of God. In turn, the sending of the Holy Spirit refers to the "return . . . of Jesus manifested in a new way"[104] after the glorification of the Son. As a result, the sending of the Son is a necessary presupposition for the sending of the Holy Spirit in the sense that both are redemptive manifestations of one God. At the same time, while it is denied that Christ preexisted in a substantial sense before the incarnation, Oneness Pentecostal doctrine upholds the preexistence of the incarnate Christ as the eternal Spirit of the one God.[105] The concepts of the "manifestations" or "roles" of the one God therefore replace the idea of the "procession" of persons in the economy and interpret the relations in a pneumatological sense and toward a christocentric proclamation of faith that stands in stark contrast to the creedal affirmation and makes the addition of the *filioque* clause unnecessary. This proposal, however, remains unacceptable to Trinitarian theology as long as its own methodological options are rooted in a necessary tension between the unity of the divine being and the division of persons that can be bridged only in terms that preserve the triadic structure. Put differently, Oneness Pentecostalism challenges contemporary theology to go beyond the structural and compositional framework of its established Trinitarian doctrine.

3. The Reformulation of Doctrine and the Play of God

This final section addresses the challenges of going beyond the structural and compositional weaknesses of Trinitarian doctrine. While the goal envisioned here is Trinitarian, Oneness Pentecostalism challenges the established tradition to revise its creedal structure and to focus its perspective on the experience of God in the economy of salvation, with particular emphasis on the implications this carries for the idea of the relations and processions of the divine persons. I wish to address this challenge in dialogue with recent Trinitarian proposals and by gathering resources from global Pentecostalism that not only help overcome the Oneness-Trinitarian polemic but also show a possible direction to avert the crisis of the doctrine of God. The goal is to offer an outline for the global theological agenda that pulls together the diverse Pentecostal and non-Pentecostal proposals in order to overcome the ecclesiological and epistemological shortcomings in the development of doctrine described in the first section. The metaphor of "play" developed in the previous chapters from the perspective of the imagination and revelation serves here to illuminate and bring together the global Pentecostal contributions to the formulation of doctrine. The ensuing invitation to join together in the theological task is necessarily painted with broad strokes. I intend to offer nothing more than a programmatic proposal for an ecumenical development of the doctrine of God.

The Doctrine of God and the Economy of Salvation

The Oneness Pentecostal doctrine of God suggests that the economy of salvation represents the primary realm of theological discourse. On the side of Trinitarian theology, Catherine LaCugna has offered a significant proposal that parallels the Oneness Pentecostal suggestion and its critique of creedal theology.[106] While I am not convinced that her negative evaluation of the historical development of Trinitarian thought will hold up to closer examination, her appraisal is helpful in situating the Oneness Pentecostal account in a broader theological context. In *God for Us,* LaCugna criticizes the distinction between economic and immanent Trinity and makes it primarily responsible for the separation of the doctrine of God from the mystery of salvation, leading to a distinction between God's self *(in se)* and God's redemptive activity in the world *(pro nobis)* (see pp. 209-41). De Régnon's oversimplified historical paradigm constitutes for her an epistemological disaster (pp. 11-12). Similar to Oneness Pentecostals, she locates the roots of the problem in the correlation of God's eternal being with God's nature in the economy of salvation and the primacy of substance metaphysics (pp. 3-4).[107] LaCugna wants to maintain the unity and equality of the divine persons without an appeal to an immanent Trinity that logically "adds" the persons and their relations to the unity of God's eternal substance. Instead, she argues that the only proper approach to the tri-unity of God's eternal being is the economy of salvation.

LaCugna locates the heart of her critique of the Trinitarian tradition at the Council of Nicaea, which she holds ultimately responsible for shifting the attention away from the revelation of God in the redemptive economy and toward the equality of the three divine persons (see p. 42). Prior to Nicaea, she contends, the doctrine of God was concerned with the unfolding of God's plan in Christ. The creedal tradition of the post-Nicene era, however, used the distinction of persons in salvation history to direct the focus to an intradivine reality that separated the eternal being of God *(theologia)* from the economy of salvation *(oikonomia)*. The preference for "speaking of God as Trinity rather than as God (Father) who comes to us in Christ and the Spirit defunctionalizes the biblical and creedal ways of speaking of God" (p. 102). The *filioque* controversy originated from this artificial separation of economic and immanent Trinity and contributed to relegating the Holy Spirit to the immanent Trinitarian relations by obscuring the property of the Spirit in the economy (pp. 298 and 373 n. 66). For LaCugna, the ultimate consequences of this decision are ecclesiological and doxological, leading to a different orientation in worship and prayer, and a substantial change in the shape of the liturgy.

In response, LaCugna suggests a return to biblical and pre-Nicene patterns of thought and a rearticulation of the link between theology and the liturgy that revises the relation between the eternal being of God and redemptive history by abandoning the terms "economic Trinity" and "immanent Trinity" and defining *oikonomia* as the only revelation of the eternal being of God.

> What we come to in the end is that if we use the term "person" of God, whether in the singular or plural, we are not giving a description of the

essence of God as it is in itself, but using a term that points beyond itself to the ineffability of God. Since person is the ecstatic and relational mode of being, then the proper focus of theology is the concrete manifestation of God's personal reality revealed in the face of Jesus Christ and the activity of the Holy Spirit. It does not so much matter whether we say God is one person in three modalities, or one nature in three persons, since these two assertions can be understood in approximately the same way. What matters is that we hold on to the assertion that God is *personal,* and that therefore the proper subject matter of the doctrine of the Trinity is the encounter between divine and human persons in the economy of salvation. (p. 305)

Most Oneness Pentecostals will have little difficulty subscribing to this proposal. The application of the principle of *perichoresis* to the economy of salvation leads LaCugna to sternly reject a separation of the doctrine of God into three articles. The separation of pneumatology from Christology, in particular, has prevented an interpenetration among theological themes: "There need not be three foci — three names, three events, three persons — for theology to be trinitarian" (p. 364). Instead, she argues that the doctrine of God should be based on a relational ontology that focuses on the notion of *perichoresis* beyond the inner life of God and opens up to a proclamation of Jesus as "the true perichoresis" (p. 296) and of the Holy Spirit as the one who "incorporates us . . . into the mystery of perichoresis" (p. 298) in the economy of redemption.

LaCugna and others suggest that for this understanding of God and for the consequential reorganization of doctrine the metaphor of *perichoresis* as "divine dance" represents "indeed an apt image of persons in communion: not for an intradivine communion but for divine life as all creatures partake and literally exist in it. . . . The one *perichoresis,* the one mystery of communion includes God and humanity as beloved partners in the dance."[108] Pentecostals have repeatedly emphasized this interdependence of Christology and pneumatology in the experience of the redemptive life and the interpenetration of the transcendence and immanence of God in the human encounter with God's Spirit. The classical Pentecostal focus on Spirit baptism, in particular, begins with the experience of the Holy Spirit in the economy of salvation and from there seeks to illuminate the perichoretic interaction of the Father, Son, and Holy Spirit in the theology of grace.[109] At the heart of the Pentecostal contribution to addressing the crisis of creedal theology stand the worship and prayer, the liturgy and doxology of the church. Daniel Albrecht has shown that the Pentecostal rituals — among them dancing, jumping, touching, swaying, waving — express not only a particular spirituality among Pentecostals but also an understanding of the human life in interaction with God in general, and thus serve to illuminate the being of God and to communicate the theological relationship between God and the faithful.[110] Central to the Pentecostal self-understanding is Christian existence that is open to freedom of expression, spontaneity, improvisation, and enthusiasm. The metaphor used to describe these relationships throughout this book is play. Its application in the present context of conceiving both God and the doctrine of God from the perspective of *perichoresis* proves helpful.

The main challenge to the theological use of "dance" is that it may be understood at heart as a performative act, that is, dance is encountered only when it is performed.[111] Similar to the concept of drama, "dance" as a thing in itself does not exist except as a type performed for others, thus providing a spatiotemporal framework on a particular stage, by particular actors, following a particular script. While this idea may add to the intention to speak theologically only from the perspective of the economy, I suggest that it carries significant implications for the identity of different performances and of those performances with the original type. Dance as a type that requires performance allows us to speak of the identity of two performances only insofar as they reflect the same type.[112] There exists thus a tripartite distinction between the original dance, its interpretation, and its performance. While the "original" dance as such does not exist unless it is performed, the uniqueness of the performance depends on the interpretation of the type, since a performance without interpretation is simply a repetition or copy.[113] As a consequence, different performances of a single dance may not be interchangeable unless they are based on the same interpretation. However, if they are based on the same interpretation they lack the creativity, spontaneity, and improvisation I have shown to be a hallmark of the imagination. Theologically, therefore, the performance of the divine dance by God in the economy of salvation leads to a distinction of three performances related only by the interpretation of the same type. In other words, the Father, Son, and Holy Spirit dance the same dance, but they do not dance with each other unless they perform simultaneously together. In the same sense, God's performance and the performance of the church are distinct and thus elide an interpenetration of the human being and the community with God's activity in the world.

The Pentecostal experience, on the other hand, corrects this performa-

tive understanding of dance and offers a perspective based not on interpretation and performance but on a Spirit-driven inspiration that imitates
diverse social and cultural worlds and thereby takes them into an encounter with Christ in the church. Dance is seen as a mediation between the human and the divine, a harmonious interplay, in which no particular type
of dance is performed.[114] Hence, dance can be an expression of praise,
worship, and celebration, as well as travail, prophecy, and spiritual warfare.[115] Different forms of expression encounter each other at the same
time without inherent contradiction and with no requirement that the
other (including God) is engaged in the same type of dance. From the perspective of global Pentecostalism, the engagement may include an adaptation of traditional ritual movements and gestures (Samoa), the reproduc-
tion of emotions (black America), expressions of a particular cultural
heritage (Latin America), ecstatic trance (southern Africa), interpretive
dance or popular urban dances (Papua), performances of biblical stories
(Kinshasa), ritual self-emptying (Ghana), or the expression of suffering
and sickness (Korea).[116] This "dancing in the Spirit" has no steps assigned,
follows no manual or premeditated movement, and thus frequently challenges established norms and expectations.[117] Those who participate follow the move of God's Spirit often with no discernible conformity in gestures or patterns of behavior. Dance, considered from this perspective, is
more closely related to play than to performance.

The notion of play sheds particular light on the formulation of the
doctrine of God. The Father, Son, and Holy Spirit, in engagement with the
world, reveal a God who is "at play" rather than "at work." Jean-Jacques
Suurmond's Pentecostal proposal of the church as the play of Word and
Spirit places the play element in the charismatic encounter *between* God
and humanity. God is not synonymous with play but "at play" with the
world. The Father, in an ecstatic movement, literally, standing outside *(ex-
stasis)* of himself, interacts through the Spirit by manifesting his identity as
the Word in the economy of salvation.[118] In this *perichoresis,* Christ becomes "paraclete" through the Spirit, while the Holy Spirit also becomes
"paraclete" through Christ, both engaging and liberating each other and
the world for dance with God as "one of the most perfect forms of play."[119]

Paul's characterization of God as "a God not of disorder" (1 Cor. 14:33),
instead of the positive affirmation as a "God of order," prompts Suurmond
to define the rules of God's play as an alternative to both extremes. It is
God's holiness poured out through the Holy Spirit and personified in
Christ that creates the ethic of play. The biblical Scriptures provide models

of this ethic but avoid prescriptive rules of either God's interaction with the world or human beings with God.[120] Suurmond is critical of a separation of Word and Spirit and the tendency of Trinitarian doctrine to identify the former strictly with the second person and the latter with a third article in the Trinitarian relations. Instead, he suggests that the doctrine of God should be understood dynamically, from the perspective of the "one God who . . . longs to share himself in the Word and the Spirit — in the creation and afterwards completely in Christ, in order after his death and resurrection to flow through them in a new way to all humankind."[121] In play with God, humanity is filled with God's Word and Spirit and, in turn, gives itself (Word and Spirit) to others and God in a "reciprocal permeation"[122] that foreshadows the eschatological union with God.

This contrast of play and performance questions the common terminology of God's activity in the world as "work" or "operations" in the "economy" of redemption. As a consequence of the dominance of purposefulness, productivity, and order, *perichoresis* is interpreted as a choreographed routine rather than a "dancing around" *(perichoreuō)*, a joyful, ecstatic, or self-emptying movement of God's existence beyond God's self. The Latin translation, *circumincessio* (to move around), is seen as a purposeful "circular" activity rather than a playful "roundabout."[123] Its alternative, *circuminsessio* (to sit around), characterizes a passivity in the divine interpenetrations instead of a different aspect in the movement of the divine persons.[124] In turn, traditional Trinitarian doctrine assigns to the divine choreography of the Son and the Spirit only a "moving forward" *(processio)*, a dance in one direction following a single order *(taxis)*, and while applying the principle of *perichoresis* to the unity of being, does not also apply the same principle to the movement of the Father, Son, and Holy Spirit in the economy of salvation. The metaphor of dance as a forward and backward movement, an exclusion and embrace, a sending and receiving, is reflected only with difficulty in the creedal structure and manifests that a reformulation of doctrine is one of the most urgent tasks of contemporary theology.

Toward a Reformulation of the Doctrine of God

The liturgical foundation of the formulation of doctrine evident in classical Pentecostalism suggests that a response to the crisis of the creed from among Pentecostals is likely formulated on the basis of the affections that saturate the Pentecostal experience. While this perspective does not reject as irrelevant the idea of God apart from the creation, a distinction is not formally made between the economic and immanent reality of God but, more experientially, between what Pentecostal theologian Terry Cross calls the perfection of God and the relationality of God. "We need not start our consideration of this God in the abstract philosophical realm of being and substance, but rather in the arena of incarnation. From the cue given us about God in the life of Christ, we understand that our God is a being who desires relationship with his creatures. This breaks down the static models of divinity (regardless of their origin) and forces our thought into the dynamic realm of relationality."[125] The static nature of the creedal formulation of the doctrine of God is a fundamental starting point for the Pentecostal reformulation of doctrine. Samuel Solivan holds the static, philosophical formulations of post-Nicene doctrine largely responsible for creating an apathetic image of God that ultimately suppressed modalistic monarchianism because of its teaching on the divine suffering (patripassionism).[126] While Solivan does not embrace Oneness Pentecostal doctrine, he does suggest that the theological motivation behind the Oneness model emerges from an affectionate encounter with God rather than a reflection of doctrine. Whereas the theological tradition applies the affections in principle only to Christ, God's eternal being is conceptualized as self-sufficient, unmoved, and dispassionate. God's involvement in the world is the result of "work" *(ergon)* as an extension of God in creation, not of "passion" *(pathos)* as the expression of the essence of God's being.[127] In contrast, Solivan suggests that pathos is not only an economic but also a theological term that refers to both a "redemptive expression of compassion" and a "liberating passion" *(orthopathos)* in God's nature, communicated by the Holy Spirit and most fully revealed in Jesus Christ.[128] Pathos is seen as the bridge between praxis and doctrine, since it portrays God in dynamic, relational, and affectionate ways that adequately express God's being from the experience of God in the economy of salvation. From the perspective of the affections, the task of theology necessitates a reformulation and redefinition of doctrine that takes account of the participation of creation in the one God who is moved by a liberating passion to go beyond the divine life in itself to an existence for others.

In this liberated divine and human relationship, the Father, Son, and Holy Spirit are at play in the sense that they are not bound by any order or directionality necessitated by the economy of salvation. On the contrary, it is the freedom of affectionate movement in God that establishes the freedom of creation in a dynamic, interrelated activity that is not contingent upon the created order but depends entirely on the passion of the one God for the salvation of the world. LaCugna's emphasis on the soteriological dimension of God's being in the economy is complemented by Pentecostals with an emphasis on the holiness of God and the eschatological orientation of God's actions that protect the *perichoresis* of the Father, Son, and Holy Spirit from any sense of arbitrariness. The Pentecostal emphasis on *orthopathos* holds on to the revelation that the Father sent the Son and the Holy Spirit yet also opens up to the possibility of different movements of God. While the biblical witness to God's self-manifestation must be protected to be able to say anything about God at all, even the biblical texts cannot be held to offer exhaustive information about God's eternal being or the possibilities of God's continuing engagement with the world (see chapter 2). *Orthopathos* grants God's self the freedom to imagine and carry out an interaction with the world that confounds rational norms and expectations. The gospel of Christ is the prime testimony to the playfulness, disorder, and asymmetry of God's actions for the sake of the realization of God's love in the world.

Therefore, the emphasis on *orthopathos* should not be seen as granting arbitrariness and aimlessness to God's actions. Ralph Del Colle has argued "that a taxonomy of the religious affections within the Pentecostal-charismatic experience is profoundly Christocentric in its orientation."[129] More precisely, he proposes that the Pentecostal experience shared by both Oneness and Trinitarian camps reflects a pneumatologically informed Christology that has found its prime doxological expression in the doctrine of Spirit baptism. "Christologically, the grace that is Spirit-baptism, illuminates the exalted Christ as the template for both the agency of the Holy Spirit and the glorification of the Father."[130] The experience of Spirit baptism suggests that the activity of Christ and the activity of the Spirit are experienced perichoretically, so that "the agency of the risen Christ is conducted by the agency of the Spirit and the agency of the Spirit is the manifestation of the agency of Christ."[131] The Father is thus glorified and manifested in the outpouring of the Holy Spirit by the Son and, conversely, in the revelation of the Son by the Holy Spirit. The ecumenical community has reflected this suggestion with particular clarity in its testimony of Spirit baptism.[132] Pentecostal theologian Frank Macchia has suggested most emphatically that a Trinitarian formulation of Spirit baptism can indeed function as a template for a comprehensive reformulation of doctrine from a Pentecostal perspective.

Macchia confirms the mutual correlation of Christ and the Spirit in the Christian life.[133] The Oneness-Trinitarian controversy revolves, for him, precisely around the experience afforded in Spirit baptism of the fullness of God in the economy of salvation. Cross's distinction between the perfection and the relationality of God is exposed in Spirit baptism as the experience of the incarnational and eschatological manifestations of the Father in Christ and the Spirit. "The Trinitarian structure of Spirit baptism thus has a two-way movement: from the Father through the Son in the Spirit, and then from the Spirit through the Son toward the Father."[134] Since, from the perspective of the economy of salvation, "the triune life of God is not closed or self-contained but dynamic and open to creation,"[135] the mutually correlative movements of Spirit and Word are evidenced both in the life of Christ and in the Christian. This understanding has been brought into dialogue with recent proposals that speak of the Trinitarian movement as both a procession and a return.[136] What distinguishes Macchia's proposal is that his idea of the divine movement is not based on a distinction of origin but on a mutual participation in the shared, interdependent reality of the Father, Son, and Holy Spirit.

A departure from the relation of origin as foundational to orthodox Trinitarian doctrine carries significant implications for the understanding of the divine processions and the *filioque* controversy. While the fullness of these implications needs to be worked out more consistently, not only among Pentecostals, deserting the separation of the creedal confession into three articles in favor of a perichoretic formulation that emerges from a distinction between the incarnational and eschatological reality of God in the world exposes the *filioque* clause as only one side of the divine movement, and not a foundational one at that. Instead, the Holy Spirit is involved already in the conception and initiation of the mission of the Son, reflected in the story of the Spirit in the life of Christ.[137] Conversely, the Son sends the Holy Spirit at Pentecost, now transformed through his own agency, on the church, which, in turn, experiences in Spirit baptism the affective interplay of the Father, Son, and Holy Spirit.

The idea of God at play requires at base a faithful reflection in the composition of doctrine. As Wolfhart Pannenberg pointed out, the freedom of play exposes the limited power of permanent images of God in relation to the human reality.[138] Without a relation of origin as a starting point, the doctrine of God not only can but also must be able to begin anywhere in the life of God without thereby forsaking or misrepresenting any of the other movements of the divine persons. Amos Yong has suggested that the Pentecostal acknowledgment of the mutual interplay of Christ and the Spirit confirms the recent ecumenical proposals of complementing the *filioque* clause of the creed with an addition of *spirituque*. "Because of the perichoretic mutuality and reciprocity of Christ and Spirit," Yong envisions a retrieval of the narrative base of the gospel that includes "its retelling, repetition, and reenactment" as vital aspects of the reformulation of an incarnational doctrine that is oriented toward the eschatological movement of the triune God.[139] This emphasis on the narrative aspect of doctrine allows the metaphor of Spirit baptism to be one possible image for the doctrine of God by holding together in an affectionate story Christology and pneumatology as joint aspects of the activity of the Father in the economy of salvation. The second and third articles of the creed are joined together to illuminate the first, and in this interplay the articles factually cease to exist. Central to this theology "without articles" is the human being as a vital element without which the story of God cannot be told. The biblical and Pentecostal narratives correct the creedal affirmation of this aspect in speaking of God's activity "for us" by giving witness to the story of God who in Christ and the Spirit is also "among us," "with us," "in us," and "through us," and thereby invites humanity to participate in the story of redemption. In turn, the response of the church demands not only a "we believe" but also "we have encountered," "we have experienced," and "we have been transformed." The first-person plural is not an expression of a subjective observation but constitutes a moment in the ontological participation of the faithful in the life of God.

The roots of the Pentecostal imagination in the biblical story and the prophetic notion of revelation open up the formulation of doctrine to an integration of human participation beyond a confession and proclamation of faith ("credo"). Doctrine is seen not as a mere description of the content of faith but represents a vital element of the practice of faith that is characterized as much by the affections of the faithful as by the pathos of God. Consequently, the formulation of doctrine engages not only the philosophy of language, a poetological or aesthetic approach to the notion of the Trinity,[140] but also the affections of the faithful as a reflection of the passion of God for the salvation of the world. *Orthopathos* brings together in play God and the economy of salvation and thus makes the creed a dynamic expression of the Christian life. A reformulation of doctrine can begin by going beyond the performative function of the creed as a "rule" of faith, instead allowing creedal theology to speak about God in more generous terms that involve the imagination and affections.[141] The biblical witness and the testimony of the church attest to the use of dreams, visions, and prophecy as acceptable forms for the proclamation of faith, not only because they integrate the creedal intentions into their ecclesiological heritage but also because they reveal meaning beyond the disclosure of language. Doctrine, from this perspective, provides the grammar of theological discourse only insofar as it does not limit either our perception of God's activity or the manner in which we express and experience it.

The idea of doctrine as play may provoke a sense of proteophobia, "the apprehension aroused by the presence of multiform, allotropic phenomena which stubbornly defy clarity-addicted knowledge, elide assignment and sap the familiar classificatory grid."[142] After all, the performative nature of doctrine represents a safe and reliable (i.e., reproducible) procedure that tends to dislike the risks and uncertainties associated with the imagination. However, the emphasis on play should not be understood as an attempt to substitute the weight of the speculative demands of systematic theology with metaphorical language. On the contrary, play calls us into a certain interiority, both anthropological and theological, when we endeavor to enter into union with the triune life of God. This dimension of doctrine is not exhausted in the speculative, performative, or rational knowledge of redemption but demands instead a personalization and corporealization of the faith, that is, a liturgical praxis that embraces both the contemplative and the charismatic dimensions of the biblical witness and the doctrinal tradition. The present chapter has intimated this particular significance of the liturgy for the formulation of doctrine on a broad level. From a global Pentecostal perspective, the liturgy integrates and transforms orthodoxy, orthopraxy, and orthopathy. The present liturgical reality, however, often lacks the imagination, creativity, and improvisation necessary for the unfolding of these three dimensions and their full influence on the development of doctrine. The revision of the theological agenda therefore requires a different approach to liturgical celebration *(leitourgia)*, conceived not as the "work of the people" but as the "people at play." This approach forms the basis of the next chapter.

4 Beyond Ritual

Structure, Liminality,
and the Crisis of the Liturgy

The preceding chapters examined the crisis of the imagination and its impact on the role of Scripture and doctrine in the theological agenda of global Christianity. I suggested that the tension between a systematic account of theology as performance and the Pentecostal approach to theology as play represents the most fruitful contribution of Pentecostalism to a revision of the theological agenda in the late modern world. The reimagining of revelation and creed through the metaphor of play emphasizes the significance of the affective, personal, and corporeal nature of the faith. In this chapter, I wish to explore further how the notion of play can inform a theological praxis that remains fundamentally oriented toward the Word of God yet resists a rationalization and systematization of this task. I suggest that a liturgical perspective is foundational to the kind of reorientation of global Christianity approached in the previous chapters. However, the unfolding of this perspective is confronted with a number of challenges that make transparent the problems of the theological enterprise noted thus far and thereby point the way beyond the established structural notions of Christian praxis that resist improvisation, imagination, and creativity. In other words, the crisis of global Christianity is most tangible as a crisis of the liturgy.

The effort to portray the theological agenda fundamentally from a liturgical perspective is not new.[1] The twentieth century inherited two dominant approaches, one portraying the liturgy as a faithful performance of doctrine, the other seeing doctrine as emerging fundamentally from the performance of the liturgy.[2] The goal of this chapter is to bring Pentecostalism into dialogue with both traditions. To that end, I argue that the contemporary crisis of the liturgy is largely the result of understanding liturgical action in terms of performance rather than play. The first part of this chapter outlines the development of the performative understanding of the liturgy as it emerges from the medieval European context and shows the consequences of this development for a contemporary theology of the liturgy. In the second part, I proceed to an analysis of how classical Pentecostalism has exacerbated the crisis of the liturgy, and analyze what I call the "destructuralization" of established Christian rituals. In the final part I offer a constructive proposal for resolving the crisis of the liturgy by bringing resources from global Pentecostalism into dialogue with a theology of the liturgy.

The explicit suggestion made in this chapter that Pentecostalism can contribute to liturgical theology stands in sharp contrast to the stereotypical perception that portrays classical Pentecostalism as fundamentally nonliturgical. In North America, the rejection of liturgical structures is seen as a particular distinctive of Pentecostalism. In contradistinction, I argue that, although classical Pentecostals did not incorporate the established ritual culture of Christendom in their worldview and praxis of faith, the Pentecostal imagination reveals an attempt to transform the orthodox elements of the Christian liturgy into a Spirit-oriented dynamic of play rather than a rebellion against dominant liturgical structures. Put differently, instead of understanding theology as doxology in the sense of a second-order reflection on the prayers, praises, worship, and rituals of the faithful, I argue that theology emerges from the liturgy as a first-order experience of the imagination that is indistinguishable from the personal, corporeal, and kinesthetic practices of the faithful. In this sense, the liturgy is not the *product* of the church; on the contrary, as the vehicle of the imagination, the liturgy creates the life of faith.

1. The Crisis of the Liturgy

The twentieth century has exposed a long-standing liturgical crisis. This insight refers not only to the widely discussed problems of liturgical celebration in contemporary culture and society but, more importantly, to the potential for renewal that has been acknowledged in this situation. I embrace the definition of Romano Guardini, the father of the German liturgical movement, that the crisis of the liturgy is actually "a sign that the work for the liturgy . . . [is] really coming to life."[3] Guardini points out that the modern crisis of the liturgy is also a catalyst for the revival of the liturgy, since liturgical action — understood primarily as a historical reality bound to the context of particular cultural and sociological backgrounds — necessarily enters a crisis with each change of the established socio-historical structures. Exemplary of the crisis in the late modern world is the complaint that modern Christians who live in an industrial and urban civilization "find liturgical language and the ideas it contains, and even the very symbolism of the liturgy, empty of content and largely meaningless."[4] The liturgical celebrations of the church seem to have lost contact with the tangible realities of modern life and thereby have invited criticism not only of the liturgical action itself but also of the ecclesiastical communities that celebrate the liturgy as an expression of their praxis of faith. Attempts to "renew" and "modernize" the liturgy extend to the ecumenical community at large.[5] The wide-ranging signs of the liturgical crisis have become associated with the symptoms of much broader concerns about the end of Christendom, that is, a social and cultural environment no longer influenced by Christian norms and values.[6] The origins of this crisis, I argue, can be traced back to the formation of performative structures of the liturgy during the Middle Ages.

It is generally acknowledged that the liturgy of the church, although originally not intended as a dramatic performance, nonetheless emerged as such from the practices of faith in the medieval West of the ninth and tenth centuries.[7] While there is evidence of dramatic impulses in liturgical action of the patristic age, I have pointed out that the church fathers understood the imagination as a sanctified act of the community of faith (see chapter 1), which led as a consequence to a general condemnation of theatrical activities and a suppression of the development of organized drama.[8] The Middle Ages, however, transferred the condemnation of performance from the theater to the imagination itself, making the imagination instrumental to reason and thereby opening the door for dramatic performances in the church.

Theories of Dramatic Performance

The monumental work of Karl Young is among the first to consider the question of drama in medieval liturgy. Young rejects the idea that dramatic performances are defined by some form of externalities, such as the presence of dialogue or the movement and postures of participants, and instead sees the defining element of drama in the act of "impersonation."⁹

> [Drama] is, above all else, a story presented in action, in which the speakers or actors impersonate the characters concerned. Dialogue is not essential, for monologue is drama when the speaker impersonates the one from whom the utterance is represented as proceeding. Even spoken language may be dispensed with, for pantomime is a true, though limited, form of drama, provided a story is successfully conveyed, and provided the actors pretend to be the personages concerned in this story. As to the nature of impersonation in itself there can scarcely be any substantial disagreement. It consists in physical imitation. . . . It follows, then, that the dialogue and physical movements of those who participate in the liturgy will be transformed from the *dramatic* into *drama* whenever these persons convey a story and pretend to be the characters in that story.¹⁰

This definition allowed Young, and others, to distinguish different levels of dramatization in the worship of the church, reflected in a large number of dramatic pieces and subjects presented with immense variations that developed between the tenth and thirteenth centuries.¹¹ More importantly, for Young, the Mass, since it was understood as a re-creation and not a representation of an action, had to be excluded from the possibility of dramatization.¹² In this way, the Mass could be seen as the stage for drama in the medieval church by opening up the space, place, and structures for liturgical performances. The presupposition for this view, however, is a strict distinction between drama and liturgy, since the latter is understood as the possibility of the former. This feature was criticized most thoroughly in the work of O. B. Hardison.¹³ Despite the significance of Young's theory, the concept of impersonation cannot be considered the only governing principle of liturgical performance. "The ninth-century interpretation may be considered imperfectly expressed analogue of such modern theories; that is, both medieval and modern students agree that the Mass is drama, but the medieval author could only express his insight by speaking of a 'plot' and assigning to the participants the roles which they played in the history from which the 'plot' is derived. The medieval writer, unable to say that the Mass was a ritual drama, was forced to say simply that it was a drama."¹⁴ In contrast to Young, Hardison understood the Mass as a "living dramatic form" that emerged from the "dramatic instinct" of medieval Europe and found its central expression in the celebration of the liturgy.[15] The liturgy is not the possibility of dramatic performances but identical with them. The fundamental opposition between drama and liturgical action is therewith removed.

Hardison's criticism is important because it emphasizes that the liturgy understood as dramatic performance must be seen not only as a religious but also as a cultural practice that contains theological as well as sociological and anthropological foundations.[16] The recent study *The Liturgy of the Medieval Church* concluded from its findings that "it is striking . . . how many ritual activities are performed by non-specialists, often lay people, and how unmarked the boundary is between 'official' liturgical practice and what might be considered para-liturgical or even non-liturgical activities."[17] The dramatic performance of the liturgy, more than bound to the ecclesiastical culture of the medieval world, was exposed in its development to the entire historical, sociocultural, and political contexts of its time. The liturgy was not only a form of impersonation but became "the arena of intense communication of cultural values and negotiation of power within social formations at given historical moments."[18] In this sense, the idea of the "performance" of the liturgy became synonymous with the notion of "ritual."[19] Significantly, in the medieval framework, the performance of Christian rituals was often expressed with reference to the concept of play.

The names most prominently applied to liturgical performances, both in Latin and in vernacular drama, typically contained equivalents of the Latin term *ludus,* or "play."[20] This convention has survived into modern times in the performance of passion plays and nativity plays, otherwise known as Easter and Christmas plays. Even in the liturgical context, the term "play" is frequently understood as a designation associated with popular reveling.[21] Some have suggested that in "play" the idea of dramatic performance is secondary to the notion of entertainment.[22] From that perspective, it is more accurate to speak of the medieval "play" rather than the "drama" or "performance" of the liturgy. In any case, the study of the Western liturgy shows a general neglect of the playfulness of liturgical action and a preference for the interpretation of "play" as an act of dramatic performance.[23] This is most evident in the fact that the study of liturgy has been primarily a study of liturgical texts rather than of the kinesthetic and nonverbal dimension of liturgical action.

The performance of the liturgy in the Middle Ages made visible not only the theological symbolism invested in the "texts" but also the social dynamics, political structures, religious experiences, language, music, architecture, vessels, and liturgical implements that contributed to their ritual enactment.[24] Practically, liturgy means an interpenetration of the ecclesiastical rites and social and political realities of the time. The use of Latin as the language of the liturgy is less relevant than "to trace the trajectory of the ritual *doing* and to ask, not what is being said, but what is being done."[25] Thus, for example, the coronation rites of the early ninth century "present a self-conscious appropriation of Old Testament typology to the king and the 'Christian empire' of the later Carolingians."[26] The medieval development of cathedral architecture shaped the "liturgical movements of the Mass in the High Middle Ages — namely, processions, sung dialogues, and the solemn exposition of objects."[27] The rites of the church were adapted from the monastic office for devotional life in the world.[28] And the medieval culture of spectatorship eventually came to govern the dramatic performance of Christian rituals.[29] The performance of the liturgy in some cases "extended from the choir of the church into the nave; and . . . played within the building, must have taxed its entire resources."[30] This distinct fascination with the ritual performance of liturgical action encouraged "the ever-growing tendency to see in every action and gesture of the liturgy a meaning and to enhance these meanings by designing liturgical actions to carry them at every possible opportunity."[31] The historical, cultural, social, and political conditions of the ritual became virtually indistinguishable from the liturgy itself.

The ritual performance of medieval liturgical action has persisted into the late modern world. While the concept of "drama" has changed significantly, various attempts have been made to construct a historical narrative that reveals the fundamental continuities between medieval and modern liturgy.[32] However, Young notes "the gradual transference of religious drama from ecclesiastical to secular auspices . . . for an increase in the scope of the performances, for an enrichment of content, and for the use of the vernacular."[33] An important result of the secularization of ecclesiastical drama was the development of local and national drama in contrast to the international and transcultural appeal of the liturgy.[34] This led to increasing varieties in themes, literary forms, languages, and types of performances. However, a general suspicion of the new dramatic elements emerged in the church and, with it, concerns about the contamination of established liturgical practices.[35] Eventually, the Council of Trent removed the notion of drama and theater completely from the stage of the church.[36] Nevertheless, the historical, cultural, and social conditions of medieval liturgical celebration — language, scripts, actors, architecture, music, processions, movements, vestments, vessels, and liturgical implements — and with them the theological intentions of the dramatic performances, remained largely unchanged.

The preservation of the medieval conditions for liturgical action and the simultaneous expulsion of drama from the ecclesiastical stage separated the meaning invested in these conditions from their performative contexts. As the craft guilds took over dramatic presentations, they developed new forms and settings of drama independent from the churches and without the restrictions of a formal ecclesiastical setting, leading to an intensification of theatric qualities and broadening of the range of dramatic interpretation.[37] The liturgy of the church, on the other hand, characterized by an increasing clericalization and sacramentalization, separated more and more from the secular understanding and interpretation of dramatic performances.

The Sacramentalization and Clericalization of the Liturgy

The clericalization and sacramentalization of liturgical action most vividly illustrate the separation of church and drama in the modern world. The former addresses the performance of liturgical action on behalf of, rather than together with, the people; the latter concerns the concentration of liturgical performance in the sacramental rituals rather than in the overall liturgical action. As Richard McCall points out in his study of liturgy as performance, clericalization represents "a middle way between liturgy and drama proper, a stage in which . . . enactors (the priest, a deacon, the cantor) speak (chant) on behalf of the people, who are brought to a place where Christ is revealed."[38] From the Renaissance forward, the enactment by the priesthood on behalf of the laity became the principal form of impersonation in the liturgy, which now confined the laity largely to the position of spectatorship. However, with the removal of drama from the liturgy, the churches also removed the stage and story necessary to interpret the clerical enactment and its performative framework.

The celebration of the sacraments replaced the performance of drama as the conceptual and corporeal framework for the enactment of Christian rituals. Despite the postbiblical development of sacramental rites, it was not until twelfth-century scholasticism, and significantly, outside the context of ecclesiastical drama, that a theology of sacraments was developed.[39] The theological basis for the priest-centered enactment of the sacramental rituals was provided by the christocentric understanding of sacramental theology that dominated scholastic thought.[40] In the sacraments, the priest mediates the personal act of Jesus *in persona ipsius Christi,*[41] and as representative of "the whole Church by acting as liturgical leader of the local church."[42] The central position of the clergy thus reveals the hierarchical character of the liturgy as he participates in both the priesthood of Christ, who "is the fountain-head of the entire priesthood,"[43] and the priesthood of all believers, by serving as the ambassador of Christ to the people. The meaning of the liturgy is contained in the precise action of the clergy at the celebration of the sacrament (or a particular moment of it), acted out as a performance on behalf of the entire church that is independent from the particular historical and sociocultural circumstances of the participants. Impersonation came to convey the recitation and administration of a liturgical narrative that recreates the words and actions of Christ in the precise words and actions of the celebrants. The sacramental forms and rubrics of the liturgy therefore had to be strictly protected and were enforced with the Roman Breviary of 1568, the Roman Missal of 1570, and eventually the decrees of the Sacred Congregation of Rites leading to a period of rigid unification, petrification, and stagnation.[44]

This sacramentalization and clericalization of the liturgy form the basis for understanding the contemporary crisis of the liturgy. The interpretation of the liturgy as drama rather than play, and the enforcement of a uniform enactment of this drama in isolation from other social and cultural phenomena, have led to a separation of the liturgy from the context of human life in general, and from the contemporary circumstances of ecclesiastical life in particular. The separation of the liturgy from secular drama prevented the incorporation of modern dramatic qualities in the interpretation of ecclesiastical performances and disconnected the faithful from the allegorical interpretation that accompanied the medieval formation of the liturgy. In its place, the intimate connection of the saving work of God with the sacramental rites and the scripted performance of the clergy encouraged the dissolution of the liturgical community and the separation of the liturgical practices from the church's mission of evangelization.[45] Furthermore, the distinction between clergy and laity in the participation of the liturgical performances disconnected the Christian rituals from the corporeal, kinesthetic, and subjective experience of the faithful.[46]

The crisis of the liturgy can therefore be characterized as emerging essentially from a failure of the performance of the liturgy as a reenactment of medieval structures. In the global context, the symbols, actions, and gestures of the medieval liturgy often cannot be integrated into a context that has not also emerged from the European world. Moreover, at the heart of this failure stands the concern not only of adapting the liturgy to various cultures and traditions but also of opening up the liturgy within those contexts to the participation and interpretation of the people. While the notion of performance itself is open to the opportunities and challenges brought about by the crisis of the imagination, the particular framework of ritual performance that has dominated the liturgy since the Middle Ages is not transferable to every context.

Meaningful Performance of the Liturgy

Adaptation, transformation, and renewal of the liturgy require attention to the full range of ritual activities that form the basis of the late modern person's capacity for liturgical action.[47] If we agree with the influential assessment of anthropologist Victor Turner that ritual is a "transformative performance revealing major classifications, categories, and contradictions of cultural processes,"[48] then the capacity for that performance is rooted not in the ritual itself but in the broader "system" that makes possible its order and behavior in particular cultural, historical, and ecclesial contexts.[49] In this sense, performance endows with meaning not only the ritual activity but also what Mary Douglas calls the entire "grid and group"[50] of the liturgical act. This embodiment of meaning stands at the heart of the notion of performance, and its neglect forms the root of the liturgical crisis.[51] A liturgy that does not "perform" is principally seen as a ritual without purpose.

Turner's widely used study essentially ascribes transformative capacity to any ritual that is "performed well."[52] However, any transition of social, cultural, or ecclesial contexts may inhibit that performance and require the construction of a new framework within which the performance can take place and acquire new meaning. It is not only the directionality of the ritual but also the interconnectedness of performers, contexts, and media that structure this meaning and experience.[53] The liturgy thus evolves into a complex of ecclesiastical performances to an extent that the entire liturgical theology of late modernity has in principle

been constructed as a semiotic system of meaning.[54] Meaningful performance is ergotropic; it is "work" — in the modern sense of the term. Conversely, in order to "work," the liturgy must be performed within a group
and grid that is clearly assigned and consistently ordered, logical, and sensible; regulated by fixation, localization, and placement; and free from
competition and chance. In short, as Turner points out, performance understood as work lacks any aspect of the notion of play.[55] Ritual as play,
on the other hand, enters the realm of the imagination, possibility, and
subjunctivity. "It refers to what may or might be. It is also concerned with
supposition, conjecture, and assumption, with the domain of 'as-if'
rather than 'as is.'"[56] In this domain, the liturgy invites a fundamental
openness to the imagination and revelation that God is at play in the
Spirit, Word, and community. As long as the playfulness of the liturgy is
suppressed, the community is caught in the space and time of purposeful
activity and performative structures.

At the turn of the twentieth century, Guardini analyzed the European
crisis in light of the tension between the playfulness and purposefulness of
the liturgy. He suggested a solution in the attempt "not to be continually
yearning to do something, to attack something, to accomplish something
useful, but to play the divinely ordained game of the liturgy in liberty and
beauty and holy joy before God."[57] The North American context sheds
particular light on the consequences that emerged as a result of an overem-
phasis on the performative qualities of the liturgical structures indicated
in Guardini's reflections. Attempts at liturgical reform have been profoundly hampered by the pragmatism, utilitarianism, and individualism
that bring the question of the purposefulness of liturgical performance
face-to-face with the demands and expectations of the cultural and private
values of the modern person.[58] The notion of "work" as it arose in the
modern age cast the performance of the liturgy in the light of the ideas of
productivity, purposefulness, and efficiency. As much as the social and
economic aspects of "work" became disconnected from family and community, liturgy as the "work of the people" became similarly removed
from the daily lives of the faithful. Confined to the role of the audience, as
Kierkegaard observed in his analogy to the theater, people could no longer
"get anything out of the performance."[59] The liturgy experienced a crisis
because the modern world perceived its structures as unproductive, ineffi-
cient, and without purpose. It is in the midst of this crisis that we find the
emergence of classical Pentecostalism.

2. The Development of the Liturgy in Classical Pentecostalism

The situation in North America at the turn of the twentieth century was characterized by widespread ecclesiastical and liturgical diversity. European immigrants remained largely attached to the liturgical practices of their homeland churches and introduced them to the complex new reality of interacting traditions on the new continent.[60] This confrontation sheds particular light on the crisis of the liturgy outlined in the preceding section. However, while the diverse liturgical environment in general has been widely studied, little attention has been paid to the liturgical development of classical Pentecostalism within this context. This neglect is to a great extent the result of an uncritical acceptance of the conclusions offered in the classic study on Pentecostalism by Walter Hollenweger, who suggested that Pentecostalism was characterized by a black, oral liturgy.[61] The precise character of this liturgy, however, has not been examined. Hollenweger situated the liturgical origins of classical Pentecostals at the Azusa Street Mission and revival of 1906, concentrated in the black preacher William J. Seymour, who, according to Hollenweger, "inspired his congregation to develop its own liturgy."[62] Hollenweger later attributed the roots of Seymour's liturgical sensitivity to "his black heritage" yet continued to infer that it was Seymour's personal initiative that shaped the Pentecostal revivals.[63] Surprisingly, even among African American Pentecostals, little research has been done on the origins and development of a "black" Pentecostal liturgy. On the basis of contemporary research, Seymour, and even the Azusa Street revival and mission, is too insufficient a basis to explain the relationship of such a liturgy to the emergence of classical Pentecostalism. Simply to ascribe the Pentecostal liturgy to an African American heritage has no more explanatory power than to state that the crisis of the liturgy was essentially white, even though both statements are true.

The construction of a broader support for an African American basis of a Pentecostal liturgy requires two premises that have been established only recently by contemporary scholarship. First, Pentecostal origins are deeply connected with African American spirituality.[64] While the argument for African roots of classical Pentecostalism is not new, it is more precise to speak of the African roots of Pentecostal liturgy.[65] Second, this African spiritual heritage was exposed in the North American context to interracial and complex religious impulses of European, Hispanic, and other cultures.[66] From this perspective, it is clear that a Pentecostal liturgy did not develop within the medieval European context that characterizes the crisis of the liturgy. On the other hand, we cannot speak at any point of a "pure" African liturgy in the North American context. It is my hypothesis that from the plantation prayer grounds of African slaves and the camp meetings of the American South an African American spirituality was carried to the urban centers of the continent where, shaped by the social, cultural, and religious conditions of the new environment, it emerged as a new liturgical form labeled "Pentecostal."

The African Roots of the Pentecostal Liturgy

The rediscovery of slave narratives in recent scholarship shows that the African slaves formed a "unique and coherent understanding of Christianity" from often "illegal and hidden religious practices" and "in radical distinction to white Christianity . . . in their own language and idiom."[67] The forced Christianization of the slaves did little to extinguish the notions of African indigenous religion brought to the North American context, particularly the ritual sensitivities of the African life.[68] These sensitivities included a preference for nature, the field and barns, and bushes and forests over buildings, churches, and pews.[69] "Us could go to de white folk's church, but us wanted ter go whar us could sing all de way through, an' hum 'long, an' shout — yo' all know, jist turn loose lack."[70] Nature and creation formed the space of the early African American rituals. While much of this exposure to the outdoors in North America was forced upon the slaves by their white masters, the rural prayer grounds shaped significantly what was expected and what was possible in the worship experience. "We jes made er bush arbor by cutin' bushes dat was full of green leaves an' puttin' em on top of four poles reachin' from pole to pole. Den sometimes we'd have dem bushes put roun' to kiver de sides an' back from der bottom to der top. All us get together in dis arbor fer de meetin'."[71] The formal liturgies of the established churches seemed disconnected from the needs and demands of the African American faith community. As George C. L. Cummings has shown, the thematic framework was shaped decidedly by two key theological loci that I have highlighted as significant elements of the Pentecostal imagination: the presence of the Holy Spirit (pneumatology) and the expectation of the kingdom of God (eschatology).[72] "Getting religion was manifested in a variety of ways. Some slaves had visions, others shouted and walked, and still others bore witness to the creative power of the Spirit. The Spirit possessed the physical being of the slaves, and as a consequence they shouted; spoke of great visions of God, heaven, or freedom; and engaged in physical activity that manifested the Spirit's presence."[73] The presence of God's Spirit was perceived as a liberating occurrence of freedom, experienced temporally in the prayer grounds and nurturing a vision of ultimate freedom in the future. "Concomitantly," Cummings states, "the eschatological hopes and aspirations of the slave community became evident in the Spirit who guarantees the future as one of freedom and justice."[74] This orientation toward the ultimate freedom of life in the Spirit profoundly shaped the early African American liturgy, which was greatly impacted by the slave work ethic.

Work, for the African slaves, meant forced labor. As Joan Martin observes, "This made the nature of the work they were required to do evil. It was evil because it grew out of the sinful human will to subjugate and exploit others. . . . Their lives demonstrated that the result of such evil was unwarranted, unearned, and undeserved suffering."[75] This work ethic stood in contrast to the freedom and justice associated with God. For the African slaves, ritual action was not a "work" of the people but the freedom from compulsion, exploitation, duty, and performance. In the fields and bushes, the slaves were free to pray, sing, dance, shout, and "jist turn loose lack." Worship meant enthusiasm, life, and freedom — liturgy as play.

The prayer grounds lacked the structural liturgical framework of medieval liturgical performance. As Charles Joyner noted, "slaves did not so much adapt to Christianity . . . as adapt Christianity to themselves."[76] The African folk religion was based on an oral traditioning process, centered on narratives, songs, plays, and other forms of communication that preserved the story of the slaves and their values, affections, and rituals.[77] The architecture, language, movements, scripts, music, processions, vestments, and vessels of the traditional Christian liturgy did not function in the secret worship meetings. The worship of the slaves was dominated by prayer, preaching, and singing, and although oriented along European ritual, these liturgical aspects were transformed by the imagination and rhythm of their African roots.[78] Liturgy was not a "confining structure" but an "open arrangement" oriented along the necessities of the situation and the possibilities provided by the presence of God's Spirit. The liturgical arrangement invited unrehearsed participation rather than structured performance.[79] Spontaneous responses to the sermon, shouting, stomping, singing, sighing, dancing, swaying, clapping, humming, and an entire array of kinesthetic activities emerged out of a sense of spiritual liberty. "The phenomenon of spirit possession, one of the most significant features in African religion . . . , was reinterpreted in Christian terms to become a central feature of expressive behavior in African-American Christianity and a necessary part of the conversion experience. Conversion was the climax of a spiritual journey called 'seeking.' A prolonged period of praying 'in the wilderness' included an ecstatic trance without which conversion was not considered authentic."[80] The orientation toward nature, the pneumatological imagination, and the broad array of kinesthetic responses to the spiritual awareness of God's presence undoubtedly emerged from African antecedents. The experience of the presence of the Holy Spirit provided a contrast to the performance-oriented work environment of the day. The pneumatological and eschatological setting of African American worship provided a refuge from the harsh realities of everyday life and offered a sense of empowerment and freedom.[81] Here, the slaves were free to engage God in the fullness of their being and affections.

The Camp Meeting Roots of the Pentecostal Liturgy

The integration of the freed slaves into the established ecclesiastical and liturgical structures presented one of the greatest challenges after the Civil War.[82] It was the camp meeting of the rural South that provided the premier environment for the mixing of liturgical temperaments.[83] The camp meetings had already exerted a powerful influence on the conversion of the slaves to Christianity and continued to be extremely popular.[84] As Albert Raboteau states in his classic study of slave religion, the camp meetings "presented a congenial setting for slaves to merge African patterns of response with Christian interpretations of the experience of spirit possession."[85] In the traditional Christian environment, these meetings were closest in nature to the prayer-ground meetings of the African slave community, as they created room for the intermingling of different denominations, races, language groups, worship practices, and musical forms.[86] The emancipation of the slaves did not immediately prevent continued segregation, yet the camp meeting environment offered the opportunity for those who followed more expressive rituals to move to a secluded area without thereby forsaking the entire religious event.[87] The African liturgy thus came in contact with the "institutional" liturgy of those churches in North America that embraced the camp meetings as means of religious revival and evangelization.

Participants arrived at the camp meetings prepared to engage in not only a religious but also a social event. Similar to the "bush arbors" of the slave community, these events were initially held at rural, outdoor, and transient encampments that did not resemble the structural framework and liturgical environment of the established churches.[88] Arrangements were often spontaneous and haphazard, the meeting tents crowded, sleeping quarters sparse, and opportunities for eating, resting, and reflection ignored.[89] Camp meetings resisted being standardized into a particular pattern and were characterized loosely by their outdoor experience, the independent support of the participants, and the openness to all social strata among the churched and the unchurched.[90] The environment itself came to closely define the level of action and interaction for the liturgical consciousness of classical Pentecostalism. The rapidly growing Methodist and Baptist groups, and the Holiness movement in particular, carried the camp meetings to the twentieth century and into the arms of the emerging Pentecostal movement.[91]

Despite the impact of camp meeting revivals on the history of modern evangelism, the liturgical structure of the meetings has not received much theological attention. The comparative dimensions of the liturgy, however, allow for an integration of camp meetings into a heuristic framework that takes account of both liturgical and dramatic theory. Hesser and Weigert suggest that such an analysis can be divided into an actional and an interactional level.[92] If we adopt this distinction, then the camp meetings clearly reshaped the involvement of place, time, actors, gestures, objects, vestments, and language that defined the traditional liturgical setting on the actional level. The meetings were not ecclesiastical in nature but resembled more "a temporary occupancy of the summer woods where the trees and hills are especially sanctified."[93] Usually, the celebrations were temporally restricted only by the exhaustion and weariness of the participants; bad weather and nightfall rarely shortened the meetings. The language was that of the people, not of liturgical manuals. Physical structures reflected simplicity of construction rather than symbolic character. Formal liturgical vestments were absent, and liturgical "props" were limited to a few sacramental vessels.[94] As a result, the meetings were interactional on all levels, ranging from the dissolving of formal procedures and a lack of definition of the situation to spontaneous participation and unrehearsed responses to whatever the situation seemed to demand. A liturgy was not "performed"; the whole event rather "played" out as the circumstances permitted and where the Spirit of God led. Camp meetings were ordered not by formal liturgical structures but by opportunities to respond to an imagination that envisioned the campground as a sacred outdoor temple.[95] Understandably, believers from denominations that associated with the meetings, among them most prominently Baptists, Methodists, and adherents of the nineteenth-century Holiness movement, were especially attracted to African American spirituality.[96] The classical Pentecostal liturgy emerged more fully out of this environment.

The Holiness movement adopted the camp meetings not only for their effectiveness in evangelism and church growth but also for the particular purpose of propagating the message of the holiness imagination.[97] Even a superficial glance at the liturgical environment of the camp meetings reveals that the claim is unfounded that they were essentially nonliturgical. However, the outdoor environment of the camp meetings altered the performative qualities of liturgical action and interaction. Adherents to the Holiness movement frequently contrasted the ritualism of established liturgical structures with the spiritual freedom experienced at the revival meetings.[98] A structurally planned worship service was typically taken as an indication of nominal Christianity.[99] For the participants of the camp meetings, the hills, the trees, and the meadows were the sanctuary of God's Spirit. They were surrounded by a "forest temple"[100] or, liturgically speaking, a "forest of symbols."[101] Similar to the prayer-ground meetings of the African slave community, people often came directly from their work in the fields. Church buildings were replaced by tents and rough-hewn timber structures. The altar was not a place of sacramental action but of repentance and sanctification, often represented only roughly by a pulpit or the area where the Word of God was preached. Gestures were generally not visible from afar, but the spoken word traveled well in the otherwise quiet valleys and hills. Traditional liturgical vestments were avoided since they were not only impractical in the rural environment but their meaning was interpreted differently by those attending. The language was usually plain and outspoken.

The celebration of the sacraments presented a particular difficulty in the camp meeting environment. As the meeting places became established and more solid structures were built, little emphasis was placed on sacramental performance. The construction of the camp shed was influenced more heavily by the demands and potential of the moment. Central within such structures, the pulpit replaced the altar of the traditional liturgical setting. Even though worship at the pulpit was sometimes called the "altar service,"[102] this notion referred not to a sacrificial or sacramental place of worship but to a communal response to an invitation or challenge given in the sermon for the purpose of seeking salvation, repentance, or the baptism of the Holy Spirit. Considerations of performance did not influence the participation and response of the participants at these occasions. A Pentecostal camp meeting publication illustrates the event:

> As we pulled into the camp ground, which is shaded by a large grove of beautiful trees, carpeted with blue grass, surrounded by large fields of corn and alfalfa . . . , we were soon overjoyed to see the tents that were up. . . . The campers increased until the tents numbered 195 and several house cars and trucks on top of that. The estimation of the people camping is from 700 to 900 throughout the camp meeting. . . . People were surely getting through in every morning service. Many were being slain under the power, at one time I counted 22 lying under the mighty power, being filled with the Holy Ghost and power. At various times it seemed that the power just came like sheets of rain and great shouts of praise would sweep over the whole congregation. . . . A number fell under the hand of the Lord.[103]

The rural, outdoor environment of the camp meetings represented a melting pot for the amalgamation of liturgies among many Christian groups, including the open arrangement of the African American liturgy. The urbanization of the camp meetings further altered the liturgical landscape and removed the African origins of classical Pentecostalism and the camp meeting sensibility further from the established liturgical structures of the institutional churches.

The Urbanization of the Pentecostal Liturgy

While the rural adherents of the camp meetings were exposed to the African American liturgy, two main factors influenced the expansion of this mixed heritage among Pentecostals. On the one hand, the National Camp Meeting Association for the Promotion of Christian Holiness contributed to the rapid expansion of camp meetings and to the transfer of the meetings from their original rural environment to larger urban areas.[104] On the other hand, the mobility of the African American community after the emancipation of the slaves and especially with the Great Migration took the agrarian roots of the Pentecostal liturgy to the northern, northeastern, and western borders of the United States.[105] The unexpected migration of African Americans in general incurred strong, negative reactions.[106] The Holiness movement, on the other hand, "provided an unprecedented cultural context for legitimizing the African-derived liturgy of plantation praise houses."[107] The rural transplants attempted to "re-create" in the urban context the liturgical environment of the prayer grounds and camp meetings.[108] In this way, the teachings and values of the Holiness movement and the rituals of African liturgy meshed in urban areas, and exposed Pentecostals in the storefront churches to the revival rituals of the forest temples.

As a result of the urbanization, the traditional organization of the African American community was changed significantly: the cities demanded a reorganization of life and religion.[109] The urban surroundings provided a radically dissimilar environment for the actional and interactional dimensions of the rural liturgy. In the cities, the liturgy was exposed to utilitarianism, economic progress, population growth, social mobility, radical individualism, anonymity, the separation of work and residence, the emancipation of religion, as well as racial, ethnic, and religious diversity.[110] Los Angeles, often considered the birthplace of classical Pentecostalism, marked a particularly stark contrast to the environment of the rural Pentecostal communities, and the urban character of the Azusa Street Mission revival was markedly different from the roots of the Pentecostal liturgy in the camp meetings of the rural South. Nonetheless, under the leadership of William J. Seymour, the pastor of the Azusa Street Mission, together with his predominantly African American congregation, the liturgical framework of the camp meetings was kept alive in the urban environment.

The reenactment of the camp meetings at the Azusa Street Mission encountered numerous challenges. Most significantly, the openness of an outdoor sanctuary was replaced by the limitations of a city structure, a tight, hot, and sparsely illuminated enclosure. Cecil M. Robeck, Jr., paints a vivid picture of the circumstances.

> The building in which they met was "tucked away" in a transitional neighborhood. It was nothing to look at — little more than a poorly whitewashed, burned-out shell with makeshift essentials. On its sawdust-covered dirt floor sat a collection of nail kegs and boards, and an assortment of discarded chairs. Because it lacked insulation and air-conditioning, and its ground floor was built of rough-sawn studs with

only the outside lumber as walls, during the summer months the building grew intensely hot. . . . In spite of these problems — the substandard
facilities, intense heat, lack of ventilation, and swarms of flies — people
came by the thousands.[111]

The urban environment could not maintain the "open arrangement" of
the liturgical framework of the camp meetings and African American
prayer grounds. In addition, the Azusa Street congregation provided interracial impulses and a multicultural environment for liturgical celebration
that soon spread to other parts of the country.[112] Embedded in this environment were the influences of a variety of religious experiences that significantly expanded the horizon of liturgical perspectives among Pentecostals. The uniqueness of classical Pentecostalism was that its liturgical
experience differed from the Anglo-European religious and cultural arrangement, from which was crafted a new, and often radically different,
ritual arrangement on the American religious scene. The new practices
were often rejected by outsiders to the movement and were criticized even
within Pentecostal ranks. At Azusa Street, the accusations of Pentecostal
pioneer Charles F. Parham, for example, vividly illustrate the situation.
"There was a beautiful outpouring of the Holy Spirit in Los Angeles. . . .
Then they pulled off all the stunts common in old camp meetings among
colored folks. . . . That is the way they worship God, but what makes my
soul sick . . . is to see white people imitating unintelligent crude negroisms
of the Southland, and laying it on the Holy Ghost."[113] Observers frequently
reported "scenes that duplicate those of the negro revival meetings of the
South."[114] In the urban environment of the early twentieth century, the
mixture of African American worship and camp meeting tradition was
transformed into a new, Pentecostal liturgy, radically dissimilar from the
traditional Anglo-European structures. Robeck's seminal work on the
Azusa Street Mission places at the heart of the new liturgy such elements as
worship through prayer, song, singing in the Spirit, preaching and discussion, gathering at the altar, testimony, deliverance and conversion, sanctification, and the baptism in the Holy Spirit.[115] Medieval liturgical structures
were absent, established North American forms of the liturgy were not
dominant, and liturgical manuals were rarely consulted. Instead, the altar
service established itself as the heart of the urban liturgy, including opportunities for singing, testimony, conversion, deliverance, sanctification, and
Spirit baptism. Robeck vividly describes the diverse expressions of urban
Pentecostal worship.

The intensity of their encounter with God led many at the mission to respond in ways that before their encounter they could "only imagine." It
was a life-changing moment, a transformative time that produced a
range of responses. There were those who . . . broke into dance. Others
jumped, or stood with hands outstretched, or sang or shouted with all
the gusto they could muster. Others were so full of awe when they encountered God that their knees buckled — they fell on the floor, "slain
in the Spirit." Some spoke, rapid-fire, in a tongue they did not know,
while others were struck entirely speechless.[116]

The established churches in the urban environment were ill-prepared
to engage the emerging Pentecostal liturgy, which was seen as differing in
both form and substance from orthodox Christian worship.[117] The ecstatic
ritual practices were generally seen as "a symbolic rebellion on the part of
socially disenfranchised Pentecostals."[118] These Pentecostals, however, were
themselves unsure about the complexity of the liturgical practices emerging
among them. Their liturgy had been shaped by African roots that were confronted with the sociocultural context of slavery in North America, exposed
to the religious impulses of camp meetings and the Holiness movement,
and transformed in the multicultural context of migration and urbanization. A Pentecostal liturgy did therefore not develop in conscious opposition to or rejection of established forms of liturgical celebration. Nonetheless, the origins of the classical Pentecostal liturgy in isolation from
the dominant medieval European structures and the exposure to the North
American cultural and ecclesiastical context contributed to a destructuralization of the conceptual framework that would allow for a traditional
composition of liturgical action.[119] In its place emerged an alternative liturgical sensitivity, born in the sanctuary of nature, shaped by a revival men-
tality, and expanded by the opportunities and challenges of urban life. In
contrast to the structural Anglo-European liturgy with its conceptually
fixed, written, priest-centered, and performance-oriented framework of
sacramental celebration, the Pentecostal liturgy emerged as a destructuralizing, flexible, oral, participation-centered, and pneumatologically oriented
"open arrangement" of worship, prayer, and praise. Liturgy, in a broad
sense, was seen as the free response to an encounter with God rather than a
structure provided for the possibility of that encounter. With this contrast,
the Pentecostal liturgy stood in sharp opposition to the sensitivities of the
emerging liturgical movement, which envisioned a conservation of the objective liturgical structures as an "organic whole"[120] rather than the

destructuralization proposed inherently by the liturgical practices of classical Pentecostalism.

The liturgical movement arrived in North America only in the 1920s and was not put into practice immediately by all Christian groups, although eventually the Roman Catholic, Episcopal, Lutheran, and United Methodist churches, and the Reformed tradition, embraced it.[121] By the time it took hold on the American continent, classical Pentecostal denominations had already been formally organized. They were largely unaffected by the problems of sacramentalization and clericalization that concerned the liturgical renewal in the established churches. In turn, from the perspective of the established traditions, Pentecostalism had essentially lost contact with the formal orthodox framework for a structural composition of ritual celebration. If this assessment is correct, it has been incorrectly interpreted as an indication that Pentecostalism possesses no liturgy at all — a judgment uncritically accepted by many Pentecostals.[122] As a result, the so-called nonliturgical character of Pentecostal faith and praxis became the epitome of what the liturgical movement perceived to be at the root of the liturgical crisis. At the same time, Pentecostals held the structural framework of the institutional churches responsible for the lack of freedom, openness, and flexibility in Christian worship. The fronts were hardened between the "excessive" ritual practices of classical Pentecostalism and the pneumatologically and eschatologically "dead" liturgy of Christendom.

3. The Liturgy as the Structure of Play

The origins of classical Pentecostalism consequently have been falsely construed (both inside and outside of Pentecostalism) as a rejection of liturgical theology and praxis. A first step toward resolving the crisis of the liturgy has been taken by acknowledging the formation of liturgical sensitivities in classical Pentecostalism and by contrasting them with the structural environment of the established ecclesiastical traditions. In the remainder of this chapter, I wish to provide direction for a constructive theological assessment of the contributions offered by global Pentecostalism to address the current liturgical crisis. The key metaphor for this endeavor is the proposal to understand the liturgy fundamentally as the structure of play.

At first glance, play and liturgy appear to be conceptual opposites: the liturgy as the "work" of the faithful seems to exclude the viability of play as part of any liturgical performance. At the root of this evaluation stands the tension between reason and imagination, which becomes most tangible in the consideration of liturgical action. The liturgy, although it is something *done,* is seen in its practice as a consequence of contemplation, that is, as a "mode of cognition," the rational action of the participating individual.[123] The problematic nature of this approach to liturgical action has been frequently noted; nonetheless, attempts to correct it have largely *remained* within the context of understanding the liturgy as a rational performance of symbolic actions.[124] Influenced by the medieval form of the liturgy, "play" is typically understood only in the sense of a dramatic presentation, a staging of the drama of redemption that, if interactive, invites others to join in a performance.[125] Liturgical action in this performance is defined by the rationality of the doctrine underlying the performative act.[126] The liturgy itself is an orthodox interpretation of doctrine and a "serious" performance of the life of faith — it is not a people at play.

Liturgical action defined by orthodox doctrine must be rational on a fundamental level. More precisely, the question whether liturgical action is rational in the first place is generally avoided.[127] In contrast, ritual studies have long been engaged in a rationality debate. The camps are broadly divided into universalists and relativists; the former adhere to the existence of a universal standard to judge the rationality of religious rituals, the latter emphasize the impossibility of applying one standard to all cultures and suggest that the principles of rationality are relative to particular communities.[128] While universalism has led to the rejection of many ritual practices as irrational, relativism has encouraged the development of a double standard to judge particular behaviors.[129] In addition, both options apply only with difficulty to liturgical action in the church.

The performance of the liturgy on the basis of Christian doctrine is deemed to be rational because it is defined by the rationality of orthodox doctrine. Recent cultural-linguistic and canonical-linguistic approaches suggest that doctrine acquires a propositional rationality *because* it functions performatively.[130] The former finds the basis for this performance in the cultural-linguistic framework of the faith tradition; the latter locates it in the canon itself, which functions as the script for the performative act (see chapter 1).[131] The question of the rationality of the liturgy becomes essentially a question of its purpose in the interpretation and performance of doctrine. This purpose is interpreted either as instrumental or intrinsic, that is, the liturgy either serves as the efficient means to bring about a desired goal or it is celebrated for its own sake.[132] Yet, both interpretations are problematic, the first in its construal of purpose in the terms of efficacy, the second in its understanding of purpose in the terms of fitting-ness.[133] The instrumental view reduces the liturgy to a purely mechanical act in which God is compelled to respond in a favorable way to human action, while the intrinsic view reduces the action to a purely therapeutic behavior for the sake of the faithful.[134] Both interpretations presuppose the rational behavior of the faith community.

Others have suggested the interpretation of liturgical action as "enactment" in order to escape the question of rationality.[135] In this sense liturgical action consists of "bringing to life" the drama of redemption regardless of the rationality of the performance.[136] However, this proposal essentially echoes Young's theory of *impersonation,* the conveying of a story by pretending to be the characters in that story. Liturgical action therefore is the interpretation of the biblical text through dramatic performance of a character and the embedding of the script that informs this character in human action.[137] The charismatic dimension of revelation in the prophetic community remains outside of the liturgical framework. The celebration of the liturgy remains primarily a cognitive skill. At the same time, enactment adds to the debate the idea of participation, a behavior that is central to the notion of play.

A pioneer in understanding liturgical action as play, Romano Guardini placed the question of the rationality of the liturgy in the context of examining its purpose as a praxis of faith. From the traditional perspective, the liturgy is considered "work" because liturgical action is serious and purposeful. Play, on the other hand, seems to be purposeless — and hence void of meaning.[138] Guardini attributed an intrinsic purpose to the liturgy yet emphasized that this was not to be understood in terms of the fittingness of liturgical action or the rationality of its interpretation. Instead, he suggested that the purpose of the liturgy consists of the fact that it is to be understood as the play of God's children before their God.[139] The heart of the liturgy is not the extent of its rationality but its capacity for a faithful and childlike imagination. It unites art and reality in "the imaginary sphere of representation."[140] For Guardini, liturgical action means "foregoing maturity with all its purposefulness, and confining oneself to play." "It is in this very aspect of the liturgy that its didactic aim is to be found, that of teaching the soul not to see purposes everywhere, not to be too conscious of the end it wishes to attain, not to be desirous of being over clever and grown-up, but to understand simplicity in life."[141] Although Guardini's work formed the basis for much of Roman Catholic liturgical renewal prior to Vatican II, no comprehensive theology of the liturgy was developed on the basis of his insights. The theological scholarship has pursued the relationship of liturgy and play only sporadically, often construing the notion of play as a subsidiary form of dramatic theory or aesthetics.[142] I propose that Pentecostalism offers resources to revitalize Guardini's heritage, since the development of classical Pentecostal liturgy has exposed many of the discrepancies between the traditional liturgical world of performance and the Pentecostal sensitivity to liturgical action that is best characterized as the susceptibility to engage in play.

Ritual and Play

Recent Pentecostal scholarship has focused more intensely on the observation and definition of Pentecostal rituals.[143] Common to these studies is the desire to reestablish classical Pentecostalism within a broader ritual culture while, at the same time, reconsidering the nature of ritual practiced among Pentecostals from a Spirit-oriented perspective. Daniel Albrecht explains Pentecostal rituals as "embodied affections" that are "characterized by a playful, expressive, spontaneous and free sensibility."[144] From this perspective, "ritual is best understood as a dynamic phenomenon"[145] energized by a "sensibility of improvisation" that cultivates and invents ritual practices in an openness to the work of the Holy Spirit.[146] Among Pentecostals, the pneumatological imagination is expressed kinesthetically in the liturgy as "a return to nature and body."[147] Albrecht is thus able to identify a large variety of "macrorituals" and "microrites" in Pentecostalism that range from kinesthetic expressions (e.g., standing, kneeling, dancing, jumping, clapping) to charismatic rites (e.g., laying on of hands, anointing, prophesying, speaking in tongues) and other forms of response and action.[148] The variety of the Pentecostal ritual process serves both as the expression and destructuralization of existing social structures and values, including the possibility of suspending "rational" behavior.[149] This idea of a ritual "antistructure," originally developed by Victor Turner, can offer significant insights into the Pentecostal appreciation of liturgical action. From a conceptual perspective, it is my hypothesis that the organization and configuration of the established ritual practices of Christianity are destructuralized by their engagement in play.

Central to Turner's argument is the characterization of rituals as transitional events marked by an initial phase of separation of the participants from their familiar world and a concluding state of the consummation of a new state of existence, connected by an intervening, "liminal" phase (from the Latin *limen,* "threshold").[150] The participants find themselves in this state "betwixt and between the positions assigned and arrayed by law, custom, convention, and ceremonial."[151] In this state of permanent transition the formation of a ritual antistructure is possible, more precisely, a playful, "ludic deconstruction and recombination of familiar cultural configurations."[152] For Turner, liturgical rituals involve "a play on limits, margins of a frame that are ambiguous."[153] Bonded together by this process, the participants form a *communitas* marked by undifferentiated unity and equality in which the structural assertions of the established society are suspended and transformed.[154] When the community has been thus transformed, the participants can return to society equipped by the ritual process.

Also, when it is applied to industrialized societies, Turner argues that the ritual behavior operates on a "liminoid" rather than "liminal" level. While resembling the liminal realm of agrarian cultures, the liminoid antistructure in industrial cultures is characterized by an arbitrary separation of work and play.[155] The rules and structures of work appear to be an "intrusion of normative social structure into what is potentially and in principle a free and experimental region of culture."[156] The liturgy as the "work of the people" is in this sense not actually to be considered work "but has in both its dimensions, sacred and profane, an element of 'play.'"[157] Turner considered this distinction between work and play "an artifact of the Industrial Revolution" and suggested that it is precisely in the liminoid actions of industrial culture that we can reclaim the character of liturgical action as work.[158] Turner's theory thus shows with particular clarity the importance of considering the consequences of urbanization and industrialization for an understanding of global Christianity in the late modern world.[159] In Turner's terms, urbanization or industrialization transforms the liminal character of liturgical action into liminoid behavior that stands in contrast not only to established religious structures but also to the entire sociocultural concept of work that upholds the practice of faith in the industrial world. The Pentecostal liturgy, holding on to its roots in the ritual cultures of the agrarian world, can thus be seen as an opportunity to repossess the character of "work" in the play of the people.

On the other hand, while Turner's theory accounts for transition *within* rituals, it does not explain the necessary change *of* rituals. Turner himself, in fact, rejected modifications of the Christian liturgy.[160] As Catherine Bell has pointed out convincingly, "self-consciously changing ritual presents scholars with a major conundrum, a contradiction of sorts that is rooted in the history of approaches to the study of ritual."[161] The dominant approaches to Christian rituals tend to interpret them either as the meaningful operation of particular symbolic structures or of the general structure of Christian existence, thus emphasizing the absolute invariability of ritual practice.[162] Rituals are seen as transcending historical practice, and any change or modification of the institutionalized ritual structures is typically rejected as chaotic and irrelevant (p. 34). Bell concludes that a significant "result of this orientation is the relatively little attention paid to how rituals themselves change or to why a community's sense of appropriate ritual changes" (p. 33). Instead, she suggests that liturgical studies should find an approach that focuses on identifying "dynamics intrinsic to ritual" that allow for both continuity and change (p. 34). In contrast to the strict observation of ritual structures, Bell proposes "ritual activities that orchestrate an integration of tradition and historically new circumstances" (p. 36). Pentecostalism illustrates these conclusions and suggests that one way to explore the dynamic intrinsic to the Christian liturgy is through the notion of play.

Aspects of the liminality in Pentecostal liturgy were already observed in the historical account presented above. Rooted in the imagination, which is in itself a transitional entity, the liturgy expresses this ambiguity in liminal terms. The urbanization of Pentecostalism has further consolidated the liminoid break from established sociocultural norms and expectations. Bobby Alexander has examined Turner's thesis in the context of African American Pentecostalism and focused on the Pentecostal resistance to established ritual structures.

At the heart of Alexander's study stands the practice of Spirit baptism.[163] He is critical of the established scholarly perspective that, viewed from the point of ritual, Spirit baptism is seen "as a 'symbolic manipulation,' or 'symbolic subversion,' of Pentecostals' social circumstances" and of the conclusion that Pentecostal rituals are therefore "adaptive and adjustive mechanisms by which Pentecostals sublimate their desire for social standing, equality, and power."[164] Instead, Alexander suggests that a revision of ritual structures should begin by abandoning the theoretical reference frame of structural-functional theory that makes ritual activity dependent on doctrine rather than granting it ontological status.[165] From this perspective, the liminality of Spirit baptism comes to the forefront by removing participants from established social structures and thereby creating "structural ambiguity as well as direct and egalitarian social arrangements in ritual communitas."[166] In the Pentecostal community, Spirit baptism introduces "alternative, communitarian relations that are generated in ritual liminality," and makes possible ecstatic displays of the presence of the Holy Spirit.[167] From Alexander's perspective, Pentecostal liturgy consists not of rites that induce liminal activities but of a liminal, antistructural environment in which the participants redress established behavioral norms that otherwise suppress the operation of liminality. In this suspended structural environment, the liturgy is open to the playful invention of new behavior, freedom of expression, spontaneity, and enthusiasm that characterize Christian behavior as play.

Frank Macchia has wrestled most prominently with the antistructure of Spirit baptism and pointed, in particular, to the *critical* function of tongues with regard to the ability of the established ritual symbols to capture the divine mystery.[168] For Macchia, and others, "Tongues as a mystical language plays a 'countercultural' or 'protest' function in the churches, exposing just how 'broken' all of our symbols really are."[169] Put differently, the iconoclastic function of the liminality of glossolalia is central to what many have emphasized as the "sacramentality" of the Pentecostal liturgy.[170] However, this sacramentality must be viewed from a different perspective than is supplied by the established liturgical traditions. "Glossolalia is a different kind of 'sacrament' than that which is conveyed in formalized and structured liturgies. Glossolalia accents the free, dynamic, and unpredictable move of the Spirit of God, while the liturgical traditions stress an ordered and predictable encounter with the Spirit. . . . There is implied a 'chaotic' or 'inchoate' sacramentality in Pentecostal worship that was formed in protest to any attempt at formalization or objectification of the Spirit in liturgical rites."[171] Macchia's comments highlight that the nonrational behavior typically associated with Pentecostal practices could instead be interpreted as an opposition to structural definition. In other words, Pentecostalism suggests that liturgical activity, since it constitutes a liminal realm, is not destructive, or deconstructive, but destructuralizing. The Pentecostal preference of "ordinances" in place of "sacraments" exemplifies that this inclination is a rejection not of the idea of "sacrament" but of its structural and institutional definition.[172] In Turner's terms, the "antistructure" of rituals is characterized not simply by an opposition to particular, established formal structures but by a rejection of structural performance as a whole. Destructuralization is a response to the insight that the crisis of Christianity in the late modern world consists in the conceptualization of the imagination as a purely formal, cognitive, and performative act that can be captured in particular liturgical structures.

This understanding stands in sharp contrast to the ecclesiastical traditions that have consistently defined rituals by means of their structural, institutional forms.

In contrast, Pentecostal practice exhibits a liturgical sensibility that transforms rituals into activities of pneumatological play, characterized by a freedom and enthusiasm that, to use the words of Karl Rahner, exposes "the provisional character of all that is, in the broadest sense, 'institutional' . . . and shows clearly that the whole institutional structure, although it can never disappear entirely in this life, is nevertheless in itself a sign which is destined to destroy itself and disappear at the appearance of God."[173] From a Pentecostal perspective, the church exists as a pilgrim in the liminal realm of the liturgy amidst the expectation of the coming of the kingdom of God that transcends the performative world of meaning.[174] Destructuralized, the liturgy is ignorant of its surroundings for the goal of integrating everything into play. Hence, attempts to categorize Pentecostal rituals with spatial or temporal metaphors, identities or roles, language, behaviors and gestures, or concepts of liberation and empowerment have failed to acknowledge that the liturgy fundamentally intends to encompass all areas of the life of faith. Liturgical action, conceived as the people at play, directs the attention away from the (no longer ritual) activity itself and opens the church to participation in the eschatological kingdom of God.

Jean-Jacques Suurmond has described the liturgy from a Pentecostal perspective as a liberation for eschatological play.[175] Reflecting the hallmarks of the Pentecostal imagination, holiness, and the kingdom of God, he understands the passion and joy of the liturgy as an invitation to join in play with God: "We are free to worship God for who he is; to welcome our neighbor as equal partner in the play; and to draw creation into our playing . . . [that] sets us free from our goal-oriented, play-corrupting attitude so that we can become a gift to the world."[176] As a gift of the kingdom of God, play corrects the widely acknowledged neglect of the eschatological dimension of Christian liturgical practice.[177] We may speak of this as the tendency to enlarge the playground of the liturgy.

Enlarging the Playground of the Liturgy

From the perspective of liminality, the enlarging of the playing field expands the ambiguous threshold of ritual practice to the entire realm of life and creation. This dynamic is fundamentally Spirit-oriented, as Amos Yong puts it, since in the liturgy "the Holy Spirit transforms the community of faith from moment to moment so that it can more fully realize and embody here and now the image and likeness of the eschatological Christ."[178] While Yong emphasizes the centrality of the Spirit's work in the liturgy, he also hints at the eschatological openness of the community to diverse forms of transformative experiences in the global Christian community. Pentecostal scholarship has shown that Western and non-Western constructions of Pentecostalism differ in their emphasis on the orality, indigenization, contextualization, and enculturation of Christian faith and practice.[179] While it may therefore be permissible to speak of classical Pentecostalism as an effective carrier of African American spirituality, the global Pentecostal movement shows a remarkable adaptability to any variety of different liturgical activities. A similar development can be found in the historical maturing of classical Pentecostalism in North America, which has become characterized by a number of emerging subcultures and multicultural practices.[180] Pentecostalism is, in this sense, a "movement" characterized by a liminality that exhibits what Margaret Poloma calls "the Spirit at play" in a "playful atmosphere" that continually calls for more of the presence of God.[181] As play, the liturgy encourages theological curiosity.[182] For Pentecostals, Simon Chan remarks, church is the realization of the "aimlessness" of the liturgy.[183] This atmosphere of play allows the liturgy to be subject to continual transformation, open to conservative and progressive cultural influences, the incorporation of the high church liturgy (as in the Anglo-European context), the integration of indigenous religious rituals (Pentecostalism in Korea), the mediation of ethnicity and gender (African-Caribbean Pentecostals), the appropriation of historic ecclesiastical arrangements (Pentecostalism in Africa), the acceptance of political semantics and language (Pentecostalism in Latin America), or the differentiation of diverse religious subcultures and their respective impulses (Pentecostalism in South Asia).[184]

This tendency to embrace the world in play highlights the liminal nature not only of the liturgy in general, but also of Pentecostalism in particular.[185] The task of theology, if it is to allow for the play of the imagination, is to "arrange" its liturgical sensibilities to provide opportunities for a Spirit-oriented participation of all the faithful. The question is not one of collecting an array of appropriate liturgical texts or of establishing a (however loosely defined) structural framework but of lifting the rational, structural, and performative means and expectations that have come to define Christian praxis. In this sense, the notion of play points to dimensions of the liturgy that offer a way beyond the deadlock of juxtaposing the efficacy of signs with the freedom of the Spirit, accenting freedom and sign in a way that allows them to be mutually defining in playful interaction. Nonetheless, theology from a liturgical perspective has yet to identify the realm of nonrational, kinesthetic, linguistic, and aesthetic responses to the presence of God that may characterize Christian worship in a global context. Pentecostalism suggests that the ritual field, sounds, and sights of theological practice are easily confined and restricted by structures that do not respond to the presence of the Holy Spirit in the community. In a world where the Spirit of God has been poured out "upon all flesh" (Acts 2:17) and groans together with "the whole creation" (Rom. 8:22), this pneumatological orientation means that the liturgy must ultimately be kept open to the entire creation, inviting nature and all its creatures into the celebration of play with God. The play of the liturgy is an event that embraces all of life.

Communion with one another, creation, and God are what Miroslav Volf has called "the central leisure activity" of the Christian life.[186] While work cannot be imperfect or flawed without lacking and exhausting its performance, play does not require perfection, eloquence, timing, harmony, seriousness, maturity, deliberation, or productivity (although none of these aspects are excluded from play). The liturgy succeeds as play to the degree to which it makes accessible the presence of God in the play of the creation. In this sense, play is distinct from both performance and idleness. Understood as performance, play can quickly turn into structures that limit the nature of play and restrict the scope and manner of its practice. When subject to idleness, play loosens its connection to any structures and can quickly become superfluous. The attempt to reintegrate reason in the exercise of the imagination seems to suggest that even play must exhibit a certain "structure" if it is to be intended and understood as play.

The suggestion of a structureless community may be all too readily rejected as theologically and sociologically naive.[187] Nonetheless, at first glance the challenge of integrating the concept of play into a rational account of the theological enterprise seems to lie in the general resistance of play to any formal structures. As play theorist Brian Sutton-Smith concludes, "structurally play is characterized by quirkiness, redundancy, and flexibility."[188] However, rather than this emphasis on ambiguity, the transformative character of play, or what might be called its "adaptive variability,"[189] offers a more fruitful direction. The potential to adapt should not be understood as if play simply adjusts to whatever circumstances it encounters. Rather, the adaptiveness of play consists of the potential to transform existing structural contexts for the sake of incorporating them into play. Gadamer refers to this aspect of play as "the transformation into structure."[190] Fundamental to Gadamer's perspective is the insistence not only on play as a structure in itself but also on the transformative aspect of play that provides it with an absolute autonomy.[191] In other words, if play is able to repossess the work of the people, then play in itself is transformative of reality (including itself). That means, the structure of play "is also play, because . . . it achieves its full being only each time it is played."[192] Put differently, the structure of play, as such, is characterized by the dynamic to transform other structures into play. The jazz metaphor used in previous chapters may help to elucidate this concept.

Play, in its essence, is not a performative construct of reason but an unfolding of the imagination based on the collective activity of a community characterized by a broad spectrum of improvisation. The structure of jazz, with its creative, interpretative, and extemporaneous character, illustrates how complex this spectrum can be without necessitating fixed structures. In fact, the dynamic relationship between order and chaos exhibited in complex systems may be inhibited by analytical, predictable, and standardized forms of organization.[193] Frank J. Barrett has suggested that jazz improvisation embodies not only a complex but also a self-organizing structure that embraces the risk of its own surrender for the sake of freedom, creativity, initiative, responsiveness, flexibility, and transformation.[194] Jazz play cultivates an "aesthetic of surrender" that invites openness not by negating the predictable but by affirming the creative engagement of one another.[195] This ethic is at play in the expansion of the worldwide Pentecostal communities and challenges the church as a whole to improvise its liturgy, and to surrender its comfortable rituals and predictable structures to the task of developing relationships, nourishing the habit of discernment, and cultivating the values of creativity and communion.

In the next chapter, it is necessary to address the character of the structure of theology as play more explicitly in the context of the church in general and of Pentecostalism in particular. The imaginative and transformative dynamic of play emphasized thus far indicates that the imagination takes theology beyond the rules, boundaries, and systems traditionally proposed by its self-imposed structures, genres, and concepts. While play corrects the cognitive and performative dimensions of the canonical-linguistic approach to theology, there is much in that approach that speaks to the ecclesial context necessary for defining theology as play beyond its social and cultural dimensions. Most concrete in a reimagining of the "structure" of theology is the fact that the liturgy, as the personal and corporeal expression of the life of faith, is precisely the play *of the people*. The crisis of the liturgy is therefore fundamentally a crisis of the church.

5 Beyond Church

Ecclesiality, Culture,
and the Crisis of Christendom

The foundational argument of this study has been that the integration of Pentecostalism in the theological agenda of the late modern world emphasizes the play of the imagination. This emphasis has led to a critical engagement of the orthodox notions of Scripture and doctrine in light of the affective, personal, and corporeal dimensions manifested in Pentecostalism. As a result, I suggested in the previous chapter that the task of reimagining global Christianity from the Pentecostal perspective involves a fundamental reorientation of the liturgy, now conceived in general as the people of God at play. From that liturgical perspective, the rational, structural, and performative means and expectations that have come to define Christian praxis are transformed in the play of the faithful. The task of theology, if it is to allow for the liturgical imagination to unfold, is to "arrange" its sensibilities in a way that overcomes the artificial separation of theory and praxis and invites the cognitive and existential participation of all creation. At the heart of this endeavor, amidst concepts and proposals, ministries and practices, stands the community of the faithful: the church.

Conceptually, the programmatic exercise carried out on these pages has been cast in the language of crisis. Although conceived as a positive term and prerequisite for sustaining the theological agenda in an emerging global Christianity, the notion of crisis also contains a negative connotation that implies the need for response and reconstruction. I argued in the previous chapter that a reenvisioning of contemporary theology is confronted with a crisis of the liturgy. A solution to this crisis from the perspective of play faces a twofold dynamic of the tendency of the liturgy to transform all existing structures and, as a consequence, the resistance of the liturgy to any strict, structural definition. In this chapter I propose that this dynamic calls into question the orthodox structures and institutions of Christendom. The global theological agenda is faced with an ecclesiological dilemma that emerges from the preoccupation with a structural determination of the church in a world no longer dominated by Christian norms and ideals. In other words, the crisis of global Christianity is manifested in a crisis of Christendom. This determination is inevitably connected with the profile of the churches in history and society. The purview of the present chapter can therefore be accurately described as the pursuit of a cultural ecclesiology.

The foundation for the undertaking of this chapter emerges from the notion that Christendom finds itself in a crisis, an argument made frequently and across denominational boundaries since at least the Protestant Reformation, and most sharply in the modern period. In the first part of this chapter, I examine that crisis from the perspective of the notion of "ecclesiality" and with the understanding gained from the previous chapter that the theological crisis is in principle a structural one. I here advance the hypothesis that despite the collapse of the institutional structures of Christendom, contemporary ecclesiology has conceptually remained within those structures. The second part outlines how classical Pentecostalism is a manifestation of the crisis of Christendom in its rejection of both particular ecclesiastical structures and the dominant cultural understandings of ecclesiality. The final section proposes how the cultural notion of ecclesiality can be reshaped in the late modern world by the concept of play.

1. The Crisis of Christendom

Ecclesiality — the fundamental question of what elements make up the church — is the oldest form of ecclesiology. Even before the rise of systematic treatments on the church in the modern period, the "quality" of the nature of the church was subject to theological discussion. However, the divisions among the churches ensuing from the Protestant Reformation and the new ecclesiological impulses generated by the ecumenical movement of the twentieth century have changed the methodological approach to an understanding of the church. Prominent among the earliest discussions of ecclesiality was the projection of an ideal, transcendent representation of the church. Hence, the creedal description of the church as "one, holy, catholic, and apostolic" seeks to define the nature of the community of faith in distinction to God and the world. The post-Reformation era in the West opened up this definition to critical voices within the church itself that eventually resulted in the visible separation of the churches from one another and, in that sense, from the oneness, holiness, catholicity, and apostolicity upheld by the creedal confessions.

In response, ecclesiology began the arduous task of locating the image of the ideal church in the pluralism of the visibly divided churches and of working "backwards" to the theological image of an undivided yet invisible reality of the Christian community. The latter choice became prominent in ecumenical circles as the pursuit of a *comparative* ecclesiology, what Avery Dulles calls "a systematic reflection on the points of similarity and difference in the ecclesiologies of different denominations."[1] As a result, ecclesiality became defined denominationally, and the doctrine of the church "became a discipline proper to each church and polemical in its self-definition over against other churches."[2] To escape the charge of producing mere "blueprint ecclesiologies,"[3] which project a theological model of the church that is unattainable in the pluralistic reality of the late modern world, comparative ecclesiology is intimately connected with the modern rise of sociohistorical consciousness.[4] Its goal is to arrive from the sociohistorical reality of the churches at a theological model of the one church "that all churches could recognize and in some measure claim as their own."[5] Its challenge is to reconcile that model with the ever-expanding reality of the visibly divided churches in the diverse contexts of global cultures.

The Predicament of Comparative Ecclesiology

Comparative ecclesiology takes seriously that the church as a theological entity always has a social and historical existence, dimension, and structure.[6] Ernst Troeltsch has provided perhaps the most influential analytical tools for investigating this empirical profile of the church.[7] In the introduction to his monumental work, *The Social Teaching of the Christian Churches,* Troeltsch makes a number of critical remarks on the predicament of sociology, centering on the difficulty of defining what exactly constitutes the idea of the "social."[8] Troeltsch's chief concern is the problem of arriving at a universal social theory from the diversity of social phenomena. Most importantly, he suggests that there exist essential differences between sociological entities in general, and between Christianity and other sociological groups in particular.

For Troeltsch, the predicament of a comparative sociological approach consists in its methodological choice that different sociological phenomena, "merely, for the sake of formal equality . . . are forced into one mold, and then the one is deduced from the other" (p. 27). This identification applies especially to the general idea of the "social" and the particular context of Christianity, a connection Troeltsch considers "anything but natural and obvious" (p. 27). On the one hand, Christianity cannot be simply placed as one possibility among other sociological entities. "It then becomes a contrast between the sociological group, which is organized from the viewpoint of the religious idea of love to God and man, and those sociological forces which have been organized from an entirely secular point of view" (p. 31). On the other hand, society cannot be understood as simply the sum total of individual sociological groups in order to arrive at a fundamental sociological theory. "All that can be done is to attempt to discover the possible influence of this fundamental theory in particular instances, in definite social groups. For all these social groups possess independent instincts of organization; all that we can do, therefore, is to try to discover how far the religious-sociological fundamental theory has been able to penetrate into these motives, and to what extent it has been able to assimilate these groups into itself" (p. 30). Troeltsch paints a picture of sociology aware of the incongruity of the cultural and the religious realms, and therefore unable to provide a universal social theory, as well as sufficiently attuned to the contrast between different churches and ecclesial groups, and for that reason unable to pursue a universal theory of ecclesiality. At first glance, he makes responsible for this dilemma the radical transformation Christianity endured since the Reformation and the separation of church and state that has come to characterize the post-Reformation era. At the heart of this observation lies the understanding that modern culture is fundamentally confronted with the collapse of Christendom.

> Thus, . . . in earlier days the churches found it possible to solve the social problem in their own way, because they were able to keep both Society and the State in a position of natural dependence upon themselves, and because both the State and Society willingly and entirely submitted to the power of the Faith, and the State placed itself at the disposal of the

Church for the realization of her ideal. . . . On the other hand, at the present time, to a great extent the State is inclined to look upon the churches as free associations representing private interests, and thus to regard them as part of that "Society" from which the State is differentiated. (p. 33)

Troeltsch shows a keen awareness for the modern struggle of Christianity to express itself meaningfully and coherently in a world no longer dominated by the structures of Christendom. His emphasis on the collapse of Christendom is fundamental for understanding the predicament of contemporary ecclesiology.

The term "Christendom" is in principle a cultural designation. If we follow the three senses of culture proposed by T. S. Eliot, with different emphases placed on the individual, the group, and society, "Christendom" refers primarily to the culture of a society while highlighting the influence of that society on the development of particular groups and individuals.[9] In this sense, the culture of Christendom designates in a strict sense that period of the history of Christianity when the church could enforce through its hierarchical structure submission to its authority. The dissolution of this authority was initiated by the rise of secularization, nationalism, rationalism, religious pluralism, and scientific discovery beginning with the Protestant Reformation and the Enlightenment.[10] The collapse of Christendom consequently refers to the termination of the sociopolitical structures that supported a Christian empire and integrated the authority of the church in the Western world, and to the dissolution of the customs, beliefs, and concepts that promoted and sustained a Christian culture. Confronted with this situation, the theological agenda has found itself immobilized by a definition of ecclesiality that continues to understand the church in the outdated terms of "an abstract, universal institution."[11] In its place, the postmodern "sociological imagination," to use the catchphrase, demands a revision of the empirical perspective that takes into account the challenges of the social and personal, the private and communal, power and class, economy, ecology and technology, race and gender, and work and leisure even before approaching the realm of ecclesiology.[12]

Troeltsch's own response to this situation came in the form of a classification of ecclesiality that distinguished fundamentally between "church" and "sect."[13] His methodology initiated a whole era of classifications of religious bodies that has helped shed greater light on the organization of Christian thought and praxis. On the other hand, this typological approach has received substantial criticism, especially in North American scholarship, which has lamented the inapplicability of various types to the American situation.[14] A more significant criticism, however, must be leveled against a false appropriation of Troeltsch's intentions. While Troeltsch describes his own typology as "strangely and variously interwoven and interconnected,"[15] subsequent forms of sociological ecclesiology have sharpened the distinction between classifications, leading to further diversification among different types in general, and to an explicit contrast to the "church" type in particular. Closely related to this development is the neglect of the fact that Troeltsch ended his exhaustive survey with the eighteenth century and suggested strongly that the next century represented "a new phase of existence"[16] in church history. A continuing application of Troeltsch's fundamental typology to late modern ecclesial existence implies a continuity of ecclesiality that ceased to exist with the collapse of Christendom. "Church" is seen not only as the end product of a dynamic process of history, it is at the same time upheld as the ahistorical, methodological ideal that informs all ecclesiological inquiry.

As a result, contemporary ecclesiology has to a large extent become *ecclesiocentric.* The starting point and basis of modern typologies of ecclesiality is the notion of "church" to which all other types are placed in contrast. While classifications, such as "sect," "denomination," "ecclesiastical bodies," or "cult," are often defined negatively, indicating why and to what extent they are *not* "church," the notion of "church" itself, as the measuring stick of all other types, remains defined on the basis of the structures and patterns of Christendom.[17] Contemporary typologies are modified with regard to new religious patterns, which are nonetheless forced into an ecclesiological scheme that is oriented toward the idea of an ecclesiality that collapsed with the end of the culture of Christendom.

Limitations of an Ecclesiology of Christendom

The consequences of an ecclesiology indebted to the cultural structures of Christendom can be measured on several levels. In the first place, the "church" of Christendom is a thoroughly Western concept oriented along a premodern, prescientific, and preglobal worldview. Christendom marks the confines of a "Christian" world in contrast to the "global" world. The "church" in this world is not attuned to the awakening of Christianity in the cultures of the East and in the Southern Hemisphere.[18] Its catholicity is unaware of the demands of the multicultural, multiethnic, and multi-religious contexts of a globalized world.[19] Its apostolicity is limited to the idea of an unbroken chain of episcopal ordinations reaching back to the New Testament community that often cannot be sustained in the ecclesiastical diversity of the global cultures.[20] Its liturgy is oriented along Western medieval notions of performance rather than the universal transformation of the "ecclesial other." The structure of the Western institutional church responds only with difficulty to cultural diversity, pluralism, and change.

Second, and as a result of the former, the profile of the Western notion of "church" is formed by an institutional concept of ecclesiality that is dominated by the idea of an invisible, universal church that finds its visible expression, among other things, in an objectification of church structures, a synergy of church and state, a dialectic of whole and part, a developed bureaucracy and body of law, a distinction of ordained and laity, a patriarchal form of ministry, and a dominance of ecclesial culture, language, and liturgy.[21] The ecclesiology of Western culture, as Yves Congar observed, is essentially "a defense and affirmation of the reality of the Church as machinery of hierarchical meditation . . . , in a word, a 'hierarchology.'"[22] The hierarchical church of Christendom effectively encompassed all of Western Europe but remained largely unaware of the emergence of autonomous Christian cultures apart from its organized institution. The ecclesiastical hierarchy was legitimized as the rational element of the theology of revelation.[23] As such, it suppressed the importance of the faith of the individual, the role of women in ministry, the exercise of spiritual gifts, the need for ecumenical communion, and the dialogue among the religions, and subjected all forms of movement in the church to the dominance of the established institutional "culture."

Third, the institutional culture of the church of Christendom is dominated and justified by Christology. "Church" is essentially synonymous with the body of Christ, or more emphatically, the whole person of Christ *(totus Christus)* — a conceptual identity resulting from the prevailing understanding that the church is the continuation of the incarnation.[24] The continuing presence of the incarnate and risen Christ is concentrated in the church and reinforces its ecclesiastical structures, function, and mission. The dominance of Christology supports the argument that the church is itself divinely instituted not only in its nature but also in its structure.[25] Ecclesiology is patterned after Christology.[26] More precisely, the understanding of what constitutes the nature of the church is informed by a descending image of the Son of God, a Christology "from above," that stifles a more dynamic approach "from below" under the umbrella of the second article.[27] Consequently, as others have noted, contemporary ecclesiology renders a static, "top-down" image of "the essential nature and structure of the church that transcends any given context."[28] Instituted by Christ, the church is seen as "the summit of all religious forms, and the single, normative religion that is superior to all others. . . . In short, in an ecclesiology from above, Christocentrism has a tendency to become an ecclesiocentrism."[29] The ecclesiological imagination is narrowed fundamentally by the neglect of pneumatology and by a static view of history and humanity in the life of Christ, the Christian, and the faith community. The church as a community of God's Spirit is only a consequence of what is already accomplished in the life of Christ. The mission of the church is a performative enactment of the already established universal church in particular cultural contexts rather than an expansion and transformation of the origin of the church across cultural boundaries.[30] The church is the mover of the world, but the encounter with different cultures does not move the church.

Fourth, the ecclesiology of Christendom is essentially preecumenical. The term "ecumenical" emphasizes, at best, the "universal ecclesiastical validity"[31] of the one, invisible church in its perceived catholicity, instituted by Christ as a perfect juridical society with a hierarchical structure that rejects the authority of the separated churches.[32] The idea of a communion of churches refers to the dialectic of whole and part, of the universal and local church, not to an essential distinction in ecclesial existence. Only the debates leading up to the World Missionary Conference in Edinburgh, in 1910, began to question the ecclesiological validity of the concept of "Christendom," and with it the dominance of the church and of a Christian world and ecclesial culture.[33] Up until that time, the ecumenical task was identical with the preservation of the structures of Christendom (in a cultural and theological sense) and collapsed the historical reality of the visibly divided churches into a one-dimensional model of ecclesiality.

The rise of the ecumenical movement in the twentieth century confronted the static model of the church of Christendom with the existence and development of a variety of "ecclesiologies" or "ecclesial cultures." To integrate the diversity of sociological types into a coherent historical development of these ecclesiologies, theology has focused on the "origin" and "genesis" of the Christian community in and throughout the course of history. The result is a dispensational form of ecclesiology that portrays ecclesiality exclusively as the empirical expression of the successive, historical emergence of the church. "As a historical reality the church had a beginning in time. One can determine with relative clarity the origin of the church. This church has been and is the subject of historical development and this development must be expected to continue into the future. This historical development has been charted and studied, and while there will always be more work to be done, one can point to a great deal of consensus on the basic turning points of this history."[34]

The "dispensational" charts and illustrations of the church demonstrate with particular clarity the fundamental weakness of contemporary ecclesiology as the inability to take as normative in a post-Christendom world any one historical account of the church. Instead, the pluralism of "ecclesiologies" has come to manifest not the transformation and consistency but the competitive claim of the idea of the church in history. The ecclesiology of Christendom is radically performative in its portrayal of all ecclesial existence as a competition for occupancy of the singular term "church." The notion that the church *is* one is interpreted to mean that there *can be* only one church. Methodologically, this ecclesiology functions on the basis of "additions" to a singular historical beginning of the church. The church's journey through history unveils new denominations and ecclesiastical bodies that are added on to each other in an increasingly complex picture of cultural and historical relations.[35] This line of development is built on the premise of the divisions of the church without which it could not be constructed.

The weakness of this ecclesiology can be illustrated particularly with regard to its cultural and historical selectivity and consequent neglect of a number of significant events that contributed to the genesis of the church.[36] The emergence of Pentecostalism in North America serves as an illuminating example of the challenges faced by an ecclesiology oriented along the structures of Christendom. An integration of classical Pentecostalism into the established classifications and patterns of ecclesiality is notoriously difficult, since the rise of classical Pentecostalism at the turn of the twentieth century did not substantially impact the ecclesiology of the European churches.

Comparative ecclesiology can conceptualize the origin and development of classical Pentecostalism only in terms of an "event" that, as Roger Haight puts it in his seminal work, *Christian Community in History*, "is almost preecclesiological in any academic sense."[37] Although comparative ecclesiology acknowledges the dynamic character of Pentecostalism and hints at the possibility that it may elude established ecclesiological patterns, the comparative method forces it to categorize Pentecostalism within existing structures of an ecclesiastical development shaped by the norms of Christendom. Understood as a preecclesiological entity, Pentecostalism is consequently categorized as exhibiting a "sectarian" or "separatist" rather than "ecclesial" identity.[38] However, its inherent development as a movement that has shifted from sectarian tendencies to recognizable ecclesiastical practices has lifted Pentecostalism into the established ecclesiological scheme.[39] As such, classical Pentecostalism is identified as an add-on to the landscape of North American church history, an addition at the end of an ecclesiastical line, an outgrowth of the Holiness movement, an example of the Evangelical and Free Church traditions, or, more generally, the most recent expression of Protestantism and the Reformation movements.[40] Granted ecclesiological status, Pentecostalism has become one entity among others, a movement *in* the church but not characteristic *of* the church. Thus integrated into the established ecclesiological paradigm, Pentecostalism, as much as any "new" community in the history of the church, is swallowed up by the competitiveness of the ecclesiological scheme and destined to be overcome by subsequent additions that continue to add to the diversity of ecclesial existence in the late modern world. Among the pluralism of ecclesial communities and cultures, the understanding of what constitutes the essence of "church" is lost.

2. Classical Pentecostalism and Post-Christendom Ecclesiology

Classical Pentecostalism emerged in a complex ecclesiastical North American environment that was itself already reactionary to the European culture of Christendom. A diverse mix of circumstances — immigration, migration, urbanization, fundamentalism, revivalism, the advance of liberal religion, and the rise of modern Protestantism — formed the seedbed for an understanding of the church that is perhaps best described as "post-Christendom," surfacing at the end of and in conscious response to the ideas of ecclesiality upheld by the established churches of the colonial period.[41] In this context, following the revival at the Azusa Street Mission, Pentecostalism was immediately designated as a "movement,"[42] albeit without a concrete theological definition of this designation.[43] A closer look at the terminology, I suggest, shows that it is, at heart, an ecclesiological description. Based on this insight, this section dispels the popular notion that classical Pentecostalism did not develop an ecclesiology.[44] On the contrary, early Pentecostal literature indicates a dominant interest in the question of ecclesiality that is concentrated in the designation of Pentecostalism as a "movement." Pentecostals, much like the apostles, saw themselves as "men and women moved by the Holy Spirit" (2 Pet. 1:21). The understanding of this Spirit-directed "movement" was thoroughly dominated by ecclesiological concerns.

Pentecostalism as Movement: Rejection of the Structures of Christendom

The notion of "movement" as a designation of Pentecostal ecclesiality arose from the concrete experience of what was frequently described as the "stagnation" and "institutionalism" of the so-called old churches. Pentecostals found the existing use of the term "church" itself to be a sectarian designation, since it was typically attached to a particular form of ecclesiastical institution in order to validate its own authority.[45] In contrast, classical Pentecostalism emerged from historical roots that were already commonly designated as "movements" within the church — most prominently the Holiness movement and the Apostolic Faith movement. Both movements were nourished by the revivalism and popularity of restorationist ideas in the nineteenth century.[46] Similarly, the Pentecostal movement sought the reinstatement of "the old time religion, camp meetings, revivals, missions, street and prison work and Christian Unity everywhere."[47] Nourished by a holiness and eschatological imagination, Pentecostals understood their own identity in radical opposition to the historical consciousness of the established churches:

> We believe with all our hearts in the "Apostolic Movement" not as a name for a church, but as a religious "reform movement" composed of all clean people who will join in our battle cry and reform slogan of "Back to Christ and the apostles!" . . . But this is only a "reform movement," not a church, not the church, not the churches of God. As many churches as like can belong to this reform movement, as many do; but it is not a church, the church nor the churches; and it is a mistake we ought to get out of to call a Bible congregation of believers set in divine order by any sort of sector nickname.[48]

The repeated distinction of the term "movement" from the designation "church" highlights both the awareness of ecclesiastical categories among Pentecostals and the rejection of established classifications. The dismissal of the term "church" as an identifier of Pentecostalism was rooted in the conviction that "church" was fundamentally the title of an eschatological, not doctrinal, community. In this sense, Pentecostals were convinced that no particular faith community could claim the right to be called "church."[49] This conviction was a consolation for most Pentecostals who generally found themselves as "outcasts from the ecclesiastical camps."[50] From the perspective of these Pentecostal pioneers, the distinctions were drawn primarily on a methodological basis:

> The older denominations have a past which is their own in a peculiar sense; they can trace the beginnings of their church and the course of its history subsequent to its foundation. The time between the beginning and the present has been sufficient to establish precedent, create habit, formulate custom. In this way they have become possessed of a two-fold inheritance, a two-fold guide of action, a two-fold criterion of doctrine — the New Testament and the church position. The Pentecostal Movement has no such history; it leaps the intervening years crying, "Back to Pentecost!"[51]

As a movement, Pentecostals understood themselves as carriers of the transformation and change brought about by the biblical "Pentecost" — a watchword that referred at once to the historical events recorded in Acts 2, the operation of the Holy Spirit in the apostolic community, and the continuing outpouring of the Spirit in Christian history.[52] The slogan "Back to Pentecost!" expressed the desire to revive an event that was suppressed in its unfolding by the habits, customs, and structures of the church. Pentecostals understood themselves as thoroughly placed in history — albeit from an eschatological perspective that questioned the extent of history's jurisdiction.[53] This perspective exposed the weaknesses of the ecclesiogenesis of Christendom, which portrays classical Pentecostalism as a contradiction of historic tradition. Pentecostals, on the other hand, saw their own identity not at all in terms of historicality and thereby undermined the use of established ecclesiological patterns.

In light of their eschatological imagination, classical Pentecostals found any ecclesiastical designation misleading as long as it remained within the boundaries of normative sociohistorical jurisdiction. Since Pentecostals saw themselves as part not of a historical organization but of an eschatological movement in history, the revival of Pentecost was taken as the eschatological continuation and completion of the historical work of God who "started this movement in A.D. 33."[54] To designate their ecclesiality from an eschatological perspective, Pentecostals typically identified the contemporary revival with the day of Pentecost and used the term "Latter Rain Movement" to indicate that "the first Pentecost started the church, the body of Christ, and this, the second Pentecost, *unites* and *perfects* the church into the coming of the Lord."[55] Pentecostalism as a movement was not the fulfillment of God's work but the work *itself,* not an organization or institution but a tangible "forward moving"[56] expression of the outpouring of the Holy Spirit and the forming of the church as an eschatological community through history and the world. The editors of the *Weekly Evangel* expressed the sentiment succinctly: "In speaking of the present 'movement' it is to be noted that this is not a 'movement' in the ordinary sense in which the word is used. The chief justification for using the word is that the Blessed Holy Spirit is moving in anew upon men, women, and children mightily. There is no human leader or head and no organization at the back of it."[57] This resistance to established classifications is characteristic of the early history of classical Pentecostalism. Pentecostals criticized the "formalism," "institutionalism," "ritualism," and "ecclesiasticism" of "human organizations."[58] The heart of the criticism was leveled at the existence of the "many different religious organizations each enclosed by its own particular sectarian fence."[59] The origins of Pentecostal ecclesiology were deeply rooted in an ecumenical reading of history rather than an isolated structural criticism.

Despite the broad appeal to the apostolic faith community, Pentecostals made no serious effort to trace and develop a historical connection with the primitive church.[60] The reason for this neglect was rooted in the conviction that any bonds of apostolic succession had been severed by the organizational efforts of the Constantinian church to prescribe its faith and praxis in the form of creeds (see chapter 3).[61] Pentecostals adamantly proclaimed that they were "not fighting men or churches, but seeking to displace dead forms and creeds or wild fanaticisms with living, practical Christianity."[62] The concerns were as much structural as they were ecumenical. However, at the root stood an ecumenical idea that differed radically from the dominant definition.

The main effect of the primitivism of classical Pentecostals was what historian Grant Wacker has called an "antistructuralist impulse" that culminated in "a determination to destroy the arbitrary conventions of denominational Christianity in order to replace them with a new order of primal simplicity and purity."[63] Pentecostals illustrated their antistructuralist impulses by drawing a sharp distinction between the "mechanistic" church of Christendom and an "organic" notion of the church.[64] The chief contrast was painted between the "institutional structures" of the visible church and the "spiritual dynamic" that animates the whole Christian body.[65] "The rise or fall of Christianity depends upon where we put the emphasis. It is either upon organization or Spirit-filled men. If upon organization, then Christianity is dominated by stagnation. If upon Spirit-filled men, whose lives are yielded to God's will for the need of the world, then the church grows and the Kingdom expands with accelerated power."[66] With the invocation of episcopal authority over spiritual decision-making and creedal authority over the use of Scripture, the creeds represented the prime event where the church had "*organically fallen*."[67] This "organic" characterization of "church" was based on two biblical images, the body of Christ and the bride of Christ. The first served to define the ecumenical depth of the church, the second its eschatological dimension. Fused by a pneumatological imagination, both images were joined together by a common concern for Christian unity. "We must have unity of the Spirit. Getting everybody into one church organization would not settle the world's problems, nor the problems that confront religious leaders. Everybody in one church organization would not mean spiritual unity, but would make for spiritual disaster."[68] It was the pneumatological aspect that distinguished the church as an organism from a mere human organization. As a human structure, the church was formed by "creeds, doctrines, and ceremonies"[69] that yoked the spiritual freedom and general priesthood of believers and were to be abandoned because they had led to separation. Healing of the divisions was found in the unity of the Spirit (Eph. 4:13), interpreted as the sanctification of the carnal nature of the church (Rev. 19:7-8), and the liberation from the entanglement of organized institutions.[70] The oneness of the church was heralded among Pentecostals as an eschatological reality made possible in history by the outpouring of God's Spirit. This pneumatological perspective stood in sharp contrast to the Christocentrism and ecclesiocentrism of the established ecclesiology. In the eschaton, the kingdom of God and the church of God are identical. Until then, however, the name "church" designated "more a movement of the Spirit than a structure wedded to the present age."[71]

As a movement, classical Pentecostalism existed in ecclesial grassroots communities that generated a new sense of ecclesiality. The established ecclesiology of Christendom was confronted not "with the expansion of an existing ecclesiastical system . . . but with the emergence of another form of being church."[72] More precisely, Pentecostals understood themselves as *becoming* church. A particular community, or even the current state of the Pentecostal movement as a whole, was considered transitory and expected to be surpassed by the continuing outpouring of the Holy Spirit and the resulting transformation of Christianity.[73] "So all Christendom, made up of many parts, is aiming to become one gigantic, organized movement."[74] As this expectation met reality, the challenge of how this movement could be organized led to a reconsidering of the entire thought world of early Pentecostal ecclesiology.

Pentecostal Churches: Return to the Structures of Christendom

At the beginning of the twentieth century, the official ecclesiological use of the term "movement" was not very well established. It derived its identity from European political language that associated movements generally with asymmetry, mobilization, and revolution.[75] The ecclesiology of Christendom, which identified the church with the cultural habits and traditions that supported its authority, discussed ecclesial movements largely in terms of their cultural dissidence and religious instability.[76] From a sociohistorical perspective, "movements" were synonymous with "sects" and existed only on the fringes of the ecclesiastical spectrum. As the Pentecostal movement began to expand with unprecedented force during the first decades of the twentieth century, the question of the structure and organization of the movement rose to the forefront. In 1916 the *Weekly Evangel* observed: "There is every indication of a growing stability and settledness in the movement all over the country."[77] Pentecostalism was shaping itself into a national movement that reached far beyond the structural organization of the original local communities. Moreover, the worldwide expansion of "Pentecost" fueled the debates about the ecclesiality of the movement in the global context. However, the dominance of the ecclesiology of Christendom has stifled the full development of a Pentecostal ecclesiology. Four aspects exerted the most critical influence: the numerical and geographical expansion of Pentecostalism, the occurrence of internal divisions, the demands of global missionary activity, and an increasing ecumenical exposure of the Pentecostal movement worldwide.

First, the growth of Pentecostalism initially confirmed its self-understanding as a movement. The expansion of the small base communities was seen as mimicking the growth of the apostolic community from Jerusalem, to Judea and Samaria, "and to the ends of the earth" (Acts 1:8). Pentecostalism was seen as the movement of the Spirit that swept *across* the church and thus *became* the church. On the other hand, Pentecostals also found much resistance to growth, not only from outsiders to the movement but from internal observation, and further expansion often seemed prevented by a lack of organization.[78] By the second decade of the twentieth century, the movement had become "a composition of several branches of Pentecostal bodies."[79] The "inconsistencies and failures and counterfeits and different grades of experience following along with this movement"[80] demanded the development of structures that would bring coherence and unity. As a result, Pentecostals turned to the visible structures of organized religion surrounding them. This consideration influenced, in the first place, the designation of leaders following the apostolic pattern of apostles, prophets, evangelists, pastors, and teachers (see Eph. 4:11).[81] However, the establishment of this form of organized leadership was specifically connected with the Christian assembly, which in Scripture carries the explicit name "church." An adaptation to the ecclesiology of Christendom therefore supported the use of the explicit title, and "church" or "assembly" became the designation of choice for most organized Pentecostal bodies.[82] This ecclesiological choice significantly hampered an unfolding of the eschatological self-understanding of Pentecostalism as a movement toward its global realization of becoming church. The use of the title "church" for the local assembly competed with the original concept of a "movement" and prevented that concept from becoming part of a more fully developed ecclesiology.

Second, classical Pentecostalism was plagued by internal debates, fractures, and divisions. The growing movement divided over disagreements on doctrine, personalities, church politics, and praxis.[83] In response, many Pentecostals noted that "the conviction is growing all over the movement that the God of order . . . has order in the church. That if there be no order in the church, it is the only place in all God's creation where it is absent."[84] In the effort to establish the necessary order, most Pentecostals began to interpret the designation "church" ecclesiocentrically and in distinction to those groups who "have run wild after that which is new and sensational."[85] The eschatological orientation of the early-movement ecclesiology was overshadowed by the structural demands of the rapidly expanding Pentecostal communities. Traditional ecclesiology could not hold step with this development: the identification of churches with the stability and survival of the movement nourished an ecclesiology of competition. As a result, and mimicking the ecclesiological patterns of Christendom, the title "church" moved from the local assembly to the group of assemblies that associated one another with like doctrine, personalities, politics, and spiritual life. Others designated this group as a denomination.[86] Internal dissension and schism hastened the process of institutionalization on various levels.[87] The conceptual shift of Pentecostal ecclesiality to the realm of denominations complicated the use of the designation "church" and effectively shut the door to a more pronounced eschatological and ecumenical ecclesiology.

The ecumenical exposure of Pentecostalism represents a third influence on the shaping of the ecclesiology of the movement. Recent scholarship has established the fact that the origins of classical Pentecostalism are thoroughly steeped in ecumenical practices.[88] As a movement, Pentecostalism was almost universally regarded as the fulfillment of Jesus' prayer for Christian unity (John 17:21).[89] The designation "church," however, could not sustain the same ecumenical impulse. Rather, the adoption of the traditional ecclesiological classification inevitably led to confrontation internally as well as with other "churches." Since Pentecostals were adamant that they did not "desire to tear down churches but to make new churches out of old ones,"[90] the understanding of Pentecostal ecclesiality had to be altered to allow for the existence of multiple "churches." This decision, however, further consolidated a sense of competition and exclusivist attitude toward non-Pentecostal communities.[91] Much in response to a widespread rejection by the established traditions, Pentecostalism reverted to a "spiritual" ecumenism, and its self-understanding as a movement became ecclesiastically invisible. The use of the term "church" signaled the adoption of an ecclesiology of Christendom that was irreconcilable with the sense of ecclesiality that had originated with the Pentecostal grassroots communities.

Finally, classical Pentecostals understood themselves fundamentally as a missionary movement of the Holy Spirit. Publications were filled with accounts of men and women who had left their homes to preach the gospel in other cultures.[92] The understanding of Pentecostalism as a "movement" was largely synonymous with the idea of the church's "mission."[93] However, as the movement expanded, the missionary workers suffered most visibly from the disorganization and divisions. As Allan Anderson observes, "Many of them were independent, without financial or organizational backing, and they related only loosely to fledgling Pentecostal congregations in their home country. After all, the Spirit had set them free from human ecclesiastical institutions."[94] The initial, and spontaneous, confidence that Pentecostals possessed "the simple but effective Scriptural Plan for evangelizing the world"[95] eventually made room for the somber realization that the absence of plans and support structures severely hampered the growth and effectiveness of the Pentecostal movement. The establishment of missionary structures therefore represented the primary catalyst for the institutionalization of classical Pentecostalism. The designation "church" promised growth, stability, and survival and dramatically reshaped the missional ecclesiology of early Pentecostals. Designated as "churches," Pentecostal communities were seen not as the anticipation but as the realization of the kingdom of God in the world. Missionary activity became an ecclesial rather than eschatological endeavor. The movement no longer journeyed *toward* its full realization as the church of God; the church was now located *within* the Pentecostal movement.[96] This perspective not only juxtaposed ecclesiology and eschatology, it also had a profound impact on the cultural self-understanding of an ever-expanding Pentecostal movement.

Despite the growth and worldwide exposure of classical Pentecostalism, the ecclesiology of Christendom has been unable to define the ecclesiality of the "movement" from either a grassroots or a global perspective. The change of self-designation from "movement" to "church," and the neglect to provide a sustained definition of its ecclesiality, supported the interpretation of Pentecostalism as a movement in terms of a simple sect-church development — characteristic of a variety of religious communities and not distinctive of Pentecostalism.[97] If Pentecostalism was a movement, the question arose whether it was "useful or valid to talk about ecclesiology at all."[98] In this debate, classical Pentecostalism avoided the crucial question of culture in defining its own ecclesiality and thereby sidestepped the debate on the impact of modernism, modernity, and cultural formation, supporting the separation of the religious realm from the arena of politics, economics, and the secular, and strengthening the autonomy of culture.[99] As a result of the undeveloped account of the theological identity and ecclesiological role of culture, the organic ecclesiality of Pentecostalism as a movement, its pneumatological basis, and its eschatological orientation have remained largely underdeveloped. While the origins of classical Pentecostalism serve to illustrate the crisis of Christendom, the neglect of the concept of culture in the definition of the nature and purpose of the church is not limited to Pentecostals.[100] It suggests that an answer to the question of culture in the context of global Christianity represents one of the most significant tasks of contemporary ecclesiology.

3. Church as the Playground of Cultures

The relationship of church and culture is a precarious one because it touches the Christian community at its core, questioning the authenticity of its doctrines and practices. The foremost challenge is the appropriateness of the formulation and communication of the faith in terms that meet the demands and needs of particular cultural contexts. The limitations of the ecclesiology of Christendom show that the path ahead inevitably leads to a reconsideration of ecclesiality in the global arena. Theology has discussed the challenges of this task since the 1970s under the headings "contextualization" and "inculturation."[101] The focus of the debates has been on the formation of doctrine and the proclamation of the faith, in other words, the relation of Christianity, culture, and theology. Surprisingly, however, the nature of the church is rarely the subject of the discussion. On the contrary, church and culture are seen as two distinct realms, and it is their association and integration that is presented as the chief problem.[102] Ecclesiology is the subject but not the object of consideration. Culture, in turn, is often seen as "thoroughly ambiguous and therefore something in need of purification and redemption."[103] In this view, culture is not part of the church — it is part of the mission of the church, an object of evangelization. Only converted culture possesses an ecclesial dimension.[104] As a result, the encounter of church and culture is seen as a cultural and not an ecclesial phenomenon. At this time, there exists no ecclesiological model of contextualization.

Arguably one of the most significant documents of the twentieth century on the relation of church and culture, the Roman Catholic "Pastoral Constitution on the Church in the Modern World" *(Gaudium et spes)*, has offered one of the most influential proposals for the development of a contextual theology of the church. The ecclesiological dynamic of the text was captured in the conciliar slogan *aggiornamento,* which referred to "an updating or development of theological resources to provide a coherent critique of the culture of modernity."[105] *Aggiornamento* became an ecclesiological catchphrase, symbolic of the dynamic nature of the church, its renewal, renovation, and rejuvenation.[106] Yet, despite its immediate and wide reception, the term and its ecclesiological implications have also met significant criticism.

The most substantial criticism has come recently from Tracey Rowland, who demonstrated that one major element of the failure was the neglect to provide a theological definition of culture that, in turn, would allow for an understanding of the cultural formation of the church.[107] For Rowland, this failure is intimately connected with the absence of a further development of the pneumatological dimension of culture. The result, she argues, is an "accommodation" of the church to the culture of modernity rather than a critical engagement and response to the modern world. "The polyvalent character of the *aggiornamento* concept . . . offered no guidance for a philosophical or theological interpretation of the 'spirits' of the 'modern world.'"[108] In reply, she suggests the need for "a well-developed account of the role of culture in the formation of the soul."[109] In other words, the notion of ecclesiality depends not primarily on the culture of a society, as the ecclesiology of Christendom suggests, but on the culture of the individual and the group. In addition, the development of a cultural ecclesiology demands more extensive and precise criteria of spiritual discernment. In Pentecostal terms, the relationship of church and culture is not primarily a matter of the right doctrines and praxis but of right pathos. The concept of orthopathy, however, cannot be defined in the abstract. The affections are always bound to the particular context of a group and the individual.

In global Pentecostalism, the concept of *aggiornamento* finds concrete application and definition in diverse forms. One of the consistent elements in the worldwide development of Pentecostal ecclesiality has been the emphasis on orthopathy, interpreted in pneumatological, ecclesiological, and anthropological terms. As the previous chapters have shown, orthopathy as a carrier of the imagination forms a bridge between the conceptual and the practical and thus opens the church to the playfulness of the affections and the critical, countercultural function of the liturgy. This function of orthopathy is understood as the location where culture is brought into dialogue with orthodoxy and orthopraxy. The liturgy thus becomes the very possibility of contextualization *within* the church.

Pentecostal Liturgy in the Global Cultures

The most sustained development of a theology of inculturation has come from Africa, where the ecclesiality of Pentecostal communities has been widely discussed.[110] With Africa's large diversity of cultures, worldviews, and religions, the expansion of the Pentecostal movement is to a large extent characterized as a cross-cultural phenomenon. Ogbu Kalu, for example, interprets the growth and transformation of Pentecostalism in Africa as a response to the cultural domination of the West and a sign that African Christianity is leaving its adolescence.[111] Kalu observes that the character of Pentecostal churches has changed repeatedly as the movement engaged cultural shifts on the continent.[112] This *aggiornamento* of the movement's ecclesiality finds expression in a liturgical diversification that ranges from meetings in fields and forests among the poor, healing and feeding crusades, and the building of schools, clinics, and seminaries, to televangelism and the rise of megachurches. These changes reflect the diverse social, economic, and political demands of African cultures and have led to several shifts in the perception of Pentecostal ecclesiality.[113] An organic understanding of "church" allows for the transformation of the meaning of "church."[114] At the same time, the cultural interpretation must not conflict with the theological interpretation of being "church."

The definition of Pentecostal ecclesiality in Africa remains transient, including forms of primal religiosity, independent indigenous churches, parachurch ministries, neo-Pentecostal churches, and the expansion of charismatic spirituality among the traditional mainline churches.[115] This *aggiornamento* is characterized by a liturgical flexibility and innovativeness that seek to preserve continuity with primal African culture while remaining firmly rooted in biblical and apostolic patterns of Christianity.[116] At the same time, the churches "brand beliefs, customs and practices such as the mediatorial role of ancestors, the use of charms and amulets, pouring of libation, aspects of naming ceremony and puberty rites as 'doorways' to demonic possession or oppression of a person or a place."[117] This continuity and discontinuity of the liturgy demand a careful discernment of Christian cultural identity.

In liturgical celebration, Pentecostal churches equip the faithful to examine and retell their sociohistorical identity and to become incorporated into a contextual environment. Line Marie Onsrud has described this idea in the context of East Africa as a "self-historising" of the Pentecostal community by narrating its identity contextually.[118] The oral character of Pentecostal liturgy and the significance of testimony and story play a significant role in this task. Liturgical activity does not serve primarily to integrate the story of the faithful into the story of the church; rather, the story told by the faithful establishes the story of the church in the context of the particular culture and tradition.[119] This equipment for self-contextualization provides a cultural and ecclesial identity to the individual and the community in a dynamic liturgical interaction with both culture and church. In the liturgy takes place the reshaping of culture and re-

ligion through a revisioning of the daily life of the self, the individual, and
the community, in the social, religious, and public domains.[120] This is
manifested theologically through a strong emphasis on the priesthood of
all believers and practically through a high level of volunteer participation.[121] A high visibility of the churches in culture *and* of culture in the
churches opens up the possibility of mutual interplay between the local
and the global, the individual and the group, the group and society as a
whole. The liturgy is of an ad hoc nature that is sensitive to the interchange
of cultural needs and ecclesiastical improvisation.[122] In many situations,
the understanding of "church" is "not so much a thematized theology as a
lived reality"[123] that expresses the liminality of ecclesial existence. The
concept of church has no priority over the notions of salvation, redemption, liberation, transformation, and renewal. Ecclesiality is not defined in
an ecclesiocentric manner but through what might be called a "cultural
ecclesiality."

A similar picture emerges of Pentecostal ecclesiality in other cultures.
Pentecostals in Korea speak to the forming of a liturgy oriented along Korean history and religious practices transformed by the faith and practices
of the church.[124] Emerging in the context of the devastations of the Pacific
War and the suffering caused by a grueling civil war, Pentecostal praxis has
focused on the release of suffering and oppression *(minjung)*, a role traditionally assigned to Korean shamanism, and thereby has granted the
churches a fundamental role in the spiritual formation of the people.[125]
The Pentecostal imagination incorporates the history and culture of the
country, particularly the use of mountains and hills — already firmly established in the religious traditions of Korean culture — as places of
prayer, fasting, pilgrimage, and spiritual reflection. The receptivity to indigenous spirituality ranks among the most significant factors for the
growth and dynamism of Pentecostalism, particularly in Korean urban areas.[126] At the same time, the rejection of traditional shamanism and the
revolutionary use of women in leadership challenge the traditional elements of Korean culture and religion.[127] In a context where Christian
theological terms can only with difficulty be applied, "church" refers to a
communal process of self-awareness and transformation that involves
people in a critical discernment and spiritual formation of their existence.
The notion of "church" ranges from grassroots communities to mega-
churches, from dedicated buildings to places of nature, from continuity
with history to liberation from oppressive spiritual traditions.

In India, Pentecostalism has emerged in the established ecclesiastical

context of the Indian Orthodox Church and the experience of Western colonial missions embedded in a complex religious environment and caste
society.[128] Pentecostal communities are frequently considered indigenous
churches and seen at the margins of the social and religious landscape.[129]
It is there, particularly among the Dalit, the so-called untouchables who
constitute almost 25 percent of the Indian population, that the Pentecostal
churches have flourished.[130] In the wake of independence and modernization, many Dalits face often insurmountable obstacles to escape their situation.[131] While many have turned to Christianity for liberation, the institutional structures of the established churches have confronted them with
a persistence of social segregation and barriers to upward mobility. Pentecostals, in turn, directed the Dalits, first, not to the "church" but to the liturgy as a fellowship of equals where they are called not *dalit* (literally,
"crushed," "destroyed") but "brothers" and "sisters."[132] While traditional
ecclesiology is often identified with the persistence of class distinctions,
Pentecostals understand the church as a movement out of the caste system.[133] *Aggiornamento* means the bringing of an awareness of social, economic, and psychological change into the liturgy, addressing the emo-
tional needs of social outcasts, the dignity of the poor, and the identity of
the masses.[134] The ideal of this transformation has met the harsh reality
that such an undertaking cannot proceed without the support of the ecumenical community.[135] While the Dalits have moved *into* the church, Pentecostals have not yet succeeded in moving them *through* the churches. The
task of inculturation in the churches is confronted with the difficulty of
reconciling the culture of the people with the cultures of the divided
churches.

The most explicit debate about the tension between popular and
ecclesial culture has occurred in Latin and Central America, where ecumenical ecclesiology is confronted with an established Latino Catholic culture, a growing Pentecostal and evangelical movement, and a complex reality of diverse ecclesial grassroots communities.[136] According to Leonardo
Boff, the continent is experiencing the building of a living church, an
"ecclesiogenesis," from a multiplicity of church base communities.[137]
These communities exist in a cultural and ecclesiastical melting pot *between* the traditional "church" and "parachurch" communities. Boff views
the "theological problem" in the "ecclesial character of the basic community," which "must be seen within a context of the recovery by these communities of a true ecclesiological dimension."[138] Rather than a branching
out of the one church into particular churches, the grassroots communi-

ties reflect "the ongoing birth and creation of the church."[139] As a result, the base communities often do not reflect the ecclesiality of a mother church but "there are as many ecclesiologies as there are basic ecclesial structures."[140] For global Pentecostalism, this means that there exist a number of cultural images of the church that reflect the dynamic of a group or individual rather than the culture of the whole society. From the perspective of these base ecclesiologies, the church might be called "a mosaic within a mosaic," a "bricolage under construction," or an "immense laboratory"[141] that is reshaping the structures of Christian community.

Global Pentecostalism, not only in Latin America, emerged in the form of these ecclesial base communities "as alternative religious societies" that "were generated quasi-spontaneously and quasi-autochthonously . . . from national Protestant churches . . . , from Catholicism, and . . . intra-Pentecostal divisions."[142] It is therefore more accurate to speak of Pentecostal ecclesiality as "movements," in the plural. Despite their diversity, A. Gaxiola suggests that these different groups have found a common ecclesiality in their confrontation with the dominant cultural problems.[143] Classical Pentecostalism upheld the idea of the indigenous church as a self-governing, self-supporting, and self-propagating entity that proclaims an unchanging gospel to all cultures and contexts.[144] The global expansion of Pentecostalism has turned the focus instead to the contextualization of ecclesiality on the grassroots level and to an experience of being church that seeks to be relevant and meaningful in a particular context while being fundamentally shaped by its culture. For Gaxiola, "the Pentecostal movements propose an integral salvific project to the degree in which they incorporate into their cultural and liturgical practice the elements which belong to their culture."[145] Put differently, the ecclesiality of the "movements" is gained not by an expansion of (classical) Pentecostal origins but by the birth of new Pentecostal communities from within different cultural contexts and as a result of particular cultural phenomena. The immediate focus of these groups is a movement into the social life and culture of the individual and the family.[146] Their theological imagination finds expression through cultural agency and relational transformation that form the very essence of their ecclesiality.[147] To be sure, "church" is invested with theological meaning. However, this meaning is "cultivated," to use Eugene Halton's idea, not in the church as an abstract and figurative religious system but in the living reality of personal, social, economic, and political relations. "The question is not whether culture is a 'system' or not but whether we shall continue to conceive of culture as an inert, mechanical system or code, incapable of self-critical cultivation, or as a 'living system' — a way of living fully open to contingency, spontaneity, purposive growth and decay."[148] Halton highlights the nonperformative and unproductive elements of culture as a living system. Base ecclesial communities are meaningful and valuable in this environment only if they function as cultural agents that are open to imagination, creativity, improvisation, and change.

The preceding collection of admittedly highly selective examples of the global Pentecostal engagement of cultures encounters at least two significant concerns. First, a form of *aggiornamento* that is sensitive to the grassroots level involves the possibility of displacement by newly emerging base communities if the original relationship with the sociocultural environment is weakened or lost. Second, the cultural sensitivity of the churches involves the risk of syncretism and the more serious charge that the Christian community seeks cultural relevance at the cost of theological commitment. The Pentecostal response to these concerns has come as an emphasis on spiritual discernment and the development of a multicultural sense of ecclesiality.

Toward Multicultural Ecclesiality

From a global Pentecostal perspective, the churches cannot afford to be antagonistic or ambivalent to culture but must invite it into the ecclesial environments where spiritual discernment can take place. The notions of "spiritual discernment" and "discerning the spirit(s)" are complementary terms in Pentecostal praxis. They emphasize that the spiritual powers involved encompass both the ecclesial and cultural dimensions without making a strict distinction between the two realms. From a pneumatological perspective, the Holy Spirit is seen as present not only in the church but in some way also in the environments of cultures, societies, and religions.[149] Spiritual discernment as an ecclesiological tool is thus located both in the church directed toward culture and in the culture directed toward the church. Liberation theology has emphasized with particular clarity the need for a reconciliation of the two realms.[150] One of the most significant proposals is Paulo Freire's notion of "conscientization,"[151] a concept that has been further expanded by Pentecostals.

Key to Freire's concept is the presupposition that cultures themselves are in continuous transition.[152] In conscientization human beings become attuned to this process and act as conscious agents of the transformation of culture, a "*consciousness of* and *action upon* reality" that ultimately results in "cultural action" and "cultural revolution."[153] For Freire, this engagement serves to negate oppressive elements and to create a new cultural reality. While Freire associated this process primarily with the rise of a popular consciousness, Pentecostals have applied the concept to the ecclesial realm and endowed it with a pneumatological orientation.

Beyond the notion of liberation theology, Cheryl Bridges Johns has argued that Pentecostalism in general can be understood as a movement of conscientization.[154] She interprets conscientization in the Pentecostal environments as a form of discernment "initiated and maintained by the Holy Spirit who unveils reality in a manner which incorporates but supersedes human praxis."[155] Johns links conscientization with the theological dynamic of conversion, sanctification, and Spirit baptism that leads to social action. While the theological framework is formed by an interpenetration of orthopathy, orthodoxy, and orthopraxis, she locates the primary opportunities for conscientization in the church's liturgy.[156] Building on the suggestion by Walter Hollenweger that cultural, ethnic, and economic dialogue take place in worship, as well as the insight of Harvey Cox that worship both enacts and demonstrates social and cultural ideals, Johns defines the liturgy as an experiential, praxis-oriented, Spirit-filled context with the capacity for creation.[157] "Pentecostal liturgy is a liturgy in the making, constantly being shaped and reshaped by God's people. The key element of such a liturgy is the full participation of every person. This participation may take a variety of forms, with the intention of bestowing a capacity for action. Therefore, Pentecostal liturgy is revolutionary, serving for the conscientization of the people of God."[158]

In the previous chapter, I suggested that theology from the perspective of the liturgy has yet to identify the realm of responses to the presence of God that may characterize Christian worship in a global context. The notion of conscientization further adds to this task the challenge to see the churches as both the object of God's work and the subject of culture. Pentecostal ecclesiality suggests that the awareness of this interplay of both realms requires not only the reflective-critical power of human consciousness but also an action-reflection in the Holy Spirit that bridges the tension between conversion and empowerment, evangelism and social action, spiritual formation and social transformation, ecclesial movement and cultural transition.[159] However, Pentecostals have lamented the fact that there exists no developed pneumatological approach to a discernment of these isues.[160] From a Pentecostal perspective, pneumatology drives the church toward the kingdom of God and already actualizes the presence of that kingdom in the world through the manifestation of the gifts of the Spirit. In the midst of this confrontation, a pneumatological orientation "helps the church's self-diagnosis"[161] in the encounter of the gospel with society, culture, and religion. While the ecclesiality of the church as movement is inseparable from the cultural dynamic, the churches are incompatible with any element of culture that is ungodly, hostile to the Christian environment, unreceptive of the gospel, and destructive of ecclesial community.

Amos Yong has persistently developed a theology of discernment from a broader pneumatological perspective.[162] He suggests that spiritual discernment should be understood as both a gift of the Holy Spirit and the cultivation of "physical, cognitive, and affective sensibilities in order to more accurately perceive the assorted features of the natural world and of socio-institutional and interpersonal relationships."[163] While the discipline of discernment is attainable by all Christians, and as such is an exercise of the whole church, Yong understands the task not from an ecclesiocentric perspective. Rather, spiritual discernment is "a holistic activity focused on the various dimensions of human life"[164] and engages, as a "hermeneutics of life,"[165] personal and social phenomena not only critically but also creatively. The pneumatological imagination, by engaging the spiritual, affective, and volitional dimensions of life, both shapes the identity of the discerning community and engages in the process of world making.[166] Put differently, the church exists as a community of discernment, but it is not the exclusive realm in which discernment takes place. Yong envisions the task not as an in-house dialogue of a restricted community disengaged from the world but as the courageous and charismatic engagement of God's Word and Spirit in the public square, inviting others into the arena of discernment and thereby building the church in the particularity of the cultural situation.[167] Discernment is not an ecclesiastical performance but takes place in the interplay of church and world. While Yong's focus derives from the framework of a foundational pneumatology, the ecclesiological implications of his work can be further expanded by the thought of Jean-Jacques Suurmond on the notion of play.

Suurmond describes the church as a liberated community in which the world is invited into play with the Word and the Spirit.[168] Like Yong, he understands this interaction fundamentally as a relationship with which all creation is endowed and which therefore demands a critical discernment of the whole of life. Suurmond is critical of an ecclesiocentric use of the gospel and Christian doctrine that forces the relationship with the Spirit and the world to the periphery of the church. From a global Pentecostal perspective, the Spirit represents a critical counterpart to the institutional structures of the church and the tendencies of ecclesiastical authority to assure conformity to the church's teachings and organization (pp. 61-74). Yet, Suurmond does not advocate the widely accepted antagonism between Spirit and institution. Rather, he proposes that the structures of the church should be seen as the movement of the Spirit where the world is brought into relationship with God and the faithful. The metaphor that best describes this relationship for Suurmond is the notion of play, which always takes place in particular sociocultural contexts with their own particular arrangements. Suurmond finds this aspect reflected with particular clarity in the praxis of the churches.

Following Gadamer's notion of play as self-transcendence, Suurmond describes the church as a form of existence that "puts people in a position to surpass themselves to a degree that normally lies outside their reach" (p. 180). He interprets the Pentecostal ecclesiality as a "movement" from a cultural perspective as the result of an ongoing tension between the churches' own "ordered recognizable identity and change in relationship to the world" (p. 76). This process is in essence a charismatic event that includes the gifts of the Spirit and the human encounter with one another. The charisms are the "power of encounter" that overcomes the boundaries between church and world, and the "power of weakness" that exposes Christians to the world in service to their neighbor. Both church and world are thus built up and transformed through the charismatic encounter: while the world is changed through a confrontation with the gospel and encounter with the Spirit of God, the churches are separated from a false self-image and drive toward self-preservation (pp. 182-88). By going outside of themselves in mission to the world, the churches become the subject of "a transformation that will be worked out in the world" (p. 188). Pentecostals thus recognize the play of Word and Spirit also outside of the churches in other cultures and religions, abolishing the divisions between holy and worldly, church and culture, play and work, celebration and life (pp. 198-203).[169] The discernment of these encounters is not performed by the church on the world but engages both church and world in "a playful attitude to life in which, in interaction with the ethical demand and the concrete situation which is always new, choices must constantly be made."[170] Building on this insight, Simon Chan similarly suggests that the reality of play can only be discerned in its proper place in the larger context

of everyday life.[171] Here, "play" becomes an activity of discernment beyond an ecclesiocentric perspective for the purpose of reconciling social,
cultural, ethnic, and religious differences in which the Christian is involved as both subject and object.

As these accounts show, the question of ecclesiality is the primary
place where global Pentecostalism intersects with traditional ecclesiology.
Pentecostal thought and praxis reflect the diversity of ecclesial situations
in global contexts and suggest a linking of church, culture, and charisms in
defining the nature of the church in the world. The concept of *koinonia* is
particularly fruitful in this regard because of its wide ecumenical reception. Classical Pentecostalism has interpreted the concept most emphatically in its charismatic dimension but has remained subject to the limitations of an ecclesiology of Christendom.[172] In contrast, the global
Pentecostal landscape suggests that the contemporary task of ecclesiology
is faced with a definition of the church as both charismatic and cultural
fellowship. The ecclesiological task includes not only "experiences, understandings, symbols, words, judgments, statements, decisions, actions, relationships, and institutions which *distinguish* the group of people called
'the church'"[173] but which *establish* and *integrate* that group in the cultural
environment by which it is shaped and to which it speaks. In contrast, contemporary ecclesiology has the tendency to "ecclesiasticize" Christian faith
and praxis and to reduce the traditioning process to established, institutional structures.[174] From a global Pentecostal perspective, the widely received ecumenical consensus statements, *Baptism, Eucharist, and Ministry*
and *The Nature and Mission of the Church,* leave a discussion of culture
largely untouched and are more interested in establishing the boundaries
of the church *ad intra* than its openness to the world.[175] At the heart of the
ecclesiological debate therefore stands the question of the structures of the
church in a particular cultural context.

Global Pentecostalism suggests that cultural ecclesiality in the late
modern world is radically different from the concepts developed in the
singular context of Christendom. The ecumenical notion of *koinonia* has
yet to take account of these changes, and the biblical roots of the concept
demand a more concrete integration with the social, cultural, and ethical
demands of the twenty-first century.[176] The fact that Pentecostalism supports the speaking of "ecclesiologies," in the plural, further highlights the
dynamic and dialogical dimensions of ecclesiality and the need to resolve
the deep-rooted antagonism between charism, culture, and church structures.[177] From a Pentecostal perspective, *koinonia* refers not only to the

flexibility of a particular structure but also to the interplay among the diversity of ecclesial forms. Cultural ecclesiality, in light of the aforementioned jazz metaphor, does not place different ecclesiologies simply next to each other but invites all ecclesial rhythms into play, because the church in the global arena exists only as the propulsive, syncopated interaction of all ecclesial movements. Global Pentecostalism does not propose one particular (Pentecostal) structure but suggests that ecclesiality is experienced most concretely in a diversity of liturgical rhythms where church and culture meet in a mutual movement that shapes the ecclesial community in that particular context. The concept of "movement" thus has to be integrated and defined more firmly from an ecumenical perspective that reenvisions the sociohistorical definitions outside of the sect-church dialectic of Christendom and within the multicultural contexts of the liturgy.

The integration of Pentecostalism in the theological agenda suggests that the notion of "movement" is the ecclesiological equivalent of the cultural term "play" and applies not only to Pentecostalism but also, in principle, to all churches. It is a dynamic theological concept that espouses the ecclesiology shaped by and pertinent to a particular cultural context. In this sense, the doctrine of the church is not ecclesiocentric but encompasses the whole of life. The envisioning of the church as the playground of living cultures can help overcome the typical separation of church and culture, charism and institution, community and individual.[178] The church as playground demands an ecclesiology that takes account of the church as everyday "places" and "situations" of transformation, which open up the world for an encounter with God and humanity in ways not accounted for by traditional ecclesiological genres and classifications.[179] The churches as movements exist in the midst of the play of the Holy Spirit's transforming and renewing work to which the churches themselves are subject. The final chapter of this volume attends to the implication of this idea with particular focus on the transformation of Christian orthodoxy and the application of theology as play.

6 Beyond Orthodoxy

Pentecostalism, Renewal,
and the Crisis of Play

The previous chapters presented various dimensions of the crisis of global Christianity. The purpose has been to show not only the form and extent of various critical moments but also to point a way forward to a transformation of the present circumstances. In response, I suggested that the future of theology in the late modern world involves both the development of the theological task in its global proportions and the integration of worldwide Pentecostalism in the global theological agenda. The chief goal has been to present Pentecostalism as an indispensable catalyst in the revision of this agenda. This joint venture is possible, I have argued, because global Pentecostalism and theology feature a sensitivity that can be described by the notion of play. This metaphor has allowed me to portray the contours of the theological agenda in the late modern world beyond the confines of classical Pentecostalism and in contrast to the crisis that characterizes the current theological enterprise.

The present chapter ties together the constructive proposals of the previous chapters by offering a critical analysis of the idea of play as a proper image for the global theological task. After all, this approach seeks to join together play and theology in a manner not widely established in theological discourse. In fact, the titles of the previous chapters may have given the impression that play stands in rather sharp contrast to the orthodox theological discourse, method, and scope, leading astray the theological enterprise beyond the orthodox pillars of reason, Scripture, doctrine, ritual, and church. While play is thoroughly embedded in psychology, sociology, education, art, literature, and even mathematics and the natural sciences,[1] theology has hardly made use of the concept or its practices. More precisely, the integration of the idea of play in the theological land-scape has been carried out generally by offering a theology *of* play rather than by seeking an understanding of how theology itself may proceed *as* play. This immediate theologizing of play, however, is confronted with a general lack of prolegomena regarding the essential nature of play in the history and method of Christian theology and thus avoids the immediate confrontation with the question of Christian orthodoxy.

In this final chapter, I address the relationship of orthodoxy and play on three interrelated levels. In the first part, I highlight the predicament of understanding and realizing theology as play. While the previous chapters have accomplished this task from the perspective of the crisis of Christian orthodoxy and presented play as a way of improvement, this chapter shows that the application of play to the concerns of theological orthodoxy is itself shaped by the conflicts of global Christianity. In other words, Christian orthodoxy is ultimately faced with a crisis of play. The second part presents the confrontation of orthodox theology and play in the particular context of classical Pentecostalism and shows how the crisis of play confronts Pentecostals with the boundaries of their own orthodoxy. This criti-cal analysis is carried out through the lens of the popular notion of revival as a possible but ultimately untenable equivalent of the notion of play. The third part addresses the wider dimensions of Christian orthodoxy and suggests that the notion of renewal offers the most far-reaching challenge to the orthodox theological agenda by being sensitive to both global and Pentecostal voices and practices. The conclusion of this chapter addresses the potential directions for a renewal of global Christianity beyond the lens of classical Pentecostal and Christian orthodoxy and toward the idea of a *renewal theology* that is open to the unlimited possibilities of play.

1. The Crisis of Play

The most significant challenge the notion of play presents to Christian or-thodoxy is its expansive character. Any attempt to provide an overview of the idea of play fails inevitably to do justice to the broad variety of ideas and disciplines involved.[2] On the one hand, studies in philosophy, cultural anthropology, pedagogy, and psychoanalysis argue that play constitutes a foundational, diverse, but omnipresent component of human life.[3] The pretheoretical, cross-disciplinary, and multicultural ubiquity of play therefore seems to put the concept at the forefront of the global theological agenda. On the other hand, the popular understanding of "play" stands in sharp contrast to the seriousness of creation or the somber reality of the crucifixion and thus seems to pervert the idea of human freedom and the purposefulness of life.[4] Reflections on a praxis of play in pastoral theology since the early twentieth century, and an accumulation of theological texts on play during the 1960s and 1970s, have not helped to produce a comprehensive theology of play, much less an understanding of how to perceive theology itself as play.[5] While the accessibility and immediacy of play in everyday life offer various opportunities for the use of the concept for theological purposes, the vagueness of the character of play seems to elude a precise and systematic application to the concerns of the orthodox theological agenda.

In the history of Christian thought, play represents a relatively recent and widely contested phenomenon. The notion of play seems foreign to orthodox theological discussion and has entered the contemporary argument primarily through the lens of anthropological, psychological, and philosophical concerns. Most influential to the theological conversation have been the cultural history of play by Johan Huizinga, the psychological studies of Jean Piaget, and the philosophical writings of Eugen Fink. While these, and other studies, generally serve as a foundation for theological reflection on the idea of play, each of these thinkers also sheds particular light on the crisis of play in the late modern world and the challenges of integrating play in the orthodox theological landscape.

The Cultural Decline of Play

Johan Huizinga's cultural history, *Homo Ludens*, has been widely influential for the development of the concept of play.[6] Attempting to locate the "play-element" in culture, Huizinga is interested in formulating a general theory of culture on the basis of the concept of play. Reacting to dominant psychological, behavioral, and phylogenetic theories,[7] Huizinga calls play "a free activity standing quite consciously outside 'ordinary' life as being 'not serious,' but at the same time absorbing a person intensely and utterly."[8] In the complete disinterestedness of play in anything other than itself, play not only transcends but actually becomes culture. While the purpose of play lies outside the realm of human life, the execution of play as a cultural phenomenon assumes particular forms that can be transmitted, traditioned, and repeated without being thereby assigned to the rationality of ordinary reality. Rather, in shaping its own reality, the execution of play casts its own rhythm over the world of nonplay, creating a different order entirely and inviting all to share in the "illusion" (from Latin, *illusio*, literally, "in-play") (p. 11).[9] Play creates the images, rituals, and traditions of ordinary life from the extraordinary resources of the imagination.

Consequently, Huizinga defines the essence of play as the resistance to any form of causality, utilitarianism, and rationality that shapes the ordinary (p. 17). The whole point of play is to do so without seeking to perform an established human desire, fulfilling a given material goal, or attending to some logical cosmic cause. Playing emerges not from human instinct, which would be dominated by the human order of life, but from the activity of what Huizinga calls the "spirit" of play that transcends the ordinary realm of mind and matter — areas that constantly seek to reassert their dominance over the enchantment of the imagination. Play and culture are interwoven at a level that permeates life in all its possible dimensions:

> Law and order, commerce and profit, craft and art, poetry, wisdom and science. All are rooted in the primaeval soil of play. . . . Ritual grew up in sacred play; poetry was born in play and nourished on play; music and dancing were pure play. Wisdom and philosophy found expression in words and forms derived from religious contests. The rules of warfare, the conventions of noble living were built up on play-patterns. We have to conclude therefore, that civilization is, in its earliest phases, played. It does not come *from* play like a babe detaching itself from the womb: it arises *in* and *as* play, and never leaves it. (pp. 5, 173)

The spirit of play is thus characterized by the risk, uncertainty, and tension that are necessary to challenge and overcome the ordinary conditions of a utilitarian, materialistic, and performative world (p. 51). *Homo ludens* refers to the human being existing in a civilization that arises in and as play, that is, in tension between the element of play inherent in culture and its actualization in the ordinary patterns of life.

This tension between the play-element in culture and the actualization of play in various cultural functions has experienced a radical transformation in Western civilization in general, and the twentieth century in particular. Huizinga concludes his influential study with a critical evaluation of the actualization of play that emphasizes the dominance of orthodox tendencies, which run "directly counter to all that we mean by play"

(p. 191). With the Industrial Revolution, work, productivity, efficiency, and welfare emerged as the ideals of the age. "Henceforth, the dominants of civilization were to be social consciousness, educational aspirations, and scientific judgment" (p. 192). Culture is taken with the utmost seriousness; philosophy, religion, economy, and politics are carried out in deadly earnest. The twentieth century further submitted to the dominance of competition, performance, and productivity as well as the increasing systematization, structuralization, and differentiation of rules, processes, and goals. Play is replaced by professionalism, a calculated and false form of play, which defunctionalizes the characteristics of the true play-elements in human life (p. 206). For Huizinga, access to play is lost in the constant submission to the meaning, purpose, and logic of the human product. As a result, contemporary human culture has become void of play.

The Psychological Accommodation of Play

The research of Jean Piaget on the developmental psychology and genetic epistemology of play contributes a further dimension to an understanding of the crisis of play.[10] With a focus on the prevalence of play among children, Piaget observes the diminishing of play in similar proportions to Huizinga. Reacting to dominant theories that attribute play to purely functional or teleological categories, Piaget locates the origin of play in the psychological structures of assimilation and accommodation.[11] For him, "play manifests the peculiarity of a primacy of assimilation over accommodation which permits it to transform reality in its own manner . . . without becoming subordinated to accommodative imitation."[12] That means, although there is no assimilation without accommodation, play is characterized primarily by the transformation of the external into the internal world of the players for the sake of subordinating all reality that can potentially be assimilated. Significantly, Piaget finds imaginative assimilation, the essential property of play, to diminish with age and give way to the structures of logical accommodation and intelligent adaptation.[13] In this development, play itself diminishes.

Piaget discusses the formation of logical structures in a later work on the history and theory of structuralism where he defines structure as "a system of transformations,"[14] thereby rejecting the idea of the universal preexistence of structure in favor of a continuous construction and discovery of structural properties in human life. In other words, logical and formal structures are always in the process of composition. The origin of structure is found not in the assembly of preexistent structures but in the continual formation and organization of reality through the process of assimilation.[15] The realization and operation of structures are located in the epistemic subject, or more precisely, in the subject's operation of assimilation, which eventually gives rise to structures. As a result, "structures are inseparable from performance,"[16] since assimilation is the functional operation of the formation of structures by the acting (i.e., playing) subject. As structures arise, however, they tend to become detached from the subject and are governed autonomously by "a self-regulation whose conditions become more stringent as it steers toward an equilibrium that is mobile and stable at the same time."[17] The human subject is confronted with the ever-increasing complexity of structures that demand adaptation, logic, construction, and systematization in order to adequately adjust to reality. In this sense, play becomes increasingly differentiated within structures and ultimately diminishes under the pressures of accommodation.

Unlike Huizinga, Piaget therefore explains the decline of play not merely as a result of the contrast of the culture of play with the culture of nonplay but as a consequence of the reciprocal interconnection between both realms.[18] The crisis of play is characterized not by the complete disappearance of play but by the human adaptation to a new understanding of reality dominated by symbolic constructions and rules. Play devolves into the structural performance of a game with rules formed by the pressures of the socialized being.[19] Spontaneous play is diminished when the rules of the game "become 'institutional' in the sense that they are social realities which are passed on through the pressure of one generation on the next."[20] Piaget thus asserts to have found an explanation for the decline of play in "the extent to which the child attempts to adjust to reality rather than to assimilate."[21] While he did not make the further consequences of this adjustment in the adult life a topic of his study, Piaget's work does suggest that the absence of play in the social world of adults finds its explanation in the institutionalization of accommodation, that is, the lack of motivation to transform the conditions of equilibrium between the self and the world.

The Ontological Depreciation of Play

Influenced by the studies of Huizinga and Piaget, the philosophical discussion regarding play arose in the 1960s as an attempt to describe the metaphysical implications of play as a philosophical problem. Influential in particular are the writings of Eugen Fink, which connect the anthropological and psychological concerns of the previous generations with the sobriety of the postwar industrialized world. In three related works, Fink examines the position of play as a primary phenomenon of human existence, in the structures of the world, and in the relationship of world and humanity.[22] His overall corpus is guided by a fundamental critique of traditional ontology and its dependence on the principles of permanence and performance that cannot be found in or derived from the increasingly complex and transitional realities of human life.[23] For Fink, the *homo laborans* and its underlying condition of work and production, one of the most pervasive ideas of the late modern age, contradict the reality of play in any form and manner.[24] As a result, the *homo ludens* is isolated from the existential reality of ordinary life.[25] At the root of this dilemma stands the fact that play, unlike all other activity, is not fundamentally task-oriented. This peculiarity marks not only the essence but also the crisis of play, since the realization of play in everyday life has become essentially irreconcilable with the goal-oriented, performative, and productive mode of being that characterizes the late modern world.

> Unlike other activities, play does not fit into this style of life. It contrasts conspicuously with the futuristic mode of being, and it cannot easily be fitted into the complex structure of goals. . . . In contrast with the restless dynamism, the obscure ambiguity and relentless futurism of our life, play is characterized by calm, timeless "presence" and autonomous, self-sufficient meaning. . . . [T]he *immanent* purpose of play is not subordinate to the ultimate purpose served by all other human activity. Play has only internal purpose, unrelated to anything external to itself. Whenever we play "for the sake of" physical fitness, military training, or health, play has been perverted and has become merely a means to an end.[26]

For Fink, the world is unable to play because the dominant structures of the world have become defined by authenticity, continuity, purpose, seriousness, and work that do not allow the unfolding of play within these structures. Fink is intentional in defining the world itself as the potential playground of play. In other words, play needs the world to be played.[27] The established dominant structures of the world, however, dismiss the relevance of play.

At the root of this crisis stands the human rejection of the "worldliness" of play. With this idea, Fink points to play as an activity that relates the world to the meaning of all existence by allowing the world as a whole to reflect back on everything that exists. In play, the human person transcends the conventional structures set to define human existence. Play is "an ecstasy of existence to the world."[28] This ecstasy presents the heart of the crisis of play, since it demands a balance, or equilibrium (in Piaget's terms), of "not only the clear apollonian moment of free self-determination, but also the dark dionysian moment of panic self-abandon."[29] Play requires the realization of living between reality and illusion, in a realm of the already and not-yet, that is simultaneously in the world and out of the world. More precisely, play requires the imagination, which is lost to the human person engulfed in the structures of purposive, productive, and performative existence.

> The play world is an imaginary dimension, whose ontological meaning presents an obscure and difficult problem . . . for here we find a quite peculiar "schizophrenia," a kind of split personality that is not to be mistaken for a manifestation of mental illness. . . . Here we must distinguish between the real man who "plays" and the man created by the role within the play. The player hides his real self behind his role and is submerged in it. He lives *in* his role with a singular intensity, and yet not like the schizophrenic, who is unable to distinguish between "reality" and "illusion." The player can recall himself from his role; while playing, man retains a knowledge of his double existence, however greatly reduced this knowledge may be. Man exists in two spheres simultaneously . . . because this double personality is essential to play.[30]

This essential demand on the human existence fully uncovers the crisis of play. To the late modern person, the world of play seems "unreal." Play is ontologically devalued and characterized as mere reflection or imitation of a particular object of life.[31] The world of play cannot be perceived in its full potential as the full representation of the real world since it has neither place nor duration in the purely rational, conceptual, teleological, and performative dimensions of reality but can be perceived only by the exercise of the imagination. Since this faculty is unique to humanity, the human being is able to both participate in and comprehend the world of play. Therefore, if "the essence of the world is conceived as play, the logical consequence for man is that he is the only creature in the entire universe who can relate to and reproduce the working of the whole of Being."[32] However, the late modern person is conditioned to distinguish strictly between truth and appearance, real and unreal, orthodox and unorthodox, purpose and meaninglessness, and can no longer imagine joining these dimensions in a world dominated by work, productivity, and competition.[33] The crisis of play in the late modern person is constituted by a fundamental imbalance of the realities of existence in the world.

The Theological Contours of the Crisis of Play

This cursory overview of the crisis of play from anthropological, psychological, and philosophical perspectives represents the backdrop for the sparse theological discussion that has occurred since the second half of the twentieth century.[34] Multidisciplinary approaches to the notion of play show a general hesitancy to turn to theological questions or methodology, whereas in theological circles, on the other hand, the attempt to formulate a theology of play, at the frequent expense of nontheological factors, has overshadowed questions of the determinability of theology itself as play. In the quest to understand the phenomenon of play from the perspective of Christian orthodoxy, the question whether play is an appropriate mode of the theological task is simply answered in the negative. While theologians have ignored much of the general literature on play, the often sharp response by those who intentionally reject play as a proper metaphor for the theological enterprise further illuminates the theological contours of the crisis of play.

The ambiguity of play presents a chief reason for the rejection of the fruitfulness of the idea for theological purposes. Play is not orthodox. The absence of a consistent definition of play and the eclecticism of those who choose particular facets of play that predetermine compatibility with their given project have led to a general attitude of distrust and skepticism toward the credibility of play.[35] The lack of credibility is rooted in the frequent characterization of play as useless, unproductive, and inconsequential.[36] Play is seen as immature and not serious, an ambiguous and even frivolous behavior that contradicts orthodox theological sensibilities.[37] In its basic sense, play is seen as romantic at best, or trivial at worst.[38] In its romantic nature, play is characterized as an intangible and inauthentic form of life that contradicts the prevailing economic spirit of competition, the Protestant work ethic, and the idea of progress, and that resists dominant scientific attitudes.[39] In its trivial form, play eludes the significance and consequences inherent to theology: play simply does not seem applicable to the idea of God.[40] The dominant estimate in contemporary theology sees the only possibility to harness the notion of play for the intentions of Christian orthodoxy in a performative interpretation or corporealization of playful activity.[41] Essential to this aspect is its symbolizing potential, a function by which the human person is continually integrated in and confronted with the larger context of reality and the realm of the more-than-necessary. Yet the idea of the orthodoxy of play has also received substantial criticism. Werner Jetter summarizes the essential concerns. "This kind of choice makes . . . life a play at the boundaries: . . . the more the possibilities gained in play become necessary, the more the person must care for and utilize them, the player becomes a servant of his own self-produced necessities. The play with possibilities turns into their exact control and the human being into the compulsory executor of his own play."[42]

In response to these challenges, a more robust understanding of play and its application to the orthodox mode of theology has yet to be produced. One way forward is the proper distinction between the boundaries that are constitutive of play and the limitations brought from the outside to the actualization of play. Harvey Cox has addressed these complex connections in a sequence of writings, *The Secular City, The Feast of Fools,* and *The Seduction of the Spirit,* that illustrate the escalating inability of the modern person to access the full reality of life.[43] In a reflection on the development of his thought, Cox remarks on the methodological difficulties that the notion of play presents to contemporary theology.

> *Feast* [*of Fools*] is not a recantation of *Secular City;* it's an extension, a recognition that the changes we need are much more fundamental . . . and that the method for achieving them must be much more drastic. Man actually took charge of his own history back in the 19th Century. In *City* I was trying to help us face that fact — defatalization — on the conscious level and work out the consequences. In *Feast* the point is that we can't handle the burden of making history if we are ourselves buried in it, unaware of the timeless dimension that we touch only in fantasy and festivity.[44]

This search for the foundational dimensions of human life is characterized by the fundamental imbalance noted already in the works of Huizinga, Piaget, and Fink, and concentrated for Cox in the religious life. The task of theology is a restoration of the balance of life found in play. Cox's theology of play and observations on the human loss of playfulness are echoed in a number of other theological works.[45] Yet, unlike many of his contemporaries, he is also uniquely aware of the need to understand "theology *itself* as a playful activity."[46] At the end of *The Spirit of Seduction*, he outlines the theological contours of the crisis of play. For him, the drastic methodological changes necessary in Christian orthodoxy to confront the crisis consist of an understanding of play in three interrelated dimensions.

First, theology cannot function as play unless theologians understand themselves as "fools" and "jesters" who criticize, expose, and demythologize the facade of meaningless systems, empty symbols, and overbearing institutions. Theology is faced with the task to criticize the reigning constructs of the powerful, "dismantling and deflating auras, halos and nimbuses . . . undercutting the magical authority of sacred texts and the spurious legitimacy of proud rulers" (pp. 319-20). Late modern theology has ceased to be critical by making fun of existing structures in favor of succumbing to their seeming dominance and magnanimity. Second, theology must be seen as "making believe, as fantasizing, pretending or imagining" (p. 320) God and the world in a manner that liberates from the predominance of existing patterns, old systems, and outdated metaphors void of "prayers, confessions, visions, imaginary dialogues, improbable puns and wild speculations" (p. 322). The task of religion is not the elaboration of a new comprehensive system but a playful sharing of the experiences and imagination of people's lives. Theologians are faced with the challenge "to learn how to experience one another's spiritual traditions from the inside" (p. 323). The success of this task, however, is jeopardized by the third problematic: the inability to conceive of theology as a noninstrumental, nonproductive, and "useless" activity. Theology betrays itself "when it accepts the industrial-technical closure of the world of human meaning, or tries to blend into the one-dimensional flatland" (p. 328). For Cox, the crisis of play is fundamentally a crisis of Christian orthodoxy.

Cox's suggestions are indicative of the magnitude of challenges facing the global theological agenda in the late modern world. With these observations Cox apparently concluded his formal discussion of play and did not return to the subject. More recently, however, Cox has suggested that religion in the twenty-first century is reshaped most dynamically by Pentecostalism, a global movement that exhibits many of the characteristics of play.[47] In Pentecostalism he finds a liberating spirit, a shift in religious sensibility, marked by the playful recovery of primal speech and primal piety, the revival of an eschatological vision and prophetic witness, and the exuberance of worship that takes on diverse cultural forms. For Cox, the diverse forms of global Pentecostalism present the opportunities to experience the global spiritual traditions from the inside. In so doing, Cox shatters not only existing stereotypes of Pentecostalism but also classical Pentecostal assumptions about the essential makeup of their own movement. Pentecostalism represents, in its diverse global manifestations, an alternative to the limitations of orthodox theology in the secular city. I have elaborated on these alternatives in the final sections of the preceding chapters and portrayed global Pentecostalism as a catalyst for the renewal of the theological agenda. However, despite these similarities, Cox's account assumes a homogeneous development of Pentecostalism from its North American form to the global proportions of the movement that I have dispelled throughout this volume. As the following section will show, classical Pentecostalism is itself an exemplary manifestation of the crisis of play. Before we can ascertain the opportunities for play in the Pentecostal movement, we have to identify its most immediate challenges.

2. The Institutionalization of Classical Pentecostalism

In this section I describe the crisis of play in the particular context of classical Pentecostalism. The previous chapters already highlighted the manifestations of the diverse critical moments in the history of the Pentecostal movement in North America, which is itself affected by the crisis of play. In this final chapter I focus more precisely on the loss of playfulness as a result of the institutionalization of classical Pentecostalism. Surprisingly little research has been done on the institutional forms and routinizations of Pentecostal thought and praxis.[48] I can therefore offer only an initial description of the dilemmas of institutionalization and its impact on the playfulness of classical Pentecostalism, which, I propose, proceeded in three broad stages: (1) a selective focus on glossolalia as a forced representative of the early Pentecostal revivals, (2) the institutionalization of these revivals through the formulation of the doctrine of Spirit baptism, and (3) the solidification of classical Pentecostalism through the pressures of socialization. Contrary to the notion that the origins of classical Pentecostalism in the revivals of the early twentieth century represent the heart of the movement, I argue that global Pentecostalism — in becoming conscious of these roots — is in the process of going beyond them to the new and unexplored boundaries of global Christianity.

The Dilemmas of Institutionalization

The theological use of the notion of institutionalization is an extension of Max Weber's widely used theory of the routinization of charisma.[49] In an application of Weber's theory, Thomas F. O'Dea has offered a well-known reflection on the five institutional dilemmas of religion.[50] These reflections illustrate the dimensions of the central dilemma of routinization and institutionalization inherent in the development of all religions and offer particular insight into the history of Pentecostal and charismatic groups.

> Since such institutionalization involves the symbolic and organizational embodiment of the experience of the ultimate in less-than-ultimate forms and the concomitant embodiment of the sacred in profane structures, it involves in its very core a basic antinomy that gives rise to severe functional problems for the religious institution. . . . Moreover, since the religious experience is spontaneous and creative and since institutionalization means precisely reducing these unpredictable elements to established and routine forms, the dilemma is one of great significance for the religious movement. . . . The founded religions display this fundamental antinomy in their histories. They begin in "charismatic moments" and proceed in a direction of relative "routinization." (pp. 31-32)

The first dilemma in this development is the presence of mixed motivation, an ambiguity toward the criteria that motivate the existence and development of the religious movement between self-interest, on the one hand, and disinterested motivation, on the other hand. The functional needs of the organization and the institutional structures "emphasize performance and therefore will not distinguish very finely between the two types of motivation involved" (p. 33). The second dilemma is the objectification and alienation of symbolism from the subjective experience of the participants. The loss of the symbolic dimension leads to the disappearance of "the resonance between the external and the internal" (p. 35). Worship and liturgy devolve into objectified rituals, semimagical clichés that serve strictly utilitarian and performative ends. The third dilemma is the emergence and formalization of administrative order that includes "an elaboration and standardization of procedures and the emergence of statuses and roles within a complex of offices" (p. 35). The charismatic movement is transformed into an array of administrative organizations and functions that tend to become complicated and confusing mechanisms that shroud the genuine character of the original charismatic event. The fourth dilemma is the process of concretization, the translation of the beliefs and practices of the movement into relevant terms that can be incorporated in the patterns of existing social organizations. The religious experience of the movement is submitted to the concrete rules and definitions that tend to transform "the original insight into a complicated set of legalistic formulae and the development of legalistic rigorism" (p. 36). Finally, the fifth dilemma is the interpenetration of religion and power. The institutionalization of the religious movement leads to a confusion of religious values with cultural and political concerns that exchange interior conviction with external pressures (p. 37). Ultimately, the relation and legitimization of established authority and power structures weaken the bonds of the religious community and threaten to dissolve the fascination of the original movement.

The central sections of the previous chapters have outlined the contours of these various dilemmas in the history of classical Pentecostalism, emphasizing the motivational, performative, structural, liturgical, ecclesiastical, organizational, and cultural transformation of the movement in the North American context. I suggested that these changes are exemplary of the broader transformations of global Christianity. O'Dea proposes that these dilemmas of institutionalization are paradigmatic of religion in general, and form unavoidable elements in the development of all religious movements. The history of classical Pentecostalism initially seems to confirm these assumptions.

Margaret Poloma has argued most forcefully for the applicability of O'Dea's paradigm to classical Pentecostalism.[51] Beginning her research with a detailed study of the particular situation in the Assemblies of God, she recently suggested more broadly that "each of the five dilemmas — *mixed motivation, symbolic, delimitation, power,* and *administrative order* — provides a unique vantage point to explore the essence and future of Pentecostalism."[52] Poloma takes Weber's notion of "charisma" as "the social psychological key" to understanding the Pentecostal movement and assesses the degree to which routinization and institutionalization have obscured the original charismatic event that led to the rise of classical Pentecostalism.[53] She observes the tensions between charismatic experience and religious organization, creativity and efficiency, spontaneity and stability, and warns about the presence of institutional forces that are able to quench the charismatic spirit. Echoing Piaget's concerns about accommodation, Poloma describes classical Pentecostalism as a movement where "pragmatism, efficiency, wealth, and power continue to make significant accommodative gains."[54] While the flexibility of Pentecostalism is able to sustain the spirit of charisma, the heterogeneity of contemporary Pentecostal institutions contains the very forces that threaten to quench the viability of the original movement.

What Poloma calls the spirit of charisma, I have included within the more broadly conceived notion of play. Poloma's study underscores the significant impact of institutionalization on the charismatic dimensions of classical Pentecostalism. For the broader purposes of this chapter, however, I suggest using the notion of "revival," since it includes not only the idea of "charisma" but also the importance of noncharismatic factors contributing to the development of classical Pentecostalism. Revival marks a point of contact between orthodoxy and play. As I have shown in previous chapters, the playfulness of Pentecostalism is captured in the idea of revival, a notion that embraces the movement's self-understanding in a variety of ways. The term is more genuine to classical Pentecostal language than "charisma" and representative of an overwhelming amount of popular and academic literature, pamphlets, handbooks, leaflets, manuals, and sermons. Revival has consistently been seen as the lifeblood of the early Pentecostal movement. In a broad sense, the term "revival" has been applied to classical Pentecostalism as a whole.[55] It designates the understanding that "Pentecostalism" is in its essence perceived as bringing to life again the biblical event of "Pentecost." In addition, revival is also applied to the events that together constitute the historical origins of classical Pentecostalism in North America, such as the revival at Camp Creek (1886), the revival at Topeka (1901), and the Azusa Street revival (1906).[56] Moreover, the notion of revival has been used to designate a particular activity or a period of time set aside for the revitalization of worship, prayer, and praise. Classical Pentecostals adopted the broad use of the term from the rich history of revivalism in North America.[57] I have described the intellectual, sociological, theological, and liturgical contexts of this history throughout the previous chapters and characterized the various elements in general with reference to the metaphor of play. The crisis of play in classical Pentecostalism is most evident in the institutionalization of the early Pentecostal revivals.

The Institutionalization of Revival

The idea of the institutionalization of religious revivals has been the subject of much controversy at least since the revivals associated with Charles

Finney.[58] The early history of Pentecostal revivals, however, shows little use of the techniques and methods proposed by Finney. Rather, the institutionalization of Pentecostal revivals was a gradual process in response to the pressures of initial persecution and eventual socialization. Its origins are particularly evident in the emergence of early anti-Pentecostal arguments. Attacks and persecution were generally not caused by doctrinal disagreements. Instead, the overwhelming target was the practices and experiences that presented the most immediately accessible and tangible manifestations of the revivals.

> Within a short time . . . the Pentecostal revival became the object of scurrilous attacks. It was denounced as "anti-Christian," as "sensual and devilish," and as "the last vomit of Satan." Its adherents were taunted and derided from the pulpit as well as in the religious and secular press. Some leaders were actually subjected to violence. Those ministers and missionaries from the old-line denominations who embraced the doctrine of the Holy Spirit baptism were removed from their pulpits or dismissed by their mission boards.[59]

The revivals among Pentecostals were seen as immoral, childish, deluded, frivolous, insane, and even demonic.[60] Few critics actually sought to substantiate their judgments with concrete evidence. Exceptions typically pointed to the controversial physical manifestations that accompanied the revivals and that earned Pentecostals the pejorative nickname "holy rollers."[61] This label was often indiscriminately used to describe the unorthodox practices of jumping, jerking, falling, and rolling on the floor that contradicted established social norms and religious expectations. Yet, the nickname did not capture the complexity of Pentecostal beliefs, practices, doctrines, and ethics that influenced and supported the events nor the affections, passions, and desires that accompanied the revivals. Despite their interest in detracting from those outward manifestations, Pentecostals typically responded directly to the allegations and thereby helped pinpoint the discussion on what they perceived to be slanderous and malignant accusations.[62] Monikers such as "holy rollers" solidified the public image of the revivals as paradigmatic of unorthodox patterns and practices. While drawing attention from the public, these and other attempts to describe and define Pentecostals focused on one exceptional element at the expense of the overall dynamic of the revivals. Eventually, these isolated elements came to be synonymous with the revivals themselves and displaced them with concepts that seemed to present better the identity of the Pentecostal ethos. The most significant characteristic of these descriptors was speaking in tongues.

Speaking in tongues as a descriptor of the Pentecostal revivals, unlike the pejorative "holy rollers," did not meet any resistance from Pentecostals. As I have shown previously, glossolalia quickly manifested itself as a universal phenomenon of the Pentecostal movement, not restricted in cultural, historical, racial, ethnic, or linguistic dimensions, that was identified by the utterance of sounds, syllables, or songs generally not attributed to any known language and not understood by the audience or the speaker.[63] For Pentecostals it was an exuberant manifestation of the "play" of the Holy Spirit; for those opposed to the revivals, speaking in tongues represented the "work" of the devil. Pentecostals saw the entire event as embedded in a larger experience of transformation in the life of the individual, the church, and society. To the opposition, speaking in tongues served no discernible purpose and had no apparent meaning; glossolalia did not follow particular laws and often interrupted existing rules and regulations.[64] Through the lens of glossolalia, the revivals exhibited a freedom that confronted the dominant religious and social structures with the realization that the orthodox Christian norms and categories were unable to comprehend or categorize the events. At the same time, Pentecostals themselves were unable to disassociate the unorthodoxy of the revivals from the singularity of one charismatic manifestation.

Pentecostals soon began to describe the revivals in the particular terms of speaking in tongues, which made them the structural basis of the meetings and the center of public attention. Pentecostals who had followed the direction of the moment, spontaneous, improvising, and imaginative, began to plan the revival meetings with particular attention to maintaining the physical manifestations. Those who had been fools and jesters that criticized, exposed, and demythologized the dominant structures of religion and society, now began to shape the revivals by the performance of the gifts of the Spirit. While the original Pentecostal revivals had occurred for their own sake — with no intention to shape the growing number of participants into a coherent movement — the idea that the revivals could be maintained led to deliberate forms and structures intended to capture the meetings' central activities.

The institutionalization of the revivals became more evident with the second phase of persecution and opposition, which focused less on experiential manifestations than on "a rational polemic based on doctrine."[65]

The theological pressure on early Pentecostals shaped the direction of their own teachings in response to the doctrinal accusations. Since the early revivals did not follow prescriptive doctrines or premeditated forms of practice, Pentecostals were hard pressed to offer their own theological explanations. Ad hoc descriptions typically answered the challenges from orthodox circles using the same terminology and theological framework in which they were presented.[66] The rigorous theological agenda demanded the continuing vitality of the revivals and made it necessary to provide a teaching consistent with the emerging Pentecostal ethos. Consequently, Pentecostals turned to existing sources and concepts to develop their own theological perspectives, particularly with reference to the phenomenon of speaking in tongues. Key to this development was the doctrine of Spirit baptism. Pentecostals found in this doctrine a theological grid that allowed them to reflect the apparent key dimensions of the movement. The history of that engagement is well documented.[67] However, less attention has been paid to the implications of choosing the doctrine of Spirit baptism as a framework for the Pentecostal movement altogether.

The adoption of the doctrine of Spirit baptism solidified glossolalia as the premier expression of the theological identity of the revival movement — an emphasis supported by both Pentecostals and their opposition. Classical Pentecostalism thus emerged in a more dramatic sense as "the modern tongues movement."[68] Internal debates were often dominated by the question of the primacy of glossolalia, couched in the performative language of initial evidence.[69] On a larger scale, however, the entire debate also affected the ecumenical perception and integration of Pentecostalism in the theological landscape of the early twentieth century. Donald Dayton summarizes the immediate consequences:

> In the first place, glossolalia fails to define the movement adequately in such a way as to distinguish it fully from other religious movements. . . . Second, such a concentration on glossolalia among interpreters of Pentecostalism precludes an adequate understanding of the movement by encouraging the ahistorical claims of its advocates that Pentecostalism emerged *de novo*. . . . Third, the attention given to the practice of glossolalia has diverted interpreters from theological categories of analysis. . . . Even when theological analysis has been attempted, the concentration on glossolalia has foreshortened the theological analysis by restricting the type of questions considered. The result has been that typical theological analysis of Pentecostalism has centered almost

exclusively on questions of pneumatology, especially the doctrine of the baptism in the Holy Spirit and the gifts of the Spirit.[70]

As a result, classical Pentecostalism was essentially understood as "pneumatobaptistocentric" (Spirit-baptism centered), a characterization that only recently has been alleged "to miss the point altogether."[71] The enshrining of glossolalia and the elevation of the doctrine of Spirit baptism imprisoned the emerging Pentecostal theology in a matrix of one particularly exuberant practice. The isolation of glossolalia neglects other manifestations of the imagination characteristic of Pentecostalism, such as prophecies, dreams, and visions; words of knowledge; and divine healing. In turn, attempts to uncover the full dimensions of the Pentecostal imagination have inevitably led to a displacement and dispersion of the doctrine of Spirit baptism among a diversity of other so-called distinctives.[72] The point is that these other characteristics, although not as flamboyant as glossolalia, were now forced to a marginal position. The narrow focus and inconsistent definition of the doctrine of Spirit baptism among early Pentecostals not only isolated them further from the theological mainstream but also separated them from their own genuine roots in the history of the Holiness movement and the doctrine of sanctification.[73] The pneumatobaptistocentric identification of the revivals shifted the self-understanding of Pentecostals and led them to perform the revivals in a manner consistent with their theological interpretation. Spirit baptism now became a necessary element that defined the orthodoxy of the movement and shaped the pressures of the social and religious realities to be passed on to subsequent generations. In the terms of play, classical Pentecostals became the servants of their own self-produced necessities. The playfulness of the revivals turned into a compulsory performance of the normalization of particular religious experiences.

The Future of Pentecostalism

From the perspective of non-Pentecostals, the routinization of Spirit baptism and the doctrinal integration of glossolalia made classical Pentecostalism theologically more predictable and socially more acceptable. The borrowing of orthodox theological concepts and vocabulary allowed Pentecostals to fashion a straw identity that fit the existing theological systems, even if it did not adequately express Pentecostal sensitivities. The acceptance of Pentecostals into scholarly associations and religious organizations reinforced the adapted theological matrix. Moreover, the pressures of socialization accompanying the growing popularity of Pentecostals and the rise of the movement into the American middle and upper middle classes led to the continuing formalization of dominant Pentecostal practices and solidified the borrowed theological systems. While this development can be seen as a decline of the charismatic enthusiasm or a relaxing of the ethical rigor of the past,[74] its broader impact is more clearly seen in an assessment of the future of Pentecostalism.

In the wake of the centenary of the Azusa Street revival in 2006, a group of Pentecostal scholars set out to assess the future of Pentecostalism in the United States.[75] The outlook among the contributors was dominated by a rather pessimistic attitude questioning whether "there is the will or vitality left in classical Pentecostal denominations to project a spiritually vital Pentecostalism into the decades ahead."[76] The negative evaluation confirms many of the elements of the crisis of play outlined in the previous section. The institutionalization of classical Pentecostalism delayed Pentecostals from entering frontiers, such as international ecumenical relations or the dialogue with the religions, as well as the nontheological métier, such as the natural sciences, technology, medicine, and academia or the challenges of ecology and political or social justice.[77] The "creative chaos"[78] of the early Pentecostal revivals has made room for an increasing structuralization and routinization of the movement submitted to the orthodox ideals of performance, purpose, order, and meaning. Pentecostal denominations, churches, and ministries have become characterized by an increasing systematization and differentiation of rules, processes, and goals dominated by calculation and competition. The increasing complexity of structures demands logic and systematization following the principles of accommodation, imitation, and adaptation. In contrast to the origins of the movement, Pentecostalism in North America has become a task- and goal-oriented set of institutions governed by the matrix of productivity, efficiency, usefulness, and welfare. Classical Pentecostalism is the outcome of an institutionalization of revival and, as such, has become inimical to play. The future of global Pentecostalism lies beyond the confines of the classical Pentecostal institution.

From the perspective of the crisis of play, the pressures of socialization and institutionalization have diminished the imagination and spontaneity of classical Pentecostalism and shaped the playfulness of the early revivals into a necessary and pragmatic exercise with performative rules. Succumbing to the idea of permanence, Pentecostals began to emphasize authenticity, continuity, purpose, and seriousness at the expense of the nonrational, spontaneous, unexpected, meaningless, and playful aspects of the original revivals. Adjusting to the demands of reality rather than to the possibilities of the imagination, the movement accepted the dominant criticism of play and abandoned its unorthodox role in favor of assuming a more prominent place as the motor of religious progress. Threatening the equilibrium between reality and imagination, classical Pentecostalism has become adaptive and imitative of the concepts and systems of the dominant theological traditions. The worldliness and meaninglessness of the original movement have given way to the pursuit of power and politics. Classical Pentecostalism is no longer seen as anti-intellectual or anti-ecumenical, and although this assessment is correct, the precise intellectual and ecumenical contributions of Pentecostal thought and praxis have eluded global Christianity.

This analysis may suggest that I am advocating the end of classical Pentecostalism. O'Dea indeed repeatedly speaks of the inherent inevitability of institutionalization and routinization that seem to represent the main causes for the crisis of play. However, despite the critical observations made throughout this volume that seem to confirm O'Dea's judgment, the idea of the inevitable triumph of institutional forces and organizational patterns has encountered some critical voices.[79] Poloma implies this disapproval in her concluding suggestions that the spirit of charisma is threatened but not obliterated among Pentecostals.[80] I attribute this persistence to the dynamic of play inherent in the Pentecostal ethos as a whole, and in the diverse forms of global Pentecostalism in particular. Since the crisis of play in classical Pentecostalism is manifested in the formalization, routinization, and institutionalization of revival, this popular notion does not represent a viable option for a revision of the global theological agenda.[81] Revival, generally considered the heart of Pentecostalism, is not able to sustain the movement in its global proportions. Instead, I suggest that the resources to overcome the limitations of revivalism are found in the global Pentecostal emphasis on renewal. Beyond Pentecostalism lies the renewal, not the revival, of the orthodox theological agenda.

3. The Renewal of the Theological Agenda

In the previous chapters I sketched out a revision of the theological agenda with the help of the image of play beyond orthodox structures and expectations. My excursions into the various dimensions of the theological landscape approached this integration of orthodoxy and play from the perspective of global Pentecostalism. I suggested that Pentecostal thought and praxis provide indispensable resources for addressing the contemporary crisis of global Christianity. In this chapter, it has become evident that these resources do not consist of a revival of classical Pentecostalism, which is plagued by many of the same ailments. The history of classical Pentecostalism shows that the notion of revival cannot be applied consistently to the intersection of orthodoxy and play. In contrast, I presented global Pentecostalism as a catalyst in the renewal of global Christianity. This distinction between classical and global does not emerge from the existence of two innately different Pentecostalisms but from a radical transformation experienced by the Pentecostal movement in its emergence as a worldwide phenomenon. In the concluding reflections of this final chapter, I suggest that foundational to this dynamic quality is the notion of renewal, which is not a simple correlate of revival but represents a fundamentally different dimension of Christian theology.

Theology and Renewal

The significance of renewal in the place of the dominant notion of revival lies in its different functional quality. The manifestations of revival can be observed as historical and sociocultural phenomena, typically understood with reference to an unusual demonstration of God's presence and power (usually from a pneumatological perspective) and as manifesting a significant stage in God's overall redemptive plan.[82] In this sense, the history of Christianity is comprised of a continuing series of spiritual revivals, each significant for the stage it represents yet always remaining a partial manifestation that anticipates the more universal realization of God's redemptive activity. Revival is different from normative Christian experiences, yet this distinction is merely "a difference in degree, not in kind."[83] In its historical advancement, as in the case of classical Pentecostalism, the deployment of revival is subject to the ideology of revivalism — the use of techniques in order to perform and sustain the manifestations of revival.[84] From this functional perspective, revivalism is primarily an instrument of evangelism and tool of Christian mission, often with separatist tendencies.[85] The immediate goal of revivalism is the conversion of the individual and the growth of the revivalist group with little immediate concerns for the broader theological agenda. Revivals are concentrated on theological and religious issues that may initiate social reform and cultural change.[86] Revivalism, however, does not possess the scope, vision, structure, and methods to engage nontheological and cross-disciplinary concerns on a global scale.

In contrast, the term "renewal" exceeds the functional aspects, scope, and theological focus of revival and is more akin to the identity and self-understanding of a religious movement. The choice of a more expansive notion than revival is well documented in the designations for the Pentecostal movement in the early twentieth century (see my introduction), which included terms such as "classical Pentecostal" or "first wave" for the early forms of the movement, and "second wave," "third wave," or "neo-Pentecostal" for subsequent manifestations.[87] The new terminology illustrates the struggle to integrate the phenomenon of Pentecostal revivals beyond their origins in the growing awareness that they were not limited to a particular form of Christianity.[88] The growing consciousness of the expansion of the Pentecostal revivals has come with the realization that the accompanying phenomena are more extensive than the notion of "revival" communicates. Although the diverse terminology has been applied to other movements, such as the so-called Catholic Pentecostals,[89] neither the term "revival" nor the identifier "Pentecostals" is able to convey the broad changes of identity, cultural values, social behaviors, and religious practices that are characteristic of the changing global face of Christianity.[90] Instead, the term preferred to document the expansive changes in religious life, institutions, structures, liturgy, catechesis, worship, preaching, ecumenical relations, and theological parlance is "renewal."

Roman Catholic historian and theologian Peter Hocken has remarked extensively on this distinction between revival and renewal.[91] As an important aspect of the history of Pentecostalism, he suggests that the change of language from revival to renewal is much more significant than the widely known alteration from Pentecostal to charismatic. Renewal encompasses a more expansive "network of trends and convictions"[92] than conveyed by either "Pentecostal" or "charismatic" terminology. The idea of renewal focuses on what is essential and foundational to the worldwide effectiveness of the gospel: the outpouring of God's Spirit on all flesh.[93] For Hocken, this global pneumatological perspective helps distinguish revival as an essential component from the broader reality of renewal, and in the historical and theological sense of this observation, identifies the Pentecostal movement as an essential but transitional component of the larger phenomenon of renewal, for which there exists no single, dominant model. In other words, it is difficult to institutionalize renewal or to infer its practical applications from particular techniques and functions. Hocken's observations highlight the irreducible character of renewal that makes the notion particularly helpful for the concerns of global Christianity.

The irreducibility of renewal to particular phenomena and methods allows the concept to function as a theological representative of the notion of play. Whereas revival sheds light on the particularity of play at various moments of Christian history and illuminates the empirical reality of theology during the events and seasons that characterize the revival (a posteriori), renewal is able to project a transcendental theological method that makes possible (a priori) the knowledge and experience of any given particularity.[94] In other words, the contribution of renewal as a theological equivalent of play lies primarily in its methodological quality.

From a methodological perspective, renewal can be described as the imagination of play. Renewal directs play away from a purely intrinsic motivation to the demands and resources of particular contexts and moments. Theologically, each of these particularities is embedded in reality as creation made possible, initiated, and sustained by God. One could say that renewal is the purpose of life. The Pentecostal imagination, among others, describes the renewal of life from the perspective of the story of the Holy Spirit.[95] This pneumatological orientation is embedded in the penetrating reality of God's own imagination manifested in the interplay of Spirit, Word, and community. Renewal reflects the passion of God for the salvation of creation, not in abstract, transcendent terms, but in the imagination of the concrete and personal experiences of all the living. Renewal is in its purpose transformative of all reality and the whole of life.

However, it is somewhat misleading to speak of the "purpose" of renewal, since there exists no objectively quantifiable reality that would define that purpose. Put differently, the moment we ascertain a particular purpose of renewal, this purpose in turn becomes subject to the dynamics of the renewal.[96] Theology as play, confronted with a particular purpose, will either cease to be play or transform and assimilate any particular purpose. The ultimate purpose of the renewal of life is hidden in the depths of the imagination of God, which only God's Spirit searches and reveals (see 1 Cor. 2:10-12). At the same time, the emphasis on purpose highlights that renewal can function in performative and institutionalized environments, as in the contexts of classical Pentecostalism and the charismatic movement. Nonetheless, renewal employed as an instrument of performative endeavors is limited in scope and energy and likely to be sustained only until the stated goals have been reached. This distinction between instrument and method has to be clearly maintained for a theological appreciation of renewal. The former limits theology in its phenomenological dimensions and principal purpose to the normative patterns and goals of Christian orthodoxy. The latter opens up the theological imagination to unlimited (and often unorthodox) possibilities.

Renewal as method resists the instrumentalization of religious experiences, their patterns of observation and interpretation, as orthodox praxis. Global Pentecostalism illustrates this resistance in the multiplicity of practices that allow for the ritual, even sacramental, use of glossolalia, prophecies, healing, dreams, and visions, patterned after scriptural practices, on the one hand, and the indigenous, spiritual beliefs and practices that seem to border on syncretism, on the other hand.[97] However, it is precisely this mixture of normative and exceptional patterns that Pentecostals have emphasized and defended in the contexts of global Christianity.[98] Global Pentecostalism seeks to explore the frontiers of science, technology, politics, ethics, and academia left untouched by classical Pentecostals, often blurring the lines between theology and these other disciplines.[99] Pentecostals worldwide have begun to see themselves not only as a movement of the margins but also as a "movement in transition," a community "at a crossroads," a "religion made to travel," and a "global culture."[100] From the perspective of the global Pentecostal movement, renewal is determinative of a holistic worldview and imagination, as Allan Anderson notes of Pentecostalism in Africa, "and does not accommodate the Western tendency to separate physical and spiritual, natural and supernatural, personal and social — there is a presumed interpenetration of each."[101] This interpenetration represents God's joyful involvement in all of life, and it is the breaking through of God's Spirit into all dimensions of creation that constitutes much of the attraction and relevance of global Pentecostalism. Similarly, Amos Yong calls attention to the seemingly syncretistic practices of Pentecostalism in Asia "as a complex phenomenon, one that sits not in contrast to, but across a fluid spectrum"[102] of global expressions of the Christian faith. These and other Pentecostal scholars are hesitant to accept the predominantly negative understanding of exceptional patterns and practices and emphasize, instead, that a "theologically responsible syncretism"[103] should define the character of global Christianity in the diverse contexts of the unavoidable and necessary encounter between different communities, cultures, religions, disciplines, thoughts, and imaginations. Responsibility here refers to a commitment to the past, the teachings and practices of orthodox Christianity and the Christian spiritual tradition — all emphasized by the idea to re-new (not to reinvent) the theological agenda. As I have illustrated, this task is confronted with the twofold challenge of protecting orthodox Christian thought and praxis while reaching out to the boundaries of orthodox theological (and nontheological) discourse.

Global Christianity as Generous, Radical Orthodoxy

The challenge to renew orthodox patterns and practices inevitably leads to the tendency to distinguish between orthodox and unorthodox, or in less confrontational terms, between the center and the margins of orthodoxy. Christianity, by virtue of its mission, is always oriented toward the margins of the world. Theology seeks to extend the witness to the gospel of Jesus Christ beyond Jerusalem, Judea, and Samaria, to the ends of the world (see Acts 1:8). It is not the center but the margins that are the mark of global Christianity. Broadly speaking, these margins include any area, state, or condition outside the mainstream of contemporary theology. Predominant boundaries remain not only at the long-standing geographical and cultural margins but also at the thresholds of theology and science, theology and spirituality, the dialogue among the religions, the reconciliation of the churches, and the dichotomy between scholars and laity.[104] Renewal occurs at these margins wherever we encounter a "creative re-visioning"[105] of what is considered conventional, normal, or orthodox. Global Christianity is shaped by these margins and moved forward in the attempt to bring balance to the global state of affairs.

The margins of Christianity are the birthplace of renewal. They constitute a place of risk, tension, and uncertainty less prone to the domination of meaning, purpose, and logic and open to a critical assessment of the utilitarian, materialistic, and performative theological agendas developed at the center. The margins resist the complexity of structures that demand accommodation, systematization, and institutionalization and instead submit everything to an imagination of renewal of the fundamental imbalances of existence in the world. In this sense, global theology depends on the voices from the margins in order to remain grounded in the realities of life as a whole. Nonetheless, in the same sense, the worldwide theological development is not an exclusive "journey at the margins" — an idea that has been applied to a variety of particular contexts, among them Asian American theology, Latino/Latina theologies, liberation theology, and classical Pentecostalism.[106] The particularities of these perspectives are not interchangeable with one another or with the agenda of global theology itself. Any theology that remains at the margins is theology in exile.[107] In turn, a theology that listens to the margins is global only if it reaches out beyond itself to the ends of the world. The same vision must also account for a theology of the center.

Theology in the twentieth century was long described as a theology of the center, what Fernando F. Segovia calls the "traditional Eurocentric perspective."[108] Global theology, in this sense, has been "a movement away from the longstanding control of theological production by European and Euro-American voices and perspectives toward the retrieval and revalorization of the full multiplicity of voices and perspectives at the margins."[109] However, global Christianity does not forsake the European perspective in favor of the margins. The current shift in Christianity toward the East and the Southern Hemisphere retrieves the voices from the margins only if those voices speak to the center. At the same time, this move from the margins to the center is plausible and productive only if the center has been transformed by the public witness and missionary presence of those on the margins.[110] Global Christianity issues a call forward from the margins to the universe.[111] This task constitutes the greatest challenge of the renewal of the theological agenda in the twenty-first century.

The renewal of the theological agenda from the margins is a goal, not a state of being. It is ruled by the desire for balance between what is considered central and what appears marginal to the dominant worldview. From a Pentecostal perspective, global Christianity invites everyone to play. However, as the playground shifts and expands, so does the center of theology. As a result, the margins of Christianity also do not stay the same. New margins emerge as old margins widen the global perspective. Those who remain at the old margins inevitably position themselves on the outside of the playground. Many voices from the margins see their position as outsiders to be integral and essential to their theological identity and authority. Classical Pentecostals have frequently subscribed to that perspective. However, marginal theology that disappears if it ceases to be at the margins does not move global theology forward; it remains a hindrance to the global agenda as long as it celebrates its own oppression and marginalization. Theology from the margins can challenge everybody only if it becomes globally oriented. The margins must not be romanticized. Suffering, oppression, and persecution of the marginalized are real, and need to be abolished. Holding on to the margins stifles theological productivity and creativity and solidifies the insider/outsider status that the renewal of theology seeks to overcome. In other words, the renewal of theology must ultimately produce *renewal theology* as its central "expression of theological revitalization."[112] The difficulties of this task are well illustrated in the recent debate among evangelicals about the "renewing" or "reclaiming" of the center that resists both the notion of play and the development of a renewal theology.

Similar to Pentecostalism (and partially because of it), Evangelicalism has become a movement in transition faced by the crisis of global Christianity. In reaction to the challenges of postmodernism, Stanley J. Grenz issued an extended call to evangelicals to embrace Hans Frei's vision of a "generous orthodoxy."[113] Grenz interpreted Frei's idea as a theological program that demands and evokes "the renewal of a 'generous orthodoxy' that is as 'orthodox' as it is 'generous.'"[114] What Grenz proposed was a renewed center of evangelical theology that would overcome the "conservative/liberal" rhetoric of the twentieth century and thus be able to meet the challenges of the postmodern world.[115] He envisioned this task as a movement of renewal that would overcome the dichotomy between theology at the margins and the center and thus provide a new identity to the whole church. For Grenz, "the crucial importance of this balance between center and margin for the vitality of the church" has become evident in the theological "task of serving as a renewal movement within and toward the church as a whole."[116] The generosity of this task is manifest in its global, catholic theological vision "that engages with all of life and embraces all of creation."[117] Pentecostals play an important role in this vision of a global theology. The voices from the margins, Grenz points out, "above all Pentecostal and charismatic contributions . . . are now shaping Evangelicalism."[118] Grenz's vision of a balanced Christianity brings Pentecostalism to the heart of the renewal of the theological agenda in the late modern world.

The significant position of renewal in evangelical theology is highlighted by the critical responses to the generous orthodoxy project that demand a "reclaiming" rather than a "renewing" of the center.[119] The critics interpret generous orthodoxy not as a forsaking of the center/margin dichotomy but as an attempt to steer between the two poles, thus creating a new center within a new set of dichotomies.[120] Providing a voice for their rebuttal of generous orthodoxy, Millard Erickson proposes instead a new conservative theology that is objective, practical, postcommunal, metanarratival, dialogical, futuristic, and global.[121] In contrast to Grenz, the new conservative theology is global only in reaction to theological shifts by conserving and reclaiming orthodox tradition before the shift, not as a result of a deliberate pursuit of renewal in light of the shift.[122] While both sides emphasize the importance of orthodoxy, a reclaiming of the center is less "generous" in its departure from historic orthodox patterns and practices than the renewal theology envisioned by Grenz, whose proposal the conservative position views as accommodating postmodern tendencies and destroying the foundational orthodox center of Evangelicalism. This critique solidifies the current situation as the most far-reaching impasse in the further development of global Christianity. Orthodox thought and praxis, it may appear, do not allow for renewal and play.

This impasse in the discussion among evangelicals raises questions about the significance attributed to orthodoxy with regard to both global Christianity in general and confessional theological contributions in particular. The dilemma is essentially characterized by a debate about the limits and possibilities of Christianity in the late modern context set by the parameters of historical orthodoxy. The situation is therefore not unique to evangelicals. Since the late 1990s, a similar inquiry has taken place among largely Catholic and Anglican theologians from the perspective called "Radical Orthodoxy."[123] Where generous orthodoxy calls for a critical appropriation of so-called postmodern sensitivities, and its opponents speak of the certain demise of the postmodern, Radical Orthodoxy attempts to walk both paths, albeit with a different goal. While it attempts, similar to a generous orthodoxy, to overcome the modern use of dualisms, Radical Orthodoxy turns not to the postmodern but to the premodern. On the other hand, while it rejects, similar to the opponents of a generous orthodoxy, the nihilistic absurdity of postmodernism, Radical Orthodoxy often deliberately speaks in the language of the postmodern. In fact, Radical Orthodoxy is more "radical" than generous orthodoxy precisely in its understanding of the broadness of what constitutes Christian orthodoxy and allows even for the possibility to speak about *orthodoxies*.[124] While the debate about generous orthodoxy is concerned primarily with the renewal of theology, Radical Orthodoxy also engages the renewal of the social, cultural, anthropological, historical, political, and metaphysical realms of Christianity. If the goal of a generous orthodoxy can be described as "turning around the center,"[125] and that of its opponents as "turning back to the

center," then the goal of Radical Orthodoxy lies clearly beyond concerns
about a particular theological mainline. In this sense, the concepts advanced by this perspective further illustrate the broader dimensions of renewing the theological agenda beyond the constraints of orthodox
thought and praxis.

Often seen as a manifesto for the agenda of Radical Orthodoxy, John
Milbank's *Theology and Social Theory* criticized the roots of modernity's
"secular, scientific" convictions.[126] Rooted in a pretentious rejection of
Christian orthodoxy while remaining indebted to essentially religious and
fundamentally theological positions, secular modernity has posited its
own confession of reality and, for Milbank, "is actually *constituted* in its
secularity by 'heresy' in relation to orthodox Christianity."[127] Hence, Radical Orthodoxy, in response to secular modernity, understands itself as a
substantial "postsecular" critique of what may be described "as a 'parody'
of Christian faith and the church."[128] The renewal of the theological
agenda is therefore "radical" in the sense that it seeks to rigorously retrieve
and rethink the "roots" *(radix)* of Christian orthodoxy and their significance for an understanding of the modern (and postmodern) world.[129] Introducing the project to the North American audience, James K. A. Smith
lists five essential concerns: (1) a critique of modernity and liberalism, (2) a
quest for the postsecular, (3) an emphasis on participation and embodiment, (4) a renewed appreciation of sacramentality, liturgy, and aesthetics,
and (5) the pursuit of a constructive critique and transformation of culture.[130] In this broad field of interests, Smith has suggested that global
Pentecostalism offers a particular appropriation of the sensitivities underlying a radical orthodox agenda.[131]

Smith argues that Radical Orthodoxy and global Pentecostalism pursue
a similar theological agenda by sharing a rejection of modernity, modern
dualism, the myth of secularity, and pure reason, and offering in their place
an alternative to postmodernism, an unapologetically confessional theology,
and "an emphasis on the affectivity of religious experience and knowledge."[132] Global Pentecostalism, he suggests, is perhaps better equipped to
develop the cultural criticism envisioned by proponents of Radical Orthodoxy.[133] In his response to Smith, Graham Ward further emphasizes the importance of pneumatology shared by Pentecostals.[134] Indeed, Pentecostal
spirituality pushes beyond the premodern resources of the Radical Orthodoxy project to the roots of Christianity in the New Testament, to a prophetic appraisal of reality in light of the biblical texts, and to the spiritual discernment of the present world.[135] Pentecostalism has many similarities with

the postmodern worldview.[136] Nonetheless, it maintains a radical (i.e., neither modern nor postmodern) commitment to the sovereign and transforming presence of God. Although Pentecostalism is not associated with Radical Orthodoxy, a renewal of global theology developed through an encounter with Pentecostalism has all the sensitivities of the project. In this sense, one might answer positively to Smith's inquiry whether Pentecostals might not "be more radical than the radically orthodox."[137]

Ultimately, it is misleading to separate the terms "radical" and "orthodox" in the context of renewal. The notion of global Pentecostalism that I advocate on these pages always tends toward both being grounded in the rules of orthodoxy and experimenting with the radical extension of those rules for the sake of renewal. In fact, global theology as play, from a Pentecostal perspective, is radical precisely in its insistence on orthodoxy — not its departure from it. Global Christianity is radically orthodox in its generous understanding of what constitutes the boundaries of the orthodox playing field. Pentecostal faith and practices extend those boundaries because global Pentecostalism moves across the playing field of theology not only from the center but also from the margins of the world. In this sense, a Pentecostal perspective is globally oriented because of both its worldwide presence and its location at the margins, which allow Pentecostal sensitivities to traverse global Christian faith and practices in their entirety.

Global Pentecostalism offers a multiplicity of resources to understand and engage in the worldwide renewal of theology at the beginning of the twenty-first century. Pentecostal history, theology, spirituality, and praxis are interwoven in the challenges and opportunities faced by global Christianity. Pentecostalism manifests the playful character of a generous, radical orthodoxy necessary to engage the challenges of the late modern world. As such, global Pentecostalism is an instrument of renewal, not its final goal. The playful courage and curiosity of renewal ultimately lead also beyond Pentecostalism. Those who dare look beyond the Pentecostal movement will find that renewal theology is not situated in one particular center of activity or thematic locus. Its method proceeds from a theological imagination not bound to theological questions and concerns. Renewal theology is not the property of one particular discipline, institution, or practice. Rather, renewal, as the imagination of play, serves as the inherent method of a theology that pushes the boundaries of the orthodox agenda from the traditional occupation with the doctrine of God outward and throughout all theological and nontheological dimensions to the margins of life and creation.

Postscript

The nature of the arguments presented in this volume does not allow for a conclusion, which might give the impression that Christianity can now take a step forward to embrace its global dimensions. The preceding chapters have given no more than an outline of the diverse forms of crises that face the global theological agenda. The crises of the imagination, revelation, creed, liturgy, Christendom, and play paint the picture of Christianity in transition, a radical and deep-seated transformation that affects most of all the manner and mode of how Christian theology is envisioned and carried out in the late modern world. I have criticized contemporary theology for its mechanistic, utilitarian, productive, performative, and competitive nature. In contrast, I used the metaphor of play to illustrate an alternative image of Christian thought and praxis. It seems therefore more appropriate to conclude with a postlude, in the sense of a playful epilogue or afterword.

In many ways, writing (and, I am sure, reading) the preceding chapters has been a battle with the performative and task-oriented character that defines the contemporary theological enterprise. To many readers, it will not go unnoticed that I have consistently described a way beyond the crisis of global Christianity as the "task" of theology while emphasizing, at the same time, that the realization of theology as play is not oriented toward the ideals of purpose, productivity, and performance. While I have attempted to reconcile the notion of play with the concept of work, the final chapter has shown that the lack of balance between these realms constitutes a major challenge to the renewal of the theological agenda. Global

Christianity has not even begun to play, except perhaps in the communities and churches of what I have called global Pentecostalism.

Beyond Pentecostalism, the title of this book, is arguably the most playful aspect of the entire project. It neither elevates nor demotes Pentecostalism but, to the best of my abilities, plays with Pentecostal sensitivities and introduces them in a playful manner to the realm of global Christian theology. In the same sense, I have challenged the global theological agenda to open up to the resources of Pentecostalism. The lengthy arguments of this volume should not distract from the idea that this project is intended as an invitation to play. In so doing, it shows all the shortcomings of someone who is not used to jesting or fantasizing or any activity done simply for the joy of doing it and motivated by a universal vision of renewal. The contours of the crisis of global Christianity I have presented mark only the introduction to succeeding movements, a small selection of motifs and rhythms that recur throughout the entire discussion, an improvisation that anticipates the joining of other voices and rhythms. In this sense, we really have arrived only at the end of a prelude . . .

Notes

Notes to the Introduction

1. Cf. Robert J. Schreiter, *The New Catholicity: Theology between the Global and the Local* (Maryknoll, NY: Orbis, 2000), pp. 1-27.

2. Cf. Hans Schwarz, *Theology in a Global Context: The Last Two Hundred Years* (Grand Rapids: Eerdmans, 2005), pp. 472-539; William A. Dyrness, ed., *Emerging Voices in Global Christian Theology* (Grand Rapids: Zondervan, 1994).

3. I use the phrase "late modern" in contrast to "postmodern" to indicate the continuity of the contemporary world with the structures and developments of modernity that are, as the following chapters will show, characterized by an ambiguity or reshaping rather than a rejection or abandoning of the elements of the modern world. I am following, among others, Jock Young, *The Vertigo of Late Modernity* (London: Sage, 2007); Robert Cummings Neville, *Religion in Late Modernity* (Albany: SUNY Press, 2002); Zygmunt Bauman, *Liquid Modernity* (Malden, MA: Blackwell, 2000); Anthony Giddens, *The Consequences of Modernity* (Stanford: Stanford University Press, 1990).

4. See, for example, Harvey Cox, *The Secular City: Secularization and Urbanization in Theological Perspective* (New York: Macmillan, 1965); Roger Aubert, *Sacralization and Secularization* (New York: Paulist, 1969); Heribert Mühlen, *Entsakralisierung: Ein epochales Schlagwort in seiner Bedeutung für die Zukunft der christlichen Kirchen* (Paderborn: Ferdinand Schöningh, 1971).

5. Heribert Mühlen, *Kirche wächst von innen: Weg zu einer glaubensgeschichtlich neuen Gestalt der Kirche* (Paderborn: Bonifatius, 1996), p. 40, translation mine.

6. Cf. Wolfgang Vondey, *Heribert Mühlen: His Theology and Praxis; A New Profile of the Church* (Lanham, MD: University Press of America, 2004).

7. Ludek Broz, "The Task Facing Theology in Europe," *ER* 45, no. 2 (1993): 169-72, here p. 171.

8. Broz, "The Task Facing Theology," p. 172.

9. See, for example, Gary J. Dorrien, "American Liberal Theology: Crisis, Irony, De-

cline, Renewal, Ambiguity," *CC* 55, no. 4 (2006): 456-81; Daniel Johnson, "The Catholic Crisis," *Commentary* 115, no. 2 (2003): 25-32; Edward T. Oakes, "Evangelical Theology in Crisis," *FT* 36 (October 1993): 38-44; Brevard S. Childs, *Biblical Theology in Crisis* (Philadelphia: Westminster, 1970); Cecil Wayne Cone, *The Identity Crisis in Black Theology* (Nashville: AMEC, 1975).

10. See Manuel Jesus Mejido Costoya, "Theology, Crisis and Knowledge-Constitutive Interests, or Towards a Social Theoretical Interpretation of Theological Knowledge," *SC* 51, no. 3 (2004): 381-401; Vítor Westhelle, "The Current Crisis in Latin American Theology," *Di* 34 (Winter 1995): 39-43.

11. See John W. de Gruchy, *Theology and Ministry in Context and Crisis: A South African Perspective* (Grand Rapids: Eerdmans, 1986); John W. de Gruchy, *The Church Struggle in South Africa,* 2nd ed. (Grand Rapids: Eerdmans, 1986); Charles Villa-Vicencio and John W. de Gruchy, eds., *Apartheid Is Heresy* (Grand Rapids: Eerdmans, 1983).

12. See Hwa Yung, *Mangoes or Bananas: The Quest for an Authentic Asian Christian Theology* (Oxford: Regnum, 1997); Chris Sugden, *Seeking the Asian Face of Jesus: The Practice and Theology of Christian Social Witness in Indonesia and India, 1974-1996* (Oxford: Regnum, 1997); R. S. Sugirtharajah, ed., *Frontiers in Asian Christian Theology: Emerging Trends* (Maryknoll, NY: Orbis, 1994).

13. H. Emil Brunner, *The Theology of Crisis* (New York: Scribner, 1929), p. 1.

14. Brunner, *The Theology of Crisis,* p. 3.

15. See Peter Lange, *Konkrete Theologie? Karl Barth und Friedrich Gogarten "Zwischen den Zeiten" (1922-1933)* (Zürich: Theologischer Verlag, 1972).

16. Edmund Husserl, *The Crisis of European Sciences and Transcendental Phenomenology: An Introduction to Phenomenological Philosophy,* trans. David Carr (Evanston, IL: Northwestern University Press, 1970). See also James Dodd, *Crisis and Reflection: An Essay on Husserl's Crisis of the European Sciences,* Phaenomenologica 174 (New York: Kluwer Academic, 2005).

17. Dodd, *Crisis and Reflection,* p. 48.

18. Husserl, *Crisis of European Sciences,* p. 12.

19. Martin Heidegger, *On Time and Being,* trans. Joan Stambaugh (New York: Harper and Row, 1972), pp. 56-57.

20. See Thomas S. Kuhn, *The Structure of Scientific Revolutions,* 3rd ed. (Chicago: University of Chicago Press, 1996), pp. 66-91.

21. Cf. Rex Ambler, *Global Theology: The Meaning of Faith in the Present World Crisis* (London: SCM, 1990).

22. Steven J. Land, *Pentecostal Spirituality: A Passion for the Kingdom,* JPTS 1 (Sheffield: Sheffield Academic, 1994), p. 79.

23. Cf. Horace S. Ward, "The Anti-Pentecostal Argument," in *Aspects of Pentecostal-Charismatic Origins,* ed. Vinson Synan (Plainfield, NJ: Logos International, 1975), pp. 99-122.

24. See Kuhn, *Structure of Scientific Revolutions,* p. 82.

25. Kuhn, *Structure of Scientific Revolutions,* p. 85.

26. Brunner, *The Theology of Crisis,* p. 18.

27. Early examples of this argument are Walter J. Hollenweger, "The Critical Tradition of Pentecostalism," *JPT* 1 (1992): 7-17; Land, *Pentecostal Spirituality,* p. 13; D. William Faupel, *The Everlasting Gospel: The Significance of Eschatology in the Development of Pentecostal Thought,* JPTS 10 (Sheffield: Sheffield Academic, 1996), p. 309.

28. Cf. Michael Wilkinson, "What's 'Global' about Global Pentecostalism?" *JPT* 17, no. 1 (2008): 96-109.

29. See Allan Anderson, *An Introduction to Pentecostalism: Global Charismatic Christianity* (Cambridge: Cambridge University Press, 2004); Arlene Sánchez-Walsh, *Latino Pentecostal Identity: Evangelical Faith, Self, and Society* (New York: Columbia University Press, 2003); Walter J. Hollenweger, *Pentecostalism: Origins and Developments Worldwide* (Peabody, MA: Hendrickson, 1997); Cheryl Bridges Johns, "The Adolescence of Pentecostalism: In Search of a Legitimate Sectarian Identity," *Pneuma* 17 (1995): 3-17.

30. Wolfgang Vondey, "Presuppositions for Pentecostal Engagement in Ecumenical Dialogue," *EJEMR* 30, no. 4 (2001): 344-58; Wolfgang Vondey, "Christian Amnesia: Who in the World Are Pentecostals?" *AJPS* 4, no. 1 (2001): 21-39.

31. André Droogers, "Globalisation and Pentecostal Success," in *Between Babel and Pentecost: Transnational Pentecostalism in Africa and Latin America,* ed. André Corten and Ruth Marshall-Fratani (Bloomington: Indiana University Press, 2001), pp. 41-61, here p. 46.

32. See Nils Bloch-Hoell, *The Pentecostal Movement: Its Origin, Development, and Distinctive Character* (Oslo: Universitetsforlaget, 1964), pp. 172-77.

33. William K. Kay and Anne E. Dyer, eds., *Pentecostal and Charismatic Studies: A Reader* (London: SCM, 2004), pp. 25-234; Robert Mapes Anderson, *Vision of the Disinherited: The Making of American Pentecostalism* (Peabody, MA: Hendrickson, 1979), p. 4; Edward D. O'Connor, *The Pentecostal Movement in the Catholic Church* (Notre Dame, IN: Ave Maria, 1971), pp. 263-86.

34. See Ward, "The Anti-Pentecostal Argument," pp. 99-122.

35. See Donald Dayton, *Theological Roots of Pentecostalism* (Peabody, MA: Hendrickson, 1987), p. 21.

36. See Vondey, "Christian Amnesia," pp. 33-35.

37. Hollenweger, *Pentecostalism,* p. 1. See also Walter Hollenweger, *The Pentecostals: The Charismatic Movement in the Churches* (Minneapolis: Augsburg, 1972), pp. 71-72.

38. Allan Anderson, *An Introduction to Pentecostalism,* p. 1.

39. *NIDPCM,* p. xx.

40. Allan Anderson, *An Introduction to Pentecostalism,* pp. 13-14; Allan Anderson, "Diversity in the Definition of 'Pentecostal/Charismatic' and Its Ecumenical Implications," *MS* 19, no. 2 (2002): 40-55.

41. Allan Anderson, "Introduction: World Pentecostalism at a Crossroads," in *Pentecostals after a Century: Global Perspectives on a Movement in Transition,* ed. Allan H. Anderson and Walter J. Hollenweger, JPTS 15 (Sheffield: Sheffield Academic, 1999), pp. 19-31, here p. 20.

42. One of the first to make this suggestion was Cecil M. Robeck, Jr., "Making Sense of Pentecostalism in a Global Context" (paper presented at the Twenty-eighth Annual Meeting of the Society for Pentecostal Studies, Springfield, MO, 1999), pp. 1-34; Cecil M. Robeck, Jr., "Taking Stock of Pentecostalism: The Personal Reflections of a Retiring Editor," *Pneuma* 15, no. 3 (1993): 35-60.

43. See Peter Beyer, *Religions in Global Society* (London: Routledge, 2006), pp. 147-50; Daniel Chiquete, "Latin American Pentecostalisms and Western Postmodernism: Reflections on a Complex Relationship," *IRM* 92, no. 364 (2003): 29-39.

44. Patrick Johnstone and Jason Mandryk, *Operation World: 21st Century Edition* (Carlisle, U.K.: Paternoster, 2001), p. 757.

45. See Veli-Matti Kärkkäinen, "'Anonymous Ecumenists'? Pentecostals and the Struggle for Christian Identity," *JES* 37, no. 1 (2000): 13-27.

46. Amos Yong, *The Spirit Poured Out on All Flesh: Pentecostalism and the Possibility of Global Theology* (Grand Rapids: Baker Academic, 2005), pp. 18-19. The use of capitalization is problematic when the term is found at the beginning of a sentence, since this position forces a capitalization of the word. See Vondey, "Pentecostalism and the Possibility of Global Theology: Implications of the Theology of Amos Yong," *Pneuma* 28, no. 2 (2006): 289-312.

47. See Amos Yong, "Performing Global Pentecostal Theology: A Response to Wolfgang Vondey," *Pneuma* 28, no. 2 (2006): 313.

48. The different spelling of the terms "pentecostal" and "Pentecostal" helps distinguish two groups on a general scale but obscures the distinctions that continue to exist within each group. The terminology suggests not a descriptive but an essential difference in being Pentecostal.

49. On the concept of performance in religion, see Peter Beyer, *Religion and Globalization* (London: Sage, 1994), pp. 79-93; Niklas Luhmann, *The Differentiation of Society*, trans. Stephen Holmes and Charles Larmore (New York: Columbia University Press, 1982), pp. 238-42.

50. See the literature on play throughout this volume. For a detailed overview of the theological approaches to the concept of play, see Sabine Bobert-Stützel, *Frömmigkeit und Symbolspiel: Ein pastoralpsychologischer Beitrag zu einer evangelischen Frömmigkeitstheorie*, Arbeiten zur Pastoraltheologie 37 (Göttingen: Vandenhoeck & Ruprecht, 2000); Thomas Klie, *Zeichen und Spiel: Semiotische und spieltheoretische Rekonstruktion der Pastoraltheologie* (Gütersloh: Kaiser, 2003).

51. This tradition stretches from the early Christian creeds and councils to the various contemporary works of systematic theology. Particular significance in modern and late modern theology has accrued to the works of Peter Lombard *(Liber sententiarum)*, Thomas Aquinas *(Summa theologiae)*, Philipp Melanchthon *(Hypotyposes theologicæ seu loci communes)*, John Calvin *(Institutes of the Christian Religion)*, Karl Barth *(Church Dogmatics)*, and Karl Rahner *(Theological Investigations)*.

Notes to Chapter 1

1. See, for example, Douglas Hedley, *Living Forms of the Imagination* (London: T. & T. Clark, 2008); Garrett Green, *Theology, Hermeneutics, and Imagination: The Crisis of Interpretation at the End of Modernity* (Cambridge: Cambridge University Press, 2000); John Llewelyn, *The Hypocritical Imagination: Between Kant and Levinas* (London: Routledge, 2000); J. M. Cocking, *Imagination: A Study in the History of Ideas*, ed. Penelope Murray (London: Routledge, 1991); Garrett Green, *Imagining God: Theology and the Religious Imagination* (Grand Rapids: Eerdmans, 1989); Richard Kearney, *The Wake of Imagination: Toward a Postmodern Culture* (Minneapolis: University of Minnesota Press, 1988); James P. Mackey, ed., *Religious Imagination* (Edinburgh: Edinburgh University Press, 1986); Murray Wright Bundy, *The Theory of Imagination in Classical and Medieval Thought*, University of Illinois Studies in Language and Literature 12 (Urbana: University of Illinois Press, 1927).

2. See Kearney, *The Wake of Imagination*, pp. 79-118; Green, *Imagining God*, pp. 9-27;

Green, *Theology, Hermeneutics, and Imagination,* pp. 1-107; Mary Warnock, *Imagination* (Berkeley: University of California Press, 1976), pp. 13-71.

3. Bundy, *The Theory of Imagination,* p. 58.

4. Cf. Bundy, *The Theory of Imagination,* pp. 30-31.

5. Cf. J. P. Vernant, "Image et apparence dans la théorie Platonicienne de la mimesis," *JP* 2 (April-June 1975): 133-60.

6. See *Republic* 6.509d-513e and 7.514a-520a.

7. *Republic* 7.532c. Cf. Kearney, *The Wake of Imagination,* p. 91.

8. On the Platonic legacy, see Hedley, *Living Forms,* pp. 9-37.

9. Cf. Gerard Watson, "Imagination and Religion in Classical Thought," in *Religious Imagination,* pp. 29-54; Kearney, *The Wake of Imagination,* pp. 99-105; Bundy, *The Theory of Imagination,* pp. 48-54.

10. Kearney, *The Wake of Imagination,* p. 99.

11. Cf. Watson, "Imagination and Religion," p. 31.

12. Cf. Watson, "Imagination and Religion," pp. 35-44; Kearney, *The Wake of Imagination,* pp. 106-13; Bundy, *The Theory of Imagination,* pp. 60-92, 117-34.

13. See Kearney, *The Wake of Imagination,* pp. 37-78.

14. See Walter Brueggemann, "Imagination as a Mode of Fidelity," in *Understanding the Word: Essays in Honor of Bernard W. Anderson,* JSOTSup 37 (Sheffield: JSOT, 1985), pp. 13-36; Kearney, *The Wake of Imagination,* pp. 39-49.

15. Brueggemann, "Imagination," p. 27, italics in original.

16. Tertullian, *On the Soul* 17.5, in *The Fathers of the Church, Tertullian, Apologetical Works,* trans. R. Arbesmann (Washington, DC: University of America Press, 1950), p. 215.

17. Irenaeus, *Against Heresies* 4.20.6, in *Ante-Nicene Fathers,* 1:489.

18. Irenaeus, *Against Heresies* 4.20.6, in *Ante-Nicene Fathers,* 1:489.

19. See Hilary of Poitiers, *The Trinity* 2.49; Pseudo-Clementine, *Recognitions* 2.65.

20. See Basil of Caesarea, *Homily 14, On Psalm 29* 5; Gregory of Nyssa, *On Virginity* 1.

21. See Augustine, *Confessions* 10.27.38.

22. See Augustine, *Letter to Paulina (The Book of the Vision of God)* 47-48, in *The Fathers of the Church, Saint Augustine, Letters,* vol. 3, trans. Wilfrid Parsons (Washington, DC: Catholic University of America Press, 1953), p. 216.

23. See Augustine, *On the Trinity* 11.2.

24. Bundy, *The Theory of Imagination,* p. 162.

25. See Augustine, *Commentary on Genesis* 12.11-24; cf. Bundy, *The Theory of Imagination,* p. 169.

26. Augustine, *Commentary on Genesis* 12.23-24.

27. Augustine, *Commentary on Genesis* 12.9, 20.

28. Cf. Bundy, *The Theory of Imagination,* p. 173. See, for example, Boethius, *The Consolation of Philosophy* 5.4.

29. Cf. Kearney, *The Wake of Imagination,* p. 120.

30. Kearney, *The Wake of Imagination,* p. 131.

31. Cf. Jacques Le Goff, *The Medieval Imagination,* trans. Arthur Goldhammer (Chicago: University of Chicago Press, 1988), pp. 181-231.

32. Cf. Bundy, *The Theory of Imagination,* pp. 202-3.

33. See Richard of St. Victor, *The Mystical Ark* 6, in *The Twelve Patriarchs, The Mystical*

Ark, Book Three of the Trinity, trans. and ed. Grover A. Zinn (New York: Paulist, 1979), pp. 161-64.

34. See Richard of St. Victor, *Selected Writings on Contemplation,* trans. Clare Kirchberger (London: Faber and Faber, 1957), pp. 82-85, 93-94. Cf. Kearney, *The Wake of Imagination,* p. 121.

35. Bonaventure, *The Soul's Journey to God,* trans. and ed. Ewert Cousins (New York: Paulist, 1978), pp. 75-78.

36. *STh* Ia, q. 5. Cf. Kearney, *The Wake of Imagination,* pp. 119-32; Bundy, *The Theory of Imagination,* pp. 199-224.

37. *STh* Ia, 2, q. 27; 2a 2ae, q. 145.

38. Cf. Patrick Grant, "Imagination in the Renaissance," in *Religious Imagination,* pp. 86-101.

39. See, for example, Jane Kneller, *Kant and the Power of Imagination* (New York: Cambridge University Press, 2007); Gary Banham, *Kant's Transcendental Imagination* (New York: Macmillan, 2006); Sarah L. Gibbons, *Kant's Theory of Imagination: Bridging Gaps in Judgment and Experience* (New York: Oxford University Press, 1994); Martin Heidegger, *Kant and the Problem of Metaphysics,* trans. James S. Churchill (Bloomington: Indiana University Press, 1962), pp. 144-208.

40. See Kant, *Critique of Pure Reason,* A11 and A118; cf. Warnock, *Imagination,* pp. 26-30; Kearney, *The Wake of Imagination,* pp. 167-71.

41. F. W. J. Schelling, *System of Transcendental Idealism* (1800), trans. Peter Heath (Charlottesville: University Press of Virginia, 1978), p. 12.

42. Johann Gottlieb Fichte, *Fichtes Werke,* vol. 1, *Zur theoretischen Philosophie I,* ed. Immanuel Hermann Fichte (Berlin: De Gruyter, 1971), p. 284, translation mine.

43. Cf. John Sallis, *Spacings of Reason and Imagination in Texts of Kant, Fichte, Hegel* (Chicago: University of Chicago Press, 1987), pp. 132-57.

44. See *Critique of Pure Reason,* B153-54. Cf. Kearney, *The Wake of Imagination,* p. 168; Bernard Freydberg, *Imagination in Kant's Critique of Practical Reason* (Bloomington: Indiana University Press, 2005), p. 12.

45. Cf. Banham, *Kant's Transcendental Imagination,* pp. 143-44.

46. Kant, *Critique of Pure Reason,* B154.

47. Cf. Warnock, *Imagination,* pp. 56-59; Kearney, *The Wake of Imagination,* pp. 174-77; Gibbons, *Kant's Theory of Imagination,* pp. 124-51.

48. Kant, *Critique of Judgment,* §28. Cf. Gibbons, *Kant's Theory of Imagination,* pp. 152-92.

49. Kant, *Critique of Judgment,* §59. See the discussion in Freydberg, *Imagination in Kant's Critique,* pp. 141-46.

50. Cf. Kneller, *Kant,* pp. 104-13.

51. Philip J. Rossi, *The Social Authority of Reason: Kant's Critique, Radical Evil, and the Destiny of Human Kind* (New York: SUNY Press, 2005), p. 161.

52. Paul Ricoeur, *Freud and Philosophy: An Essay on Interpretation* (New Haven: Yale University Press, 1970); Paul Ricoeur, "The Critique of Religion," *USQR* 28 (1973): 205-12.

53. Cf. Wolfgang Vondey, "Introduction to the New Edition," in Ludwig Feuerbach, *The Essence of Christianity,* Library of Essential Reading Series (New York: Barnes and Noble, 2004), pp. ix-xvi.

54. Vondey, "Introduction," pp. xii-xiv.

55. Friedrich Heinrich Jacobi, "David Hume on Faith or Idealism and Realism: A Dialogue," in *The Main Philosophical Writings and the Novel Allwill: Friedrich Heinrich Jacobi,* trans. and ed. George di Giovanni (Montreal and Kingston: McGill-Queen's, 1994), p. 583.

56. See Nietzsche, *The Antichrist,* A 5-7. Cf. Green, *Theology, Hermeneutics, and Imagination,* pp. 122-25.

57. Kearney, *The Wake of Imagination,* pp. 196-217.

58. See Heidegger, *Kant,* pp. 201-8; cf. Kearney, *The Wake of Imagination,* pp. 222-24.

59. Heidegger, *Kant,* p. 171.

60. Heidegger, *Kant,* p. 173.

61. Heidegger, *Kant,* pp. 181-208, 233-38.

62. Jean-Paul Sartre, *The Psychology of Imagination* (Secaucus, NJ: Citadel, 1972), pp. 12-27. Cf. Kearney, *The Wake of Imagination,* pp. 224-29.

63. Kearney, *The Wake of Imagination,* pp. 237-38.

64. Kearney, *The Wake of Imagination,* p. 251.

65. Cf. Kearney, *The Wake of Imagination,* p. 253.

66. See Ferdinand de Saussure, *Course in General Linguistics,* trans. Wade Baskin (New York: Philosophical Library, 1959), p. 80. Cf. Wolfgang Vondey, "The Symbolic Turn: A Symbolic Conception of the Liturgy of Pentecostalism," *WTJ* 36, no. 2 (2001): 223-47.

67. De Saussure, *Course in General Linguistics,* pp. 159-60.

68. See Jean Baudrillard, *Symbolic Exchange and Death,* trans. Iain Hamilton Grant (London: Sage, 1993), p. 7.

69. Cf. Kearney, *The Wake of Imagination,* pp. 256-95.

70. Jean-François Lyotard, *The Postmodern Condition: A Report on Knowledge,* trans. Geoff Bennington and Brian Massumi (Minneapolis: University of Minnesota Press, 1984), p. xxiv.

71. Cf. James K. A. Smith, *Who Is Afraid of Postmodernism? Taking Derrida, Lyotard, and Foucault to Church* (Grand Rapids: Eerdmans, 2006), p. 65.

72. Cf. Brueggemann, "Imagination," pp. 15-31; Walter Brueggemann, *An Introduction to the Old Testament: The Canon and Christian Imagination* (Louisville: Westminster/John Knox, 2003), pp. 1-13.

73. Cf. Smith, *Who Is Afraid?* pp. 59-79; Paul Ricoeur, *Figuring the Sacred: Religion, Narrative, and Imagination* (Minneapolis: Fortress, 1995), pp. 236-48; John McIntyre, *Faith, Theology, and Imagination* (Edinburgh: Handsel, 1987), pp. 127-57.

74. See Kwok Pui-lan, *Postcolonial Imagination and Feminist Theology* (Louisville: Westminster/John Knox, 2005), pp. 29-51.

75. On the significance of stories and imagination, see Hedley, *Living Forms,* pp. 173-244.

76. See Douglas Jacobsen, *Thinking in the Spirit: Theologies of the Early Pentecostal Movement* (Bloomington: Indiana University Press, 2003), p. 8.

77. Cf. Cecil M. Robeck, Jr., *The Azusa Street Mission and Revival: The Birth of the Global Pentecostal Movement* (Nashville: Nelson, 2006); Donald W. Dayton, *Theological Roots of Pentecostalism* (Peabody, MA: Hendrickson, 1987, 1994); Melvin E. Dieter, *The Holiness Revival of the Nineteenth Century* (Metuchen, NJ: Scarecrow, 1980).

78. See Jacobsen, *Thinking in the Spirit,* pp. 16-17; Robeck, *Azusa Street Mission,* pp. 17-128.

79. See Horace S. Ward, "The Anti-Pentecostal Argument," in *Aspects of Pentecostal-Charismatic Origins,* ed. Vinson Synon (Plainfield, NJ: Logos International, 1975), pp. 99-122.

80. Cf. Melvin E. Dieter, "The Wesleyan/Holiness and Pentecostal Movements: Commonalities, Confrontation, and Dialogue," *Pneuma* 12, no. 1 (1990): 4-13; Randall J. Stephens, *The Fire Spreads: Holiness and Pentecostalism in the American South* (Cambridge, MA: Harvard University Press, 2008), pp. 56-135.

81. Cf. Vinson Synan, *The Holiness-Pentecostal Tradition: Charismatic Movements in the Twentieth Century* (Grand Rapids: Eerdmans, 1997), pp. 143-66; D. William Faupel, *The Everlasting Gospel: The Significance of Eschatology in the Development of Pentecostal Thought,* JPTS 10 (Sheffield: Sheffield Academic, 1996), pp. 54-69.

82. See Morton T. Kelsey, *Tongue Speaking* (Garden City, NY: Waymark Books, 1968), p. 72; David A. Womack, *The Wellsprings of the Pentecostal Movement* (Springfield, MO: Gospel Publishing House, 1968), pp. 82-83.

83. Cf. Joseph Randall Guthrie, "Pentecostal Hymnody: Historical, Theological, and Musical Influences" (D.MA. diss., Southwestern Baptist Theological Seminary, 1992), pp. 29-88.

84. C. E. Jones, "Holiness Movement," in *NIDPCM,* p. 728.

85. Joseph Campbell, *The Pentecostal Holiness Church* (Franklin Springs, GA: Publishing House of the Pentecostal Holiness Church, 1951), p. 235.

86. F. M. Graham, "We Will Sing and Preach Holiness," in *Songs of Pentecostal Power,* ed. R. E. Winsett (Dayton, TN: R. E. Winsett, 1908), p. 213.

87. Cf. Dayton, *Theological Roots of Pentecostalism,* pp. 65-73; Guthrie, "Pentecostal Hymnody," pp. 30-47.

88. See Faupel, *The Everlasting Gospel,* pp. 77-306. For the idea of a "Pentecostal story," see Kenneth J. Archer, *A Pentecostal Hermeneutic for the Twenty-first Century: Spirit, Scripture, and Community,* JPTS 28 (London: T. & T. Clark, 2004); Kenneth J. Archer, "Pentecostal Story: The Hermeneutical Filter for the Making of Meaning," *Pneuma* 26, no. 1 (2004): 36-59. Archer interprets the story exclusively from the eschatological perspective of the "Latter Rain" motif.

89. L. E. Jones, "Rally Round the Standard," in *Pentecostal Hymns,* vol. 1, ed. Henry Date et al. (Chicago: Hope Publishing Co., 1894), p. 398.

90. Susan A. Duncan, "What Is It?" *WW* (August 1910): 239.

91. Cf. Steven J. Land, *Pentecostal Spirituality: A Passion for the Kingdom,* JPTS 1 (Sheffield: Sheffield Academic, 1993), 58-121; Faupel, *The Everlasting Gospel,* pp. 264-70.

92. Sam C. Perry, "An Ideal Church," *COGE* 9, no. 14 (April 6, 1918): 4.

93. See "The Great Crisis Near at Hand," *ELCGE* 1, no. 15 (October 1, 1910): 1; A. J. Tomlinson, *The Last Great Conflict* (Cleveland, TN: Walter E. Rogers, 1913), p. 172.

94. See D. William Faupel, "The Function of Models in the Interpretation of Pentecostal Thought," *Pneuma* 2, no. 1 (1980): 51-71; Faupel, *The Everlasting Gospel,* pp. 27-41.

95. See Simon Chan, *Pentecostal Theology and the Christian Spiritual Tradition,* JPTS 21 (Sheffield: Sheffield Academic, 2000), pp. 23-24; Archer, *A Pentecostal Hermeneutic,* pp. 117-18; Deborah McCauley, *Appalachian Mountain Religion: A History* (Urbana: University of Illinois Press, 1995), pp. 45-142.

96. Cf. Jacobsen, *Thinking in the Spirit,* p. 17; Land, *Pentecostal Spirituality,* pp. 47-48.

97. Maria Beulah Woodworth-Etter, "Sermon on Visions and Trances," in *A Reader in*

Pentecostal Theology: Voices from the First Generation, ed. Douglas Jacobsen (Bloomington: Indiana University Press, 2006), p. 26.

98. Cf. Jerry Horner, "The Credibility and the Eschatology of Peter's Speech at Pentecost," *Pneuma* 1, no. 3 (1980): 22-31.

99. Land, *Pentecostal Spirituality,* p. 72.

100. Land, *Pentecostal Spirituality,* p. 174.

101. I resist here the distinction between glossolalia and xenolalia, since these are conceptual terms foreign to the Pentecostal imagination and insignificant for an integration of the imaginative function of tongues in the broader network of theological meaning.

102. Land, *Pentecostal Spirituality,* p. 134.

103. Land, *Pentecostal Spirituality,* p. 136.

104. Land, *Pentecostal Spirituality,* p. 139.

105. See Robeck, *Azusa Street Mission,* pp. 235-80; Allan H. Anderson, "Spreading Fires: The Globalization of Pentecostalism in the Twentieth Century," *IBMR* 31, no. 1 (2007): 8-12, 14; Gary B. McGee, "'The New World of Realities in Which We Live': How Speaking in Tongues Empowered Early Pentecostals," *Pneuma* 30, no. 1 (2008): 108-35.

106. See, for example, William K. Kay and Anne E. Dyer, *Pentecostal and Charismatic Studies: A Reader* (London: SCM, 2004), pp. 83-117.

107. See Vondey, "The Symbolic Turn," pp. 223-47.

108. See Frank D. Macchia, "Sighs Too Deep for Words: Towards a Theology of Glossolalia," *JPT* 1 (1992): 47-73.

109. See J. R. Williams, "Baptism in the Holy Spirit," in *NIDPCM,* pp. 354-63.

110. H. L. Gilmour, "Like a Mighty Sea," in *Evangel Songs* (Springfield, MO: Gospel Publishing House, 1931), pp. 14-15.

111. See Kay and Dyer, *Pentecostal and Charismatic Studies,* pp. 83-123.

112. Cf. Vinson Synan, *In the Latter Days: The Outpouring of the Holy Spirit in the Twentieth Century* (Ann Arbor: Servant, 1984), pp. 75-78.

113. Cf. Frank Macchia, "Tongues as a Sign: Towards a Sacramental Understanding of Pentecostal Experience," *Pneuma* 15, no. 1 (1993): 61-76.

114. See Steve Durasoff, *Bright Wind of the Spirit: Pentecostalism Today* (Englewood Cliffs, NJ: Prentice-Hall, 1972), p. 4.

115. See *STh* III. A.9, ad 1; Augustine, *In Johannis Evangelium Tractatus* 6.1.7; *Sacrosanctum Concilium* 7.

116. See Macchia, "Tongues as a Sign," pp. 61-76.

117. See Amos Yong, "'Tongues of Fire' in the Pentecostal Imagination: The Truth of Glossolalia in Light of R. C. Neville's Theory of Religious Symbolism," *JPT* 12 (1998): 39-65; Amos Yong, "The Truth of Tongues Speech: A Rejoinder to Frank Macchia," *JPT* 13 (1998): 107-15; Frank Macchia, "Discerning the Truth of Tongues Speech: A Response to Amos Yong," *JPT* 12 (1998): 67-71.

118. John Thomas Nichol, *Pentecostalism* (New York: Harper and Row, 1966), p. 70.

119. Cf. Ward, "The Anti-Pentecostal Argument," pp. 99-122.

120. See Jean-Daniel Plüss, "Azusa and Other Myths: The Long and Winding Road from Experience to Stated Belief and Back Again," *Pneuma* 15, no. 2 (1993): 189-201; Timothy B. Cargal, "Beyond the Fundamentalist-Modernist Controversy: Pentecostals and Hermeneutics in a Postmodern Age," *Pneuma* 15, no. 2 (1993): 163-88.

121. Cargal, "Fundamentalist-Modernist Controversy," p. 168.

122. See Vondey, "Christian Amnesia: Who in the World Are Pentecostals?" *AJPS* 4, no. 1 (2001): 21-39.

123. See Vondey, "Christian Amnesia," p. 33.

124. Cf. Steven M. Studebaker, "Pentecostal Soteriology and Pneumatology," *JPT* 11, no. 2 (2003): 248-70; D. Lyle Dabney, "Saul's Armor: The Problem and the Promise of Pentecostal Theology Today," *Pneuma* 23, no. 1 (2001): 115-46.

125. Besides the works cited above, see Henry Duméry, *Imagination et religion: Éléments de judaïsme, éléments de christianisme* (Paris: Belles lettres, 2006); Paul Avis, *God and the Creative Imagination: Metaphor, Symbol, and Myth in Religion and Theology* (London: Routledge, 1999); Gillian Robinson and John Rundell, eds., *Rethinking Imagination: Culture and Creativity* (London: Routledge, 1994); David Bryant, *Faith and the Play of the Imagination: On the Role of the Imagination in Religion,* Studies in American Biblical Hermeneutics 5 (Macon, GA: Mercer University Press, 1989); Gordon Kaufman, *The Theological Imagination: Constructing the Concept of God* (Philadelphia: Westminster, 1981); Julian Hartt, *Theological Method and Imagination* (New York: Seabury Press, 1977); Edward S. Casey, *Imagining: A Phenomenological Study* (Bloomington: Indiana University Press, 1976).

126. Considered among the original proposals of narrative theology are generally Hans Frei, *The Eclipse of Biblical Narrative: A Study in Eighteenth and Nineteenth Century Hermeneutics* (New Haven: Yale University Press, 1974); George Lindbeck, *The Nature of Doctrine: Religion and Theology in a Postliberal Age* (Philadelphia: Fortress, 1984); Ronald F. Thiemann, *Revelation and Theology: The Gospel as Narrated Promise* (Notre Dame, IN: University of Notre Dame Press, 1985); Stanley Hauerwas and L. Gregory Jones, eds., *Why Narrative? Readings in Narrative Theology* (Grand Rapids: Eerdmans, 1989).

127. Hans W. Frei, *Theology and Narrative: Selected Essays,* ed. George Hunsinger and William C. Placher (New York: Oxford University Press, 1993), p. 112.

128. Lindbeck, *The Nature of Doctrine,* p. 120.

129. Lindbeck, *The Nature of Doctrine,* pp. 32-41; George Lindbeck, "The Story-Shaped Church: Critical Exegesis and Theological Interpretation," in *Scriptural Authority and Narrative Intepretation,* ed. Garrett Green (Philadelphia: Fortress, 1987), pp. 161-78.

130. Lindbeck, *The Nature of Doctrine,* pp. 40-41.

131. Cf. Reinhard Hütter, *Suffering Divine Things: Theology as Church Practice* (Grand Rapids: Eerdmans, 2000), p. 26.

132. Kevin J. Vanhoozer, *The Drama of Doctrine: A Canonical-Linguistic Approach to Christian Theology* (Louisville: Westminster/John Knox, 2005), p. 16. Parenthetical page references to this work have been placed in the text.

133. See especially Samuel Wells, *Improvisation: The Drama of Christian Ethics* (Grand Rapids: Brazos, 2004); Samuel Wells, "Improvisation in the Theatre as a Model for Christian Ethics," in *Faithful Performances: Enacting the Christian Tradition,* ed. Trevor A. Hart and Steven R. Guthrie (Aldershot: Ashgate, 2007), pp. 147-65.

134. Vanhoozer defines discernment as a cognitive virtue rather than a spiritual discipline. See Vanhoozer, *The Drama of Doctrine,* pp. 332-35.

135. Vanhoozer, *The Drama of Doctrine,* pp. 336-40.

136. Vanhoozer, *The Drama of Doctrine,* pp. 340-41. See also Michael Horton, *Covenant and Eschatology: The Divine Drama* (Louisville: Westminster/John Knox, 2002).

137. Vanhoozer, *The Drama of Doctrine,* p. 341.

138. Vanhoozer, *The Drama of Doctrine,* p. 344, italics in original.

139. See Casey, *Imagining,* p. 19.

140. Casey, *Imagining,* p. 53. Casey himself also sees this margin within the cognitive realm.

141. Cf. David Smilde, "Skirting the Instrumental Paradox: Intentional Belief through Narrative in Latin American Pentecostalism," *QS* 26, no. 3 (2003): 313-29.

142. See the definition of "Pentecostal believers" in Ludwig David Eisenlöffel, *Freikirchliche Pfingstbewegung in Deutschland: Innenansichten 1945-1985,* Kirche — Konfession — Religion 50 (Göttingen: V. & R. Unipress, 2006), p. 27.

143. See Vanhoozer, *The Drama of Doctrine,* pp. 256-63.

144. The following summary is based on Amos Yong, *Spirit-Word-Community: Theological Hermeneutics in Trinitarian Perspective* (Eugene, OR: Wipf and Stock, 2002), pp. 123-217. Page references have been placed in the text.

145. See Amos Yong, *The Spirit Poured Out on All Flesh: Pentecostalism and the Possibility of Global Theology* (Grand Rapids: Baker Academic, 2005), pp. 254-55. Yong picks up the idea of theology as performance in *Hospitality and the Other: Pentecost, Christian Practices, and the Neighbor* (Maryknoll, NY: Orbis, 2008).

146. The following mark some of the changes: Bradley T. Noel, "Gordon Fee and the Challenge to Pentecostal Hermeneutics: Thirty Years Later," *Pneuma* 26, no. 1 (2004): 60-80; Veli-Matti Kärkkäinen, "Pentecostal Hermeneutics in the Making: On the Way from Fundamentalism to Postmodernism," *JEPTA* 18, no. 1 (1998): 76-115; Kenneth J. Archer, "Pentecostal Hermeneutics: Retrospect and Prospect," *JPT* 8 (1996): 63-81; Murray W. Dempster, "Paradigm Shifts and Hermeneutics: Confronting Old and New," *Pneuma* 15, no. 2 (1993): 129-36; Roger Stronstad, "Trends in Pentecostal Hermeneutics," *Paraclete* 22, no. 3 (1984): 1-12; Gordon D. Fee, "Hermeneutics and Historical Precedent — a Major Problem in Pentecostal Hermeneutics," in *Perspectives on the New Pentecostalism,* ed. Russell Spittler (Grand Rapids: Baker, 1976), pp. 118-32.

147. See Jean-Jacques Suurmond, *Word and Spirit at Play: Towards a Charismatic Theology* (Grand Rapids: Eerdmans, 1994); Jean-Jacques Suurmond, "The Church at Play: The Pentecostal/Charismatic Renewal of the Liturgy as Renewal of the World," in *Pentecost, Mission, and Ecumenism: Essays on Intercultural Theology; Festschrift in Honour of Professor Walter Hollenweger,* ed. Jan A. B. Jongeneel et al., Studien zur Interkulturellen Geschichte des Christentums 75 (Frankfurt: Peter Lang, 1992), pp. 247-59.

148. See Robert K. Johnston, *The Christian at Play* (Grand Rapids: Eerdmans, 1983); James V. Schall, *Far Too Easily Pleased: A Theology of Play, Contemplation, and Festivity* (Beverly Hills, CA: Benziger, 1976); Jürgen Moltmann, *Theology of Play,* trans. Reinhard Ulrich (New York: Harper and Row, 1972); David L. Miller, *Gods and Games: Toward a Theology of Play* (New York: World, 1970).

149. Suurmond, "The Church at Play," p. 249. His thought is based on Johan Huizinga, *Homo Ludens: A Study of Play-Elements in Culture* (London: Routledge and Kegan Paul, 1949).

150. Suurmond, "The Church at Play," p. 250.

151. Suurmond, "The Church at Play," pp. 248-50. See also Arthur E. Paris, *Black Pentecostalism: Southern Religion in an Urban World* (Amherst: University of Massachusetts Press, 1982), pp. 45-79.

152. Suurmond, *Word and Spirit,* pp. 75-83.

153. Suurmond, *Word and Spirit,* p. 76.

154. Brueggemann, *Texts under Negotiation: The Bible and Postmodern Imagination* (Minneapolis: Fortress, 1993), p. 15.

155. Cf. Richard Kearney, "Ethics and the Postmodern Imagination," *Thought* 622 (March 1987): 39-58.

156. See Suurmond, "The Church at Play," p. 251; Richard B. Hays, *The Conversion of the Imagination: Paul as Interpreter of Israel's Scripture* (Grand Rapids: Eerdmans, 2005); Terence L. Donaldson, *Paul and the Gentiles: Remapping the Apostle's Convictional World* (Minneapolis: Fortress, 1997).

157. Moltmann, *Theology of Play*, p. 12.

158. Hans-Georg Gadamer, *Truth and Method*, trans. Garrett Barden and John Cumming (New York: Seabury Press, 1975), pp. 91-119. See also Bryant, *Faith and the Play*, pp. 105-18.

159. Gadamer, *Truth and Method*, p. 94.

160. Harvey Cox, *The Feast of Fools: A Theological Essay on Festivity and Fantasy* (New York: Harper and Row, 1969).

161. Cox, *The Feast of Fools*, pp. 131-38.

162. Cf. Robert E. Neale, *In Praise of Play: Toward a Psychology of Religion* (New York: Harper and Row, 1969), p. 90.

163. See Lionel Abel, *Tragedy and Metatheatre: Essays on Dramatic Form* (New York: Holmes and Meier, 2003); Lionel Abel, *Metatheatre: A New View of Dramatic Form* (New York: Hill and Wang, 1963).

164. Cf. Darrell J. Fasching, *Narrative Theology after Auschwitz: From Alienation to Ethics* (Minneapolis: Fortress, 1992), pp. 17-47.

165. Cf. Martijn Oosterbaan, "Mass Mediating the Spiritual Battle: Pentecostal Appropriations of Mass Mediated Violence in Rio de Janeiro," *Material Religion* 1, no. 3 (2005): 358-85.

166. See Michael Horton, *A Better Way: Rediscovering the Drama of God-Centered Worship* (Grand Rapids: Baker, 2002), pp. 125-241; Horton, *Covenant and Eschatology*, pp. 99-120, 265-76.

167. Wolfhart Pannenberg, *Anthropology in Theological Perspective*, trans. Matthew J. O'Connell (Philadelphia: Westminster, 1985), pp. 322-39.

168. Suurmond, *Word and Spirit*, p. 85.

169. See Todd S. Jenkins, *Free Jazz and Free Improvisation: An Encyclopedia*, vol. 1 (Westport, CT: Greenwood, 2004), pp. xxvii-lxviii. This aspect distinguishes my proposal from similar analogies, such as Vern S. Poythress, *Symphonic Theology: The Validity of Multiple Perspectives in Theology* (Phillipsburg, NJ: P. & R. Publishing, 2001).

170. Wells, *Improvisation*, p. 12.

171. Stanley Hauerwas, *A Community of Character: Toward a Constructive Christian Social Ethic* (Notre Dame, IN: University of Notre Dame Press, 1981). For a critique of performance, see Ivan Patricio Khovacs, "A Cautionary Note on the Use of Theatre for Theology," in *Faithful Performances*, pp. 33-50.

172. See, for example, Michael Bergunder and Jörg Haustein, eds., *Migration und Identität: Pfingstlich-charismatische Migrationsgemeinden in Deutschland* (Frankfurt: Otto Lembeck, 2006); James Hosack, "The Arrival of Pentecostals and Charismatics in Thailand," *AJPS* 4, no. 1 (2001): 109-17; Hong Young-gi, "The Background and Characteristics of the Charismatic Mega-Churches in Korea," *AJPS* 3, no. 1 (2000): 99-118; Michael Wilkinson,

"The Globalization of Pentecostalism: The Role of Asian Immigrant Pentecostals in Canada," *AJPS* 3, no. 2 (2000): 219-26.

173. See Matthias Wenk, *Community Forming Power: The Socio-Ethical Role of the Spirit in Luke-Acts*, JPTS 19 (Sheffield: Sheffield Academic, 2000).

174. See particularly Heribert Mühlen, *Im-Wir-Sein: Grundlegung der Wir-Wissenschaft. Beitrag zu einer wirgemäßen Lebens- und Weltordnung*, ed. Wilhelm Maas (Paderborn: Schöningh, 2008).

175. Land, *Pentecostal Spirituality*, pp. 41-46, 119-21.

176. See Land, *Pentecostal Spirituality*, pp. 41-46; Samuel Solivan, *The Spirit, Pathos, and Liberation: Toward an Hispanic Pentecostal Theology*, JPTS 14 (Sheffield: Sheffield Academic, 1998).

177. Solivan, *Spirit, Pathos, and Liberation*, pp. 60-69.

178. Ralph Del Colle, "Aesthetics and Pathos in the Vision of God: A Catholic-Pentecostal Encounter," *Pneuma* 26, no. 1 (2004): 107-10.

179. Del Colle, "Aesthetics and Pathos," p. 110.

180. See Stephen E. Parker, *Led by the Spirit: Toward a Practical Theology of Pentecostal Discernment and Decision Making*, JPTS 7 (Sheffield: Sheffield Academic, 1996), pp. 20-38, 117-44; David R. Nichols, "The Search for a Pentecostal Structure in Systematic Theology," *Pneuma* 6, no. 2 (1984): 57-76; Cecil M. Robeck, Jr., "Written Prophecies: A Question of Authority," *Pneuma* 2, no. 2 (1980): 26-45; Yong, *Spirit-Word-Community*, p. 142.

181. See the embodiment of aesthetics in Latin American Pentecostalism; Bernice Martin, "The Aesthetics of Latin American Pentecostalism: The Sociology of Religion and the Problem of Taste," in *Materializing Religion: Expression, Performance, and Ritual*, ed. Elizabeth Arweck and William Keenan (Aldershot: Ashgate, 2006), pp. 138-60.

Notes to Chapter 2

1. See, for example, Terry L. Johnson, *The Case for Traditional Protestantism: The Solas of the Reformation* (Edinburgh: Banner of Truth Trust, 2004); Clark H. Pinnock and Barry Callen, *The Scripture Principle: Reclaiming the Authority of the Bible*, 2nd ed. (Grand Rapids: Baker Academic, 2003); Keith A. Mathison, *The Shape of Sola Scriptura* (Moscow, ID: Canon, 2001); Don Kistler, ed., *Sola Scriptura! The Protestant Position on the Bible* (Morgan, PA: Soli Deo Gloria Publications, 2000); Hans Heinrich Schmid and Joachim Mehlhausen, eds., *Sola Scriptura: Das reformatorische Schriftprinzip in der säkularen Welt* (Gütersloh: Gerd Mohn, 1991); Paul P. Kuenning, "*Sola Scriptura* and the Ecumenical Endeavor," *Dialog* 29, no. 3 (1990): 202-6.

2. See Don Thorsen, "*Sola Scriptura* and the Wesleyan Quadrilateral," *WTJ* 41, no. 2 (2006): 7-27; Craig D. Allert, "What Are We Trying to Conserve? Evangelicalism and *Sola Scriptura*," *EQ* 76, no. 4 (2004): 327-48; Burkhard Neumann, "Sola Scriptura: Das reformatorische Schriftprinzip und seine Anfrage an die katholische Theologie," *Catholica* 52, no. 4 (1998): 277-96; Robert A. Sungenis, *Not by Scripture Alone: A Catholic Critique of the Protestant Doctrine of Sola Scriptura* (Santa Barbara, CA: Queenship Publications, 1997); Randall H. Balmer, "*Sola Scriptura:* The Protestant Reformation and the Eastern Orthodox Church," *TJ* 3 (1982): 51-56.

3. See Avery Dulles, *Models of Revelation* (Garden City, NY: Doubleday, 1983); Hans Urs

von Balthasar, *The Glory of the Lord: A Theological Aesthetics,* vol. 1, *Seeing the Form,* trans. E. Leiva-Merikakis, ed. Jospeh Fessio and John Riches (San Francisco: Ignatius, 1982); Yves Congar, *The Revelation of God,* trans. A. Manson and L. C. Sheppard (New York: Herder and Herder, 1968); Edward Schillebeeckx, *Revelation and Theology* (New York: Sheed and Ward, 1967); Karl Rahner and Joseph Ratzinger, *Revelation and Tradition,* trans. W. J. O'Hara (New York: Herder and Herder, 1966); John Baillie, *The Idea of Revelation in Recent Thought* (New York: Columbia University Press, 1956); H. Richard Niebuhr, *The Meaning of Revelation* (New York: Macmillan, 1941).

4. See Pinnock and Callen, *The Scripture Principle,* pp. 15-24; Ulrich Luz, "Was heißt 'Sola Scriptura' heute? Ein Hilferuf für das protestantische Schriftprinzip," *EvT* 57, no. 1 (1997): 28-35; Colin E. Gunton, *A Brief Theology of Revelation: The 1993 Warfield Lectures* (Edinburgh: T. & T. Clark, 1995), pp. 1-19, 64-82; Carl E. Braaten, "Can We Still Hold the Principle of *Sola Scriptura?*" *Dialog* 20, no. 3 (1981): 189-94; Ted Peters, "*Sola Scriptura* and the Second Naivete," *Dialog* 16, no. 4 (1977): 268-80; Wolfhart Pannenberg, "The Crisis of the Scripture Principle," in *Basic Questions in Theology: Collected Essays,* vol. 1, trans. George H. Kehm (Philadelphia: Westminster, 1970), pp. 1-14; Gerhard Ebeling, *The Word of God and Tradition: Historical Studies Interpreting the Divisions of Christianity,* trans. S. H. Hooke (Philadelphia: Fortress, 1968), pp. 102-47.

5. To this may be added the relationship of Old and New Testament and the composition and compilation of the biblical canon. See Carl Heinz Ratschow, ed., *Sola Scriptura? Ringvorlesung der theologischen Fakultät der Philipps-Universität* (Marburg: N. G. Elwert, 1977), pp. 1-21.

6. See Yves M.-J. Congar, *Tradition and Traditions: An Historical and a Theological Essay,* trans. Michael Naseby (New York: Macmillan, 1960), pp. 107-18, 138-55; Heinrich Lennertz, "Scriptura sola?" *Gregorianum* 40, no. 1 (1959): 38-53; Friedrich Kropatscheck, *Das Schriftprinzip der lutherischen Kirche: Geschichtliche und dogmatische Untersuchungen,* vol. 1, *Die Vorgeschichte: Das Erbe des Mittelalters* (Leipzig: Georg Böhme, 1904).

7. See Heiko A. Oberman, *The Dawn of the Reformation: Essays in Late Medieval and Early Reformation Thought* (Edinburgh: T. & T. Clark, 1986), pp. 47-49, 193-94, 270-88; Jaroslav Pelikan, *Obedient Rebels: Catholic Substance and Protestant Principle in Luther's Reformation* (London: SCM, 1964), pp. 20-22; Brian A. Gerrish, "Biblical Authority and the Continental Reformation," *SJT* 10, no. 4 (1957): 337-60.

8. Cf. Oberman, *Dawn of the Reformation,* pp. 47, 194.

9. See H. Østergaard-Nielsen, *Scriptura sacra et viva vox: Eine Lutherstudie* (Munich: Kaiser, 1957); Ragnar Bring, *Luthers Anschauung von der Bibel,* Luthertum 3 (Berlin: Lutherisches Verlagshaus, 1951); Johann Michael Reu, *Luther and the Scriptures* (Columbus, OH: Wartburg, 1944); Heinrich Bornkamm, *Das Wort Gottes bei Luther* (Munich: Kaiser, 1933); Franz Rosenzweig, *Die Schrift und Luther* (Berlin: Lambert Schneider, 1926).

10. Cf. Jaroslav Pelikan, *Luther the Expositor: Introduction to the Reformer's Exegetical Writings* (St. Louis: Concordia, 1959), p. 70.

11. WA 7:98.4.

12. Formula of Concord, Solid Declaration, Rule and Norm 9.

13. See Heiko A. Oberman, *Forerunners of the Reformation: The Shape of Late Medieval Thought* (New York: Holt, Rinehart and Winston, 1966), pp. 53-66; Alister McGrath, *The Intellectual Origins of the European Reformation* (Oxford: Oxford University Press, 1987), pp. 140-51. See also David W. Lotz, "Luther and *Sola Scriptura,*" in *And Every Tongue Confess: Es-*

says in Honor of Norman Nagel on the Occasion of His Sixty-fifth Birthday, ed. Gerlad S. Krispin and Jon D. Vieker (Dearborn, MI: Nagel Festschrift Committee, 1990), pp. 250-63; Lewis W. Spitz, Sr., "Luther's *Sola Scriptura*," *CTM* 31, no. 12 (1960): 740-45.

14. Oberman, *Dawn of the Reformation,* p. 280.

15. WA 7:97.23. Cf. Walter Mostert, "*Scriptura sacra sui ipsius interpres:* Bemerkungen zum Verständnis der Heiligen Schrift durch Luther," *Lutherjahrbuch* 46 (1979): 60-96.

16. Cf. Lotz, "Luther and *Sola Scriptura,*" pp. 257-61; Spitz, "Luther's *Sola Scriptura,*" p. 742; A. Skevington Wood, "Luther's Concept of Revelation," *EQ* 35 (1963): 149-59.

17. See Jerry H. Bentley, *Humanists and Holy Writ: New Testament Scholarship in the Renaissance* (Princeton: Princeton University Press, 1983).

18. WA 7:315.24.

19. Cf. Christian Gremmels, "Der Heilige Geist als Ausleger der Schrift," in Ratschow, *Sola Scriptura,* pp. 153-77; Regin Prenter, *Spiritus Creator: Luther's Concept of the Holy Spirit,* trans. John M. Jensen (Philadelphia: Muhlenberg, 1953), pp. 101-30; Bornkamm, *Das Wort Gottes bei Luther,* pp. 9-18; Bring, *Luthers Anschauung,* pp. 13-19.

20. Wood, "Luther's Concept of Revelation," pp. 156-58; Paul Schempp, *Luthers Stellung zur heiligen Schrift,* Forschungen zur Geschichte und Lehre des Protestantismus 3 (Munich: Kaiser, 1929), pp. 79-83.

21. Cf. G. Gloege, "Schriftprinzip," in *Religion in Geschichte und Gegenwart: Handwörterbuch für Theologie und Religionswissenschaft,* vol. 5, 3rd ed. (Tübingen: J. C. B. Mohr, 1986), pp. 1540-43.

22. WA 10:1.17; 12:259; 18:136. Cf. William A. Graham, *Beyond the Written Word: Oral Aspects of Scripture in the History of Religion* (Cambridge: Cambridge University Press, 1987), pp. 141-54.

23. See the Formula of Concord, Solid Declaration, Rule and Norm 1 and 9.

24. See Lowell C. Green, "Luther on Revelation: Foundation for Proclamation and Worship," *Consensus* 9, no. 2 (1983): 3-11.

25. Pelikan, *Obedient Rebels,* p. 22.

26. Cf. Ebeling, *The Word of God,* p. 117; Bengt Hägglund, *Die Heilige Schrift und ihre Deutung in der Theologie Johann Gerhards: Eine Untersuchung über das altlutherische Schriftverständnis* (Lund: Gleerup, 1951), pp. 136-84.

27. Cf. Stephan H. Pfürtner, "Das Reformatorische 'Sola Scriptura' — Theologischer Auslegungsgrund des Thomas von Aquin," in Ratschow, *Sola Scriptura,* pp. 48-80, here p. 49.

28. Cf. Congar, *Tradition and Traditions,* p. 153.

29. Cf. Wilton Donald Ernst, "The Place of the Scriptures in the Lutheran Churches in America from the End of the First World War to the Middle of the Twentieth Century" (D.STh. diss., Temple University, 1962), pp. 47-88.

30. See Johann Reinhard, *Die Prinzipienlehre der lutherischen Dogmatik von 1700 bis 1750* (Leipzig: Deichert, 1906), pp. 43-49, 88-92.

31. Hägglund, *Die Heilige Schrift,* pp. 144-45.

32. See Hägglund, *Die Heilige Schrift,* pp. 77-81, 105-18.

33. Hägglund, *Die Heilige Schrift,* pp. 105-7. On the shift away from content, see also Pinnock and Callen, *The Scripture Principle,* pp. 45-51; Avery Dulles, *Revelation Theology: A History* (New York: Herder, 1969), chapter 3.

34. See Hägglund, *Die Heilige Schrift,* pp. 9-16; Congar, *Tradition and Traditions,* pp. 154-55.

35. Hägglund, *Die Heilige Schrift*, p. 109.

36. Johann Wilhelm Baier, *Compendium of Positive Theology*, trans. C. F. W. Walther (St. Louis: Concordia, 1877), pp. 1, 25; *Compendium theologiae positivae* was originally published in 1691.

37. Albrecht Ritschl, "Ueber die beiden Principien des Protestantismus: Antwort auf eine 25 Jahre alte Frage," *ZK* 1 (1876): 397-413. Ritschl does not consider Gerhard or Calovius in his account.

38. Johann Philipp Gabler, review of *Summa theologiae Christianae*, by Christoph Friedrich von Ammon, *JATL* 5 (1810): 587-600.

39. Gabler, review of *Summa theologiae Christianae*, pp. 594-96.

40. Gabler, review of *Summa theologiae Christianae*, p. 599.

41. Ritschl, "Ueber die beiden Principien," p. 409. Cf. Gerhard Sauter, "'Scriptural Faithfulness' Is Not a 'Scripture Principle,'" in *Revelation and Story: Narrative Theology and the Centrality of Story*, ed. Gerhard Sauter and John Barton (Aldershot: Ashgate, 2000), pp. 7-28, at p. 8.

42. Ritschl, "Ueber die beiden Principien," pp. 405-11. Cf. Ebeling, *The Word of God*, p. 117.

43. Ritschl, "Ueber die beiden Principien," p. 411.

44. Cf. Carl-Heinz Ratschow, "Einleitende Analyse der Themafrage," in Ratschow, *Sola Scriptura*, p. 4; Paul Gennrich, *Der Kampf um die Schrift in der Deutsch-Evangelischen Kirche des neunzehnten Jahrhunderts* (Berlin: Reuther & Reichard, 1898), pp. 1-9.

45. For a bibliography, see Pannenberg, "The Crisis of the Scripture Principle."

46. Pannenberg, "The Crisis," p. 4.

47. Pannenberg, "The Crisis," p. 7.

48. See Pinnock and Callen, *The Scripture Principle*, pp. 15-19; Braaten, "Can We Still Hold?" pp. 189-94.

49. See Robert Moore-Jumonville, *The Hermeneutics of Historical Distance: Mapping the Terrain of American Biblical Criticism, 1880-1914* (Lanham, MD: University Press of America, 2002), pp. 1-27; Pannenberg, "The Crisis," pp. 7-11; Congar, *Tradition and Traditions*, pp. 153-55.

50. See Eginhard Peter Meiering, "Sola Scriptura und die historische Kritik," in Schmid and Mehlhausen, *Sola Scriptura*, pp. 44-60.

51. Kevin J. Vanhoozer, *The Drama of Doctrine: A Canonical-Linguistic Approach to Christian Theology* (Louisville: Westminster/John Knox, 2005), p. 153.

52. Cf. Ebeling, *The Word of God*, p. 118; Patrick R. Keifert, "An Ecumenical Horizon for 'Canon within a Canon,'" *CurTM* 14, no. 3 (1987): 185-93.

53. Krister Stendahl, "One Canon Is Enough," in *Meanings: The Bible as Document and as Guide* (Philadelphia: Fortress, 1984), pp. 55-68.

54. Pinnock and Callen, *The Scripture Principle*, p. 248.

55. Braaten, "Can We Still Hold?" pp. 192-93.

56. See Pinnock and Callen, *The Scripture Principle*, pp. 20-21; Braaten, "Can We Still Hold?" p. 193.

57. Cf. Pinnock and Callen, *The Scripture Principle*, pp. 46-49; Richard J. Coleman, *Issues of Theological Conflict: Evangelicals and Liberals*, rev. ed. (Grand Rapids: Eerdmans, 1980), chapter 3.

58. Cf. Woodrow W. Whidden, "*Sola Scriptura*, Inerrantist Fundamentalism, and the

Wesleyan Quadrilateral: Is 'No Creed but the Bible' a Workable Solution?" *AUSS* 35, no. 2 (1997): 211-26; Paul M. Bassett, "The Theological Identity of the North American Holiness Movement: Its Understanding of the Nature and Role of the Bible," in *The Variety of American Evangelicalism*, ed. Donald W. Dayton and Robert K. Johnston (Eugene, OR: Wipf and Stock, 1997), pp. 72-108; Nathan O. Hatch, "The Christian Movement and the Demand for a Theology of the People," in *Reckoning with the Past: Historical Essays on American Evangelicalism*, ed. Darryl G. Hart (Grand Rapids: Baker, 1995), pp. 154-79.

59. See Stephen J. Lennox, "Biblical Interpretation in the American Holiness Movement, 1875-1920" (Ph.D. diss., Drew University, 1992), pp. 26-79, 153-83; Mark A. Noll, *Between Faith and Criticism: Evangelicals, Scholarship, and the Bible in America* (San Francisco: Harper and Row, 1986), pp. 11-31; George M. Marsden, "Everyone One's Own Interpreter? The Bible, Science, and Authority in Mid-Nineteenth-Century America," in *The Bible in America: Essays in Cultural History*, ed. Nathan O. Hatch and Mark A. Noll (Oxford: Oxford University Press, 1982), pp. 79-100.

60. Cf. Nathan O. Hatch, *The Democratization of American Christianity* (New Haven: Yale University Press, 1989), pp. 162-89; Hatch, "*Sola Scriptura* and *Novus Ordo Seclorum*," in *The Bible in America*, pp. 59-78.

61. Cf. Mathison, *Shape of Sola Scriptura*, pp. 152-53; Hatch, "*Sola Scriptura* and *Novus Ordo Seclorum*," pp. 62-71.

62. Noll, *Between Faith and Criticism*, p. 11.

63. Cf. Kenneth J. Archer, "Early Pentecostal Biblical Interpretation," *JPT* 18 (2001): 32-70; Scott A. Ellington, "Pentecostalism and the Authority of Scripture," *JPT* 9 (1996): 16-38; Stephen R. Graham, "'Thus Saith the Lord': Biblical Hermeneutics in the Early Pentecostal Movement," *EA* 12 (1996): 122-35; French L. Arrington, "The Use of the Bible by Pentecostals," *Pneuma* 16, no. 1 (1994): 101-7; Cecil M. Robeck, Jr., "Written Prophecies: A Question of Authority," *Pneuma* 2, no. 2 (1980): 26-45.

64. Cf. Walter J. Hollenweger, *The Pentecostals: The Charismatic Movement in the Churches* (Minneapolis: Augsburg, 1972), pp. 291-310.

65. Cf. Archer, "Early Pentecostal Biblical Interpretation," pp. 32-34; Russell P. Spittler, "Are Pentecostals and Charismatics Fundamentalists? A Review of American Uses of These Categories," in *Charismatic Christianity as a Global Culture*, ed. Karla Poewe (Columbia: University of South Carolina Press, 1994), pp. 103-16; Grant Wacker, "Functions of Faith in Primitive Pentecostalism," *HTR* 77 (1984): 353-75.

66. R. M. Evans, "Editor Tribune," *COGE* 1, no. 16 (1910): 3.

67. Cf. Randall J. Stephens, *The Fire Spreads: Holiness and Pentecostalism in the American South* (Cambridge, MA: Harvard University Press, 2008), pp. 149-50; D. William Faupel, *The Everlasting Gospel: The Significance of Eschatology in the Development of Pentecostal Thought*, JPTS 10 (Sheffield: Sheffield Academic, 1996), pp. 44-75.

68. Steven J. Land, *Pentecostal Spirituality: A Passion for the Kingdom*, JPTS 1 (Sheffield: Sheffield Academic, 1993), pp. 71-81.

69. Kenneth J. Archer, "Pentecostal Hermeneutics: Retrospect and Prospect," *JPT* 8 (1996): 63-81, here pp. 65-67; Gerald T. Sheppard, "Pentecostals and the Hermeneutics of Dispensationalism: The Anatomy of an Uneasy Relationship," *Pneuma* 6, no. 2 (1984): 5-34, here p. 22.

70. Cf. Ellington, "Pentecostalism," p. 21.

71. Cf. Keith Warrington, *Pentecostal Theology: A Theology of Encounter* (London:

T. & T. Clark, 2008), pp. 180-84; John Christopher Thomas, *Ministry and Theology: Studies for the Church and Its Leaders* (Cleveland, TN: Pathway, 1996), pp. 13-20.

72. Cf. William K. Kay, "Pentecostals and the Bible," *JEPTA* 24 (2004): 71-83, here p. 74.

73. See, for example, Aimee Semple McPherson, *This Is That: Personal Experiences, Sermons, and Writings of Aimee Semple McPherson* (Los Angeles: Echo Park Evangelistic Association, 1923). Cf. also Mark Stibbe, "This Is That: Some Thoughts concerning Charismatic Hermeneutics," *Anvil* 13, no. 3 (1998): 181-93.

74. See the exposition on revelation as spoken utterance in *Bible Training School: Study by Correspondence; Lesson One* (Cleveland, TN: Bible Training School, 1919), pp. 1-2. Cf. Veli-Matti Kärkkäinen, "Pentecostal Hermeneutics in the Making: On the Way from Fundamentalism to Postmodernism," *JEPTA* 18 (1998): 76-115, here pp. 77-80; Ellington, "Pentecostalism," pp. 26-27.

75. See Rickie D. Moore, "Canon and Charisma in the Book of Deuteronomy," *JPT* 1 (1992): 75-92, and "Deuteronomy and the Fire of God: A Critical Charismatic Interpretation," *JPT* 7 (1995): 11-33.

76. Rickie D. Moore, "A Pentecostal Approach to Scripture," *SV* 8, no. 1 (1987): 4-5, 11, here p. 4.

77. See Dorotha Erby, "The Holy Ghost Our Leader: He Does Not Lead People into Confusion, and Contrary to Scripture," *COGE* 6, no. 18 (1915): 1.

78. See Larry R. McQueen, *Joel and the Spirit: The Cry of a Prophetic Hermeneutic*, JPTS 8 (Sheffield: Sheffield Academic, 1995), pp. 99-106. For a non-Pentecostal example, see Paul Ricoeur, "Toward a Hermeneutic of the Idea of Revelation," *HTR* 70, no. 1-2 (1977): 1-37.

79. Cf. McQueen, *Joel and the Spirit*, pp. 104-6.

80. See Jaroslav Jan Pelikan, *Whose Bible Is It? A History of the Scriptures through the Ages* (New York: Viking, 2005), pp. 7-26; Susan Niditch, *Oral World and Written Word: Ancient Israelite Literature* (Louisville: Westminster/John Knox, 1996), pp. 13-24; Walter J. Ong, *Orality and Literacy: The Technologizing of the Word* (London: Routledge, 1988), pp. 139-55; William A. Graham, *Beyond the Written Word*, pp. 9-66; Lou H. Silberman, *Orality, Aurality, and Biblical Narrative* (Decatur, GA: Scholars, 1987).

81. See Robeck, "Written Prophecies," pp. 26-45.

82. See Jerry Camery-Hoggatt, "The Word of God from Living Voices: Orality and Literacy in the Pentecostal Tradition," *Pneuma* 27, no. 2 (2005): 225-55; Ellington, "Pentecostalism," pp. 20-26; Walter J. Hollenweger, "The Critical Tradition of Pentecostalism," *JPT* 1 (1992): 7-17.

83. Cf. Land, *Pentecostal Spirituality*, pp. 110-13 and 165-73.

84. Cf. Camery-Hoggatt, "The Word of God," p. 231.

85. Kärkkäinen, "Pentecostal Hermeneutics," p. 7; Timothy B. Cargal, "Beyond the Fundamentalist-Modernist Controversy: Pentecostals and Hermeneutics in a Postmodern Age," *Pneuma* 15, no. 2 (1993): 163-87.

86. Cf. George M. Marsden, *Fundamentalism and American Culture*, 2nd ed. (New York: Oxford University Press, 2006), pp. 93-96; Matthew A. Sutton, "'Between the Refrigerator and the Wildfire': Aimee Semple McPherson, Pentecostalism, and the Fundamentalist-Modernist Controversy," *CH* 72, no. 1 (2003): 159-88; Spittler, "Are Pentecostals?" pp. 3-16; C. Norman Kraus, "The Great Evangelical Coalition: Pentecostal and Fundamentalist," in *Evangelicalism and Anabaptism*, ed. C. Norman Kraus (Scottdale, PA: Herald, 1979), pp. 39-61; William W. Menzies, "The Non-Wesleyan Origins of the Pentecostal Movement," in *As-*

pects of Pentecostal-Charismatic Origins, ed. Vinson Synan (Plainfield, NJ: Logos International, 1975), pp. 83-97.

87. See A. C. Dixon and R. A. Torrey, eds., *The Fundamentals: A Testimony to the Truth,* 12 vols. (Chicago: Testimony Publishing, 1910-15). Cf. Kay, "Pentecostals and the Bible," p. 72.

88. Kraus, "The Great Evangelical Coalition," p. 56.

89. See Marsden, *Fundamentalism and American Culture,* pp. 54-57.

90. See Ernest R. Sandeen, *The Roots of Fundamentalism: British and American Millenarianism, 1800-1930* (Grand Rapids: Baker, 1970), pp. 107-12.

91. Cf. Cargal, "Fundamentalist-Modernist Controversy," p. 167.

92. See Vinson Synan, *The Holiness-Pentecostal Tradition: Charismatic Movements in the Twentieth Century* (Grand Rapids: Eerdmans, 1997), pp. 149-52; Faupel, *The Everlasting Gospel,* pp. 270-306; Donald W. Dayton, *Theological Roots of Pentecostalism* (Peabody, MA: Hendrickson, 1987), pp. 48-54, 149-53; John A. Knight, "John Fletcher's Influence on the Development of Wesleyan Theology in America," *WTJ* 13 (1978): 13-33.

93. Cf. William M. Menzies, "Non-Wesleyan Origins," p. 85.

94. Cf. James K. A. Smith, "The Closing of the Book: Pentecostals, Evangelicals, and the Sacred Writings," *JPT* 11 (1997): 49-71, here p. 50.

95. See Gary B. McGee, "'More Than Evangelical': The Challenge of the Evolving Theological Identity of the Assemblies of God," *Pneuma* 25, no. 2 (2003): 289-300; John B. Carpenter, "Genuine Pentecostal Traditioning: Rooting Pentecostalism in Its Evangelical Soil; A Reply to Simon Chan," *AJPS* 6, no. 2 (2003): 303-26; Terry L. Cross, "A Proposal to Break the Ice: What Can Pentecostals Offer Evangelical Theology?" *JPT* 10, no. 2 (2002): 44-73; Smith, "Closing of the Book," p. 60; Cargal, "Fundamentalist-Modernist Controversy," pp. 168-71.

96. See Steven M. Studebaker, "Beyond Tongues: A Pentecostal Theology of Grace," in *Defining Issues in Pentecostalism: Classical and Emergent,* McMaster Theological Studies 1 (Eugene, OR: Pickwick, 2008), pp. 46-68, and "Pentecostal Soteriology and Pneumatology," *JPT* 11, no. 2 (2003): 248-70.

97. See Charles C. Ryrie, *Dispensationalism* (Chicago: Moody Press, 1995), pp. 91-95.

98. Amos Yong, *The Spirit Poured Out on All Flesh: Pentecostalism and the Possibility of Global Theology* (Grand Rapids: Baker Academic, 2005), p. 27. See also Hollenweger, *The Pentecostals,* pp. 336-37; Dayton, *Theological Roots of Pentecostalism,* p. 23.

99. For a critical approach see Martin William Mittelstadt, "Spirit and Suffering in Contemporary Pentecostalism: The Lukan Epic Continues," in *Defining Issues in Pentecostalism,* pp. 144-73; Paul Elbert, "Pentecostal/Charismatic Themes in Luke-Acts at the Evangelical Theological Society: The Battle of Interpretive Method," *JPT* 12, no. 2 (2004): 181-215.

100. Cf. Paul Elbert, "Toward a Pentecostal Hermeneutic: Observations on Archer's Progressive Proposal," *AJPS* 9, no. 2 (2006): 320-28, and "Possible Literary Links between Luke-Acts and Paul's Letters regarding Spirit-Language," in *The Intertextuality of the Epistles: Explorations of Theory and Practice,* ed. Thomas Brodie, Stanley Porter, and Dennis MacDonald (Sheffield: Sheffield-Phoenix, 2006), pp. 226-54.

101. Cf. Kenneth J. Archer, *A Pentecostal Hermeneutic for the Twenty-first Century: Spirit, Scripture, and Community* (London: T. & T. Clark, 2004), pp. 140-48; James D. G. Dunn, "Baptism in the Spirit: A Response to Pentecostal Scholarship on Luke-Acts," *JPT* 3 (1993): 3-27.

102. Cf. Matthew S. Clark, "Pentecostal Hermeneutics: The Challenge of Relating to

(Post-)modern Literary Theory," *APB* 12 (2001): 41-67; John Christopher Thomas, "Women, Pentecostals and the Bible: An Experiment in Pentecostal Hermeneutics," *JPT* 5 (1994): 41-56; Arrington, "Use of the Bible," pp. 101-7; Joseph Byrd, "Paul Ricoeur's Hermeneutical Theory and Pentecostal Proclamation," *Pneuma* 15, no. 2 (1993): 203-14.

103. Cf. Archer, *A Pentecostal Hermeneutic*, pp. 127-55; Robert P. Menzies, "The Essence of Pentecostalism," *Paraclete* 26, no. 3 (1992): 1-9; Gordon Fee, *Gospel and Spirit: Issues in New Testament Hermeneutics* (Peabody, MA: Hendrickson, 1991); William Menzies, "The Methodology of Pentecostal Theology: An Essay on Hermeneutics," in *Essays on Apostolic Themes*, ed. Paul Elbert (Peabody, MA: Hendrickson, 1985), pp. 1-14.

104. Cf. Ellington, "Pentecostalism," pp. 36-38.

105. Cf. Mark D. McLean, "Toward a Pentecostal Hermeneutic," *Pneuma* 6, no. 2 (1984): 35-56.

106. See Najeeb George Awad, "Should We Dispense with *Sola Scriptura?* Scripture, Tradition and Postmodern Theology," *Dialog* 47, no. 1 (2008): 64-79; Victor Walter, "Beyond *Sola Scriptura:* Recovering a More Balanced Understanding of Authority," *Touchstone* 4, no. 2 (1991): 15-18; Braaten, "Can We Still Hold?" pp. 189-94; Peters, "*Sola Scriptura,*" pp. 268-80.

107. See Barth, *CD* I/2, pp. 457-740. See also Geoffrey W. Bromiley, "The Authority of Scripture in Karl Barth," in *Hermeneutics, Authority, and Canon*, ed. D. A. Carson and John D. Woodbridge (Grand Rapids: Zondervan, 1986), pp. 271-94; Klaas Runia, *Karl Barth's Doctrine of Holy Scripture* (Grand Rapids: Eerdmans, 1962).

108. Barth, *CD* I/1, p. 296.

109. Barth, *CD* I/2, p. 501.

110. Barth, *CD* I/2, p. 522. Cf. J. Mark Beach, "Revelation in Scripture: Some Comments on Karl Barth's Doctrine of Revelation," *Mid-America Journal of Theology* 17 (2006): 267-74; Runia, *Karl Barth's Doctrine*, pp. 189-219.

111. Barth, *CD* I/2, p. 532.

112. Barth, *CD* I/2, p. 533.

113. Cf. John D. Morrison, "Barth, Barthians, and Evangelicals: Reassessing the Question of the Relation of Holy Scripture and the Word of God," *TJ* 25, no. 2 (2004): 187-213, and "Scripture as Word of God: Evangelical Assumption or Evangelical Question?" *TJ* 20, no. 2 (1999): 165-90.

114. Representative of this dichotomy is the work of Gordon Kaufman, *The Theological Imagination: Constructing the Concept of God* (Philadelphia: Westminster, 1981), and *An Essay on Theological Method* (Missoula, MT: Scholars, 1975). Cf. Bruce McCormack, "Divine Revelation and Human Imagination: Must We Choose between the Two?" *SJT* 37, no. 4 (1984): 431-55.

115. See H. Richard Niebuhr, *The Meaning of Revelation* (New York: Macmillan, 1941), pp. 32-100.

116. Paul Tillich, *Systematic Theology*, vol. 1 (Chicago: University of Chicago Press, 1963), pp. 101-47, and "Theology and Symbolism," in *Religious Symbolism*, ed. F. Ernest Johnson (New York: Harper and Bros., 1955), pp. 107-16.

117. Karl Rahner, "History of the World and Salvation-History," in *Theological Investigations*, vol. 5 (Baltimore: Helicon, 1966), pp. 97-114. See Karl Rahner, "The Theology of the Symbol," in *Theological Investigations*, vol. 4 (Baltimore: Helicon, 1965), pp. 221-52. Cf. James J. Buckley, "On Being a Symbol: An Appraisal of Karl Rahner," *TS* 40, no. 3 (1979): 453-73.

118. Dulles, *Models of Revelation*, pp. 136-39.

119. David H. Kelsey, *The Uses of Scripture in Recent Theology* (Philadelphia: Fortress, 1975); Kelsey, *The Fabric of Paul Tillich's Theology* (New Haven: Yale University Press, 1967).

120. Kelsey, *Uses of Scripture*, p. 90, italics in original.

121. Kelsey, *Uses of Scripture*, p. 94.

122. Kelsey, *Uses of Scripture*, pp. 159, 170.

123. Kevin J. Vanhoozer, *The Drama of Doctrine: A Canonical-Linguistic Approach to Christian Theology* (Louisville: Westminster/John Knox, 2005), pp. 115-241; Vanhoozer, *First Theology: God, Scripture, and Hermeneutics* (Downers Grove, IL: InterVarsity, 2002), pp. 127-203; Vanhoozer, *Is There Meaning in the Text? The Bible, the Reader, and the Morality of Literary Knowledge* (Grand Rapids: Zondervan, 1998), pp. 98-147 and 281-366.

124. Vanhoozer, *The Drama of Doctrine*, p. 152.

125. See, for example, R. Schechner, *Performance Theory*, 2nd ed. (London: Routledge, 2003); Marvin Carlson, *Performance: A Critical Introduction* (New York: Routledge, 1996); Nicholas Wolterstorff, *Divine Discourse: Philosophical Reflections on the Claim That God Speaks* (Cambridge: Cambridge University Press, 1995); Nick Kaye, *Postmodernism and Performance* (New York: St. Martin's Press, 1994); Frances Young, *The Art of Performance: Towards a Theology of Holy Scripture* (London: Darton, Longman and Todd, 1990); Michael Issacharoff and Robin F. Jones, eds., *Performing Texts* (Philadelphia: University of Pennsylvania Press, 1988); Michel Benamou and Charles Caramello, eds., *Performance in Postmodern Culture* (Milwaukee: Center for Twentieth-Century Studies, University of Wisconsin–Milwaukee, 1977).

126. Vanhoozer, *The Drama of Doctrine*, p. 169. See Issacharoff and Jones, *Performing Texts*, p. 139.

127. Vanhoozer, *The Drama of Doctrine*, p. 181.

128. See Vanhoozer, *The Drama of Doctrine*, pp. 399-441.

129. Awad, "Should We Dispense?" p. 64.

130. Vanhoozer uses the taxonomy of speech acts in John Searle, *Expression and Meaning: Studies in the Theory of Speech-Acts* (Cambridge: Cambridge University Press, 1979).

131. See Kelsey, *Paul Tillich's Theology*, p. 24.

132. See Vanhoozer, *The Drama of Doctrine*, pp. 211-37; Kelsey, *Paul Tillich's Theology*, pp. 143-47.

133. Vanhoozer, *The Drama of Doctrine*, p. 401.

134. Moore, "Canon and Charisma," p. 76; See also Rick D. Moore, "'And Also Much Cattle?!' Prophetic Passions and the End of Jonah," *JPT* 11 (1997): 35-48; Moore, "Deuteronomy," pp. 11-33.

135. Moore, "Canon and Charisma," p. 90.

136. Moore, "Deuteronomy," pp. 22, 33.

137. Moore, "Canon and Charisma," pp. 90-91.

138. Moore, "Deuteronomy," p. 33.

139. Moore, "Deuteronomy," p. 33.

140. John McKay, "When the Veil Is Taken Away: The Impact of Prophetic Experience on Biblical Interpretation," *JPT* 5 (1994): 17-40, at p. 30.

141. McQueen, *Joel and the Spirit*, p. 15.

142. McQueen, *Joel and the Spirit*, p. 100.

143. Roger Stronstad, *The Charismatic Theology of St. Luke* (Peabody, MA: Hendrickson, 1984), p. 82, italics in original.

144. See Roger Stronstad, *The Prophethood of All Believers: A Study in Luke's Charismatic Theology,* JPTS 16 (Sheffield: Sheffield Academic, 1999); Stronstad, *Charismatic Theology of St. Luke,* pp. 82-83.

145. John Christopher Thomas, "Reading the Bible from within Our Traditions: A Pentecostal Hermeneutics as Test Case," in *Between Two Horizons: Spanning New Testament Studies and Systematic Theology,* ed. Max Turner and Joel B. Green (Grand Rapids: Eerdmans, 2000), pp. 108-22, 119.

146. Matthias Wenk, "The Creative Power of the Prophetic Dialogue," *Pneuma* 26, no. 1 (2004): 118-29, at p. 119.

147. Miroslav Volf, "The Church as a Prophetic Community and a Sign of Hope," *EuroJTh* 2, no. 1 (1993): 9-30.

148. Eldin Villafañe, *The Liberating Spirit: Toward an Hispanic American Pentecostal Social Ethic* (Grand Rapids: Eerdmans, 1993), pp. 216-21.

149. André Corten, *Pentecostalism in Brazil: Emotion of the Poor and Theological Romanticism,* trans. Arianne Dorval (New York: St. Martin's Press, 1999), p. 151.

150. Corten, *Pentecostalism in Brazil,* pp. 143-56. See also Walter Brueggemann, *The Prophetic Imagination,* 2nd ed. (Minneapolis: Augsburg Fortress, 2001), pp. 39-58.

151. Sunday A. Aigbe, "Cultural Mandate, Evangelistic Mandate, Prophetic Mandate: Of These Greatest Is . . . ?" *Missiology* 19, no. 1 (1991): 31-43, and Aigbe, "A Biblical Foundation for the Prophetic Mandate," *Pneuma* 11, no. 2 (1989): 77-97.

152. Aigbe, "Cultural Mandate," p. 38.

153. Madipoane Masenya, "The Bible and Prophecy in African–South African Pentecostal Churches," *Missionalia* 33, no. 1 (2005): 35-45.

154. Joseph L. Suico, "Pentecostalism and Social Change," *AJPS* 8, no. 2 (2005): 195-213.

155. Lap-yan Kung, "Globalization, Ecumenism and Pentecostalism: A Search for Human Solidarity in Hong Kong," *AJPS* 6, no. 1 (2003): 97-122.

156. See Tan-Chow May Ling, *Pentecostal Theology for the Twenty-first Century: Engaging with Multi-Faith Singapore* (Aldershot: Ashgate, 2007), pp. 39-40, 66-70.

157. May Ling, *Pentecostal Theology,* pp. 102-17.

158. See Hannah K. Harrington and Rebecca Patten, "Pentecostal Hermeneutics and Postmodern Literary Theory," *Pneuma* 16, no. 1 (1994): 109-14.

159. Cf. Mark J. Cartledge, "Charismatic Prophecy: A Definition and Description," *JPT* 5 (1994): 79-120.

160. See Kevin L. Spawn, *As It Is Written and Other Citation Formulae in the Old Testament: Their Use, Development, Syntax, and Significance* (New York: De Gruyter, 2002).

161. Lee Roy Martin, *The Unheard Voice of God: A Pentecostal Hearing of the Book of Judges,* JPTS 32 (Blandford Forum, U.K.: Deo, 2008), pp. 61-74; Camery-Hoggatt, "The Word of God," pp. 225-55; Smith, "Closing of the Book," pp. 49-71; Kärkkäinen, "Pentecostal Hermeneutics," pp. 77-80.

162. Martin, *Unheard Voice of God,* pp. 64-79.

163. James K. A. Smith, *Speech and Theology: Language and the Logic of the Incarnation* (London: Routledge, 2002), p. 154. See also Smith, "How to Avoid Not Speaking: Attestations," in *Knowing Other-wise: Theology at the Threshold of Spirituality,* ed. James H. Olthuis (New York: Fordham University Press, 1997), pp. 217-34.

164. Smith, "Closing of the Book," p. 68.

165. Archer, *A Pentecostal Hermeneutic*, pp. 156-91.

166. Archer, *A Pentecostal Hermeneutic*, pp. 189-90.

167. Amos Yong, *Spirit-Word-Community: Theological Hermeneutics in Trinitarian Perspective* (Eugene, OR: Wipf and Stock, 2002), p. 255.

168. Yong, *Spirit-Word-Community*, p. 260.

169. Yong, *Spirit-Word-Community*, p. 264.

170. Yong, *Spirit-Word-Community*, p. 315.

171. See Hans-Georg Gadamer, *Truth and Method*, trans. Garrett Barden and John Cumming (New York: Seabury Press, 1975), pp. 91-119.

172. David Bryant, *Faith and the Play of the Imagination: On the Role of the Imagination in Religion*, Studies in American Biblical Hermeneutics 5 (Macon, GA: Mercer University Press, 1989), p. 106.

173. See Margaret M. Poloma and Ralph W. Wood, Jr., *Blood and Fire: Godly Love in a Pentecostal Emerging Church* (New York: New York University Press, 2008), pp. 64-93; Michael Wilkinson, *The Spirit Said Go: Pentecostal Immigrants in Canada* (New York: Peter Lang, 2006); Ausaji Ayuk, "The Pentecostal Transformation of Nigerian Church Life," *AJPS* 5, no. 2 (2002): 189-204; Richard Shaull and Waldo Cesar, *Pentecostalism and the Future of the Christian Churches: Promises, Limitation, Challenges* (Grand Rapids: Eerdmans, 2000), pp. 209-18; Richard Shaull, "From Academic Research to Spiritual Transformation: Reflections on a Study of Pentecostalism in Brazil," *Pneuma* 20, no. 1 (1998): 71-84; Land, *Pentecostal Spirituality*, pp. 182-219.

174. See Gadamer, *Truth and Method*, pp. 100-101.

175. Cf. Gadamer, *Truth and Method*, pp. 94, 97.

176. Gadamer, *Truth and Method*, p. 93.

177. Johan Huizinga, *Homo Ludens: A Study of Play-Element in Culture* (London: Routledge and Kegan Paul, 1949), p. 9.

178. Huizinga, *Homo Ludens*, p. 15.

Notes to Chapter 3

1. See Peter Gemeinhardt, *Die Filioque-Kontroverse zwischen Ost- und Westkirche im Frühmittelalter* (Berlin: De Gruyter, 2002); Bernd Oberdorfer, *Filioque: Geschichte und Theologie eines ökumenischen Problems* (Göttingen: Vandenhoeck & Ruprecht, 2001); Yves Congar, *I Believe in the Holy Spirit*, vol. 3, *The River of the Water of Live (Rev 22:1) Flows in the East and in the West* (New York: Crossroad, 1983), pp. 3-21; Gerald Bray, "The *Filioque* Clause in History and Theology," *TynBul* 34 (1983): 91-144. For the ecumenical discussion see "The *Filioque*: A Church-Dividing Issue? An Agreed Statement of the North American Orthodox-Catholic Theological Consultation," *St. Vladimir's Theological Quarterly* 48, no. 1 (2004): 93-123; Pontifical Council for Promoting Christian Unity, ed., "The Greek and Latin Traditions regarding the Procession of the Holy Spirit," *L'Osservatore Romano* (weekly edition in English) 38 (September 20, 1995), pp. 3, 6; WCC, ed., *Spirit of God, Spirit of Christ: Ecumenical Reflections on the* Filioque *Controversy*, Faith and Order Paper 103 (Geneva: WCC, 1981).

2. Cf. Congar, *I Believe*, 3:50.

3. Cf. J. N. D. Kelly, *Early Christian Creeds*, 3rd ed. (New York: Continuum, 1981, 2006),

pp. 30-61; Jaroslav Pelikan, *Credo: Historical and Theological Guide to Creeds and Confessions of Faith in the Christian Tradition* (New Haven: Yale University Press, 2003), pp. 178-81, 377-83; Liuwe H. Westra, *The Apostles' Creed: Origin, History, and Some Early Commentaries* (Turnhout: Brepols, 2002), pp. 21-72; Bertand de Margerie, *The Christian Trinity in History*, trans. Edmund J. Fortman, SHT 1 (Still River, MA: St. Bede's Publications, 1981), pp. 57-59.

4. On the history of the term, see Kelly, *Early Christian Creeds*, pp. 52-61; Hans Jürgen Marx, *Filioque und Verbot eines anderen Glaubens auf dem Florentinum* (St. Augustin, Germany: Steyler Verlag, 1977), pp. 228-44; H. J. Carpenter, "*Symbolum* as a Title of the Creed," *JTS* 43 (1942): 1-11.

5. Rufinus, *A Commentary on the Apostles' Creed*, trans. J. N. D. Kelly, ACW 20 (New York: Newman, 1954), pp. 7-11.

6. Rufinus, *A Commentary*, p. 30.

7. Rufinus, *A Commentary*, pp. 101-2 n. 8.

8. Augustine, *Sermon 212* and *Sermon 214*. See Kelly, *Early Christian Creeds*, p. 55; Carpenter, "*Symbolum* as a Title," p. 2.

9. Marx, *Filioque und Verbot*, pp. 235-36.

10. Cf. Bruce Shelley, *By What Authority? The Standards of Truth in the Early Church* (Grand Rapids: Eerdmans, 1965), pp. 93-95. See also Marx, *Filioque und Verbot*, pp. 238-39.

11. See Marx, *Filioque und Verbot*, p. 239; Kelly, *Early Christian Creeds*, p. 54.

12. Carpenter, "*Symbolum* as a Title," p. 3.

13. Marx, *Filioque und Verbot*, p. 239; Carpenter, "*Symbolum* as a Title," p. 9.

14. Cf. Gottfried Hornig, "Analyse und Problematik der religiösen Performative," *NZSTR* 24, no. 1 (1982): 53-70.

15. Hornig, "Analyse und Problematik," pp. 62-64.

16. See, recently, Donald T. Williams, *Credo: Meditations on the Nicene Creed* (St. Louis: Chalice, 2007); L. Charles Jackson, *Faith of Our Fathers: A Popular Study of the Nicene Creed* (Moscow, ID: Canon, 2007); David Willis, *Clues to the Nicene Creed: A Brief Outline of the Faith* (Grand Rapids: Eerdmans, 2005); Luke Timothy Johnson, *The Creed: What Christians Believe and Why It Matters* (New York: Doubleday, 2003); Christopher R. Seitz, ed., *Nicene Christianity: The Future for a New Ecumenism* (Grand Rapids: Brazos, 2001).

17. Heribert Mühlen, "'We as We Ourselves Are with You': The Fundamental Promise of the New Covenant," in Wolfgang Vondey, *Heribert Mühlen: His Theology and Praxis; A New Profile of the Church* (Lanham, MD: University Press of America, 2004), pp. 323-26.

18. Mühlen, "We as We Ourselves," p. 324.

19. Heribert Mühlen, "Modelle der Einigung: Auf dem Weg zu einem universalen Konzil aller Christen," *Catholica* 27 (1973): 111-34.

20. Heribert Mühlen, "Konvergenz als Strukturprinzip eines kommenden universalen Konzils aller Christen," *ÖR* 21 (1972): 289-315, and Mühlen, "Das Konzil von Florenz (1439) als vorläufiges Modell eines kommenden Unionskonzils," *TG* 63 (1973): 184-97.

21. Pelikan, *Credo*, pp. 252-55.

22. Cf. Thomas F. Torrance, "The Deposit of Faith," *SJT* 36, no. 1 (1983): 1-28.

23. See Marx, *Filioque und Verbot*, pp. 252-58; Maria-Helene Gamillscheg, *Die Kontroverse um das Filioque: Möglichkeiten einer Problemlösung auf Grund der Forschungen und Gespräche der letzten hundert Jahre*, Das östliche Christentum 45 (Würzburg: Augustinus Verlag, 1996), pp. 27-42.

24. A notable exception is the *Agreed Statement of the North American Orthodox-*

Catholic Theological Consultation (2003), which divides the controversy among terminological, theological, and ecclesiological issues.

25. Cf. Torrance, "The Deposit of Faith," pp. 15-16. Torrance associates the origins of this development with Tertullian's notion of the rule of faith.

26. Cf. Oberdorfer, *Filioque,* pp. 129-50.

27. See R. P. C. Hanson, *The Search for the Christian Doctrine of God: The Arian Controversy, 318-381* (Grand Rapids: Baker Academic, 1988, 2005), pp. 129-78; J. N. D. Kelly, *Early Christian Doctrines,* rev. ed. (New York: Harper and Row, 1978), pp. 83-108; Bernard Lonergan, *The Way to Nicaea: The Dialectical Development of Trinitarian Theology,* trans. Conn O'Donovan (London: Darton, Longman and Todd, 1976), pp. 1-18; G. L. Prestige, *God in Patristic Thought,* 2nd ed. (London: SPCK, 1975), pp. 260-65.

28. Cf. Torrance, "The Deposit of Faith," pp. 6-11.

29. See Lorenzo Perrone, "The Impact of the Dogma of Chalcedon on Theological Thought between the Fourth and Fifth Ecumenical Councils," in *History of Theology,* vol. 1, *The Patristic Period,* ed. Angelo Di Bernadino and Basil Studer, trans. Matthew J. O'Connell (Collegeville, MN: Liturgical Press, 1997), pp. 414-30; Maurice Wiles, *Working Papers in Doctrine* (London: SCM, 1976), pp. 1-17; Jaroslav Pelikan, *The Christian Tradition: A History of the Development of Doctrine,* vol. 1, *The Emergence of the Catholic Tradition (100-600)* (Chicago: University of Chicago Press, 1971), pp. 172-225.

30. Mark Carpenter, "A Synopsis of the Development of Trinitarian Thought from the First Century Church Fathers to the Second Century Apologists," *TJ* 26, no. 2 (2005): 293-319; Pelikan, *Credo,* pp. 22-29.

31. Cf. Friedrich Loofs, "Das Nizänum," in *Patristica: Ausgewählte Aufsätze zur Alten Kirche,* ed. Christof Brennecke and Jörg Ulrich (Berlin: De Gruyter, 1999), pp. 105-21; Kelly, *Early Christian Creeds,* pp. 358-67.

32. See Deno J. Geanakoplos, "The Second Ecumenical Synod of Constantinople (381): Proceedings and Theology of the Holy Spirit," *GOTR* 27, no. 4 (1982): 407-29.

33. See John Henry Newman, *Essay on the Development of Christian Doctrine* (Baltimore: Penguin, 1878, 1960), pp. 40-41. A notable exception is Lewis Ayres, *Nicaea and Its Legacy: An Approach to Fourth-Century Trinitarian Theology* (Oxford: Oxford University Press, 2004).

34. Theodore de Régnon, *Études de théologie positive sur la Sainte Trinité,* 4 vols. (Paris: Victor Retaux, 1892/1898).

35. See Michel René Barnes, "De Régnon Reconsidered," *AS* 26, no. 2 (1995): 51-79, and "Augustine in Contemporary Trinitarian Theology," *TS* 56, no. 2 (1995): 237-50; Ayres, *Nicaea and Its Legacy,* pp. 302-4.

36. See Cyprian of Carthage, *Letter 75,* 10-11, and the discussion in Kelly, *Early Christian Creeds,* pp. 47-48.

37. Cf. Kelly, *Early Christian Creeds,* p. 96.

38. Cf. John I. Jenkins, *Knowledge and Faith in Thomas Aquinas* (Cambridge: Cambridge University Press, 1997), pp. 53-54.

39. *STh* II, ii, 1, 6-9.

40. See Scott MacDonald, "Theory of Knowledge," in *The Cambridge Companion to Aquinas,* ed. Norman Kretzmann and Eleonore Stump (Cambridge: Cambridge University Press, 1993), pp. 160-95; Frederick D. Wilhelmsen, *Man's Knowledge of Reality: An Introduction to Thomistic Epistemology* (Englewood Cliffs, NJ: Prentice-Hall, 1956).

41. *STh* II, ii, 1, 6.

42. See Tad W. Guzie, "The Act of Faith according to St. Thomas: A Study in Theological Methodology," *Thom* 29, no. 2 (1965): 239-80.

43. *STh* II, ii, 1, 6, ad 2. Cf. Reinhard Simon, *Das Filioque bei Thomas von Aquin: Eine Untersuchung zur dogmengeschichtlichen Stellung, theologischen Struktur und ökumenischen Perspektive der thomanischen Gotteslehre* (Frankfurt: Peter Lang, 1994), p. 27.

44. *STh* II, ii, 1, 8.

45. *STh* II, ii, 8, ad 3.

46. See Barnes, "De Régnon Reconsidered," pp. 58-62.

47. Cf. Walter Kasper, *The God of Jesus Christ* (New York: Crossroad, 1984), pp. 274-75.

48. Cf. Fisher Humphreys, "The Revelation of the Trinity," *PRS* 33, no. 3 (2006): 285-303.

49. This is essentially also the argument of Aquinas. See Simon, *Das Filioque bei Thomas*, pp. 26-63.

50. See David A. Reed, *"In Jesus' Name": The History and Beliefs of Oneness Pentecostals*, JPTS 31 (Blandford Forum, U.K.: Deo Publishing, 2008); Daniel L. Butler, *Oneness Pentecostalism: A History of the Jesus Name Movement* (Bellflower, CA: International Pentecostal Church, 2004); Talmadge L. French, *Our God Is One: The Story of the Oneness Pentecostals* (Indianapolis: Voice and Vision, 1999); Joseph H. Howell, "The People of the Name: Oneness Pentecostalism in the United States" (Ph.D. diss., Florida State University, 1985); Arthur L. Clanton, *United We Stand: A History of Oneness Organizations* (Hazelwood, MO: Pentecostal Publishing House, 1970).

51. A. J. Tomlinson, "Great Crisis Near at Hand," *ELCGE,* October 1, 1910, p. 1; A. S. Copley, "Pentecost in Type," *TP* 1, no. 9 (August 1909): 8.

52. See Gerald T. Sheppard, "The Nicean Creed, *Filioque,* and Pentecostal Movements in the United States," *GOTR* 31, no. 3-4 (1986): 401-16.

53. T. K. Leonard, "Prayer — as Taught by Jesus," *CE* 50 (July 18, 1914): 1.

54. R. G. Spurling, *The Lost Link* (Turtletown, TN, 1920), p. 16; *Book of Minutes: A Compiled History of the Work of the General Assemblies of the Church of God* (Cleveland, TN: Church of God Publishing House, 1922), pp. 163-64.

55. E. N. Bell, "Questions and Answers," *WE* 152 (August 12, 1916): 8.

56. W. Jethro Walthall, "The Unity of the Spirit," *WE* 153 (August 19, 1916): 12. See also Spurling, *The Lost Link,* pp. 23-26.

57. Cf. Dale M. Coulter, "The Development of Ecclesiology in the Church of God (Cleveland): A Forgotten Contribution?" *Pneuma* 29, no. 1 (2007): 64-67.

58. Cf. Howell, "People of the Name," pp. 26-30. Reed, *"In Jesus' Name,"* pp. 9-43, ascribes the experiential arena of Oneness Pentecostals to their Pietist legacy.

59. See French, *Our God Is One,* pp. 57-58; Howell, "People of the Name," pp. 30-31; Clanton, *United We Stand,* pp. 13-16.

60. See Thomas A. Fudge, *Christianity without the Cross: A History of Salvation in Oneness Pentecostalism* (Parkland, FL: Universal Publishers, 2003), pp. 150-64; David K. Bernard, "'The Whole Gospel': Oneness Pentecostal Perspectives on Christian Initiation" (paper presented at the annual meeting of the Society for Pentecostal Studies, 2001), pp. 449-68. For a historical perspective see G. T. Haywood, *The Birth of the Spirit in the Days of the Apostles* (Indianapolis: Christ Temple Book Store, 1922).

61. See Gregory A. Boyd, *Oneness Pentecostals and the Trinity* (Grand Rapids: Baker, 1992), pp. 131-46.

62. Cf. French, *Our God Is One*, pp. 48-50; Fudge, *Christianity without the Cross*, pp. 58-59; Douglas Jacobsen, *Thinking in the Spirit: Theologies of the Early Pentecostal Movement* (Bloomington: Indiana University Press, 2003), pp. 136-64; D. William Faupel, *The Everlasting Gospel: The Significance of Eschatology in the Development of Pentecostal Thought*, JPTS 10 (Sheffield: Sheffield Academic, 1996), pp. 270-306.

63. See Reed, *"In Jesus' Name,"* pp. 83-105.

64. See "Oneness-Trinitarian Pentecostal Final Report, 2002-2007," *Pneuma* 30, no. 2 (2008): 203-24, at no. 18.

65. See David Reed, "Aspects of the Origins of Oneness Pentecostalism," in *Aspects of Pentecostal-Charismatic Origins*, ed. Vinson Synan (Plainfield, NJ: Logos International, 1975), pp. 143-68; Reed, *"In Jesus' Name,"* pp. 147-66; Boyd, *Oneness Pentecostals*, pp. 139-40.

66. Cf. William B. Chalfant, *Ancient Champions of Oneness* (Hazelwood, MO: Word Aflame, 1981), pp. 137-48.

67. David K. Bernard, *Oneness and Trinity, A.D. 100-300: The Doctrine of God in Ancient Christian Writings* (Hazelwood, MO: Word Aflame, 1991), pp. 165-74; David K. Bernard, *The Trinitarian Controversy in the Fourth Century* (Hazelwood, MO: Word Aflame, 1993), pp. 9-23.

68. Bernard, *The Trinitarian Controversy*, p. 22. See also Bernard, *Oneness and Trinity*, p. 70.

69. David K. Bernard, *A History of Christian Doctrine*, vol. 1, *The Post-Apostolic Age to the Middle Ages, A.D. 100-1500* (Hazelwood, MO: Word Aflame, 1995), p. 127.

70. See Bernard, *Oneness and Trinity*, pp. 42-43, 58-59.

71. Bernard, *History of Christian Doctrine*, 1:127.

72. See Douglas Jacobsen, "Oneness Options," in *Thinking in the Spirit*, pp. 194-259, here p. 206.

73. Andrew D. Urshan, *The Almighty God in the Lord Jesus Christ* (Los Angeles, 1919), pp. 2, 10; Urshan, "The Trinity," *Witness of God*, September 1924, p. 2. Cf. Manuel Gaxiola-Gaxiola, "The Unresolved Issue: A Third-World Perspective on the Oneness Question" (paper presented at the annual meeting of the Society for Pentecostal Studies, 1987), p. 21; Reed, *"In Jesus' Name,"* pp. 246-73.

74. Bernard, *The Trinitarian Controversy*, p. 59.

75. David K. Bernard, "The Future of Oneness Pentecostalism," in *The Future of Pentecostalism in the United States*, ed. Eric Patterson and Edmund Rybarczyk (Lanham, MD: Lexington Books, 2007), pp. 123-36, at p. 123. See also Bernard, *The Oneness View of Jesus Christ* (Hazelwood, MO: Word Aflame, 1994), p. 9; Bernard, *Oneness and Trinity*, pp. 9-10; Bernard, *The Oneness of God*, rev. ed., Pentecostal Theology 1 (Hazelwood, MO: Word Aflame, 2001), pp. 246-52.

76. Bernard, *Oneness and Trinity*, pp. 121-28. See also Donald Bryan and Walter L. Copes, "Historical Development of the Trinitarian Mode of Baptism," in *Symposium on Oneness Pentecostalism, 1986*, ed. United Pentecostal Church International (Hazelwood, MO: Word Aflame, 1986), pp. 197-216.

77. See William B. Chalfant, "The Fall of the Ancient Apostolic Church," in *Symposium on Oneness Pentecostalism, 1988 and 1990* (Hazelwood, MO: Word Aflame, 1990), pp. 351-85; Thomas Weisser, "Was the Early Church Oneness or Trinitarian?" in *Symposium on Oneness Pentecostalism, 1986*, pp. 53-68.

78. Bernard, *The Oneness of God,* p. 144.

79. David K. Bernard, "A Response to Ralph Del Colle's 'Oneness and Trinity: A Preliminary Proposal for Dialogue with Oneness Pentecostalism'" (paper presented at the annual meeting of the Society for Pentecostal Studies, 1996), pp. 1-7.

80. See "Oneness-Trinitarian Pentecostal Final Report," nos. 9 and 10.

81. Bernard, *Oneness View,* p. 15.

82. "Oneness-Trinitarian Pentecostal Final Report," no. 28.

83. Butler, *Oneness Pentecostalism,* pp. 89-90, italics in original. See also David K. Bernard, *In the Name of Jesus* (Hazelwood, MO: Word Aflame, 1992), pp. 19-27.

84. Cf. Reed, *"In Jesus' Name,"* pp. 227-306; French, *Our God Is One,* p. 211; Bernard, *Oneness View,* p. 24.

85. See John Paterson, *God in Jesus Christ* (Hazelwood, MO: Word Aflame, 1966), p. 39.

86. See David A. Reed, "Oneness Pentecostalism: Problems and Possibilities for Pentecostal Theology," *JPT* 11 (1997): 73-93.

87. Bernard, *Oneness View,* p. 16.

88. Bernard, *Oneness View,* pp. 15-16.

89. "Oneness-Trinitarian Pentecostal Final Report," no. 42.

90. "Oneness-Trinitarian Pentecostal Final Report," no. 37.

91. Gordon Magee, *Is Jesus in the Godhead or Is the Godhead in Jesus?* (Hazelwood, MO: Word Aflame, 1988), p. 25.

92. See, recently, David S. Norris, *I AM: A Oneness Pentecostal Theology* (Hazelwood, MO: Word Aflame, 2009); Gary C. Rugger, *The Oneness Doctrine: Written for Easy Learning* (Bakersfield, CA: G. C. Rugger, 1997), pp. 9-11.

93. French, *Our God Is One,* p. 189.

94. David K. Bernard, *Understanding the Articles of Faith: An Examination of United Pentecostal Beliefs* (Hazelwood, MO: Word Aflame, 1992), p. 27.

95. Cf. Reed, "Aspects of the Origins," p. 152; Amos Yong, *The Spirit Poured Out on All Flesh: Pentecostalism and the Possibility of Global Theology* (Grand Rapids: Baker Academic, 2005), p. 232.

96. Bernard, *The Oneness of God,* pp. 182-83.

97. "Oneness-Trinitarian Pentecostal Final Report," no. 40.

98. See Bernard, *The Oneness of God,* pp. 128-29.

99. See Bernard, *The Oneness of God,* pp. 129-32.

100. "Oneness-Trinitarian Pentecostal Final Report," no. 39.

101. Leonardo Boff has argued that the concept provides impulses to liberation. See *Trinity and Society* (Maryknoll, NY: Orbis, 1988), p. 236.

102. Bernard, *Oneness View,* p. 74; Bernard, *The Oneness of God,* p. 184.

103. Bernard, *The Oneness of God,* p. 185.

104. Bernard, *The Oneness of God,* p. 196.

105. French, *Our God Is One,* p. 206; Bernard, *The Oneness of God,* pp. 182-84; David Campbell, *The Eternal Sonship* (Hazelwood, MO: Word Aflame, 1978), pp. 94-95.

106. Catherine Mowri LaCugna, *God for Us: The Trinity and the Christian Life* (San Francisco: Harper, 1991). The intention of this connection is also to open up dialogue between supporters and critics of LaCugna's position. For substantial criticism see Thomas Weinandy, "The Immanent and the Economic Trinity," *Thom* 57, no. 4 (1993): 655-66; Earl Muller, "The Science of Theology: A Review of Catherine LaCugna's *God for Us,*"

Gregorianum 75, no. 2 (1994): 311-41. The parenthetical page numbers in the text refer to LaCugna's *God for Us*.

107. See also the review symposium "Four Perspectives," *Horizons* 20, no. 1 (1993): 135-42.

108. LaCugna, *God for Us*, p. 274. See also Karen Baker-Fletcher, *Dancing with God: The Trinity from a Womanist Perspective* (St. Louis: Chalice, 2007); Molly T. Marshall, *Joining the Dance: A Theology of the Spirit* (Valley Forge, PA: Judson, 2003), pp. 6-9; Jürgen Moltmann, *The Trinity and the Kingdom: The Doctrine of God* (San Francisco: Harper and Row, 1981), pp. 174-76.

109. See Steven M. Studebaker, "Beyond Tongues: A Pentecostal Theology of Grace," in *Defining the Issues in Pentecostalism: Classical and Emergent* (Eugene, OR: Pickwick, 2008), pp. 46-68.

110. Daniel E. Albrecht, *Rites in the Spirit: A Ritual Approach to Pentecostal/Charismatic Spirituality*, JPTS 17 (Sheffield: Sheffield Academic, 1999), pp. 196-208.

111. See Graham McFee, *Understanding Dance* (New York: Taylor and Francis, 2003), pp. 88-111.

112. McFee, *Understanding Dance*, pp. 90-94; R. A. Sharpe, "Type, Token, Interpretation and Performance," *MQRP* 88, no. 351 (1979): 437-40.

113. Sharpe, "Type," p. 438.

114. Cf. Jean-Jacques Suurmond, *Word and Spirit at Play: Towards a Charismatic Theology* (Grand Rapids: Eerdmans, 1994), pp. 93-94.

115. See Katrien Pype, "Dancing for God or for the Devil: Pentecostal Discourse on Popular Dance in Kinshasa," *JRA* 36, nos. 3-4 (2006): 296-318.

116. See Dana L. Robert and M. L. Daneel, "Worship among Apostles and Zionists in Southern Africa, Zimbabwe," Thomas A. Kane, "Celebrating Pentecost in Leauva'a: Worship, Symbols, and Dance in Samoa," and Charles E. Farhadian, "Worship as Mission: The Personal and Social Ends of Papuan Worship in the Glory Hut," all in *Christian Worship Worldwide: Expanding Horizons, Deepening Practices*, ed. Charles E. Farhadian (Grand Rapids: Eerdmans, 2007), pp. 43-70, 156-70, and 171-95, respectively; Pype, "Dancing for God," pp. 305-8; Craig Scandrett-Leatherman, "'Can't Nobody Do Me like Jesus': The Politics of Embodied Aesthetics in Afro-Pentecostal Rituals" (Ph.D. diss., University of Kansas, 2005), pp. 229-39; Thomasina Neely-Chandler, "Modes of Ritual Performance in African-American Pentecostalism," in *The Interrelatedness of Music, Religion, and Ritual in African Performance Practice*, ed. Daniel K. Avorgbedor, African Studies 68 (Lewiston, NY: Edwin Mellen, 2002), pp. 313-45; T. Burton Pierce, "Jewishness and Pentecostal Worship," *Paraclete* 21, no. 3 (1987): 1-4.

117. Cf. F. Bixler, "Dancing in the Spirit," in *NIDPCM*, pp. 570-71.

118. Suurmond, *Word and Spirit*, pp. 180-84.

119. Suurmond, *Word and Spirit*, p. 219; J. Huizinga, *Homo Ludens: A Study of the Play-Element in Culture* (London: Routledge and Kegan Paul, 1949), p. 165.

120. Suurmond, *Word and Spirit*, pp. 194-98.

121. Suurmond, *Word and Spirit*, p. 217.

122. Suurmond, *Word and Spirit*, p. 218.

123. On the terminology see A. Deneffe, "Perichoresis, circuminsessio, circumincessio. Eine terminologische Untersuchung," *ZKT* 47 (1923): 497-532; L. Prestige, "*Perichoreō* and *perichorēsis* in the Fathers," *JTS* 29 (1928): 242-52.

124. Cf. LaCugna, *God for Us*, p. 272.

125. Terry Cross, "The Rich Feast of Theology: Can Pentecostals Bring the Main Course or Only the Relish?" *JPT* 16 (2000): 27-47, here pp. 45-46.

126. Samuel Solivan, *The Spirit, Pathos, and Liberation: Toward a Hispanic Pentecostal Theology*, JPTS 14 (Sheffield: Sheffield Academic, 1998), pp. 47-60.

127. Solivan, *The Spirit*, p. 51.

128. Solivan, *The Spirit*, p. 60.

129. Ralph Del Colle, "Oneness and Trinity: A Preliminary Proposal for Dialogue with Oneness Pentecostalism," *JPT* 10 (1997): 85-110, here p. 93.

130. Del Colle, "Oneness and Trinity," p. 94.

131. Del Colle, "Oneness and Trinity," pp. 95-96.

132. See Koo Dong Yun, *Baptism in the Holy Spirit: An Ecumenical Theology of Spirit Baptism* (Lanham, MD: University Press of America, 2003); Kilian McDonnell, ed., *Presence, Power, Praise: Documents on the Charismatic Renewal*, 3 vols. (Collegeville, MN: Liturgical Press, 1980).

133. See Frank Macchia, *Baptized in the Spirit: A Global Pentecostal Theology* (Grand Rapids: Zondervan, 2006), pp. 113-29.

134. Macchia, *Baptized in the Spirit*, p. 117.

135. Macchia, *Baptized in the Spirit*, p. 120.

136. See David Coffey, *Deus Trinitas: The Triune Doctrine of God* (Oxford: Oxford University Press, 1999), pp. 46-65. For a Pentecostal appropriation of Coffey, see Studebaker, "Beyond Tongues," pp. 46-68.

137. Cf. Macchia, *Baptized in the Spirit*, p. 118.

138. Wolfhart Pannenberg, *Anthropology in Theological Perspective*, trans. Matthew J. O'Connell (Philadelphia: Westminster, 1985), pp. 322-39.

139. Yong, *The Spirit Poured Out*, pp. 226, 233, 234.

140. See Oswald Bayer, "Poetologische Trinitätslehre," in *Zur Trinitätslehre in der lutherischen Kirche*, ed. Joachim Heubach, Veröffentlichungen der Luther-Akademie e.V. Ratzeburg 26 (Erlangen: Martin Luther Verlag, 1996), pp. 67-79.

141. See George A. Lindbeck, *The Nature of Doctrine: Religion and Theology in a Postliberal Age* (Philadelphia: Westminster, 1984), p. 95. See also John Ogden, *Believing the Creed: A Metaphorical Approach* (London: SCM, 2009).

142. Zigmund Bauman, *Postmodern Ethics* (Oxford: Blackwell, 1993), p. 164.

Notes to Chapter 4

1. For recent examples, see Louis-Marie Chauvet, *Symbol and Sacrament: A Sacramental Reinterpretation of Christian Existence*, trans. Patrick Madigan and Madeleine Beaumont (Collegeville, MN: Liturgical Press, 1995); Edward J. Kilmartin, *Christian Liturgy: Theology and Practice*, vol. 1, *Systematic Theology of Liturgy* (Kansas City, MO: Sheed and Ward, 1988), pp. 93-198.

2. Cf. Richard D. McCall, "Liturgical Theopoetic: The Acts of God in the Act of Liturgy," *WCILR* 71, no. 5 (1997): 399-401; Trevor A. Hart and Steven R. Guthrie, eds., *Faithful Performances: Enacting Christian Tradition* (Aldershot: Ashgate, 2007).

3. Romano Guardini, "An Open Letter," *Herder-Correspondence* 1.1 (1964): 25.

4. Evangelista Vilanova, "The Liturgical Crisis and Criticism of Religion," in *Concilium: Theology in the Age of Renewal,* vol. 42, *The Crisis of Liturgical Reform* (New York: Paulist, 1969), p. 6.

5. A good overview of the broadness of the liturgical crisis is gained from the essays in *Concilium,* vol. 42, *The Crisis of Liturgical Reform,* and vol. 62, *Liturgy in Transition.* For a detailed overview of the history of liturgical reforms, see Martin Klöckener and Benedikt Kranemann, eds., *Liturgiereformen: Historische Studien zu einem bleibenden Grundzug des christlichen Gottesdienstes,* 2 vols., Liturgiewissenschaftliche Quellen und Forschungen 88 (Münster: Aschendorff, 2002).

6. See James L. Halverson, ed., *Contesting Christendom: Readings in Medieval Religion and Culture* (Lanham, MD: Rowman and Littlefield, 2008); Stuart Murray, *Post-Christendom* (Carlisle, U.K.: Paternoster, 2004); Philip Jenkins, *The Next Christendom: The Coming of Global Christianity* (Oxford: Oxford University Press, 2002); Douglas John Hall, *The End of Christendom and the Future of Christianity* (Valley Forge, PA: Trinity, 1997); Malcolm Muggeridge, *The End of Christendom* (Grand Rapids: Eerdmans, 1980).

7. Among the first to make the argument were E. K. Chambers, *The Medieval Stage,* 2 vols. (Oxford: Clarendon, 1903); Karl Young, *The Drama of the Medieval Church,* 2 vols. (Oxford: Clarendon, 1933). For recent observations see Richard D. McCall, *Do This: Liturgy as Performance* (Notre Dame, IN: University of Notre Dame Press, 2007); Nils Holger Petersen, "Representation in European Devotional Rituals: The Question of the Origin of Medieval Drama in Medieval Liturgy," in *The Origins of Theater in Ancient Greece and Beyond: From Ritual to Drama,* ed. Eric Csapo and Margaret C. Miller (Cambridge: Cambridge University Press, 2007), pp. 329-60.

8. Cf. Salvatore Paterno, *The Liturgical Context of Early European Drama,* Scripta Humanistica 56 (Potomac, MD: Scripta Humanistica, 1989), pp. 7-66; McCall, *Do This,* pp. 9-40; Petersen, "Representation," p. 329.

9. Young, *The Drama,* 1:79-81.

10. Young, *The Drama,* 1:80-81, italics in original.

11. See also Walther Lipphardt, *Lateinische Osterfeiern und Osterspiele,* 9 vols. (Berlin: De Gruyter, 1975-90); Blandine-Dominique Berger, *Le drame liturgique de Paques du Xe au XIIIe siècle: Liturgie et théâtre,* Théologie Historique 37 (Paris: Beauchesne, 1976).

12. Young, *The Drama,* 1:110.

13. O. B. Hardison, Jr., *Christian Rite and Christian Drama in the Middle Ages: Essays in the Origin and Early History of Modern Drama* (Baltimore: Johns Hopkins University Press, 1965), p. 44.

14. Hardison, *Christian Rite,* p. 44.

15. Hardison, *Christian Rite,* p. 41. On the methodological approach of Hardison and Young, see Berger, *Le drame liturgique,* pp. 97-134.

16. Cf. Éric Palazzo, *Liturgie et société au Moyen Âge* (Paris: Aubier, 2000).

17. C. Clifford Flannigan, Kathleen Ashley, and Pamela Sheingorn, "Liturgy as Social Performance: Expanding the Definition," in *The Liturgy of the Medieval Church,* ed. Thomas J. Heffernan and E. Ann Matter (Kalamazoo: Medieval Institute Publications, Western Michigan University, 2001), p. 699.

18. Flannigan, Ashley, and Sheingorn, "Liturgy as Social Performance," p. 714.

19. See Catherine Bell, *Ritual: Perspectives and Dimensions* (New York: Oxford University Press, 1997); Mark Searle, "Ritual," in *The Study of Liturgy,* ed. Cheslyn Jones et al., rev.

ed. (London: SPCK, 1992), pp. 51-58. On ritual and performance see Margaret May Kelleher, "Hermeneutics in the Study of Liturgical Performance," *WCILR* 67, no. 4 (1993): 304-7; Stanley Jeyaraja Tambiah, *Culture, Thought, and Social Action: An Anthropological Perspective* (Cambridge, MA: Harvard University Press, 1985), pp. 123-66.

20. Cf. V. A. Kolve, *The Play Called Corpus Christi* (Stanford: Stanford University Press, 1966), pp. 12-13.

21. See Young, *The Drama*, 2:408.

22. Chambers, *The Medieval Stage*, 2:104.

23. See the detailed overview in Thomas Klie, *Zeichen und Spiel: Semiotische und spieltheoretische Rekonstruktion der Pastoraltheology,* Praktische Theologie und Kultur 11 (Gütersloh: Christian Kaiser, 2003).

24. See Elizabeth C. Parker, "Architecture as Liturgical Setting," in *The Liturgy of the Medieval Church*, pp. 273-326; see also, in the same volume, Elizabeth Parker McLachlan, "Liturgical Vessels and Implements," pp. 369-429; Thomas P. Campbell, "Liturgical Drama and Community Discourse," pp. 619-44; and Gabriela Ilnitchi, "Music in the Liturgy," pp. 645-71.

25. Searle, "Ritual," p. 57.

26. McCall, *Do This*, p. 11.

27. McCall, *Do This*, p. 13.

28. For example, the *Book of Hours*. Cf. Jeanne E. Krochalis and E. Ann Matter, "Manuscripts of the Liturgy," in *The Liturgy of the Medieval Church*, p. 437; in the same volume, see also Roger S. Wiek, "The Book of Hours," pp. 473-513.

29. Cf. Seth Lerer, "'Representyd Now in Yower Syght': The Culture of Spectatorship in Late Fifteenth-Century England," in *Bodies and Disciplines: Intersections of Literature and History in Fifteenth-Century England*, ed. Barbara A. Hanawalt and David Wallace (Minneapolis: University of Minnesota Press, 1996), pp. 29-62.

30. Young, *The Drama*, 2:401.

31. McCall, *Do This*, p. 17.

32. See Hardison, *Christian Rite*, pp. 284-92; Irène Slawinska, "Le théâtre liturgique aux XXe siècle (Genres et formes)," in *Problèmes, interférences des genres au théâtre et les fêtes en Europe: études,* ed. Danièle Becker and Irène Mamczarz (Paris: Presses Universitaires de France, 1985), pp. 217-34; François Lefebre, *Théâtre et liturgie,* Perspectives de théologie pratique 3 (Québec: Fides, 1998), pp. 110-15.

33. Young, *The Drama*, 2:421.

34. Young, *The Drama*, 2:425; Walther Lipphardt, "Der dramatische Tropus. Fragen des Ursprungs, der Ausführung und der Verbreitung," in *Dimensioni Drammatiche della Liturgia Medioevale,* ed. Centro di Studi sul Teatro Medioevale e Rinascimentale (Città di Castello: Bulzoni, 1977), pp. 17-31.

35. See Oscar Cargill, *Drama and Liturgy* (New York: Octagon Books, 1969), pp. 37-50.

36. Cf. Winfried Haunerland, "Einheitlichkeit als Weg der Erneuerung. Das Konzil von Trient und die nachtridentische Reform der Liturgie," in Klöckener and Kranemann, *Liturgiereformen,* 1:436-65; Theodor Klauser, *A Short History of the Western Liturgy: An Account and Some Reflection,* trans. John Halliburton, 2nd ed. (Oxford: Oxford University Press, 1979), pp. 124-29.

37. Cf. W. Moelwyn Merchant, *Creed and Drama: An Essay in Religious Drama* (Philadelphia: Fortress, 1965), pp. 28-30.

38. McCall, *Do This*, p. 15.

39. See Martin R. Dudley, "Sacramental Liturgies in the Middle Ages," in *The Liturgy of the Medieval Church*, pp. 215-43.

40. See Edward J. Kilmartin, *The Eucharist in the West*, ed. Robert J. Daly (Collegeville, MN: Liturgical Press, 1998), pp. 117-53.

41. Cf. *Mediator Dei*, nos. 40, 68, 82, 85, 91, 95; *Mystici Corporis Christi*, no. 53.

42. Kilmartin, *Eucharist in the West*, p. 135.

43. *STh* III, 22, 4c.

44. Cf. Klauser, *Short History*, pp. 117-52; Joseph A. Jungmann, *Liturgical Renewal in Retrospect and Prospect*, trans. Clifford Howell (London: Burns and Oates, 1965), pp. 10-12.

45. See Wolfgang Vondey, "New Evangelization and Liturgical Praxis in the Roman Catholic Church," *SL* 36, no. 2 (2006): 231-52.

46. Cf. David Torevell, *Losing the Sacred: Ritual, Modernity, and Liturgical Reform* (Edinburgh: T. & T. Clark, 2000), pp. 80-115.

47. Cf. Angelus Albert Häussling, "Liturgiereform und Liturgiefähigkeit," *AL* 38-39, no. 1 (1996-97): 1-24; Arno Schilson, "Liturgie und Menschsein: Überlegungen zur Liturgiefähigkeit des Menschen am Ende des 20. Jahrhunderts," *LJ* 39, no. 4 (1989): 206-27; Klemens Richter, "Die Frage nach der Liturgiefähigkeit angesichts einer erneuerten Liturgie," in *Auslegungen des Glaubens: Zur Hermeneutik christlicher Existenz*, ed. Ludger Honnefelder and Matthias Lutz-Bachmann (Berlin: Morus-Verlag, 1987), pp. 85-106.

48. Victor Turner, *The Anthropology of Performance* (New York: PAJ Publications, 1987), p. 75.

49. Cf. Wolfgang Vondey, "The Symbolic Turn: A Symbolic Conception of the Liturgy of Pentecostalism," *WTJ* 36, no. 2 (2001): 223-47.

50. Mary Douglas, *Natural Symbols: Explorations in Cosmology* (London: Barrie and Rockliff, 1970), pp. 59-65.

51. Cf. Kelleher, "Hermeneutics," p. 301.

52. Victor Turner, *From Ritual to Theatre: The Human Seriousness of Play* (New York: PAJ Publications, 1982), pp. 79-80.

53. Bruce Kapferer, "Performance and the Structuring of Meaning and Experience," in *The Anthropology of Experience*, ed. Victor W. Turner and Edward M. Bruner (Urbana: University of Illinois Press, 1986), pp. 188-203.

54. See, for example, Graham Hughes, *Worship as Meaning: A Liturgical Theology for Late Modernity* (Cambridge: Cambridge University Press, 2003).

55. Victor Turner, "Body, Brain, and Culture," *ZJRS* 18, no. 3 (1983): 232-36.

56. Turner, "Body, Brain, and Culture," p. 235.

57. Romano Guardini, *The Spirit of the Liturgy*, trans. Ada Lane (New York: Herder and Herder, 1998), pp. 71-72.

58. See Kenneth Smits, "Liturgical Reform in Cultural Perspective," *WCILR* 50, no. 2 (1976): 98-110.

59. Søren Kierkegaard, *Purity of Heart Is to Will One Thing*, trans. Douglas V. Steere (New York: Harper and Row, 1984), pp. 173-84.

60. See Karen B. Westerfield Tucker, "North America," in *The Oxford History of Christian Worship*, ed. Geoffrey Wainwright and Karen B. Westerfield Tucker (Oxford: Oxford University Press, 2006), pp. 586-632.

61. See, in particular, Walter J. Hollenweger, *The Pentecostals: The Charismatic Move-*

ment in the Churches (Minneapolis: Augsburg, 1972); Hollenweger, "Handbuch der Pfingstbewegung," 10 vols. (Ph.D. diss., University of Zurich, 1965-67); Hollenweger, "The Social and Ecumenical Significance of Pentecostal Liturgy," *SL* 8, no. 4 (1971): 207-15.

62. Hollenweger, "Social and Ecumenical Significance," p. 208.

63. Walter J. Hollenweger, "The Black Roots of Pentecostalism," in *Pentecostals after a Century: Global Perspectives on a Movement in Transition,* ed. Allan H. Anderson and Walter J. Hollenweger, JPTS 15 (Sheffield: Sheffield Academic, 1999), p. 40.

64. See, for example, Ian MacRobert, *The Black Roots and White Racism of Early Pentecostalism in the USA* (New York: St. Martin's Press, 1988); MacRobert, "The Black Roots of Pentecostalism," in *African American Religion: Interpretive Essays in History and Culture,* ed. Timothy E. Fulop and Albert J. Raboteau (New York: Routledge, 1997), pp. 295-309; Arthur E. Paris, *Black Pentecostalism: Southern Religion in an Urban World* (Amherst: University of Massachusetts Press, 1982); Cheryl J. Sanders, "African American Worship in the Pentecostal and Holiness Movements," *WTJ* 32, no. 2 (1997): 105-20.

65. A step in this direction was made by David M. Beckman, "Trance: From Africa to Pentecostalism," *CTM* 45, no. 1 (1974): 11-26.

66. See Hans A. Baer and Merrill Singer, *African American Religion: Varieties of Protest and Accommodation,* 2nd ed. (Knoxville: University of Tennessee Press, 2002), pp. 1-26. In the context of Pentecostalism, David D. Daniels, "'Everybody Bids You Welcome': A Multicultural Approach to North American Pentecostalism," in *The Globalization of Pentecostalism: A Religion Made to Travel,* ed. Murray W. Dempster et al. (Oxford: Regnum, 1999), pp. 222-52.

67. Dwight N. Hopkins, "Slave Theology in the 'Invisible Institution,'" in *Cut Loose Your Stammering Tongue: Black Theology in the Slave Narrative,* ed. D. N. Hopkins and George C. L. Cummings, 2nd ed. (Louisville: Westminster/John Knox, 2003), pp. 1-2.

68. Cf. Peter H. Wood, "'Jesus Christ Has Got Thee at Last': Afro-American Conversion as Forgotten Chapter in Eighteenth Century Southern Intellectual History," *BCSSCR* 3, no. 3 (1979): 1-7; Marcus W. Jernegan, "Slavery and Conversion in the American Colonies," *AHR* 21, no. 33 (1916): 505-27.

69. Hopkins, "Slave Theology," pp. 5-7.

70. Emily Dixon, quoted in Hopkins, "Slave Theology," p. 6.

71. Arthur Greene, quoted in Hopkins, "Slave Theology," p. 6.

72. George C. L. Cummings, "The Slave Narratives as a Source of Black Theological Discourse: The Spirit and Eschatology," in *Cut Loose Your Stammering Tongue,* pp. 33-46.

73. Cummings, "The Slave Narratives," p. 34.

74. Cummings, "The Slave Narratives," p. 43.

75. Joan Martin, "By Perseverance and Unwearied Industry," in *Cut Loose Your Stammering Tongue,* p. 127.

76. Charles Joyner, *Down by the Riverside: A South Carolina Community* (Urbana: University of Illinois Press, 1984), p. 141.

77. MacRobert, *Black Roots,* pp. 11-12; MacRobert, "Black Roots of Pentecostalism," pp. 299-301.

78. Cf. Janet Duitsman Cornelius, *Slave Missions and the Black Church in the Antebellum South* (Columbia: University of South Carolina Press, 1999), pp. 8-12, 16-20.

79. Cf. Charles Joyner, "'Believer I Know': The Emergence of African-American Christianity," in *African-American Christianity: Essays in History,* ed. Paul E. Johnson (Berkeley: University of California Press, 1994), pp. 25-36. Joyner speaks of "mutual performance."

80. Joyner, "Believer I Know," p. 30.

81. Dale P. Andrews, *Practical Theology for Black Churches: Bridging Black Theology and African American Folk Religion* (Louisville: Westminster/John Knox, 2002), pp. 34-37.

82. See Andrews, *Practical Theology*, pp. 12-30; Joyner, "Believer I Know," pp. 18-46.

83. See Charles A. Johnson, *The Frontier Camp Meeting: Religion's Harvest Time* (Dallas: Southern Methodist University Press, 1955); Paul K. Conklin, *Cane Ridge: America's Pentecost* (Madison: University of Wisconsin Press, 1990); Kenneth O. Brown, *Holy Ground: A Study of the American Tent Meeting*, Religious Information Systems Series 5 (New York: Garland, 1992); Kenneth O. Brown, *Holy Ground Too: The Camp Meeting Family Tree* (Hazelton, PA: Holiness Archives, 1997); Randall J. Stephens, *The Fire Spreads: Holiness and Pentecostalism in the American South* (Cambridge, MA: Harvard University Press, 2008).

84. See Baer and Singer, *African American Religion*, pp. 3-12; Andrews, *Practical Theology*, pp. 12-16; Albert J. Raboteau, *Slave Religion: The 'Invisible Institution' in the Antebellum South* (New York: Oxford University Press, 1978), p. 132.

85. Raboteau, *Slave Religion*, p. 72.

86. See Ellen Eslinger, *Citizens of Zion: The Social Origins of Camp Meeting Revivalism* (Knoxville: University of Tennessee Press, 1999).

87. Cf. Baer and Singer, *African American Religion*, p. 12; Percival A. Wesche, "The Revival of the Camp-Meeting by the Holiness Groups" (M.A. thesis, University of Chicago, 1945).

88. The most detailed documentation still comes from Brown, *Holy Ground Too*, pp. 26-68.

89. Eslinger, *Citizens of Zion*, pp. 233-35.

90. For a critique of formal definition, see Brown, *Holy Ground Too*, p. 27.

91. Westerfield Tucker, "North America," pp. 607-10.

92. Garry Hesser and Andrew J. Weigert, "Comparative Dimensions of Liturgy: A Conceptual Framework and Feasibility Application," *SA* 41, no. 3 (1980): 215-29.

93. Steven D. Cooley, "Manna and the Manual: Sacramental and Instrumental Constructions of the Victorian Methodist Camp Meeting during the Mid–Nineteenth Century," *RAC* 6, no. 2 (1996): 132.

94. For firsthand accounts see George Hughes, *Days of Power in the Forest Temple: A Review of the Wonderful Work of God at Fourteen National Camp-Meetings from 1867 to 1872* (Boston: John Best, 1873); Amos P. Mead, *Manna in the Wilderness; or, The Grove and Its Altar, Offerings, and Thrilling Incidents* (Philadelphia: Perkinpine and Higgins, 1860); Adam Wallace, *A Modern Pentecost: Embracing a Record of the Sixteenth National Camp-Meeting for the Promotion of Holiness Held at Landisville, Pa., July 23d to August 1st, 1873* (Philadelphia: Methodist Home Journal, 1873).

95. Cooley, "Manna and the Manual," pp. 137-45.

96. Cf. Baer and Singer, *African American Religion*, p. 11.

97. See Melvin Easterday Dieter, *The Holiness Revival of the Nineteenth Century*, 2nd ed., Studies in Evangelicalism 1 (Lanham, MD: Scarecrow, 1996), pp. 81-99.

98. Cf. Westerfield Tucker, "North America," pp. 615-16.

99. Cf. Grant Wacker, *Heaven Below: Early Pentecostals and American Culture* (Cambridge, MA: Harvard University Press, 2001), p. 100.

100. Vinson Synan, *The Holiness-Pentecostal Movement* (Grand Rapids: Eerdmans, 1971), pp. 33-54.

101. Victor Turner, *The Forest of Symbols: Aspects of Ndembu Ritual* (Ithaca, NY: Cornell University Press, 1967).

102. See Armon Newburn, "The Significance of the Altar Service," in *Conference on the Holy Spirit Digest,* vol. 2, ed. Gwen Jones (Springfield, MO: Gospel Publishing House, 1983), pp. 168-74.

103. Guy Shields, "Camp-Meeting Special," in *Pentecostal and Charismatic Studies: A Reader,* ed. William K. Kay and Anne E. Dyer (London: SCM, 2004), p. 18.

104. Dieter, *The Holiness Revival,* pp. 81-82. On the rural-urban transition, see Timothy L. Smith, *Revivalism and Social Reform in Mid-Nineteenth-Century America* (Nashville: Abingdon, 1957).

105. See Eric Arnesen, *Black Protest and the Great Migration: A Brief History with Documents,* Bedford Series in History and Culture (Boston: Bedford/St. Martin's Press, 2003); Milton C. Sernett, *Bound for the Promised Land: African American Religion and the Great Migration* (Durham, NC: Duke University Press, 1997).

106. Cf. Carole Marks, *Farewell — We're Good and Gone* (Bloomington: Indiana University Press, 1989), pp. 110-36.

107. Karen Lynell Kossie, "The Move Is On: African American Pentecostal-Charismatics in the Southwest" (Ph.D. diss., Rice University, 1998), p. 62. On the Holiness movement and the migration, see also Charles Edwin Jones, *Perfectionist Persuasion: The Holiness Movement and American Methodism, 1867-1936,* ATLA Monograph Series 5 (Metuchen, NJ: Scarecrow, 1974), pp. 79-88.

108. Cf. E. Franklin Frazier, *The Negro Church in America* (New York: Schocken, 1974), pp. 58-60.

109. See Frazier, *Negro Church in America,* pp. 52-80; Stephens, *The Fire Spreads,* pp. 67-69.

110. The difference of urban and rural revivalism in North America is one of the central arguments in Smith, *Revivalism and Social Reform in Mid-Nineteenth-Century America.* On the impact of urbanization on religion, see Harvey Cox, *The Secular City,* rev. ed. (New York: Macmillan, 1966).

111. Cecil M. Robeck, Jr., *The Azusa Street Mission and Revival: The Birth of the Global Pentecostal Movement* (Nashville: Nelson, 2006), pp. 129-31.

112. See Daniels, "Everybody Bids You Welcome," pp. 225-33. For the criticism see Synan, *The Holiness-Pentecostal Movement,* pp. 110-12; Cecil M. Robeck, Jr., "The Past: Historical Roots of Racial Unity and Division in American Pentecostalism," *CPCR* 14 (May 2005), available at http://www.pctii.org/cyberj/cyberj14/robeck.html [accessed June 1, 2008]; Synan, pp. 178-84.

113. "Sermons by Charles F. Parham," *AF,* April 1925, pp. 9-10.

114. Robeck, *Azusa Street Mission,* p. 137.

115. Robeck, *Azusa Street Mission,* pp. 138-86; David Douglas Daniels III, "'Gotta Moan Somtime': A Sonic Exploration of Earwitnesses to Early Pentecostal Sound in North America," *Pneuma* 30, no. 1 (2008): 5-32.

116. Robeck, *Azusa Street Mission,* p. 131.

117. Scholarship has only recently refuted that position; see Charles Gaede, "Pentecost and Praise: A Pentecostal Ritual?" *Paraclete* 22, no. 2 (1988): 5-8; Richard A. Baer, Jr., "Quaker Silence, Catholic Liturgy, and Pentecostal Glossolalia — Some Functional Similarities," in

Perspectives on the New Pentecostalism, ed. Russell P. Spittler (Grand Rapids: Baker, 1976), pp. 151-64.

118. Bobby C. Alexander, *Victor Turner Revisited: Ritual as Social Change,* AAR Academy Series 74 (Atlanta: Scholars, 1991), p. 71.

119. On the structural aspects see Bobby C. Alexander, "Pentecostal Ritual Reconsidered: Anti-Structural Dimensions of Possession," *JRS* 3, no. 1 (1989): 109-28.

120. See Alcuin Reid, *The Organic Development of the Liturgy: The Principles of Liturgical Reform and Their Relation to the Twentieth-Century Liturgical Movement Prior to the Second Vatican Council,* 2nd ed. (San Francisco: Ignatius, 2005).

121. Cf. John R. K. Fenwick and Bryan D. Spinks, *Worship in Transition: The Liturgical Movement in the Twentieth Century* (New York: Continuum, 1995), pp. 187-94.

122. Cf. Estrelda Y. Alexander, "Liturgy in Non-Liturgical Holiness-Pentecostalism," *WTJ* 32, no. 3 (1997): 158-93.

123. Cf. Gordon Graham, "Liturgy as Drama," *ThTo* 64, no. 1 (2007): 71-79; Warren Kliewer, "Dramatic Perception in the Liturgy," *ChrCent* 82, no. 15 (1965): 459-61.

124. See Kevin J. Vanhoozer, *The Drama of Doctrine: A Canonical-Linguistic Approach to Christian Theology* (Louisville: Westminster/John Knox, 2005), pp. 401-13; Susan K. Wood, "The Liturgy: Participatory Knowledge of God in the Liturgy," in *Knowing the Triune God: The Work of the Spirit in the Practices of the Church,* ed. James J. Buckley and Davis S. Yeago (Grand Rapids: Eerdmans, 2001), pp. 95-118; Graham, "Liturgy as Drama," pp. 71-75.

125. See, for example, Vanhoozer, *The Drama of Doctrine,* pp. 415-17; Richard D. McCall, "Liturgical Theopoetic: The Acts of God in the Act of Liturgy," *WCILR* 71, no. 5 (1997): 399-414; Lawrence A. Hoffman, "Liturgy, Drama, and Readership Strategies: Avoiding Alienation from Our Rites," *LM* 2 (Spring 1993): 49-55.

126. Vanhoozer, *The Drama of Doctrine,* p. 417.

127. Cf. Graham, "Liturgy as Drama," p. 71. This stands in contrast to the rationality debate in ritual studies; see the overview in Joel Mort and D. Jason Slone, "Considering the Rationality of Ritual Behavior," *MTSR* 18, no. 4 (2006): 424-39.

128. Cf. Mort and Slone, "Rationality of Ritual Behavior," pp. 426-27.

129. Mort and Slone, "Rationality of Ritual Behavior," p. 428.

130. See George A. Lindbeck, *The Nature of Doctrine: Religion and Theology in a Postliberal Age* (Philadelphia: Westminster, 1984), pp. 65-66; Vanhoozer, *The Drama of Doctrine,* pp. 295-305.

131. Vanhoozer, *The Drama of Doctrine,* pp. 295, 409-10.

132. Graham, "Liturgy as Drama," p. 73.

133. Graham, "Liturgy as Drama," p. 74.

134. Graham, "Liturgy as Drama," p. 74.

135. McCall, *Do This,* pp. 86-89; Graham, "Liturgy as Drama," pp. 75-77.

136. Graham, "Liturgy as Drama," p. 75.

137. Cf. Ivan Patricio Khovacs, "A Cautionary Note on the Use of Theatre in Theology," in *Faithful Performances,* p. 39.

138. Guardini, *Spirit of the Liturgy,* pp. 62-63.

139. Guardini, *Spirit of the Liturgy,* p. 71.

140. Guardini, *Spirit of the Liturgy,* p. 68.

141. Guardini, *Spirit of the Liturgy,* p. 71.

142. See, for example, Carlo F. Dumermuth, "Religio Theologia Ludens: Some Non-

Systematic Cursory Remarks," *AJT* 14, no. 1 (2000): 176-87; Don Saliers, "Liturgy as Holy Play," *Weavings* 9 (November 1994): 40-44; Kieran Flanagan, "Liturgy as Play: A Hermeneutics of Ritual Re-Presentation," *MT* 4, no. 4 (1988): 345-72; R. Ronald Sequeira, *Spielende Liturgie: Bewegung neben Wort und Ton im Gottesdienst am Beispiel des Vaterunsers* (Freiburg: Herder, 1977); P. Theodor Bogler, *Spiel und Feier: Ihre Gestaltung aus dem Geist der Liturgie,* Liturgie und Mönchtum III, 16 (Maria Laach: Ars Liturgica, 1955); Friedrich Niebergall, *Praktische Theologie: Lehre von der kirchlichen Gemeindeerziehung auf religionswissenschaftlicher Grundlage,* vol. 2 (Tübingen: J. C. B. Mohr, 1919).

143. See, especially, Daniel E. Albrecht, *Rites in the Spirit: A Ritual Approach to Pentecostal/Charismatic Spirituality,* JPTS 17 (Sheffield: Sheffield Academic, 1999); Albrecht, "Pentecostal Spirituality: Looking through the Lens of Ritual," *Pneuma* 14, no. 2 (1992): 107-25; Alexander, *Victor Turner Revisited,* pp. 67-104; Alexander, "Pentecostal Ritual Reconsidered," pp. 109-28; Jon Michael Spencer, "Isochronisms of Antistructure in the Black Holiness-Pentecostal Testimony Service," *JBSM* 2 (Fall 1988): 1-18; Gaede, "Pentecost and Praise," pp. 5-8; Paris, *Black Pentecostalism,* pp. 45-79; John Wilson and Harvey K. Clow, "Themes of Power and Control in a Pentecostal Assembly," *JSSR* 20, no. 3 (1981): 241-50.

144. Albrecht, *Rites in the Spirit,* pp. 179, 181.

145. Albrecht, *Rites in the Spirit,* p. 188.

146. Albrecht, *Rites in the Spirit,* pp. 188-89.

147. Albrecht, *Rites in the Spirit,* p. 189.

148. See Albrecht, *Rites in the Spirit,* appendixes A and B.

149. Albrecht, *Rites in the Spirit,* pp. 209-11.

150. Victor Turner, *The Ritual Process: Structure and Anti-Structure* (Chicago: Aldine, 1969), pp. 94-97.

151. Turner, *The Ritual Process,* p. 95.

152. Mathieu Deflem, "Ritual, Anti-Structure, and Religion: A Discussion of Victor Turner's Processual Symbolic Analysis," *JSSR* 30, no. 1 (1991): 14. See Turner, *The Forest of Symbols,* pp. 99-108.

153. Flanagan, "Liturgy as Play," p. 366.

154. Victor Turner, *Dramas, Fields, and Metaphors: Symbolic Action in Human Society* (Ithaca, NY: Cornell University Press, 1974), p. 46; Turner, *The Forest of Symbols,* pp. 93-111.

155. Victor Turner, "Liminal to Liminoid, in Play, Flow, and Ritual: An Essay in Comparative Symbology," *RUS* 60, no. 3 (1974): 53-92.

156. Turner, "Liminal to Liminoid," p. 61.

157. Turner, "Liminal to Liminoid," p. 63.

158. Turner, "Liminal to Liminoid," p. 65.

159. Cf. Virginia H. Hine, "The Deprivation and Disorganization Theories of Social Movements," in *Religious Movements in Contemporary America,* ed. Irving I. Zaretsky and Mark P. Leone (Princeton: Princeton University Press, 1974), pp. 646-61.

160. See Victor Turner, "Ritual, Tribal and Catholic," *WCILR* 50, no. 3 (1976): 504-26.

161. Catherine Bell, "Ritual, Change, and Changing Rituals," *WCILR* 63, no. 1 (1989): 32.

162. See the critique of these perspectives in Bell, "Ritual, Change," pp. 31-41. Page references to this article have been placed in the text.

163. Alexander, "Pentecostal Ritual Reconsidered," pp. 109-13; Bobby C. Alexander, "Correcting Misinterpretations of Turner's Theory: An African-American Pentecostal Illustration," *JSSR* 30, no. 1 (1991): 32-41.

164. Alexander, *Victor Turner Revisited*, p. 77.

165. Alexander, "Correcting Misinterpretations," pp. 34-35; Alexander, "Pentecostal Ritual Reconsidered," pp. 113-16.

166. Alexander, "Correcting Misinterpretations," p. 35.

167. Alexander, "Correcting Misinterpretations," p. 35.

168. Frank D. Macchia, "Discerning the Truth of Tongues Speech: A Response to Amos Yong," *JPT* 12 (1998): 69-70. See particularly Macchia, *Baptized in the Spirit: A Global Pentecostal Theology* (Grand Rapids: Zondervan, 2006), pp. 247-56; Macchia, "Groans Too Deep for Words: Towards a Theology of Tongues as Initial Evidence," *AJPS* 1, no. 2 (1998): 149-73; Macchia, "Tongues as a Sign: Towards a Sacramental Understanding of Pentecostal Experience," *Pneuma* 15, no. 1 (1993): 61-76.

169. Macchia, "Discerning the Truth," p. 70; see also Russell Spittler, "Glossolalia," in *NIDPCM*, p. 675; Richard A. Hutch, "The Personal Ritual of Glossolalia," *JSSR* 19, no. 3 (1980): 255-66.

170. For an introduction to the issue, see Macchia, "Tongues as a Sign," pp. 61-64.

171. Macchia, "Tongues as a Sign," pp. 63-64.

172. Cf. Richard Bicknell, "The Ordinances: The Marginalised Aspects of Pentecostalism," in *Pentecostal Perspectives*, ed. Keith Warrington (Carlisle, U.K.: Paternoster, 1998), pp. 204-22.

173. Karl Rahner, "Religious Enthusiasm and the Experience of Grace," in *Theological Investigations*, vol. 16, *Experience of the Spirit: Source of Theology*, trans. David Morland (New York: Crossroad, 1979), p. 46.

174. See Margaret M. Poloma, *Main Street Mystics: The Toronto Blessing and Reviving Pentecostalism* (Lanham, MD: Altamira, 2003), pp. 59-85.

175. Jean-Jacques Suurmond, "The Church at Play: The Pentecostal/Charismatic Renewal of the Liturgy as Renewal of the World," in *Pentecost, Mission, and Ecumenism: Essays on Intercultural Theology; Festschrift in Honour of Professor Walter Hollenweger*, ed. Jan A. B. Jongeneel et al., Studien zur Interkulturellen Geschichte des Christentums 75 (Frankfurt: Peter Lang, 1992), pp. 251-52.

176. Suurmond, "The Church at Play," p. 252.

177. See Wolfgang Vondey, *People of Bread: Rediscovering Ecclesiology* (New York: Paulist, 2008), pp. 243-89; Geoffrey Wainwright, *Eucharist and Eschatology* (London: Epworth, 1971); John D. Zizioulas, "The Eucharist and the Kingdom of God (Part 1)," *Sourozh* 58 (1994): 1-12; Zizioulas, "The Eucharist and the Kingdom of God (Part 2)," *Sourozh* 58 (1995): 22-38.

178. Amos Yong, *The Spirit Poured Out on All Flesh: Pentecostalism and the Possibility of Global Theology* (Grand Rapids: Baker Academic, 2005), p. 161.

179. See Charles Nienkirchen, "Conflicting Visions of the Past: Prophetic Use of History in Early American Pentecostal-Charismatic Movements," in *Charismatic Christianity as Global Culture*, ed. Karla Poewe (Columbia: University of South Carolina Press, 1994), pp. 119-33; see also, in the same volume, Nancy Schwartz, "Christianity and the Construction of Global History: The Example of Legio Maria," pp. 134-74.

180. See the various essays in Eric Patterson and Edmund Rybarczyk, eds., *The Future of Pentecostalism in the United States* (Lanham, MD: Lexington Books, 2007); Stanley Johannesen, "Third-Generation Pentecostal Language: Continuity and Change in Collective Perceptions," in *Charismatic Christianity as Global Culture*, pp. 175-99.

181. Poloma, *Main Street Mystics*, p. 63.

182. Cf. Flanagan, "Liturgy as Play," p. 364.

183. Simon Chan, *Liturgical Theology: The Church as Worshiping Community* (Downers Grove, IL: InterVarsity, 2006), p. 54.

184. See, for example, Ig-Jin Kim, *History and Theology of Korean Pentecostalism: Sunbogeum (Pure Gospel) Pentecostalism* (Zoetermeer, Netherlands: Uitgeverij Boekencentrum, 2003); David Martin, *Pentecostalism: The World Their Parish* (Oxford: Blackwell, 2002), pp. 132-52; André Corten, *Pentecostalism in Brazil: Emotion of the Poor and Theological Romanticism*, trans. Arianne Dorval (New York: St. Martin's Press, 1999), pp. 83-100; Ivan M. Satyavatra, "Contextual Perspectives on Pentecostalism as a Global Culture: A South Asian View," in *The Globalization of Pentecostalism*, pp. 203-21; Nicole Rodriguez Toulis, *Believing Identity: Pentecostalism and the Mediation of Jamaican Ethnicity and Gender in England* (Oxford: Berg, 1997); D. Neil Hudson, "Worship: Singing a New Song in a Strange Land," in *Pentecostal Perspectives*, pp. 177-203; Stephen D. Glazier, *Perspectives on Pentecostalism: Case Studies from the Caribbean and Latin America* (Lanham, MD: University Press of America, 1980).

185. See the negative evaluation of this ambiguity in Simon Chan, *Pentecostal Theology and the Christian Spiritual Tradition*, JPTS 21 (Sheffield: Sheffield Academic, 2000), pp. 7-16; Margaret M. Poloma, "The Symbolic Dilemma and the Future of Pentecostalism: Mysticism, Ritual, and Revival," in *The Future of Pentecostalism in the United States*, pp. 105-15.

186. Miroslav Volf, *Work in the Spirit: Toward a Theology of Work* (New York: Oxford University Press, 1991), p. 136.

187. Cf. Andrew Greeley, "Sociology and Church Structure," in *Structures of the Church*, ed. Teodoro Jiménez Urresti, Concilium 58 (New York: Herder and Herder, 1970), pp. 26-27.

188. Brian Sutton-Smith, *The Ambiguity of Play* (Cambridge, MA: Harvard University Press, 1997), p. 229.

189. See Sutton-Smith, *The Ambiguity of Play*, pp. 221-31.

190. Hans-Georg Gadamer, *Truth and Method*, trans. Garrett Barden and John Cumming (New York: Seabury Press, 1975), p. 99.

191. Gadamer, *Truth and Method*, p. 100.

192. Gadamer, *Truth and Method*, p. 105.

193. Cf. Frank J. Barrett, "Cultivating an Aesthetic of Unfolding: Jazz Improvisation as a Self-Organizing System," in *The Aesthetics of Organization*, ed. Stephen Linstead and Heather Höpfl (London: Sage, 2000), pp. 228-45; R. Chia, "From Complexity Science to Complex Thinking: Organization as Simple Location," *Organization* 5, no. 3 (1998): 341-69.

194. Barrett, "Cultivating an Aesthetic," pp. 229-37.

195. Barrett, "Cultivating an Aesthetic," p. 237.

Notes to Chapter 5

1. Avery Dulles, *Models of the Church*, expanded ed. (New York: Doubleday, 2002), p. 1.

2. Roger Haight, *Christian Community in History*, vol. 3, *Ecclesial Existence* (New York: Continuum, 2008), p. 4.

3. This is the term of Nicholas M. Healy, *Church, World, and the Christian Life: Practical-Prophetic Ecclesiology*, Cambridge Studies in Christian Doctrine 7 (Cambridge: Cambridge University Press, 2000), pp. 25-51.

4. Cf. Roger Haight, *Christian Community in History,* vol. 1, *Historical Ecclesiology* (New York: Continuum, 2004), pp. 26-66.

5. Haight, *Christian Community in History,* 3:5.

6. Recent examples are Haight, *Christian Community in History;* Joseph A. Komonchak, *Foundations in Ecclesiology* (Boston: Boston College, 1995); Eric G. Jay, *The Church: Its Changing Image through Twenty Centuries* (Atlanta: John Knox, 1978); James M. Gustafson, *Treasure in Earthen Vessels: The Church as a Human Institution* (Chicago: University of Chicago Press, 1961).

7. Cf. J. Milton Yinger, "The Sociology of Religion of Ernst Troeltsch," in *An Introduction to the History of Sociology,* ed. Harry Elmer Barnes (Chicago: University of Chicago Press, 1948), p. 314; David O. Moberg, *The Church as a Social Institution: The Sociology of American Religion,* 2nd ed. (Grand Rapids: Baker, 1962, 1984), p. 76.

8. The following is a summary of Ernst Troeltsch, *The Social Teaching of the Christian Churches,* vol. 1, trans. Olive Wyon (New York: Harper and Brothers, 1960), pp. 23-37. Page references have been placed in the text.

9. T. S. Eliot, *Notes toward the Definition of Culture* (New York: Harcourt, 1949), pp. 19-32.

10. See Douglas John Hall, *The End of Christendom and the Future of Christianity* (Valley Forge, PA: Trinity, 1996); Pablo Richard, *Death of Christendoms, Birth of the Church: Historical Analysis and Theological Interpretation,* trans. Phillip Berryman (Maryknoll, NY: Orbis, 1987).

11. Moberg, *The Church,* p. 17.

12. C. Wright Mills, *The Sociological Imagination, 40th Anniversary Edition* (New York: Oxford University Press, 2000); Steve Fuller, *The New Sociological Imagination* (London: Sage, 2005); Rhonda Levine, *Enriching the Sociological Imagination: How Radical Sociology Changed the Discipline* (Leiden: Brill, 2005).

13. See Troeltsch, *The Social Teaching of the Christian Churches,* vol. 2, trans. Olive Wyon (New York: Harper and Brothers, 1960), pp. 993-94. A third type, "mysticism," received less attention due to the absence of structural, institutional forms. Cf. Moberg, *The Church,* p. 75.

14. Moberg, *The Church,* pp. 89-90.

15. Troeltsch, *Social Teaching,* 2:993-94.

16. Troeltsch, *Social Teaching,* 2:991.

17. See William H. Swatos, Jr., "Church-Sect and Cult," *SA* 42 (1981): 17-26; Rodney Stark and William Sims Bainbridge, "Of Churches, Sects, and Cults," *JSSR* 18 (1979): 117-31; Paul Gustafson, "The Missing Member of Troeltsch's Trinity," *SA* 36 (1975): 224-26; Howard Becker, *Systematic Sociology: On the Basis of the "Beziehungslehre" and "Gebildelehre" of Leopold von Wiese* (Gary, IN: Norman Paul, 1950), pp. 624-42; J. Milton Yinger, *Religion and the Struggle for Power* (Durham, NC: Duke University Press, 1946).

18. Cf. Veli-Matti Kärkkäinen, "'The Nature and Purpose of the Church': Theological and Ecumenical Reflections from Pentecostal and Free Church Perspectives," in *Pentecostalism and Christian Unity: Ecumenical Documents and Critical Assessments,* ed. Wolfgang Vondey (Eugene, OR: Pickwick, 2010), pp. 231-42; Philip Jenkins, *The Next Christendom: The Coming of Global Christianity* (New York: Oxford University Press, 2002), pp. 107-39.

19. Cf. Robert J. Schreiter, "Globalization, Postmodernity, and the New Catholicity," in

For All People: Global Theologies in Contexts, ed. Else Marie Wiberg Pedersen et al. (Grand Rapids: Eerdmans, 2002), pp. 14, 24-31.

20. See John J. Burkhard, *Apostolicity Then and Now: An Ecumenical Church in a Postmodern World* (Collegeville, MN: Liturgical Press, 2004); Charles J. Conniry, "Identifying Apostolic Christianity: A Synthesis of Viewpoints," *JETS* 37 (1994): 247-61.

21. See Roger Haight, *Christian Community in History,* vol. 2, *Comparative Ecclesiology* (New York: Continuum, 2005), pp. 256-64; vol. 1, pp. 337-44; Hans Küng, *Structures of the Church* (New York: Nelson, 1964); WCC, ed., *Institutionalism,* Faith and Order Papers 37 (Geneva: WCC, 1963), pp. 5-22; Yves Congar, *Lay People in the Church: A Study of a Theology of the Laity,* trans. Donald Attwater (Westminster: Newman, 1963), pp. 36-48.

22. Congar, *Lay People,* p. 39.

23. Cf. Hans Dombois, *Hierarchie: Grund und Grenze einer umstrittenen Struktur* (Freiburg: Herder, 1971), p. 88.

24. Cf. Heribert Mühlen, *Una Mystica Persona: Die Kirche als das Mysterium der heilsgeschichtlichen Identität des Heiligen Geistes in Christus und den Christen: Eine Person in vielen Personen,* 2nd ed. (Paderborn: Ferdinand Schöningh, 1967), pp. 174-89; Congar, *Lay People,* pp. 61-77, 102-11.

25. Cf. Jay, *The Church,* p. 314.

26. Cf. WCC, ed., *Christ and the Church,* Faith and Order Papers 38 (Geneva: WCC, 1963), pp. 19-20.

27. Cf. Konrad Raiser, *Ecumenism in Transition: A Paradigm Shift in the Ecumenical Movement?* (Geneva: WCC, 1991), pp. 41-43. See Wolfhart Pannenberg, *Jesus — God and Man,* 2nd ed. (Philadelphia: Westminster, 1977), p. 33.

28. Stephen B. Bevans, *Models of Contextual Theology,* rev. ed. (Maryknoll, NY: Orbis, 2002), p. 50; Haight, *Christian Community in History,* 1:19.

29. Haight, *Christian Community in History,* 1:23.

30. Cf. Bevans, *Models of Contextual Theology,* p. 51.

31. Küng, *Structures of the Church,* p. 40; W. A. Visser 't Hooft, *The Meaning of Ecumenical* (London: SCM, 1954).

32. Cf. Patrick Granfield, "The Church as Institution: A Reformulated Model," *JES* 16, no. 3 (1979): 430.

33. Cf. Brian Stanley, "Defining the Boundaries of Christendom: The Two Worlds of the World Missionary Conference, 1910," *IBMR* 30, no. 4 (2006): 171-76.

34. Haight, *Christian Community in History,* 1:37.

35. See, for example, Susan Lynn Peterson, *Timeline Charts of the Western Church* (Grand Rapids: Zondervan, 1999), pp. 228-35, 238-62; Jeffrey Gros, Eamon McManus, and Ann Riggs, *Introduction to Ecumenism* (New York: Paulist, 1998), p. 14; Robert C. Walton, *Chronological and Background Charts of Church History* (Grand Rapids: Academie Books, 1986), pp. 68-76.

36. Cf. Haight, *Christian Community in History,* 1:2.

37. Haight, *Christian Community in History,* 2:477.

38. See Moberg, *The Church,* pp. 90-92; Jay, *The Church,* pp. 177-80.

39. Cf. Klaude Kendrick, "The Pentecostal Movement: Hopes and Hazards," *ChrCent* 80, no. 19 (1963): 608-10.

40. See, for example, Gros, McManus, and Riggs, *Introduction to Ecumenism,* p. 14.

41. Cf. Robert T. Handy, *A History of the Churches in the United States and Canada* (Oxford: Clarendon, 1976), pp. 136-311.

42. See "Pentecost Has Come," *AF* 1, no. 1 (September 1906): 1.

43. There is to my knowledge no publication among Pentecostals that discusses the meaning of the designation as "movement." Even the Society for Pentecostal Studies has never addressed the issue.

44. So also Dale M. Coulter, "The Development of Ecclesiology in the Church of God (Cleveland, TN): A Forgotten Contribution?" *Pneuma* 29, no. 1 (2007): 59-85.

45. See, for example, *WAW* 8, no. 6 (August 20, 1912): 2; S. D. Kinne, "The Assembly," *BM* 1, no. 22 (September 15, 1908): 2.

46. Cf. Jay Riley Case, "And Ever the Twain Shall Meet: The Holiness Missionary Movement and the Birth of World Pentecostalism, 1870-1920," *RAC* 16, no. 2 (2006): 125-59; Edith Blumhofer, "Restoration as Revival: Early American Pentecostalism," in *Modern Christian Revivals*, ed. Edith L. Blumhofer and Randall A. Balmer (Urbana: University of Illinois Press, 1993), pp. 145-61; Grant Wacker, "Playing for Keeps: The Primitivist Impulse in Early Pentecostalism," in *The American Quest for the Primitive Church*, ed. Richard T. Hughes (Urbana: University of Illinois Press, 1988), pp. 196-219.

47. *AF* 1, no. 1 (September 1906): 2.

48. *WAW* 8, no. 6 (August 20, 1912): 2.

49. See "One Church," *AF* 1, no. 2 (October 1906): 4; A. J. Tomlinson, "The Lord's Church," *BM* 2, no. 33 (May 1, 1909): 4.

50. Stanley H. Frodsham, "The Last Commission," *WE* 156 (September 9, 1916): 6.

51. B. F. Lawrence, "Apostolic Faith Restored, Article I," *WE* 121 (January 1, 1916): 4.

52. See "Transformed by the Holy Ghost," *AF* 1, no. 6 (February-March 1907): 5.

53. See Richard T. Hughes, ed., *The American Quest for the Primitive Church* (Urbana: University of Chicago Press, 1988), p. 5.

54. "Fires Are Being Kindled by the Holy Ghost throughout the World," *AF* 2, no. 13 (May 1908): 1. See Wacker, "Playing for Keeps," pp. 199-207.

55. D. Wesley Myland, *The Latter Rain Covenant and Pentecostal Power* (Chicago: Evangel Publishing House, 1910), p. 101. Cf. Donald W. Dayton, *Theological Roots of Pentecostalism* (Peabody, MA: Hendrickson, 1987), pp. 26-28.

56. See Arthur T. Pierson, *Forward Movements of the Last Half Century* (New York: Funk and Wagnalls Co., 1900).

57. B. F. Lawrence, "The Works of God, Article VII," *WE* 142 (June 3, 1916): 4. See also "Bible Pentecost," *AF* 1, no. 3 (October 1906): 1.

58. See W. F. Carothers, "Position of the Old 'Movement,'" *WE* 127 (February 19, 1916): 5.

59. Leila M. Conway, "United We Stand, Divided We Fall," *WE* 185 (April 14, 1917): 5.

60. Cf. Lawrence, "Apostolic Faith Restored, Article I," p. 4.

61. Cf. Coulter, "Development of Ecclesiology," pp. 64-67.

62. *AF* 1, no. 3 (November 1906): 2.

63. Wacker, "Playing for Keeps," pp. 209-10.

64. See "Christ and His Body," *PE*, no. 567 (October 11, 1924): 5. Cf. Walter J. Hollenweger, *The Pentecostals: The Charismatic Movement in the Churches* (Minneapolis: Augsburg, 1973), pp. 424-29.

65. See R. G. Spurling, *The Lost Link* (Turtletown, TN: n.p., 1920), pp. 12-16; Fred Lohmann, "Ye Shall Receive Power," *PE*, nos. 450-451 (June 24, 1922): 2.

66. William M. Faux, "Man Power," *PE*, no. 549 (June 7, 1924): 10. See also W. S. Norwood, "The Need of Spiritual Organization," *CE* 2, no. 13 (March 28, 1914): 5-6.

67. Spurling, *The Lost Link*, p. 8, italics mine.

68. Jonathan E. Perkins, "The Quartet That Raised the Roof," *PE*, no. 555 (July 19, 1924): 4.

69. "Letter from Bro. Seymour," *BM* 1, no. 5 (January 1, 1908): 2. See also A. J. Tomlinson, "Oneness," *BM* 2, no. 37 (May 14, 1909): 2.

70. See Tomlinson, "The Lord's Church," p. 4; A. J. Tomlinson, "Unity of the Faith," *BM* 1, no. 11 (April 1, 1908): 2; E. A. Saxton, "Organization," *BM* 5, no. 103 (February 1, 1912): 1.

71. Steven J. Land, *Pentecostal Spirituality: A Passion for the Kingdom*, JPTS 1 (Sheffield: Sheffield Academic, 1993), p. 178.

72. Leonardo Boff, *Ecclesiogenesis: The Base Communities Reinvent the Church*, trans. Robert R. Barr (Maryknoll, NY: Orbis, 1986), p. 2.

73. Carothers, "Position," p. 5.

74. A. S. Copley, "The Seven Dispensational Parables," *TP* 1, no. 7 (June 1909): 7.

75. Alberto Melloni, "Movements: On the Significance of Words," in *"Movements" in the Church*, ed. Alberto Melloni (London: SCM, 2003), pp. 7-26.

76. David Lehmann, "Dissidence and Conformism in Religious Movements: What Difference Separates the Catholic Charismatic Renewal and Pentecostal Churches?" in *"Movements" in the Church*, pp. 122-38.

77. *WE* 134 (April 8, 1916): 1.

78. David G. Roebuck, "Restorationism and a Vision for World Harvest: A Brief History of the Church of God (Cleveland, Tennessee)," *CPCR* 5 (February 1999), available at http://pctii.org/cyberj/cyberj5/roebuck.html, accessed July 10, 2008.

79. "We Are One," *PHA* 1, no. 3 (May 17, 1917): 8.

80. "We Are One," p. 8.

81. See E. A. Saxton, "Do Pentecostal People Need to Be Shepherded?" *BM* 2, no. 44 (August 15, 1909): 1.

82. The name "Church of God" is among the most popular. Cf. Vinson Synan, *The Holiness-Pentecostal Movement in the United States* (Grand Rapids: Eerdmans, 1971), pp. 77-93.

83. Cf. Robert Mapes Anderson, *Vision of the Disinherited: The Making of American Pentecostalism* (New York: Oxford University Press, 1979), pp. 192-94; Land, *Pentecostal Spirituality*, pp. 178-79.

84. B. F. Lawrence, "The Works of God, Article IV," *WE* 139 (May 13, 1916): 5.

85. J. H. King, "From the General Superintendent," *PHA* (September 6, 1917): 10.

86. See Wolfgang Vondey, "The Denomination in Classical and Global Pentecostal Ecclesiology: A Historical and Theological Contribution," in *"Denomination": Between the Church Local and Universal*, ed. Paul M. Collins and Barry Ensign-George, Ecclesiological Investigations 4 (London: T. & T. Clark, 2010), pp. 60-78.

87. Robert Mapes Anderson, *Vision of the Disinherited*, p. 194.

88. See Vondey, *Pentecostalism and Christian Unity*; Veli-Matti Kärkkäinen, "'Anonymous Ecumenists?' Pentecostals and the Struggle for Christian Identity," *JES* 37, no. 1 (2000): 13-27; Jeffrey Gros, "Pentecostal Engagement in the Wider Christian Community," *MEJ* 38, no. 4 (1999): 26-47; Cecil M. Robeck, Jr., "Pentecostals and the Apostolic Faith: Implications for Ecumenism," *Pneuma* 9, no. 1 (1987): 61-84.

89. Cf. Cecil M. Robeck, Jr., "Name and Glory: The Ecumenical Challenge" (paper presented at the Annual Meeting of the Society for Pentecostal Studies, Cleveland, Tenn., March 1983), pp. 12-19.

90. *AF* 1, no. 1 (September 1906): 4.

91. Cf. Kärkkäinen, "Anonymous Ecumenists?" pp. 15-18.

92. See, for example, *AF* 2, no. 13 (May 1908): 1-4.

93. Cf. Allan Anderson, *Spreading Fires: The Missionary Nature of Early Pentecostalism* (London: SCM, 2007); Michael Bergunder and Jörg Haustein, eds., *Migration und Identität: Pfingstlich-charismatische Migrationsgemeinden in Deutschland* (Frankfurt: Lembeck, 2006), pp. 155-69.

94. Allan Anderson, "Spreading Fires: The Globalization of Pentecostalism in the Twentieth Century," *IBMR* 31, no. 1 (2007): 10.

95. *WW* 29, no. 4 (April 1907): 117.

96. E. A. Saxton, "Increasing Missionary Activity," *BM* 3, no. 69 (September 1, 1910): 1; *PE*, no. 580 (January 17, 1925): 3.

97. See Luther P. Gerlach, "Pentecostalism: Revolution or Counter-Revolution," in *Religious Movements in Contemporary America*, ed. Irving I. Zaretsky and Mark P. Leone (Princeton: Princeton University Press, 1974), pp. 669-99; Bryan R. Wilson, "Role Conflict and Status Contradiction of the Pentecostal Minister," *AJS* 64 (1959): 494-504.

98. Paul D. Lee, "Pneumatological Ecclesiology in the Roman Catholic–Pentecostal Dialogue: A Catholic Reading of the Third Quinquennium (1985-1989)" (Ph.D. diss., Pontificia Studiorum Universitas a S. Thoma Aq. in Urbe, 1994), p. 15.

99. See Susie C. Stanley, "Wesleyan/Holiness Churches: Innocent Bystanders in the Fundamentalist/Modernist Controversy," in *Re-forming the Center: American Protestantism, 1900 to the Present,* ed. Douglas Jacobsen and William Vance Trollinger, Jr. (Grand Rapids: Eerdmans, 1998), pp. 172-93.

100. See Tracey Rowland, *Culture and the Thomist Tradition after Vatican II* (London: Routledge, 2003), pp. 11-34; Aidan Nichols, *Christendom Awake: On Re-energizing the Church in Culture* (Grand Rapids: Eerdmans, 1999), pp. 1-2.

101. Sigurd Bergmann, *God in Context: A Survey of Contextual Theology* (Aldershot: Ashgate, 2003), pp. 1-20; Bevans, *Models of Contextual Theology.*

102. Cf. Joseph P. Fitzpatrick, *One Church, Many Cultures: Challenge of Diversity* (Kansas City, MO: Sheed and Ward, 1987), p. 169.

103. Bevans, *Models of Contextual Theology,* p. 50.

104. Cf. Francis E. George, *Inculturation and Ecclesial Communion: Culture and Church in the Teaching of Pope John Paul II* (Rome: Urbania University Press, 1990), p. 245.

105. Rowland, *Culture,* p. 19.

106. Cf. John W. O'Malley, "Reform, Historical Consciousness, and Vatican II's Aggiornamento," *TS* 32, no. 4 (1971): 584-89; John W. O'Malley, *Tradition and Transition: Historical Perspectives on Vatican II,* Theology and Life 26 (Wilmington, DE: Michael Glazier, 1988), pp. 44-81; Manfred Hoffmann, "Church and History on Vatican II's Constitution on the Church: A Protestant Perspective," *TS* 29, no. 2 (1968): 191-214.

107. Rowland, *Culture,* pp. 11-50.

108. Rowland, *Culture,* p. 20.

109. Rowland, *Culture,* p. 161.

110. See Allan H. Anderson, *African Reformation: African Initiated Christianity in the 20th Century* (Trenton, NJ: Africa World, 2001), pp. 167-90.

111. Ogbu Kalu, "The Third Response: Pentecostalism and the Reconstruction of Church Experience in Africa, 1970-1995," *SHE* 24, no. 2 (1998): 1-34; Ogbu Kalu, "Peter Pan Syndrome: Aid and Selfhood of the Church in Africa," *Missiology* 3, no. 1 (1975): 15-29.

112. Ogbu Kalu, "Pentecostalism and Mission in Africa," *MS* 24, no. 1 (2007): 9-45.

113. Kalu, "Pentecostalism and Mission," pp. 27-28, 31-33; Jeffrey S. Hittenberger, "Globalization, 'Marketization,' and the Mission of Pentecostal Higher Education in Africa," *Pneuma* 26, no. 2 (2004): 182-215; Paul Gifford, *African Christianity: Its Public Role* (Bloomington: Indiana University Press, 1998), pp. 31-39.

114. Ogbu Kalu, "Not Just New Relationships but a New Body," *IRM* 64, no. 254 (1975): 143-47.

115. See J. Kwabena Asamoah-Gyadu, *African Charismatics: Current Developments within Independent Indigenous Pentecostalism in Ghana* (Leiden: Brill, 2005); Paul Gifford, *Ghana's New Christianity: Pentecostalism in a Globalising African Economy* (London: Hurst and Co., 2004); Cephas Omenyo, *Pentecost Outside Pentecostalism: A Study of the Development of Charismatic Renewal in the Mainline Churches in Ghana* (Zoetermeer: Uitgeverij Boekecentrum, 2002); and the essays in *Pneuma* 24, no. 2 (2002): 110-224.

116. Cf. Cephas Omenyo, "Charismatic Churches in Ghana and Contextualization," *EJEMR* 31, no. 3 (2002): 265-68.

117. Omenyo, "Charismatic Churches," p. 268.

118. Line Marie Onsrud, "East Africa Pentecostal Churches: A Study of 'Self-Historisation' as Contextualisation," *SM* 87, no. 3 (1999): 419-46.

119. Cf. G. C. Oosthuisen, "The Use of Oral Information in the Writing of the History of African Indigenous Churches," *SHE* 19, no. 1 (1993): 64-80.

120. Ogbu Kalu, "Pentecostal and Charismatic Reshaping of the African Religious Landscape in the 1990s," *MS* 20, no. 1 (2003): 84-111.

121. Cf. Stephan Hunt, "'A Church for All Nations': The Redeemed Christian Church of God," *Pneuma* 24, no. 2 (2002): 200.

122. Cf. Michael Harper, "The Holy Spirit Acts in the Church, Its Structures, Its Sacramentality, Its Worship and Sacraments," *OIC* 12 (1976): 322; Veli-Matti Kärkkäinen, *An Introduction to Ecclesiology: Ecumenical, Historical, and Global Perspectives* (Downers Grove, IL: InterVarsity, 2002), p. 73.

123. Lee, "Pneumatological Ecclesiology," p. 16.

124. See Dongsoo Kim, "The Healing of Han in Korean Pentecostalism," *JPT* 15 (1999): 123-39; Lee Hong Jung, "*Minjung* and Pentecostal Movements in Korea," in *Pentecostals after a Century: Global Perspectives on a Movement in Transition,* ed. Allan H. Anderson and Walter J. Hollenweger, JPTS 15 (Sheffield: Sheffield Academic, 1999), pp. 139-60.

125. Walter J. Hollenweger, *Pentecostalism: Origins and Development Worldwide* (Peabody, MA: Hendrickson, 1997), pp. 99-105; Myung Soo Park, "David Yonggi Cho and International Pentecostal/Charismatic Movements," *JPT* 12, no. 1 (2003): 107-28; Kim, "Healing of Han," pp. 132-37.

126. Sung Hoon Myung, "Spiritual Dimension of Church Growth as Applied in Yoido Full Gospel Church" (Ph.D. diss., Fuller Theological Seminary, 1990).

127. Allan Anderson, "The Contextual Pentecostal Theology of David Yonggi Cho," *AJPS* 7, no. 1 (2004): 110-16.

128. See George Oommen, "Growth of Pentecostalism in Central Kerala from 1921-47: A Paradigm for Pentecostal Growth of Churches in North India," *ICHR* 35, no. 2 (2001): 131-67; Ivan Satravatra, "Contextual Perspectives on Pentecostalism as Global Culture: A South Asian View," in *The Globalization of Pentecostalism: A Religion Made to Travel,* ed. Murray Dempster et al. (Oxford: Regnum, 1999), pp. 203-21.

129. See G. B. McGee and S. M. Burgess, "India," in *NIDPCM,* pp. 118-26; Amos Yong, *The Spirit Poured Out on All Flesh: Pentecostalism and the Possibility of Global Theology* (Grand Rapids: Baker, 2005), pp. 54-58.

130. See Roger E. Hedlund, ed., *Christianity Is Indian: The Emergence of an Indigenous Community* (Delhi: ISPCK, 2004), pp. 361-449.

131. Cf. James Massey, ed., *Indigenous People: Dalits; Dalit Issues in Today's Theological Debate* (Delhi: ISPCK, 1994).

132. See T. S. Samuel Kutty, *The Place and Contribution of Dalits in Select Pentecostal Churches in Central Kerala from 1922 to 1972* (Delhi: ISPCK, 2000), pp. 84-88.

133. P. G. Abraham, *Caste and Christianity: A Pentecostal Perspective* (Kumbazha: Crown Books, 2004), compares two approaches to the caste system.

134. See, for example, Siga Arles, "Indigenous Pentecostal Church Growth at KGF (Kolar Gold Fields), Karnataka," in *Christianity Is Indian,* pp. 387-98.

135. Kutty, *Place and Contribution,* pp. 119-33.

136. See Anne Motley Hallum, *Beyond Missionaries: Toward an Understanding of the Protestant Movement in Central America* (Lanham, MD: Rowman and Littlefield, 1996); Mike Berg and Paul Pretiz, *Spontaneous Combustion: Grass-Roots Christianity, Latin American Style* (Pasadena, CA: William Carey Library, 1996); David Lehmann, *Struggle for the Spirit: Religious Transformation and Popular Culture in Brazil and Latin America* (Cambridge: Polity, 1996).

137. Boff, *Ecclesiogenesis,* pp. 1-9.

138. Boff, *Ecclesiogenesis,* p. 13.

139. Boff, *Ecclesiogenesis,* p. 23.

140. Boff, *Ecclesiogenesis,* p. 23.

141. Cf. Jean-Pierre Bastian, *Le protestantisme en Amérique Latine: Une approche socio-historique,* Histoire et société 27 (Geneva: Labor et Fides, 1994), pp. 257-70; Manuel J. Gaxiola-Gaxiola, "Latin American Pentecostalism: A Mosaic within a Mosaic," *Pneuma* 13, no. 2 (1991): 107-29.

142. Adoniram Gaxiola, "Poverty as a Meeting and Parting Place: Similarities and Contrast in the Experiences of Latin American Pentecostalism and Ecclesial Base Communities," *Pneuma* 13, no. 2 (1991): 170-71.

143. Gaxiola, "Poverty," p. 171.

144. See, for example, the influential works by Melvin L. Hodges: *The Indigenous Church* (Springfield, MO: Gospel Publishing House, 1976); *A Theology of the Church and Its Mission: A Pentecostal Perspective* (Springfield, MO: Gospel Publishing House, 1977); *The Indigenous Church and the Missionary: A Sequel to the Indigenous Church* (Springfield, MO: Gospel Publishing House, 1978).

145. Gaxiola, "Poverty," p. 172.

146. See Hallum, *Beyond Missionaries,* pp. 129-34; David Smilde, *Reason to Believe: Cultural Agency in Latin American Evangelicalism* (Berkeley: University of California Press, 2007), pp. 3-15.

147. See Smilde, *Reason to Believe*, pp. 153-222.

148. Eugene Halton, *Bereft of Reason: On the Decline of Social Thought and Prospects for Its Renewal* (Chicago: University of Chicago Press, 1995), p. 82.

149. Cf. Amos Yong, *Beyond the Impasse: Toward a Pneumatological Theology of Religions* (Grand Rapids: Baker, 2003), pp. 129-61; Amos Yong, *Discerning the Spirit(s): A Pentecostal-Charismatic Contribution to Christian Theology of Religions*, JPTS 20 (Sheffield: Sheffield Academic, 2000), pp. 96-148.

150. Cf. Christián Parker, *Popular Religion and Modernization in Latin America: A Different Logic*, trans. Robert R. Barr (Maryknoll, NY: Orbis, 1996), pp. 247-64.

151. See Paulo Freire, *Pedagogy of the Oppressed*, thirtieth anniversary ed., trans. Myra Bergman Ramos (New York: Continuum, 2000).

152. Cf. Moacir Gadotti, *Reading Paulo Freire: His Life and Work*, trans. John Milton (Albany: SUNY Press, 1994), pp. 41-43.

153. Paolo Freire, *Cultural Action for Freedom* (Cambridge, MA: Harvard Educational Review, 1970), pp. 28, 42.

154. Cheryl Bridges Johns, *Pentecostal Formation: A Pedagogy among the Oppressed*, JPTS 2 (Sheffield: Sheffield Academic, 1993), pp. 62-110.

155. Johns, *Pentecostal Formation*, p. 62.

156. Johns, *Pentecostal Formation*, p. 90.

157. Johns, *Pentecostal Formation*, pp. 89-91. See Walter Hollenweger, "Creator Spiritus," *Theology* 81 (1978): 32-40; Harvey Cox, *The Feast of Fools: A Theological Essay on Festivity and Fantasy* (New York: Harper and Row, 1969), pp. 81-95.

158. Johns, *Pentecostal Formation*, p. 100.

159. Cf. Charles E. Self, "Conscientization, Conversion, and Convergence: Reflections on Base Communities and Emerging Pentecostalism in Latin America," *Pneuma* 14, no. 1 (1992): 59-72; Lidia Susana Vaccaro de Petrella, "The Tension between Evangelism and Social Action in the Pentecostal Movement," *IRM* 75, no. 297 (1985): 34-38.

160. See Veli-Matti Kärkkäinen, "Are Pentecostals Oblivious to Social Justice? Theological and Ecumenical Perspectives," *Missionalia* 29, no. 3 (2001): 387-404; Cecil M. Robeck, Jr., "Discerning the Spirit in the Life of the Church," in *The Church in the Movement of the Spirit*, ed. William R. Barr and Rena M. Yocom (Grand Rapids: Eerdmans, 1994), pp. 29-49; Richard J. Mouw, "Life in the Spirit in an Unjust World," *Pneuma* 9, no. 2 (1987): 109-28.

161. Lee, "Pneumatological Ecclesiology," p. 277.

162. See Yong, *Beyond the Impasse*, pp. 129-92; Amos Yong, *Spirit-Word-Community: Theological Hermeneutics in Trinitarian Perspective* (Eugene, OR: Wipf and Stock, 2002), pp. 123-49; Amos Yong, *Discerning the Spirit(s)*, pp. 96-148.

163. Amos Yong, "Spiritual Discernment: A Biblical-Theological Reconsideration," in *The Spirit and Spirituality: Essays in Honour of Russell P. Spittler*, ed. Wonsuk Ma and Robert P. Menzies, JPTS 24 (London: T. & T. Clark, 2004), pp. 98-99; Yong, *Beyond the Impasse*, p. 130.

164. Yong, "Spiritual Discernment," p. 99.

165. Yong, *Beyond the Impasse*, pp. 149-61.

166. Yong, *Spirit-Word-Community*, pp. 146-49. See Nelson Goodman, *Ways of Worldmaking* (Indianapolis: Hackett, 1978), pp. 7-17.

167. Yong, *Spirit-Word-Community*, pp. 275-310.

168. Jean-Jacques Suurmond, *Word and Spirit at Play: Towards a Charismatic Theology* (Grand Rapids: Eerdmans, 1994). Page references have been placed in the text.

169. See also Walter J. Hollenweger, "All Creatures Great and Small: Towards a Pneumatology of Life," in *Strange Gifts? A Guide to Charismatic Renewal*, ed. David Martin and Peter Mullen (Oxford: Blackwell, 1984), pp. 41-53.

170. Suurmond, *Word and Spirit*, p. 195.

171. Simon Chan, *Pentecostal Theology and the Christian Spiritual Tradition*, JPTS 21 (Sheffield: Sheffield Academic, 2000), pp. 116-19.

172. Cf. Veli-Matti Kärkkäinen, "The Church as the Fellowship of Persons: An Emerging Pentecostal Ecclesiology of *Koinonia*," PS 6, no. 1 (2007): 1-15. See also the essays on the Pentecostal–Roman Catholic dialogue on *koinonia* in *Pneuma* 12, no. 2 (1990): 77-183.

173. Komonchak, *Foundations in Ecclesiology*, p. 57, italics mine.

174. Cf. Franz-Xaver Kaufmann, *Kirche begreifen: Analysen und Thesen zur gesellschaftlichen Verfassung des Christentums* (Freiburg: Herder, 1979), pp. 100-104.

175. See my essays, "Pentecostal Perspectives on *The Nature and Mission of the Church*: Challenges and Opportunities for Ecumenical Transformation," in *Receiving "The Nature and Mission of the Church": Ecclesial Reality and Ecumenical Horizons for the Twenty-first Century*, ed. Paul M. Collins and Michael A. Fahey, Ecclesiological Investigations 1 (New York: Continuum, 2008), pp. 55-68; "Point de vue pentecôstiste. (Dossier à propos du document Nature et Mission de L'Église)," UDC 149 (January 2008): 23-26; and "A Pentecostal Perspective on *The Nature and Mission of the Church*," ET 35, no. 8 (2006): 1-5.

176. For my approach to this task, see Wolfgang Vondey, *People of Bread: Rediscovering Ecclesiology* (New York: Paulist, 2008).

177. See Veli-Matti Kärkkäinen, "Church as Charismatic Fellowship: Ecclesiological Reflections from the Pentecostal–Roman Catholic Dialogue," *JPT* 18 (April 2001): 100-121.

178. See Clark H. Pinnock, "Church in the Power of the Holy Spirit: The Promise of Pentecostal Ecclesiology," *JPT* 14, no. 2 (2006): 147-65.

179. See, for example, Mary McClintock Fulkerson, *Places of Redemption: Theology for a Worldly Church* (Oxford: Oxford University Press, 2007).

Notes to Chapter 6

1. Cf. Brian Sutton-Smith, *The Ambiguity of Play* (Cambridge, MA: Harvard University Press, 1997), pp. 1-17.

2. See David Cohen, *The Development of Play* (London: Routledge, 1993); Janet R. Moyles, *Just Playing: The Role and Status of Play in Early Childhood Education* (Philadelphia: Open University Press, 1989); Catherine Garvey, *Play* (Cambridge, MA: Harvard University Press, 1977).

3. See, for example, Donald E. Lytle, *Play and Educational Theory and Praxis* (Westport, CT: Praeger, 2003); Jean Piaget, *Play, Dreams, and Imitation in Childhood*, trans. C. Gattegno and F. M. Hodgson, International Library of Psychology 25 (1951; reprint, London: Routledge, 1999); Erik Erikson, *Toys and Reasons: Stages in the Ritualization of Experience* (New York: Norton, 1977); Donald W. Winnicott, *Playing and Reality* (New York: Basic Books, 1971); Hugo Rahner, *Man at Play* (New York: Herder and Herder, 1967).

4. Cf. Michael Roth, *Sinn und Geschmack fürs Endliche: Überlegungen zur Lust an der*

Schöpfung und der Freude am Spiel (Leipzig: Evangelische Verlagsanstalt, 2002), pp. 14-37; François Euvé, *Penser la creation comme jeu* (Paris: Cerf, 2000), pp. 127-50; Karl-Heinrich Bieritz, "'Freiheit im Spiel': Aspekte einer praktisch-theologischen Spieltheorie," *BTZ* 10, no. 2 (1993): 164-74; Robert E. Neale, *In Praise of Play: Toward a Psychology of Religion* (New York: Harper and Row, 1969), pp. 98-125.

5. See, for example, Michel S. Koppel, *Open-Hearted Ministry: Play as Key to Pastoral Leadership* (Minneapolis: Fortress, 2008); Thomas Klie, *Zeichen und Spiel: Semiotische und spieltheoretische Rekonstruktion der Pastoraltheologie*, Praktische Theologie und Kultur 11 (Gütersloh: Christian Kaiser, 2003); Sabine Bobert-Stützel, *Frömmigkeit und Symbolspiel: Ein pastoralpsychologischer Beitrag zu einer evangelischen Frömmigkeitstheorie*, Arbeiten zur Pastoraltheologie 37 (Göttingen: Vandenhoeck & Ruprecht, 2000); Jürgen Moltmann, *Theology of Play*, trans. Reinhard Ulrich (New York: Harper and Row, 1972); Gordon Dahl, *Work, Play, and Worship* (Minneapolis: Augsburg, 1972); Harvey Cox, *The Feast of Fools* (New York: Harper and Row, 1969).

6. Johan Huizinga, *Homo Ludens: A Study of the Play-Element in Culture* (London: Routledge and Kegan Paul, 1949).

7. For example, F. J. J. Buytendijk, *Het spel van mensch en dier als ofenbaring of levensdriften* (Amsterdam: Kosmos, 1932); H. Zondervan, *Het spel bij dieren, kinderen en volwassen menschen*, Nederlandsche bibliotheek 533 (Amsterdam: Maatschappij, 1928); Karl Groos, *Das Spiel: Zwei Vorträge* (Jena: Fischer, 1922); Herbert Spencer, *The Principles of Psychology* (London: Longman, Brown, Green, and Longmans, 1855).

8. Huizinga, *Homo Ludens*, p. 13. Page numbers have been placed in the text.

9. From the Latin, *inlusio*, *illudere*, or *inludere*.

10. See Piaget, *Play, Dreams, and Imitation in Childhood*.

11. Piaget, *Play, Dreams, and Imitation*, pp. 150-68. Cf. Klie, *Zeichen und Spiel*, p. 98; Cohen, *The Development of Play*, pp. 40-48.

12. Jean Piaget, "Response to Brian Sutton-Smith," *PR* 73, no. 1 (1966): 111-12, here p. 111.

13. Treatment of this development can be found in Piaget, *Play, Dreams, and Imitation*, pp. 215-91, and his previous works, *The Child and Reality: Problems of Genetic Psychology*, trans. Arnold Rosin (New York: Penguin Books, 1972), pp. 63-91; *The Child's Conception of Physical Causality*, trans. Marjorie Gabain (London: Routledge, 1930; reprint, 1999), pp. 281-91; *Judgment and Reasoning in the Child*, trans. Marjorie Warden (London: Routledge, 1928; reprint, 1999), pp. 244-52.

14. Jean Piaget, *Structuralism*, trans. Chaninah Maschier (New York: Harper and Row, 1970). See also Jean Piaget, *The Development of Thought: Equilibration of Cognitive Structures*, trans. Arnold Rosin (New York: Viking, 1977), p. 5.

15. Piaget, *Structuralism*, pp. 60-68.

16. Piaget, *Structuralism*, p. 69.

17. Piaget, *Structuralism*, p. 67; Piaget, *The Development of Thought*, pp. 81-135. Cf. Usha Goswami and Ann L. Brown, "Higher-order Structure and Relational Reasoning: Contrasting Analogical and Thematic Relations," in *Critical Readings on Piaget*, ed. Leslie Smith (London: Routledge, 1996), pp. 209-28.

18. Cf. Ken Richardson, *Models of Cognitive Development* (Hove, U.K.: Psychology Press, 2003), pp. 94-118; Barry J. Wadsworth, *Piaget's Theory of Cognitive and Affective Development*, 4th ed. (New York: Longman, 1989), pp. 115-42; Jeanette McCarthy Gallagher and

D. Kim Reid, *The Learning Theory of Piaget and Inhelder* (Monterey, CA: Brooks/Cole, 1981), pp. 40-57.

19. Piaget, *Play, Dreams, and Imitation*, p. 142.

20. Piaget, *Play, Dreams, and Imitation*, p. 143.

21. Piaget, *Play, Dreams, and Imitation*, p. 145.

22. Eugen Fink, *Grundphänomene des menschlichen Daseins* (Freiburg: Alber, 1979); *Spiel als Weltsymbol* (Stuttgart: Kohlhammer, 1960); *Oase des Glücks: Gedanken zu einer Ontologie des Spiels* (Freiburg: Alber, 1957).

23. For an English synopsis, see Eugen Fink, "The Oasis of Happiness: Toward an Ontology of Play," *YFS* 41 (1968): 19-30. Cf. Algis Mickunas, "Philosophical Anthropology of E. Fink," *Problemos* 73 (2008): 167-78. See also Eugen Fink, *Traktat über die Gewalt des Menschen* (Frankfurt: Klostermann, 1974), pp. 145-220.

24. See Fink, *Grundphänomene des menschlichen Daseins*, pp. 216-66 and 352-419.

25. Fink, *Grundphänomene des menschlichen Daseins*, p. 357.

26. Fink, "The Oasis of Happiness," pp. 20-21; Fink, *Oase des Glücks*, pp. 22-23.

27. Fink, *Spiel als Weltsymbol*, pp. 207-30. Cf. Yoshihiro Nitta, "Der Weltaufgang und die Rolle des Menschen als Medium," in *Eugen Fink: Sozialphilosophie — Anthropologie — Kosmologie — Pädagogik — Methodik*, ed. Anselm Böhmer (Würzburg: Königshausen & Neumann, 2006), pp. 183-92.

28. Fink, *Spiel als Weltsymbol*, p. 231.

29. Fink, "The Oasis of Happiness," p. 25; Fink, *Oase des Glücks*, p. 39. See also Fink, *Grundphänomene des menschlichen Daseins*, pp. 386-402.

30. Fink, "The Oasis of Happiness," p. 23; Fink, *Oase des Glücks*, pp. 34-35.

31. Fink, *Spiel als Weltsymbol*, pp. 112-24.

32. Fink, "The Oasis of Happiness," pp. 29-30; Fink, *Oase des Glücks*, p. 51.

33. Fink, *Spiel als Weltsymbol*, pp. 230-42. Cf. also Rahner, *Man at Play*, pp. 26-45.

34. See Euvé, *Penser la creation comme jeu*, pp. 123-247; Robert Kent Johnston, "Theology and Play: A Critical Appraisal" (Ph.D. diss., Duke University, 1974), pp. 155-205.

35. Cf. Klie, *Zeichen und Spiel*, pp. 59-60; Johnston, "Theology and Play," pp. 43-52.

36. Cf. Roth, *Sinn und Geschmack fürs Endliche*, pp. 159-73.

37. Cf. Sutton-Smith, *The Ambiguity of Play*, pp. 201-13.

38. Cf. Diana Kelly-Byrne, "The Meaning of Play's Triviality," in *The Masks of Play*, ed. Brian Sutton-Smith and Diana Kelly-Byrne (New York: Leisure, 1984), pp. 165-70; Gerhard Marcel Martin, "Eine neue Genitiv-Theologie? Giebt es so etwas wie eine 'Theologie des Spiels'?" *WPKG* 60 (1971): 516-23.

39. Cf. Johnston, "Theology and Play," pp. 19-28.

40. Cf. Moltmann, *Theology of Play*, p. 112; William Wesley Lites, "Play as a Metaphor for the Process of Perceiving God" (Ph.D. diss., Southern Baptist Theological Seminary, 1992), chapter 3.

41. See, for example, Marcus A. Friedrich, *Liturgische Körper: Der Beitrag von Schauspieltheorien und -techniken für die Pastoralästhetik* (Stuttgart: Kohlhammer, 2001); A. Ronald Sequeira, *Spielende Liturgie: Bewegung neben Wort und Ton im Gottesdienst am Beispiel des Vaterunsers* (Freiburg: Herder, 1977).

42. Werner Jetter, *Symbol und Ritual: Anthropologische Elemente im Gottesdienst* (Göttingen: Vandenhoeck & Ruprecht, 1978), pp. 69-70.

43. See Harvey Cox, *The Seduction of the Spirit: The Use and Misuse of People's Religion*

(New York: Simon and Schuster, 1973); *The Feast of Fools: A Theological Essay on Festivity and Fantasy* (New York: Harper and Row, 1969); *The Secular City: Secularization and Urbanization in Theological Perspective* (New York: Macmillan, 1965).

44. T. George Harris, "Religion in the Age of Aquarius: A Conversation with Harvey Cox," *PT* 3, no. 11 (1970): 45-47 and 62-67, here p. 62.

45. See, for example, Wolfhart Pannenberg, *Anthropology in Theological Perspective*, trans. Matthew J. O'Connell (Philadelphia: Westminster, 1985), pp. 322-39; Robert K. Johnston, *The Christian at Play* (Grand Rapids: Eerdmans, 1983), pp. 16-52; Moltmann, *Theology of Play*, pp. 1-75; Sam Keen, *To a Dancing God* (New York: Harper and Row, 1970); Rahner, *Man at Play*, pp. 26-64; Neale, *In Praise of Play*, pp. 19-41; Walter Kerr, *The Decline of Pleasure* (New York: Simon and Schuster, 1962), pp. 9-42.

46. Cox, *Seduction of the Spirit*, p. 319. Page references have been placed in the text.

47. Harvey Cox, *Fire from Heaven: The Rise of Pentecostal Spirituality and the Reshaping of Religion in the 21st Century* (Reading, MA: Addison-Wesley, 1995).

48. To my knowledge, research is limited to the essays in Michael Wilkinson, *Canadian Pentecostalism: Transition and Transformation* (Montreal: McGill-Queen's University Press, 2009), pp. 197-276; Margaret M. Poloma, "The Symbolic Dilemma and the Future of Pentecostalism: Mysticism, Ritual, and Revival," in *The Future of Pentecostalism in the United States* (Lanham, MD: Lexington Books, 2007), pp. 105-21; Margaret M. Poloma, *Main Street Mystics: The Toronto Blessing and Reviving Pentecostalism* (Walnut Creek, CA: Altamira, 2007); Margaret M. Poloma, "The 'Toronto Blessing': Charisma, Institutionalization, and Revival," *JSSR* 36, no. 2 (1997): 257-71; Gerard Roelofs, "Charismatic Christian Thought: Experience, Metonymy, and Routinization," in *Charismatic Christianity as a Global Culture*, ed. Karla O. Poewe (Columbia: University of South Carolina Press, 1994), pp. 217-33; Roy Arthur Grindstaff, "The Institutionalization of Aimee Semple McPherson: A Study in the Rhetoric of Social Intervention" (Ph.D. diss., Ohio State University, 1990), pp. 276-322; Margaret M. Poloma, *The Assemblies of God at the Crossroads: Charisma and Institutional Dilemmas* (Knoxville: University of Tennessee Press, 1989); Luther P. Gerlach and Virginia H. Hine, *People, Power, Change: Movements of Social Transformation* (Indianapolis: Bobbs-Merrill, 1970), pp. 33-78.

49. See Max Weber, *The Theory of Social and Economic Organizations*, trans. A. M. Henderson and Talcott Parsons (New York: Free Press, 1947), pp. 358-92.

50. Thomas F. O'Dea, "Five Dilemmas of the Institutionalization of Religion," *JSSR* 1, no. 1 (1961): 30-39, and two revisions: "Sociological Dilemmas: Five Paradoxes of Institutionalization," in *Sociological Theory, Values, and Sociological Change: Essays in Honor of Pitirim A. Sorokin*, ed. Edward A. Tiryakian (Glencoe, IL: Free Press, 1963), pp. 71-89, and *The Sociology of Religion* (Englewood Cliffs, NJ: Prentice-Hall, 1966), pp. 90-97. The page references in the following text are to O'Dea, "Five Dilemmas of the Institutionalization of Religion."

51. See Poloma, "The Symbolic Dilemma," pp. 105-21; Poloma, *Main Street Mystics*, pp. 15-20, 160-63, 181-91; Poloma, "The 'Toronto Blessing,'" pp. 257-71; Poloma, *Assemblies of God*, pp. 94-98, 101-212.

52. Poloma, "The Symbolic Dilemma," p. 105.

53. Poloma, *Assemblies of God*, p. 88; Poloma, "The 'Toronto Blessing,'" p. 259.

54. Poloma, *Assemblies of God*, p. 209.

55. Cf. Peter Hocken, "The Pentecostal-Charismatic Movement as Revival and Re-

newal," *Pneuma* 3, no. 1 (1981): 31-47. See, for example, Stanley H. Frodsham, *With Signs Following: The Story of the Pentecostal Revival in the Twentieth Century* (Springfield, MO: Gospel Publishing House, 1946).

56. See, for example, Walter J. Hollenweger, *The Pentecostals: The Charismatic Movement in the Churches* (Minneapolis: Augsburg, 1972), pp. 21-26.

57. See Edith L. Blumhofer, "Restoration as Revival: Early American Pentecostalism," in *Modern Christian Revivals*, ed. Edith L. Blumhofer and Randall Balmer (Urbana: University of Illinois Press, 1993), pp. 145-60.

58. See Ian Hamish Murray, *Revival and Revivalism: The Making of American Evangelicalism, 1750-1858* (Edinburgh: Banner of Truth Trust, 1994); Keith Hardman, *Seasons of Refreshing: Evangelism and Revivals in America* (Grand Rapids: Baker, 1994).

59. John Thomas Nichol, *Pentecostalism* (New York: Harper and Row, 1966), p. 70.

60. Cf. Horace S. Ward, "The Anti-Pentecostal Argument," in *Aspects of Pentecostal-Charismatic Origins*, ed. Vinson Synan (Plainfield, NJ: Logos International, 1975), pp. 99-122.

61. See Cecil M. Roebeck, Jr., "Sanctified Passion or Carnal Pleasure? A Review Essay," *Pneuma* 29, no. 1 (2007): 103-11; Ann Taves, *Fits, Trances, and Visions: Experiencing Religion and Explaining Experience from Wesley to James* (Princeton: Princeton University Press, 1999), pp. 226-49, 328-41.

62. See, for example, Harry Morse, "Holy Rollers vs. Pentecostal Movement," *CE* 56 (August 29, 1914): 3, and G. C. Morris, "Eleventh Annual Assembly," *COGE* 6, no. 47 (1915): 1.

63. Cf. Wolfgang Vondey, "Glossolalia," in *Global Dictionary of Theology*, ed. William A. Dyrness and Veli-Matti Kärkkäinen (Downers Grove, IL: InterVarsity, 2008), pp. 343-45.

64. On the frequent accusation of disruptive behavior and teachings, see Cecil M. Robeck, Jr., *The Azusa Street Mission and Revival: The Birth of the Global Pentecostal Movement* (Nashville: Nelson, 2006), pp. 129-86.

65. Horace S. Ward, "The Anti-Pentecostal Argument," p. 107.

66. See Wayne E. Warner, *Revival! Touched by Pentecostal Fire: Eyewitnesses to the Early-Twentieth-Century Pentecostal Revival* (Tulsa: Harrison House, 1978).

67. See Roland Wessel, "The Spirit Baptism, Nineteenth Century Roots," *Pneuma* 14, no. 2 (1992): 127-57; Donald W. Dayton, *Theological Roots of Pentecostalism* (Peabody, MA: Hendrickson, 1987); Richard Lovelace, "Baptism in the Holy Spirit and the Evangelical Tradition," *Pneuma* 7, no. 2 (1985): 101-23; Harold D. Hunter, *Spirit-Baptism: A Pentecostal Alternative* (Lanham, MD: University Press of America, 1983); Donald R. Wheelock, "Spirit Baptism in American Pentecostal Thought" (Ph.D. diss., Emory University, 1983).

68. Robert G. Gromacki, *The Modern Tongues Movement* (Philadelphia: Presbyterian and Reformed, 1967).

69. See Gary B. McGee, ed., *Initial Evidence: Historical and Biblical Perspectives on the Pentecostal Doctrine of Spirit Baptism* (Peabody, MA: Hendrickson, 1991).

70. Dayton, *Theological Roots of Pentecostalism*, pp. 15-16.

71. Steven Jack Land, *Pentecostal Spirituality: A Passion for the Kingdom*, JPTS 1 (Sheffield: Sheffield Academic, 1993), p. 63, in response to Frederick Dale Bruner, *A Theology of the Holy Spirit: The Pentecostal Experience and the New Testament Witness* (Grand Rapids: Eerdmans, 1970).

72. Cf. Frank D. Macchia, *Baptized in the Spirit: A Global Pentecostal Theology* (Grand Rapids: Zondervan, 2006), pp. 20-28.

73. See Macchia, *Baptized in the Spirit*, pp. 61-88.

74. Cf. Hollenweger, *The Pentecostals*, pp. 29-46.

75. See Eric Patterson and Edmund Rybarczyk, *The Future of Pentecostalism in the United States* (Lanham, MD: Lexington Books, 2007).

76. Eric Patterson, "Conclusion: Back to the Future? U.S. Pentecostalism in the 21st Century," in *The Future of Pentecostalism in the United States*, pp. 189-209, here p. 206.

77. See Amos Yong, ed., *The Spirit Renews the Face of the Earth: Pentecostal Forays in Science and Theology of Creation* (Eugene, OR: Pickwick, 2009); Donald E. Miller and Tetsunao Yamamori, *Global Pentecostalism: The New Face of Christian Social Engagement* (Berkeley: University of California Press, 2007); Veli-Matti Kärkkäinen, "Are Pentecostals Oblivious to Social Justice? Theological and Ecumenical Perspectives," *Missionalia* 29, no. 3 (2001): 387-404; Grant Wacker, "Searching for Eden with a Satellite Dish: Primitivism, Pragmatism, and the Pentecostal Character," in *The Primitive Church in the Modern World*, ed. Richard T. Hughes (Urbana: University of Illinois Press, 1995), pp. 139-66.

Notes to Pages 190-93

78. D. William Faupel, *The Everlasting Gospel: The Significance of Eschatology in the Development of Pentecostal Thought*, JPTS 10 (Sheffield: Sheffield Academic, 1996), p. 222.

79. James A. Mathisen, "Thomas O'Dea's Dilemmas of Institutionalization: A Case Study and Re-evaluation after Twenty-five Years," *SA* 47, no. 4 (1987): 302-18; J. Milton Yinger, "Comment," *JSSR* 1, no. 1 (1961): 40-41.

80. Poloma, *Assemblies of God*, pp. 241-43.

81. Cf. Tony Gray, "An Anatomy of Revival," *EQ* 72, no. 3 (2000): 249-70.

82. Cf. Gray, "An Anatomy of Revival," pp. 255-63.

83. Murray, *Revival and Revivalism*, p. 23; Gray, "An Anatomy of Revival," p. 263.

84. See Gray, "An Anatomy of Revival," pp. 255-58; Russel E. Richery, "Revivalism: In Search of a Definition," *WTJ* 28, no. 1 and 2 (1993): 165-75.

85. See C. C. Goen, *Revivalism and Separatism in New England, 1740-1800: Strict Congregationalists and Separate Baptists in the Great Awakening* (New Haven: Yale University Press, 1962), pp. 36-114; William Warren Sweet, *Revivalism in America* (Nashville: Abingdon, 1944), pp. 140-61.

86. For examples, see George M. Thomas, *Revivalism and Cultural Change: Christianity, Nation Building, and the Market in the Nineteenth-Century United States* (Chicago: University of Chicago Press, 1989); Timothy L. Smith, *Revivalism and Social Reform: American Protestantism on the Eve of the Civil War* (Baltimore: Johns Hopkins University Press, 1980); John L. Hammond, *The Politics of Benevolence: Revival Religion and American Voting Behavior* (Norwood, NJ: Ablex, 1979); William G. McLoughlin, *Revivals, Awakenings, and Reform* (Chicago: University of Chicago Press, 1970), pp. 1-23.

87. See the articles "Classical Pentecostalism," "Neo-Pentecostals," "Neo-Charismatics," and "Third Wave," in *NIDPCM*.

88. Cf. Hocken, "Pentecostal-Charismatic Movement," p. 37.

89. See Jan Kerkhofs, *Catholic Pentecostals Now* (Canfield, OH: Alba, 1977); J. Massyngberde Ford, *Which Way for Catholic Pentecostals?* (New York: Harper and Row, 1976); Kevin Ranaghan and Dorothy Ranaghan, *Catholic Pentecostals* (New York: Paulist, 1969).

90. See Joseph Michael Ryan, "'Life in the Spirit': Cultural Values and Identity Changes among Catholic Pentecostals" (Ph.D. diss., University of Pennsylvania, 1978).

91. See Peter Hocken, "Revival and Renewal," *JEPTA* 18 (1998): 49-63; Peter Hocken,

Streams of Renewal: The Origins and Early Development of the Charismatic Movement in Great Britain (Exeter, Devon, U.K.: Paternoster, 1986); Hocken, "Pentecostal-Charismatic Movement," pp. 31-47; Peter Hocken, *The Strategy of the Spirit? Worldwide Renewal and Revival in the Established Church and Modern Movements* (Guildford, Surrey, U.K.: Eagle, 1966).

92. Hocken, "Pentecostal-Charismatic Movement," p. 42.

93. Hocken, "Pentecostal-Charismatic Movement," p. 44.

94. I use the phrase "transcendental method" in the Kantian sense as employed by Bernard Lonergan, *Method in Theology* (Toronto: University of Toronto Press, 1971; reprint, 2003), pp. 13-20.

95. See my treatment in chapter 1. See also Jürgen Moltmann, *The Source of Life: The Holy Spirit and the Theology of Life,* trans. Margaret Kohl (Minneapolis: Fortress, 1997), pp. 22-25; Michael Welker, *God the Spirit,* trans. John F. Hoffmeyer (Minneapolis: Fortress, 1994), pp. 52-65.

96. This challenge is illustrated by the history of the journal *Theological Renewal;* see Mark J. Cartledge, *"Theological Renewal* (1975-1983): Listening to an Editor's Agenda for Church and Academy," *Pneuma* 30, no. 1 (2008): 83-107; Mark Stibbe, "The Theology of Renewal and the Renewal of Theology," *JPT* 3 (1993): 71-90.

97. Julie C. Ma, *When the Spirit Meets the Spirits: Pentecostal Ministry among the Kankan-ey Tribe in the Philippines* (Berlin: Peter Lang, 2001); Julie C. Ma, "Santuala: A Case of Pentecostal Syncretism," *AJPS* 3, no. 1 (2000): 61-82; André Droogers, "The Normalization of Religious Experience: Healing, Prophecy, Dreams, and Visions," in *Charismatic Christianity as a Global Culture,* pp. 33-49; Mark R. Mullins, "Japanese Pentecostalism and the World of the Dead: A Study of Cultural Adaptation in Iesu no mitama kyokai," *JJRS* 17, no. 4 (1990): 353-74.

98. See Amos Yong, "Going Where the Spirit Goes: Engaging the Spirit(s) in J. C. Ma's Pneumatological Mission," *JPT* 10, no. 2 (2002): 110-28; Allan Anderson, "Stretching the Definitions? Pneumatology and 'Syncretism' in African Pentecostalism," *JPT* 10, no. 1 (2001): 98-119.

99. Cf. Yong, *The Spirit Renews the Face of the Earth;* James K. A. Smith, "Is the Universe Open for Surprise? Pentecostal Ontology and the Spirit of Naturalism" *ZJRS* 43, no. 4 (2008): 879-96; Andrew K. Gabriel, "Pneumatological Perspectives for a Theology of Nature: The Holy Spirit in Relation to Ecology and Technology," *JPT* 15, no. 2 (2007): 195-212; Paul Elbert, "Genesis 1 and the Spirit: A Narrative-Rhetorical Ancient Near Eastern Reading in Light of Modern Science," *JPT* 15, no. 1 (2006): 23-72; Rick M. Nañez, *Full Gospel, Fractured Minds? A Call to Use God's Gift of the Intellect* (Grand Rapids: Zondervan, 2005).

100. Cf. the essays in Allan H. Anderson and Walter J. Hollenweger, eds., *Pentecostals after a Century: Global Perspectives on a Movement in Transition,* JPTS 15 (Sheffield: Sheffield Academic, 1999), and in Murray W. Dempster et al., eds., *The Globalization of Pentecostalism: A Religion Made to Travel* (Oxford: Regnum, 1999). For the Pentecostal sensitivity for the margins, see Doug Petersen, *Not by Might Nor by Power: A Pentecostal Theology of Social Concern in Latin America* (Oxford: Regnum, 1996); Samuel Solivan, *The Spirit, Pathos, and Liberation: Toward an Hispanic Pentecostal Theology,* JPTS 14 (Sheffield: Sheffield Academic, 1998); Cheryl J. Sanders, *Empowerment Ethics for a Liberated People* (Minneapolis: Fortress, 1995).

101. Anderson, "Stretching the Definitions?" p. 102.

102. Amos Yong, *The Spirit Poured Out on All Flesh: Pentecostalism and the Possibility of Global Theology* (Grand Rapids: Baker Academic, 2005), p. 49.

103. Walter J. Hollenweger, *Pentecostalism: Origins and Developments Worldwide* (Peabody, MA: Hendrickson, 1997), pp. 132-41.

104. Many of these aspects were noted already by Richard F. Lovelace, *Dynamics of the Spiritual Life: An Evangelical Theology of Renewal* (Downers Grove, IL: InterVarsity, 1979); Edward Schillebeeckx, *The Concept of Truth and Theological Renewal*, trans. N. D. Smith (London: Sheed and Ward, 1968); Karl Rahner, *Theology for Renewal: Bishops, Priests, Laity*, trans. Cecily Hastings and Richard Strachan (New York: Sheed and Ward, 1964).

105. Cf. S. F. Sugirtharajah, ed., *Voices from the Margin: Interpreting the Bible in the Third World* (Maryknoll, NY: Orbis, 2004), pp. 1-8.

106. See Jeorg Rieger, *Opting for the Margins: Postmodernity and Liberation in Christian Theology*, Reflection and Theory in the Study of Religion (Oxford: Oxford University Press, 2003); Peter C. Phan and Jung Young Lee, eds., *Journeys at the Margin: Towards an Autobiographical Theology in American-Asian Perspective* (Collegeville, MN: Order of Saint Benedict, 1999); Edith L. Blumhofer, Russell P. Spittler, and Grant A. Wacker, eds., *Pentecostal Currents in American Protestantism* (Urbana: University of Illinois Press, 1999).

107. See Cheryl J. Sanders, *Saints in Exile: The Holiness-Pentecostal Experience in African American Religion and Culture*, Religion in America (Oxford: Oxford University Press, 1996).

108. Fernando F. Segovia, *Decolonizing Biblical Studies: A View from the Margins* (Maryknoll, NY: Orbis, 2000), p. 85.

109. Segovia, *Decolonizing Biblical Studies*, p. 123.

110. Cf. Marian Ronan, "From the Margins to the Universe," *CC* 42, no. 1 (1992): 102-10; Cheryl Bridges Johns, "From the Margins to the Center: Exploring the Seminary's Leadership Role in Developing the Public Presence of Pentecostalism," *TE* 38, no. 1 (2001): 33-46.

111. Cf. Denise M. Ackermann, "Forward from the Margins: Feminist Theology for Life," *JTSA* 99 (November 1997): 63-67; Ronan, "From the Margins," pp. 102-10.

112. J. Rodman Williams, *Renewal Theology: Systematic Theology from a Charismatic Perspective; Three Volumes in One* (Grand Rapids: Zondervan, 1996), p. 12. On the unfinished nature of this task, see Terry L. Cross, "Toward a Theology of the Word and the Spirit: A Review of J. Rodman Williams's *Renewal Theology*," *JPT* 3 (1993): 113-35.

113. Stanley J. Grenz, *Renewing the Center: Evangelical Theology in a Post-Theological Era*, 2nd ed. (Grand Rapids: Baker Academic, 2006), pp. 333-59.

114. Grenz, *Renewing the Center*, p. 334.

115. See Douglas Jacobsen and William Vance Trollinger, Jr., eds., *Re-forming the Center: American Protestantism, 1900 to the Present* (Grand Rapids: Eerdmans, 1998).

116. Grenz, *Renewing the Center*, p. 344.

117. Grenz, *Renewing the Center*, p. 359.

118. Grenz, *Renewing the Center*, p. 187.

119. So the title of Millard J. Erickson, Paul Kjoss Helseth, and Justin Taylor, *Reclaiming the Center: Confronting Evangelical Accommodation in Postmodern Times* (Wheaton, IL: Crossway, 2004).

120. Taylor, "An Introduction to Postconservative Evangelicalism," in *Reclaiming the Center*, p. 18.

121. Millard J. Erickson, "On Flying in Theological Fog," in *Reclaiming the Center,* pp. 323-49.

122. See Erickson, "On Flying," p. 328.

123. See John Milbank, Catherine Pickstock, and Graham Ward, eds., *Radical Orthodoxy: A New Theology* (New York: Routledge, 1999); Laurence Paul Hemming, ed., *Radical Orthodoxy? — a Catholic Enquiry* (Aldershot: Ashgate, 2000); James K. A. Smith, *Introducing Radical Orthodoxy: Mapping a Post-Secular Theology* (Grand Rapids: Baker Academic, 2004).

124. Graham Ward, "Radical Orthodoxy and/as Cultural Politics," in *Radical Orthodoxy?* p. 106.

125. This phrase is adapted from Thomas C. Oden, *Turning around the Mainline: How Renewal Movements Are Changing the Church* (Grand Rapids: Baker Academic, 2006).

126. John Milbank, *Theology and Social Theory: Beyond Secular Reason,* 2nd ed. (Oxford: Blackwell, 2006).

127. Milbank, *Theology and Social Theory,* p. 3.

128. James K. A. Smith, *Introducing Radical Orthodoxy,* p. 131.

129. Cf. Milbank, Pickstock, and Ward, *Radical Orthodoxy,* p. 2; Ward, "Radical Orthodoxy," p. 103.

130. James K. A. Smith, *Introducing Radical Orthodoxy,* pp. 70-80.

131. James K. A. Smith, "What Hath Cambridge to Do with Azusa Street? Radical Orthodoxy and Pentecostal Theology in Conversation," *Pneuma* 25, no. 1 (2003): 97-114.

132. James K. A. Smith, "What Hath Cambridge?" p. 111; see also pp. 109-14.

133. James K. A. Smith, "What Hath Cambridge?" p. 112.

134. Graham Ward, "In the Economy of the Divine: A Response to James K. A. Smith," *Pneuma* 25, no. 1 (2003): 115-20.

135. James K. A. Smith, "What Hath Cambridge?" pp. 101, 112.

136. Cf. Jackie David Johns, "Pentecostalism and the Postmodern Worldview," *JPT* 7 (1995): 73-96.

137. James K. A. Smith, "What Hath Cambridge?" p. 101.

Name Index

Subject Index